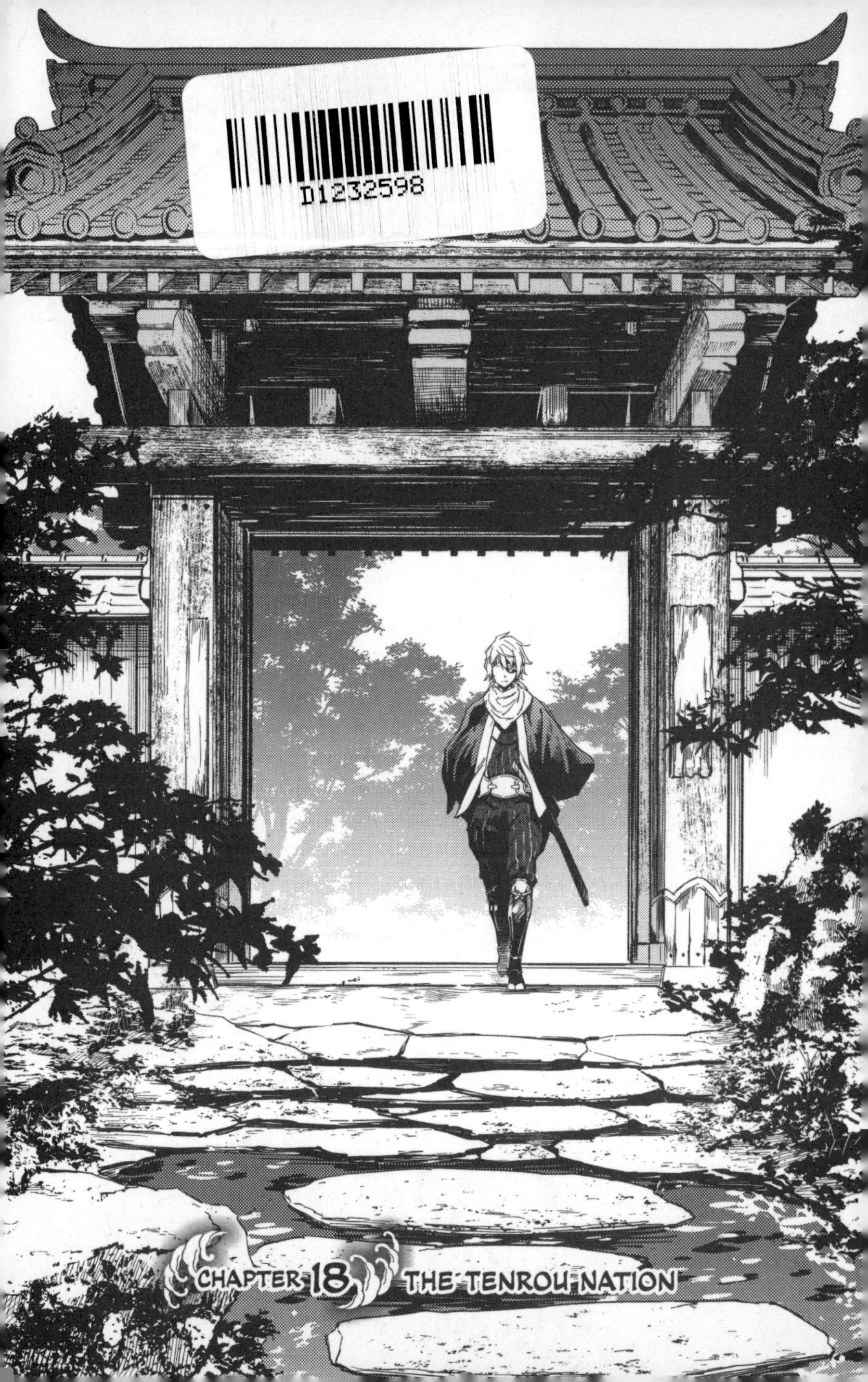
CHAPTER 18 THE TENROU NATION

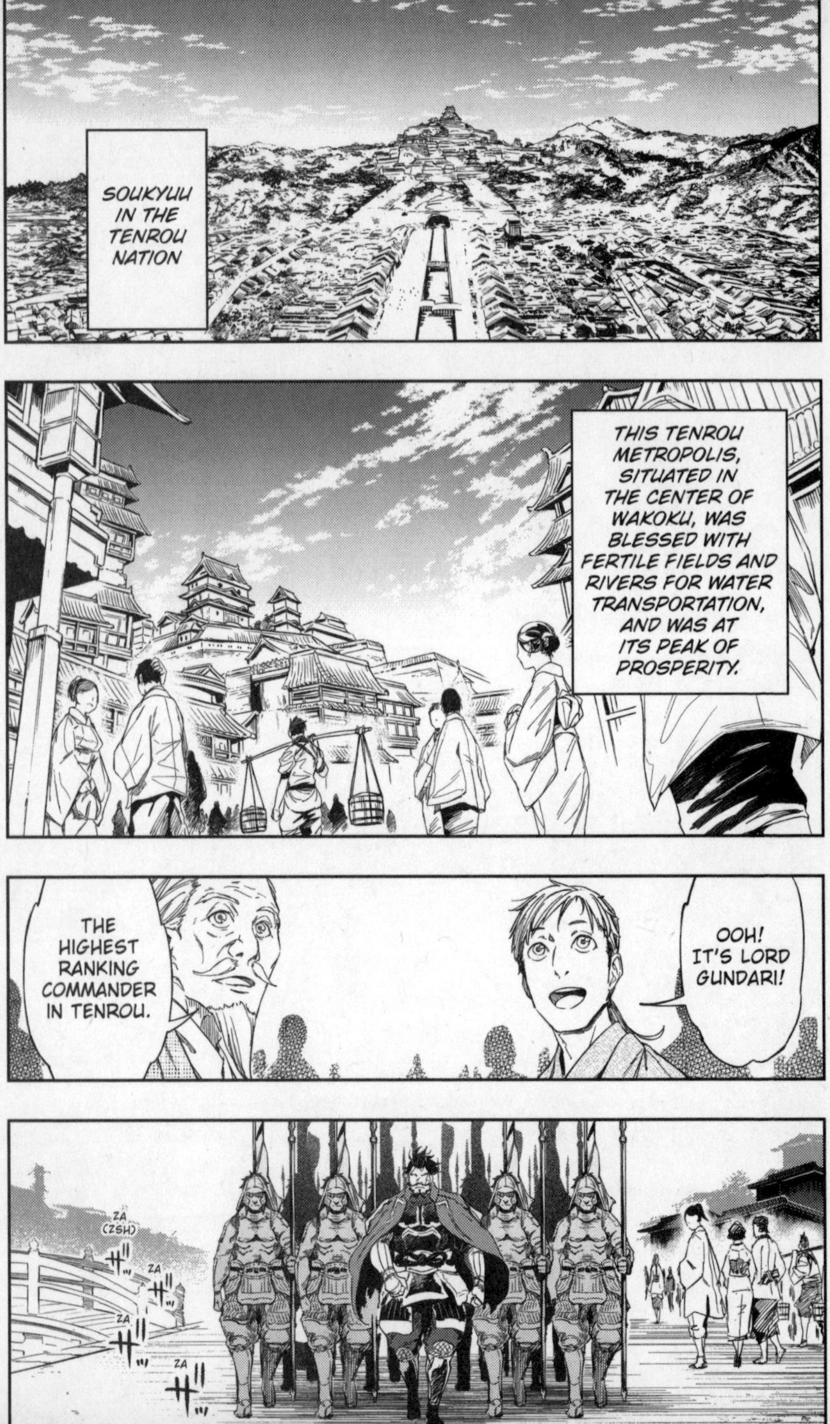
SOUKYUU IN THE TENROU NATION
THIS TENROU METROPOLIS, SITUATED IN THE CENTER OF WAKOKU, WAS BLESSED WITH FERTILE FIELDS AND RIVERS FOR WATER TRANSPORTATION, AND WAS AT ITS PEAK OF PROSPERITY.
OOH! IT'S LORD GUNDARI!
THE HIGHEST RANKING COMMANDER IN TENROU.
ZA (ZSH)
ZA
ZA
ZA

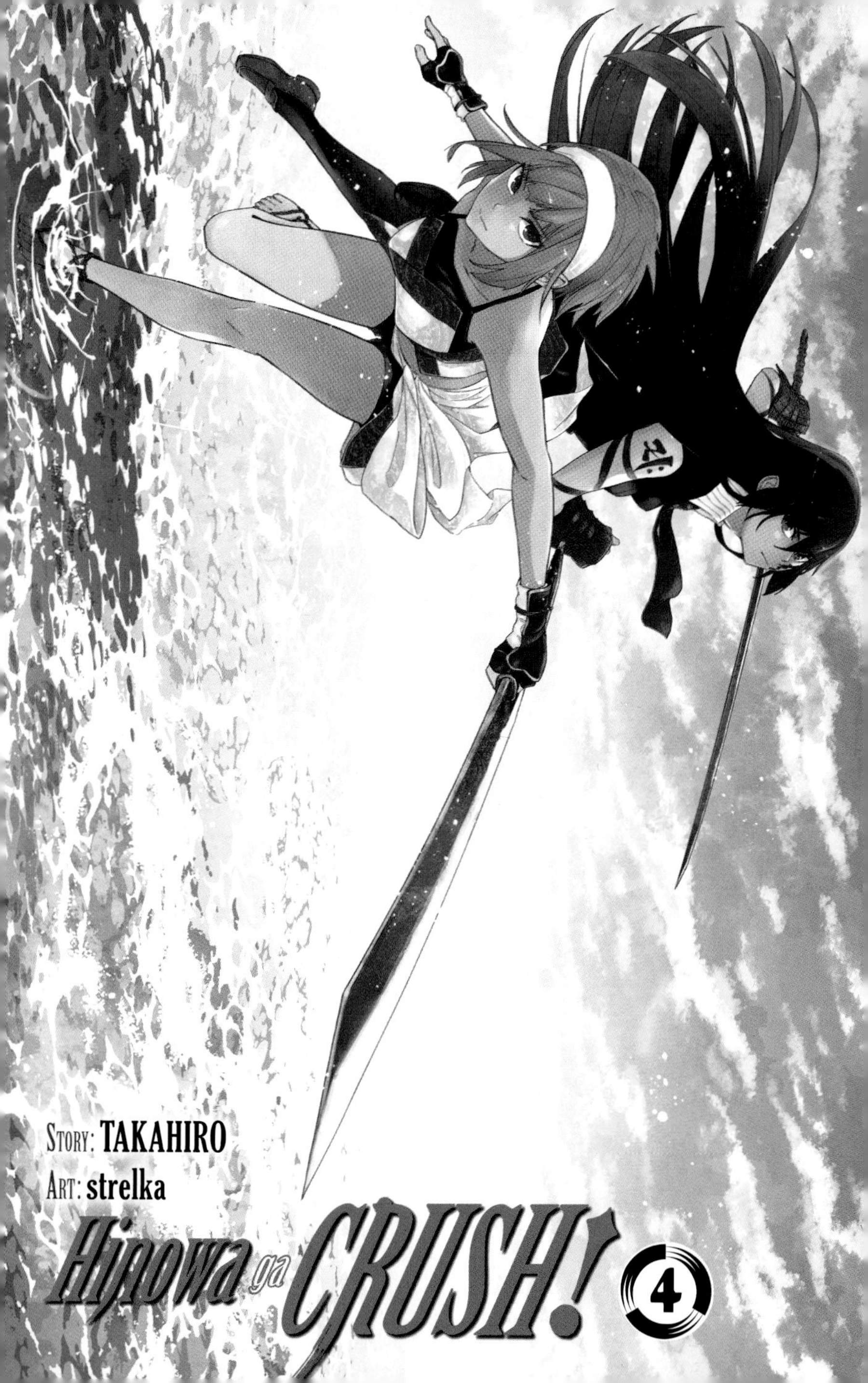
STORY: TAKAHIRO
ART: strelka
Hinowa ga CRUSH! 4

Contents

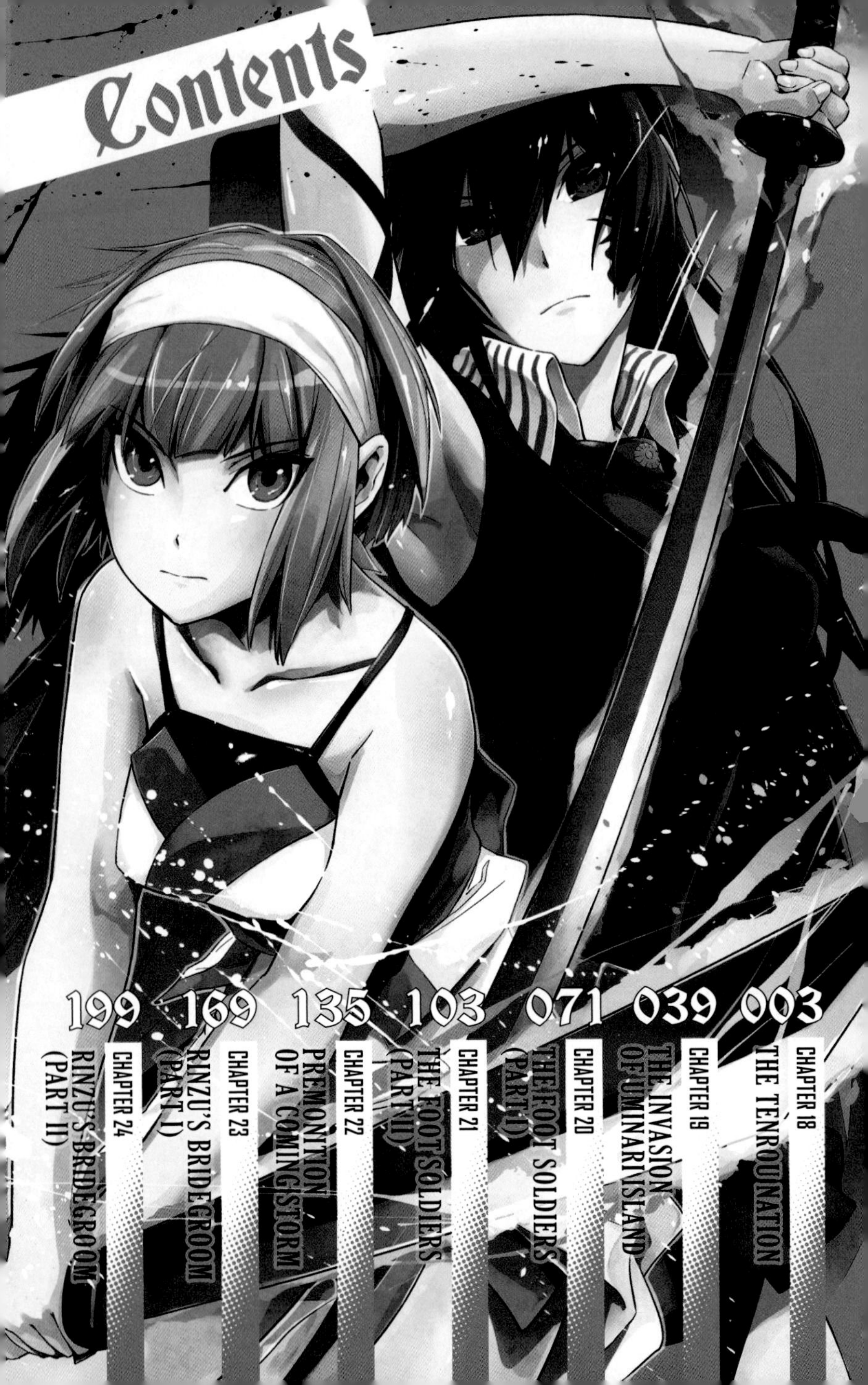

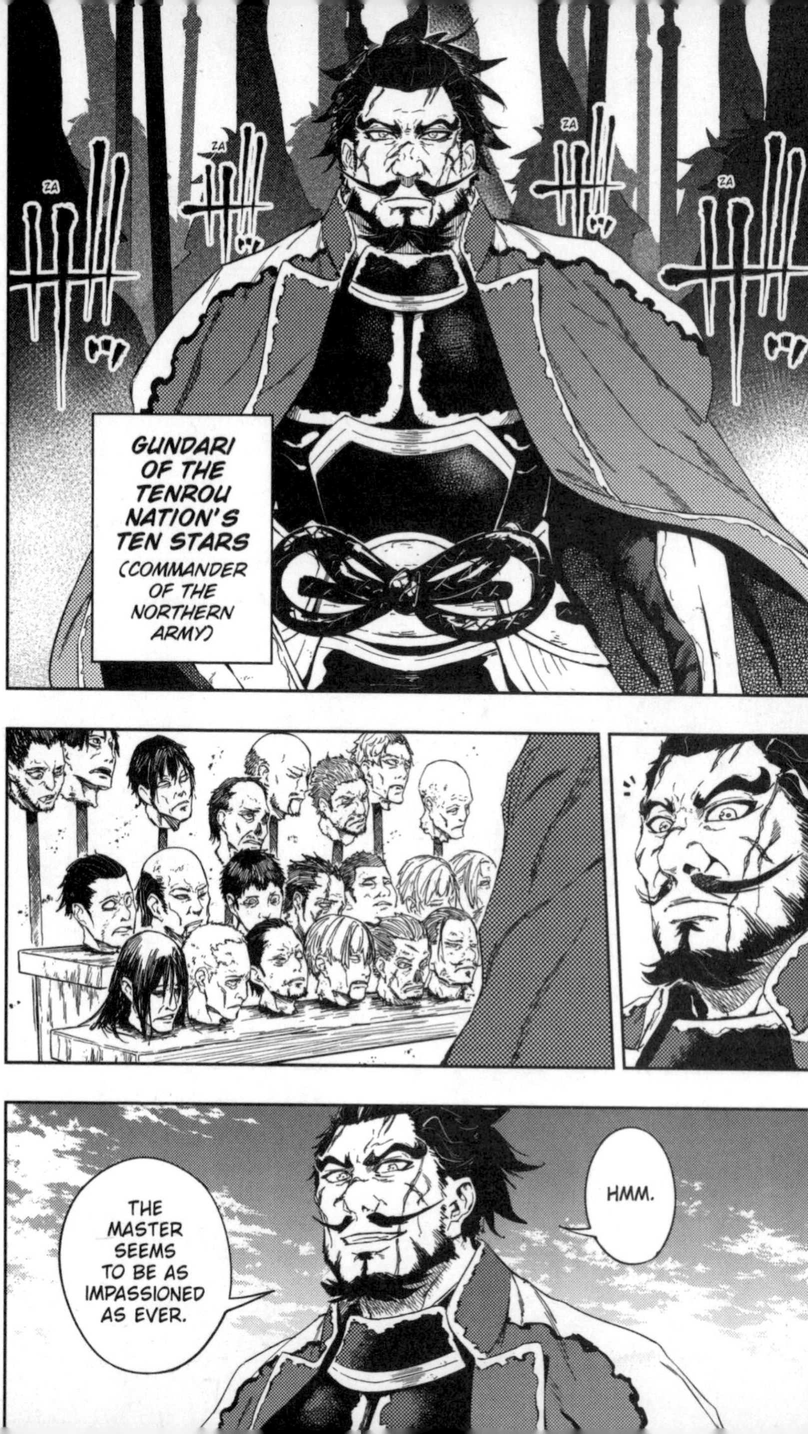
ZA
ZA
ZA
ZA
GUNDARI OF THE TENROU NATION'S TEN STARS (COMMANDER OF THE NORTHERN ARMY)
HMM.
THE MASTER SEEMS TO BE AS IMPASSIONED AS EVER.

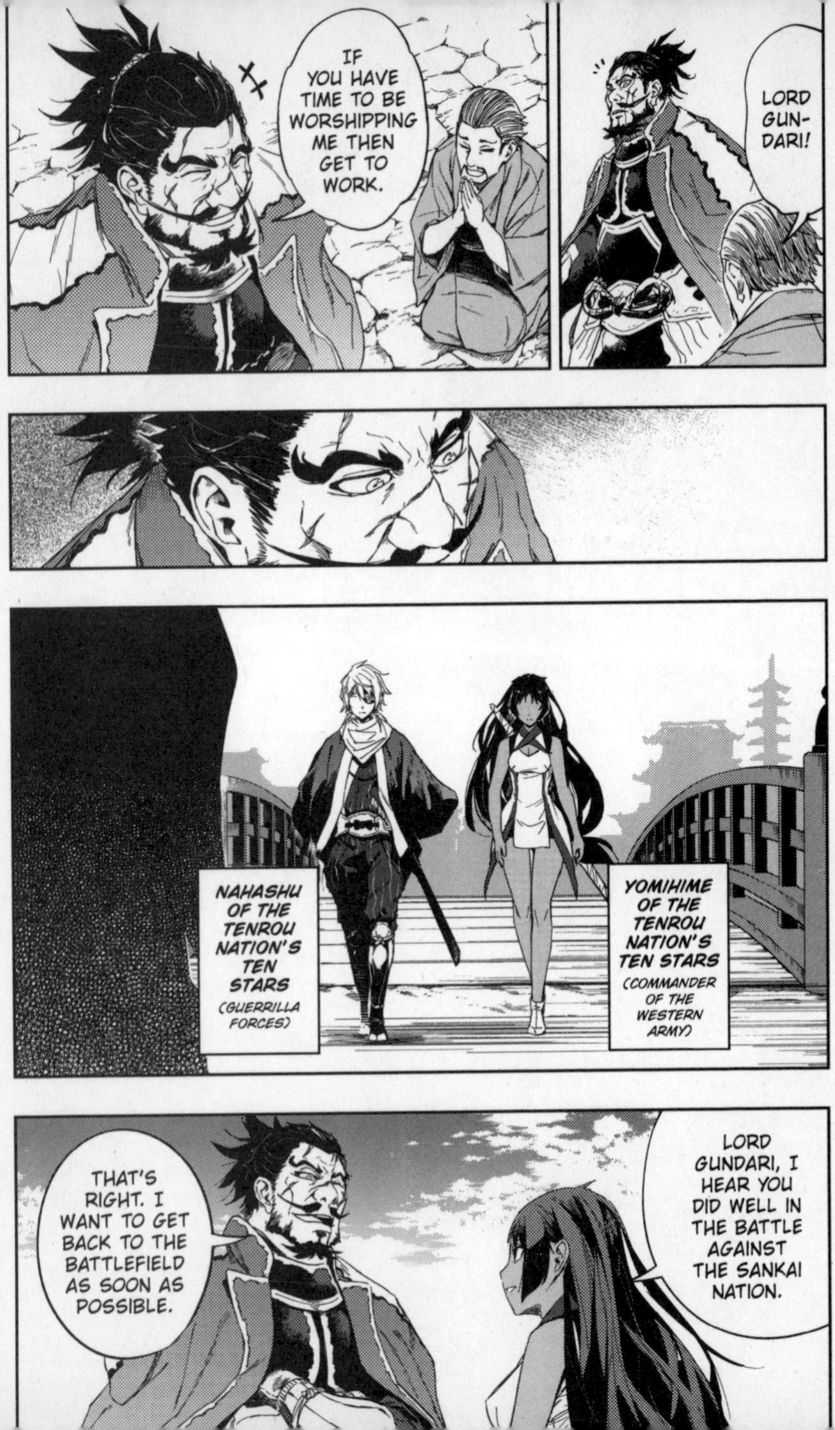
LORD GUNDARI!
IF YOU HAVE TIME TO BE WORSHIPPING ME THEN GET TO WORK.
YOMIHIME OF THE TENROU NATION'S TEN STARS (COMMANDER OF THE WESTERN ARMY)
NAHASHU OF THE TENROU NATION'S TEN STARS (GUERRILLA FORCES)
LORD GUNDARI, I HEAR YOU DID WELL IN THE BATTLE AGAINST THE SANKAI NATION.
THAT'S RIGHT. I WANT TO GET BACK TO THE BATTLEFIELD AS SOON AS POSSIBLE.

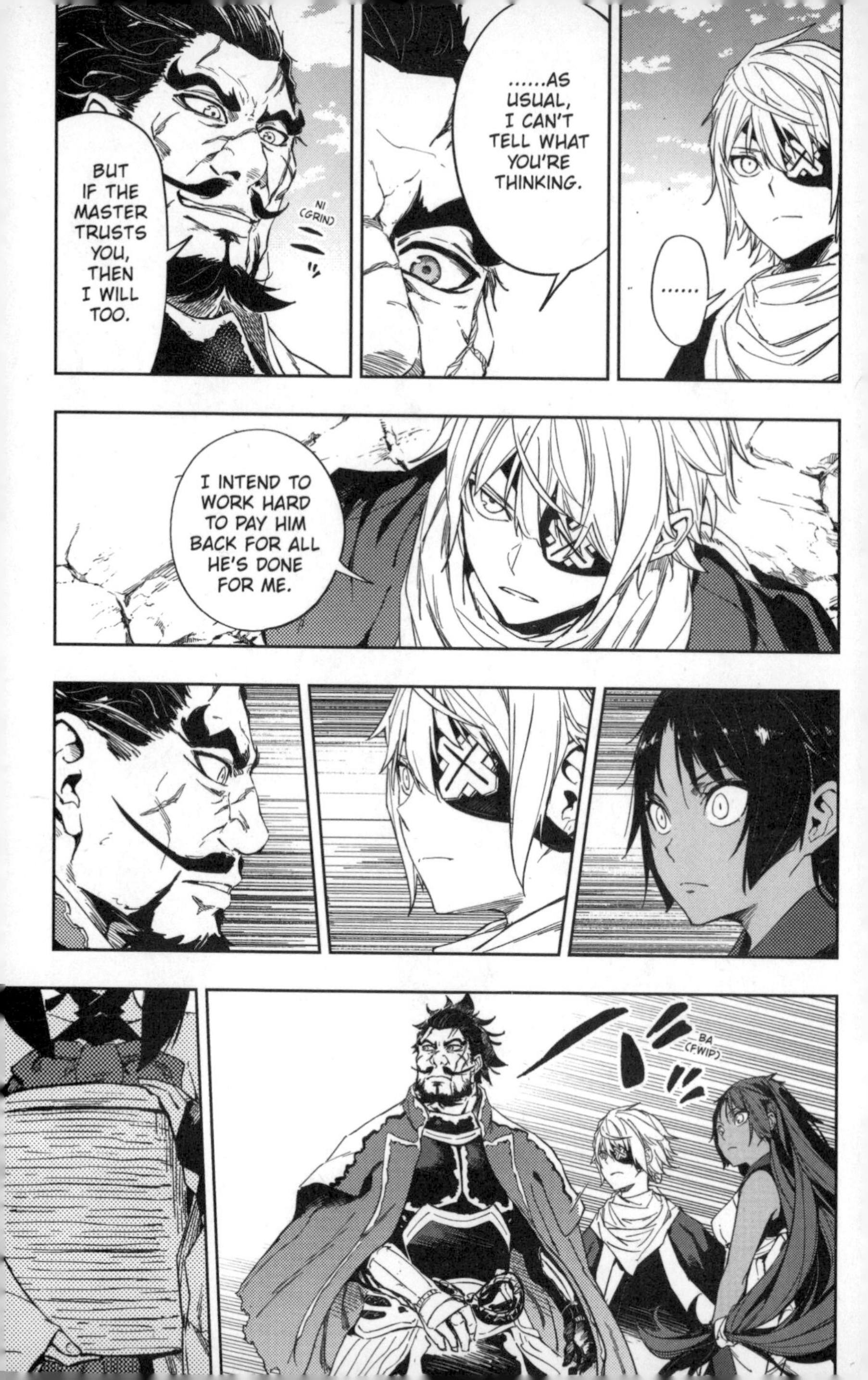
......
......AS USUAL, I CAN'T TELL WHAT YOU'RE THINKING.
NI (GRIN)
BUT IF THE MASTER TRUSTS YOU, THEN I WILL TOO.
I INTEND TO WORK HARD TO PAY HIM BACK FOR ALL HE'S DONE FOR ME.
BA (FWIP)

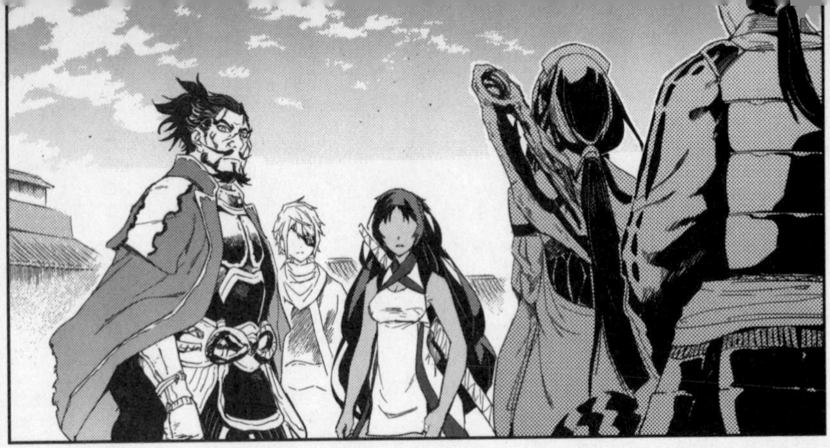

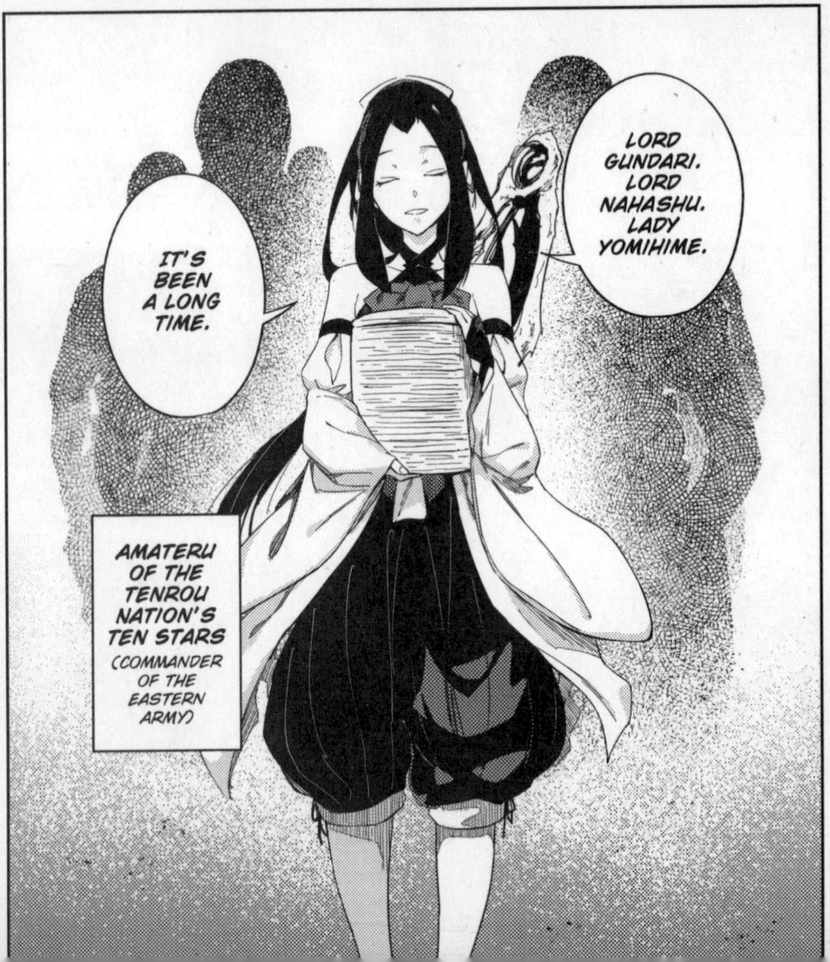
LORD GUNDARI. LORD NAHASHU. LADY YOMIHIME.
IT'S BEEN A LONG TIME.
AMATERU OF THE TENROU NATION'S TEN STARS
(COMMANDER OF THE EASTERN ARMY)

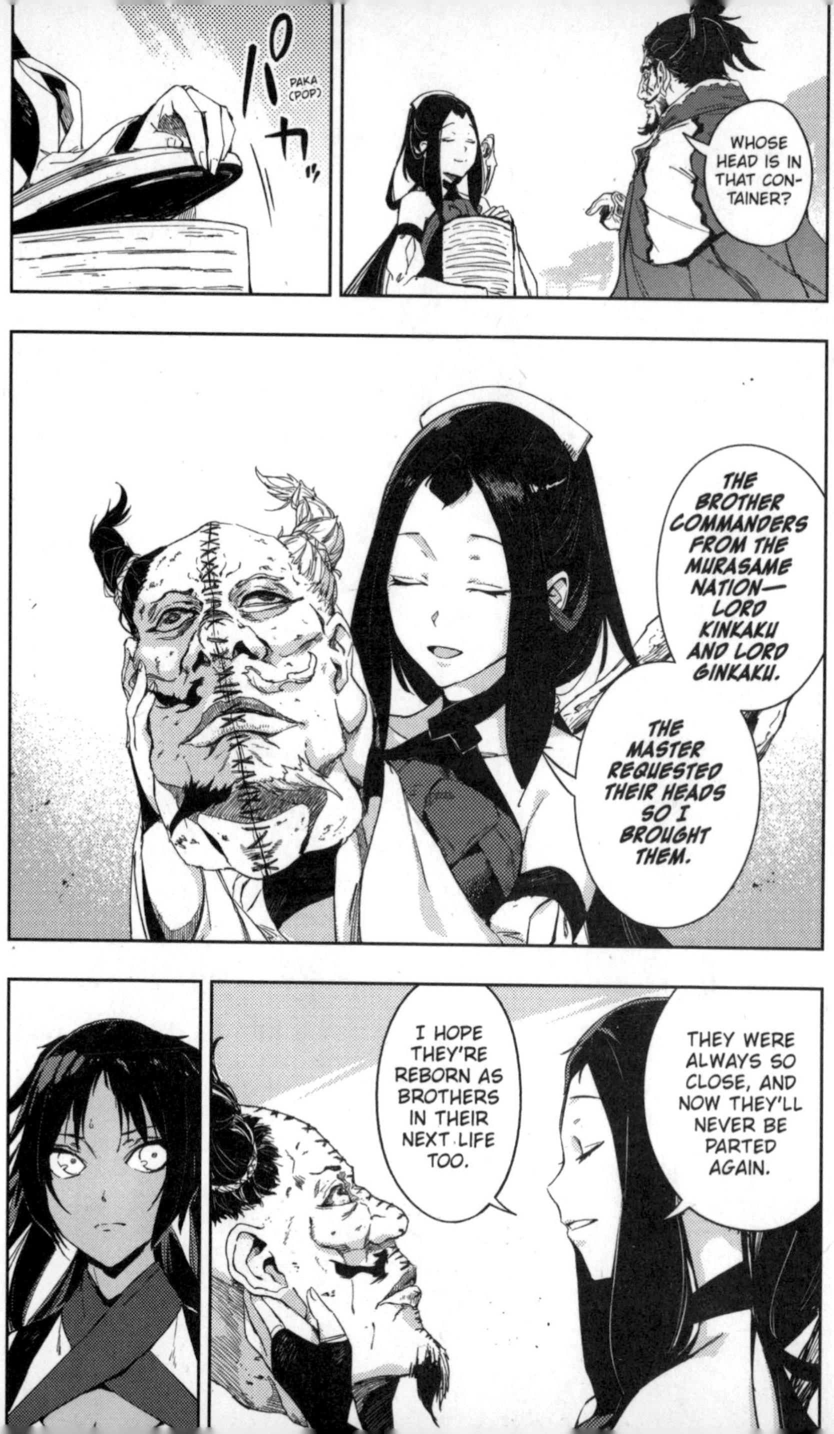
WHOSE HEAD IS IN THAT CONTAINER?
パカ
PAKA (POP)
THE BROTHER COMMANDERS FROM THE MURASAME NATION—LORD KINKAKU AND LORD GINKAKU.
THE MASTER REQUESTED THEIR HEADS SO I BROUGHT THEM.
THEY WERE ALWAYS SO CLOSE, AND NOW THEY'LL NEVER BE PARTED AGAIN.
I HOPE THEY'RE REBORN AS BROTHERS IN THEIR NEXT LIFE TOO.

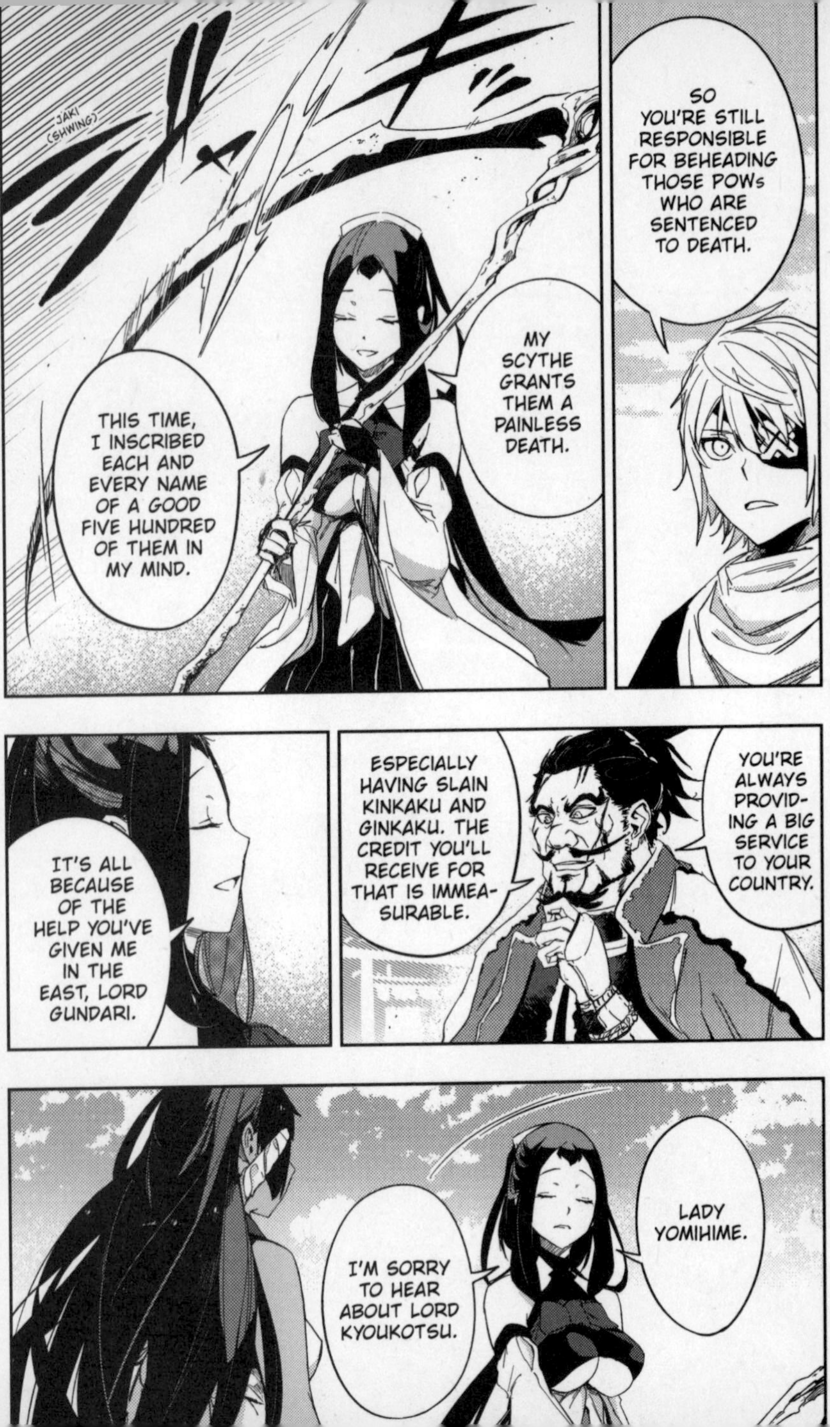
SO YOU'RE STILL RESPONSIBLE FOR BEHEADING THOSE POWs WHO ARE SENTENCED TO DEATH.
JAKI (SHWING)
MY SCYTHE GRANTS THEM A PAINLESS DEATH.
THIS TIME, I INSCRIBED EACH AND EVERY NAME OF A GOOD FIVE HUNDRED OF THEM IN MY MIND.
YOU'RE ALWAYS PROVIDING A BIG SERVICE TO YOUR COUNTRY.
ESPECIALLY HAVING SLAIN KINKAKU AND GINKAKU. THE CREDIT YOU'LL RECEIVE FOR THAT IS IMMEASURABLE.
IT'S ALL BECAUSE OF THE HELP YOU'VE GIVEN ME IN THE EAST, LORD GUNDARI.
LADY YOMIHIME.
I'M SORRY TO HEAR ABOUT LORD KYOUKOTSU.

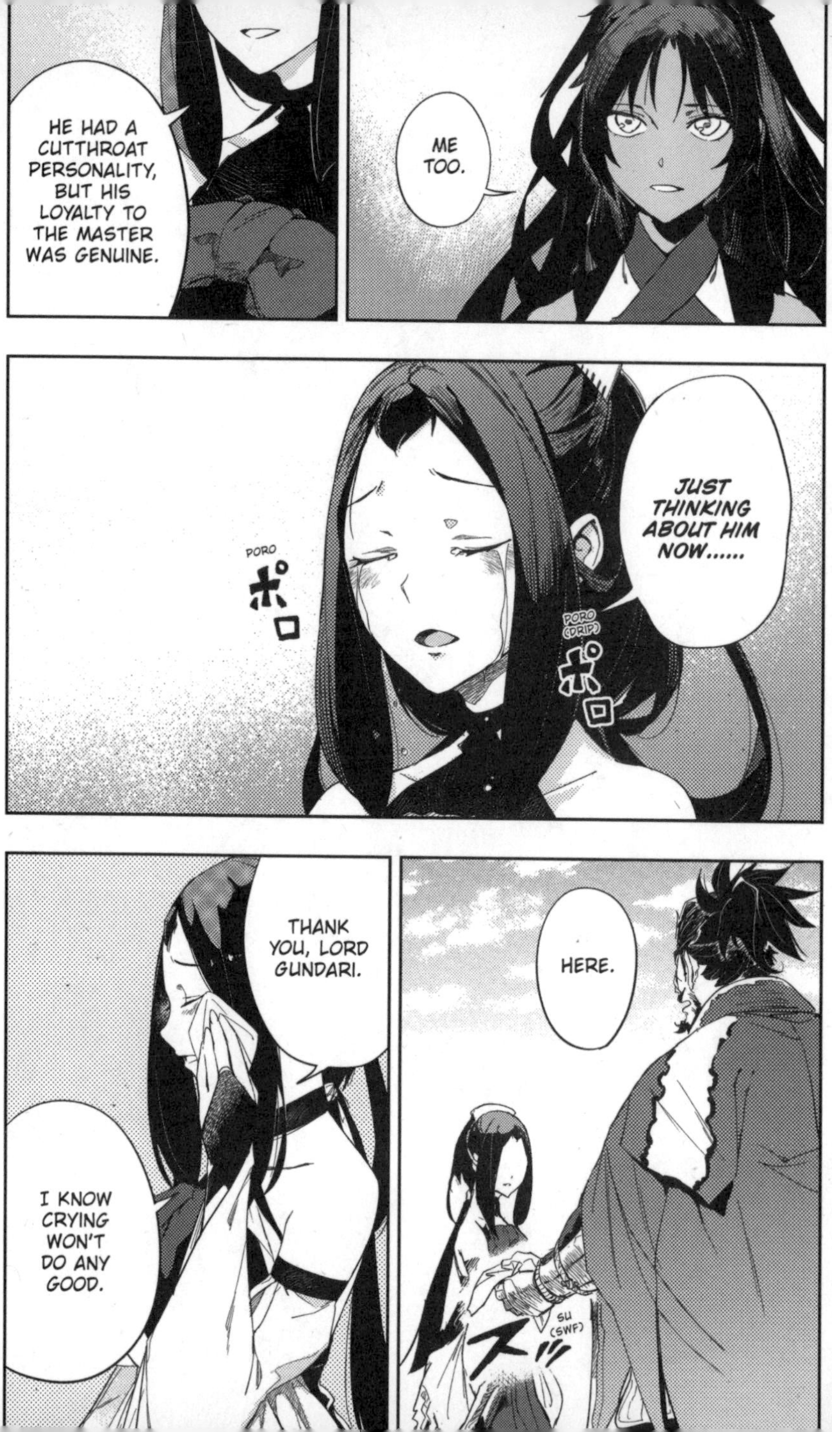
ME TOO.
HE HAD A CUTTHROAT PERSONALITY, BUT HIS LOYALTY TO THE MASTER WAS GENUINE.
JUST THINKING ABOUT HIM NOW......
PORO (DRIP)
ポロ
PORO
ポロ
HERE.
SU (SWF)
ス
THANK YOU, LORD GUNDARI.
I KNOW CRYING WON'T DO ANY GOOD.

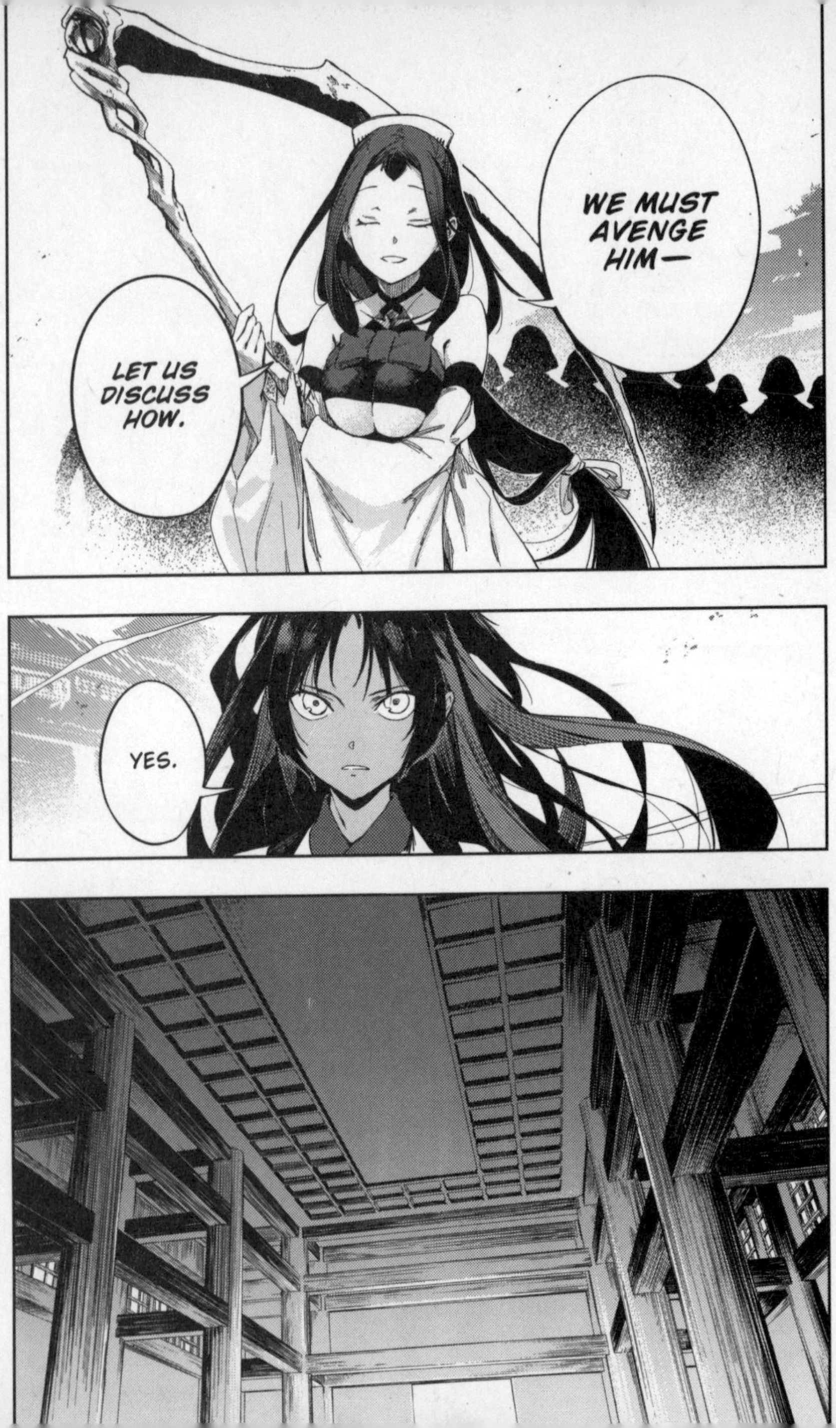
WE MUST AVENGE HIM—
LET US DISCUSS HOW.
YES.

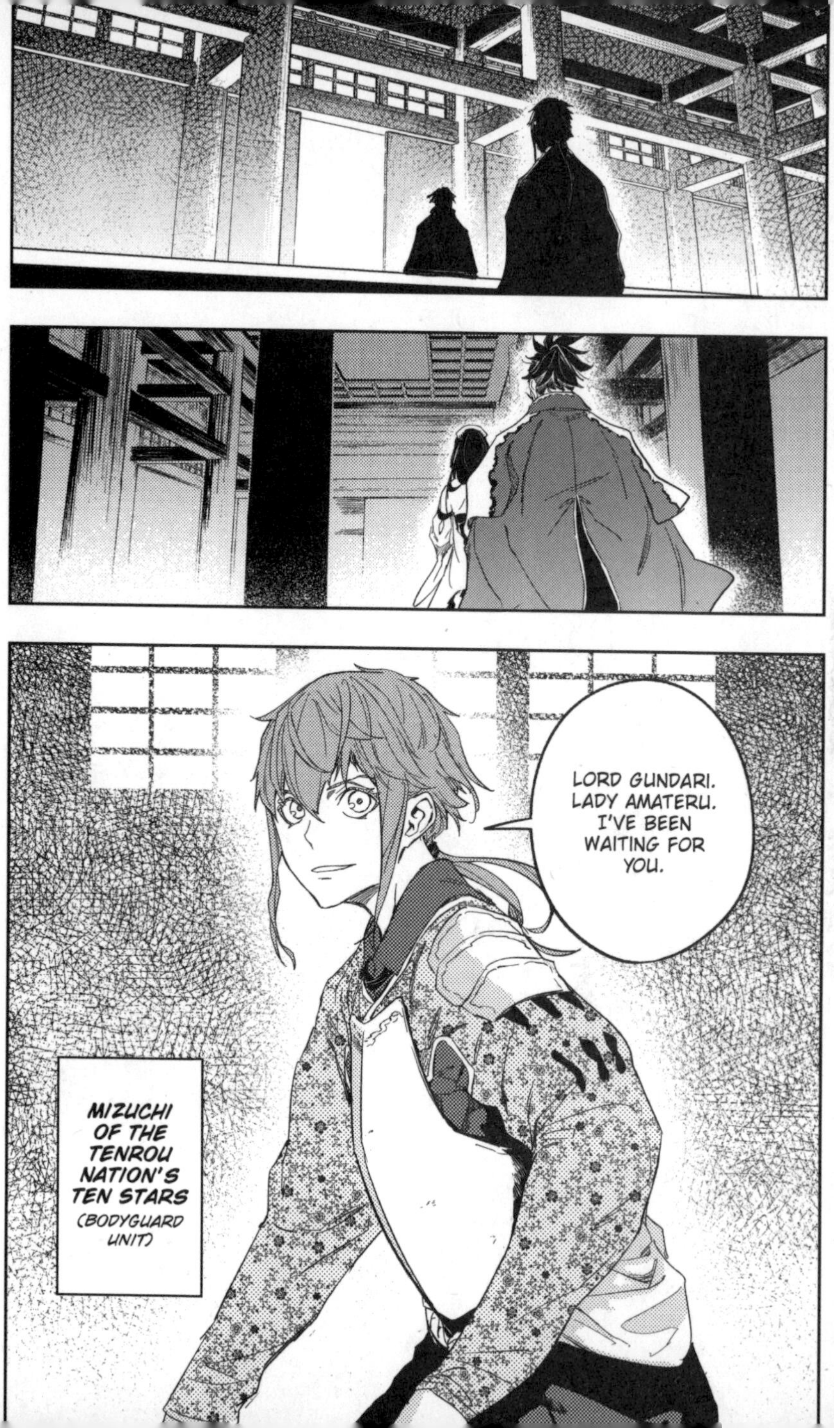
LORD GUNDARI. LADY AMATERU. I'VE BEEN WAITING FOR YOU.
MIZUCHI OF THE TENROU NATION'S TEN STARS (BODYGUARD UNIT)

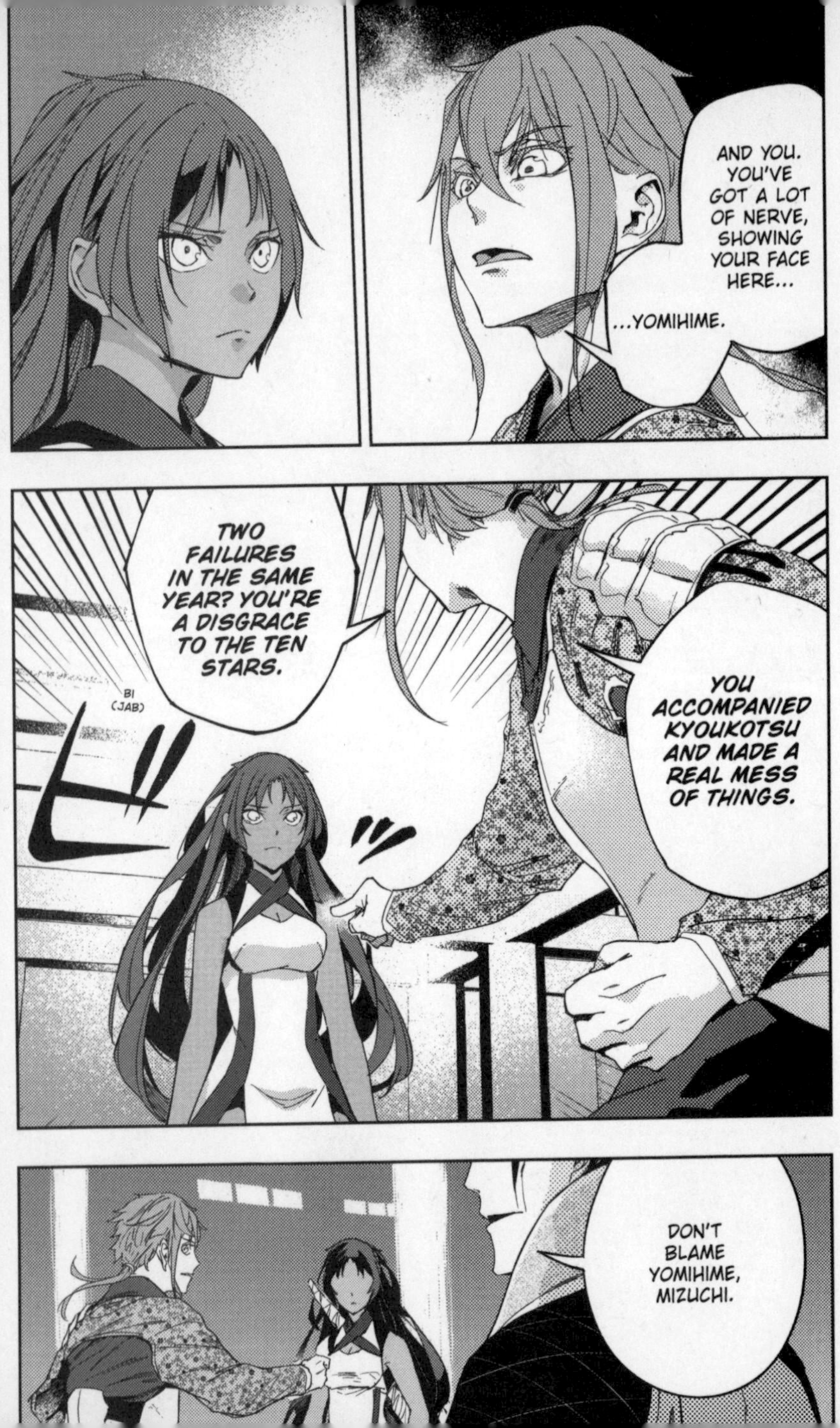
AND YOU. YOU'VE GOT A LOT OF NERVE, SHOWING YOUR FACE HERE...
...YOMIHIME.
YOU ACCOMPANIED KYOUKOTSU AND MADE A REAL MESS OF THINGS.
TWO FAILURES IN THE SAME YEAR? YOU'RE A DISGRACE TO THE TEN STARS.
BI (JAB)
DON'T BLAME YOMIHIME, MIZUCHI.

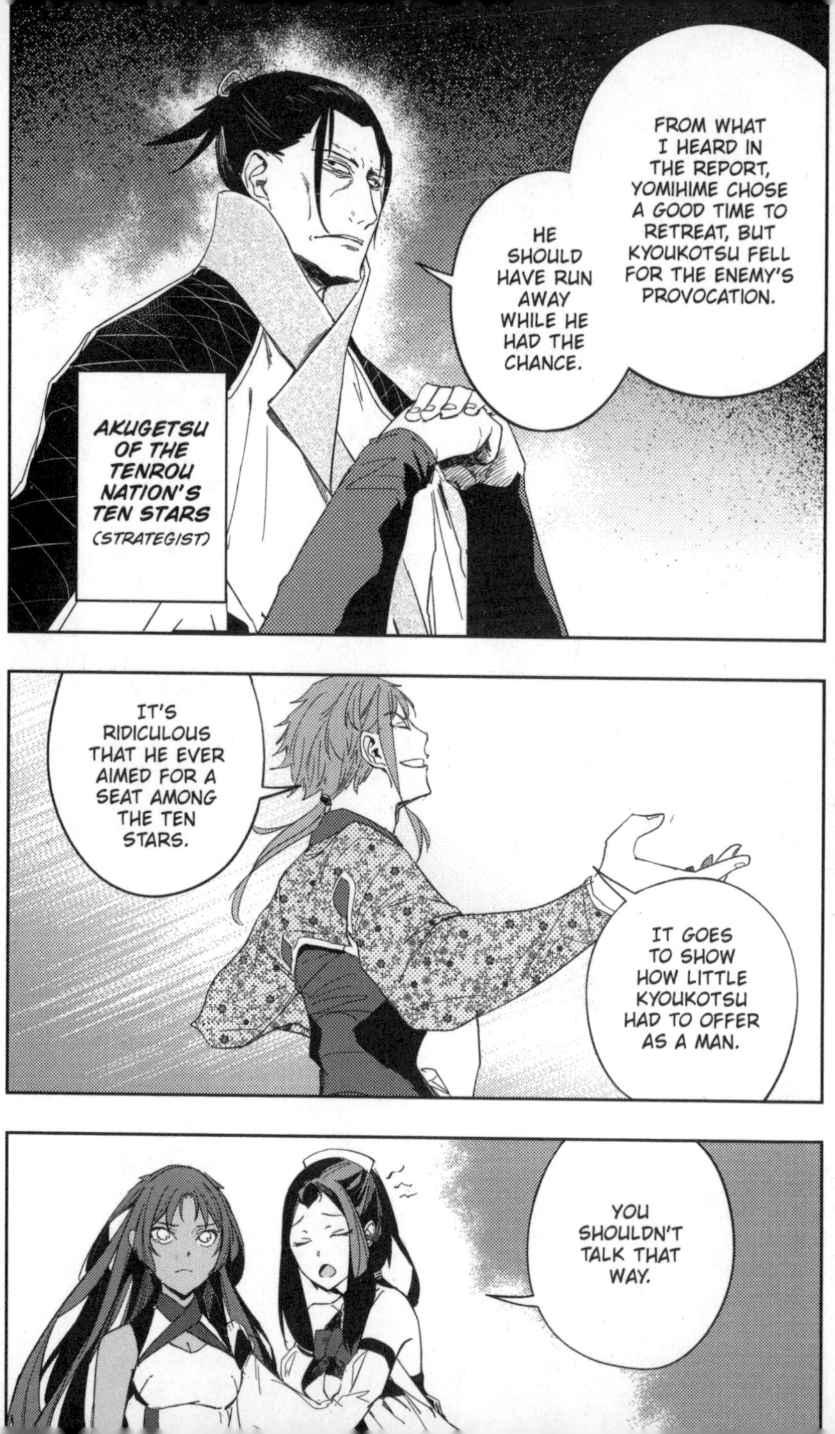
FROM WHAT I HEARD IN THE REPORT, YOMIHIME CHOSE A GOOD TIME TO RETREAT, BUT KYOUKOTSU FELL FOR THE ENEMY'S PROVOCATION.
HE SHOULD HAVE RUN AWAY WHILE HE HAD THE CHANCE.
AKUGETSU OF THE TENROU NATION'S TEN STARS (STRATEGIST)
IT'S RIDICULOUS THAT HE EVER AIMED FOR A SEAT AMONG THE TEN STARS.
IT GOES TO SHOW HOW LITTLE KYOUKOTSU HAD TO OFFER AS A MAN.
YOU SHOULDN'T TALK THAT WAY.

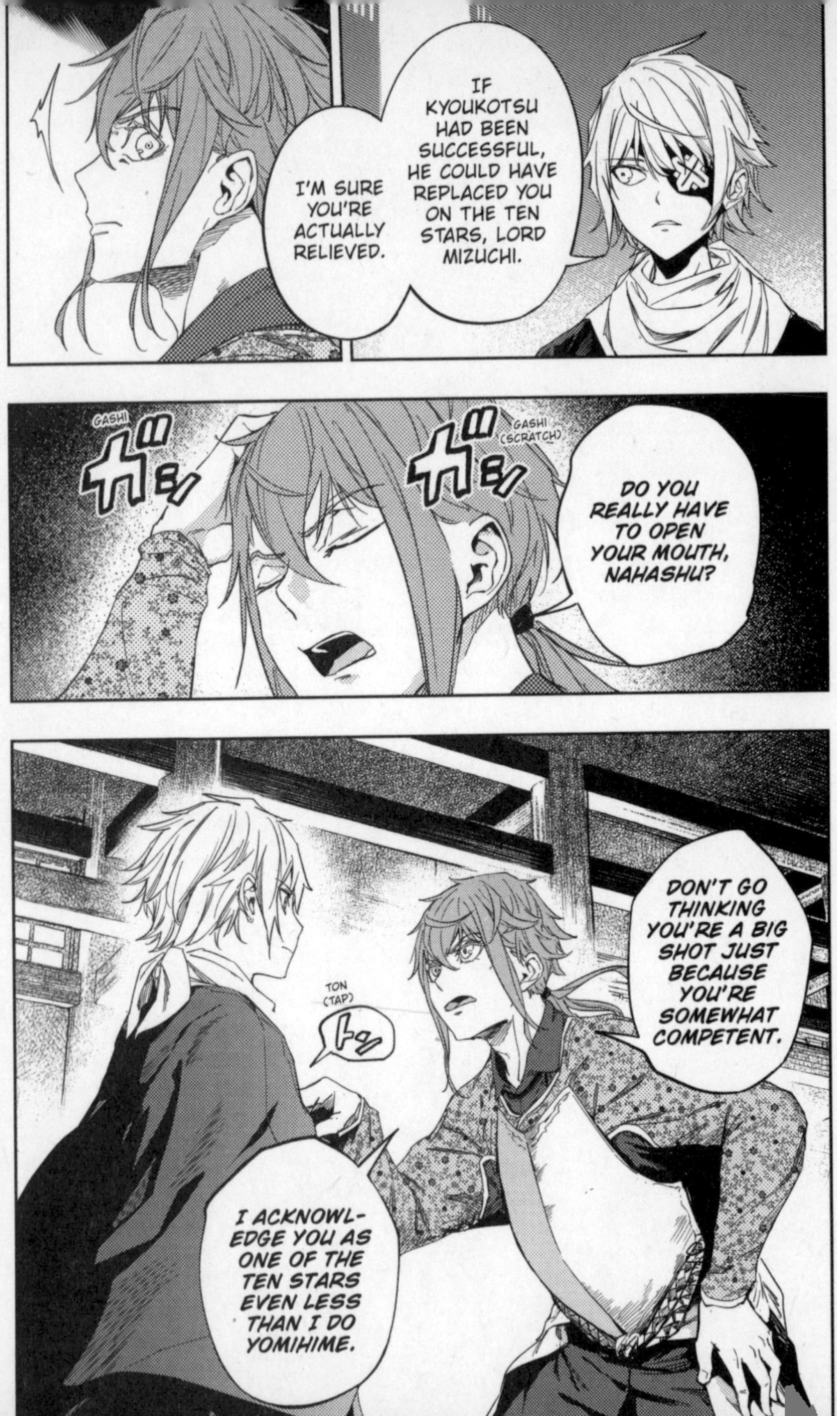
IF KYOUKOTSU HAD BEEN SUCCESSFUL, HE COULD HAVE REPLACED YOU ON THE TEN STARS, LORD MIZUCHI.
I'M SURE YOU'RE ACTUALLY RELIEVED.
DO YOU REALLY HAVE TO OPEN YOUR MOUTH, NAHASHU?
GASHI (SCRATCH)
GASHI
DON'T GO THINKING YOU'RE A BIG SHOT JUST BECAUSE YOU'RE SOMEWHAT COMPETENT.
TON (TAP)
I ACKNOWL-EDGE YOU AS ONE OF THE TEN STARS EVEN LESS THAN I DO YOMIHIME.

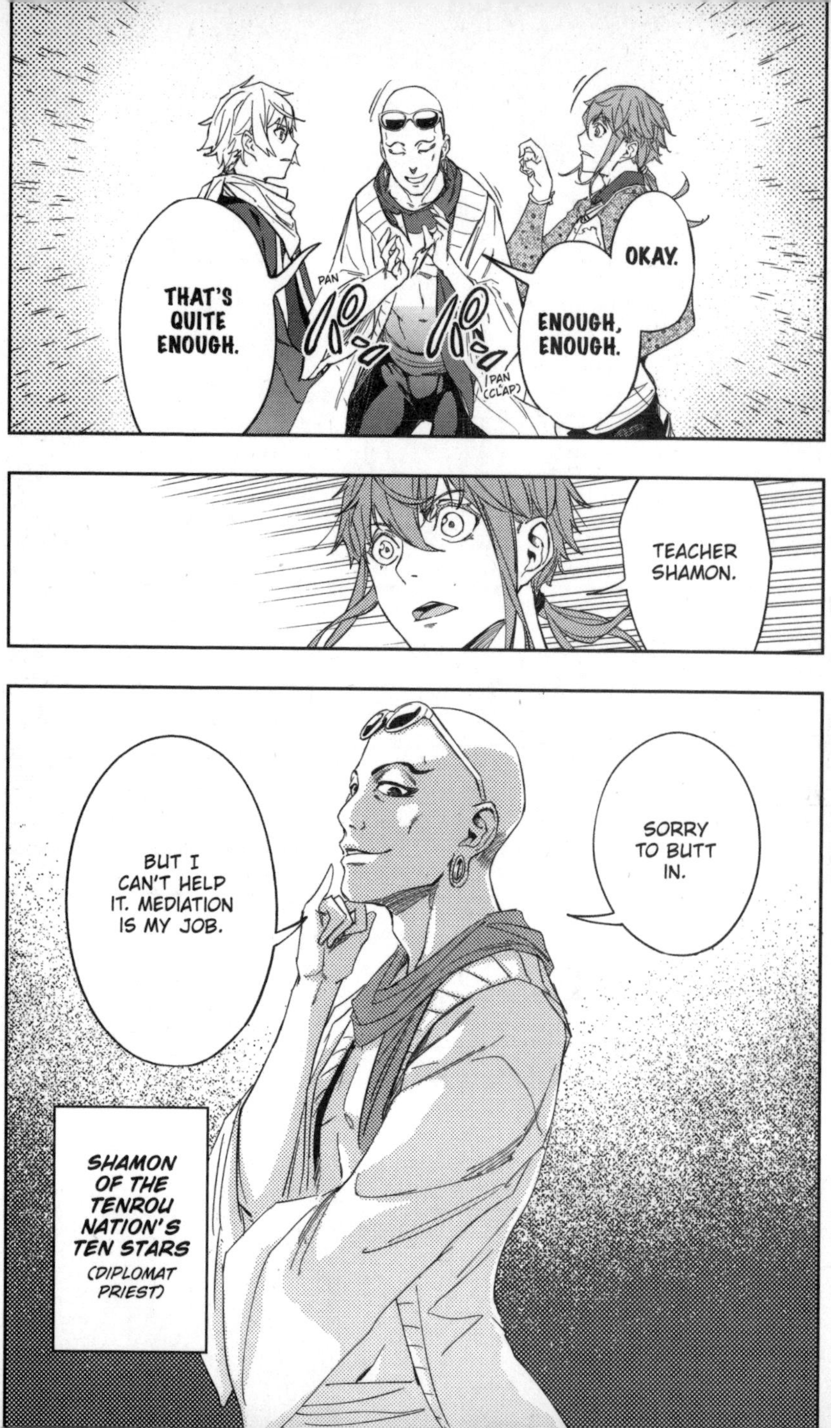
OKAY.
ENOUGH, ENOUGH.
PAN
PAN (CLAP)
THAT'S QUITE ENOUGH.
TEACHER SHAMON.
SORRY TO BUTT IN.
BUT I CAN'T HELP IT. MEDIATION IS MY JOB.
SHAMON OF THE TENROU NATION'S TEN STARS (DIPLOMAT PRIEST)

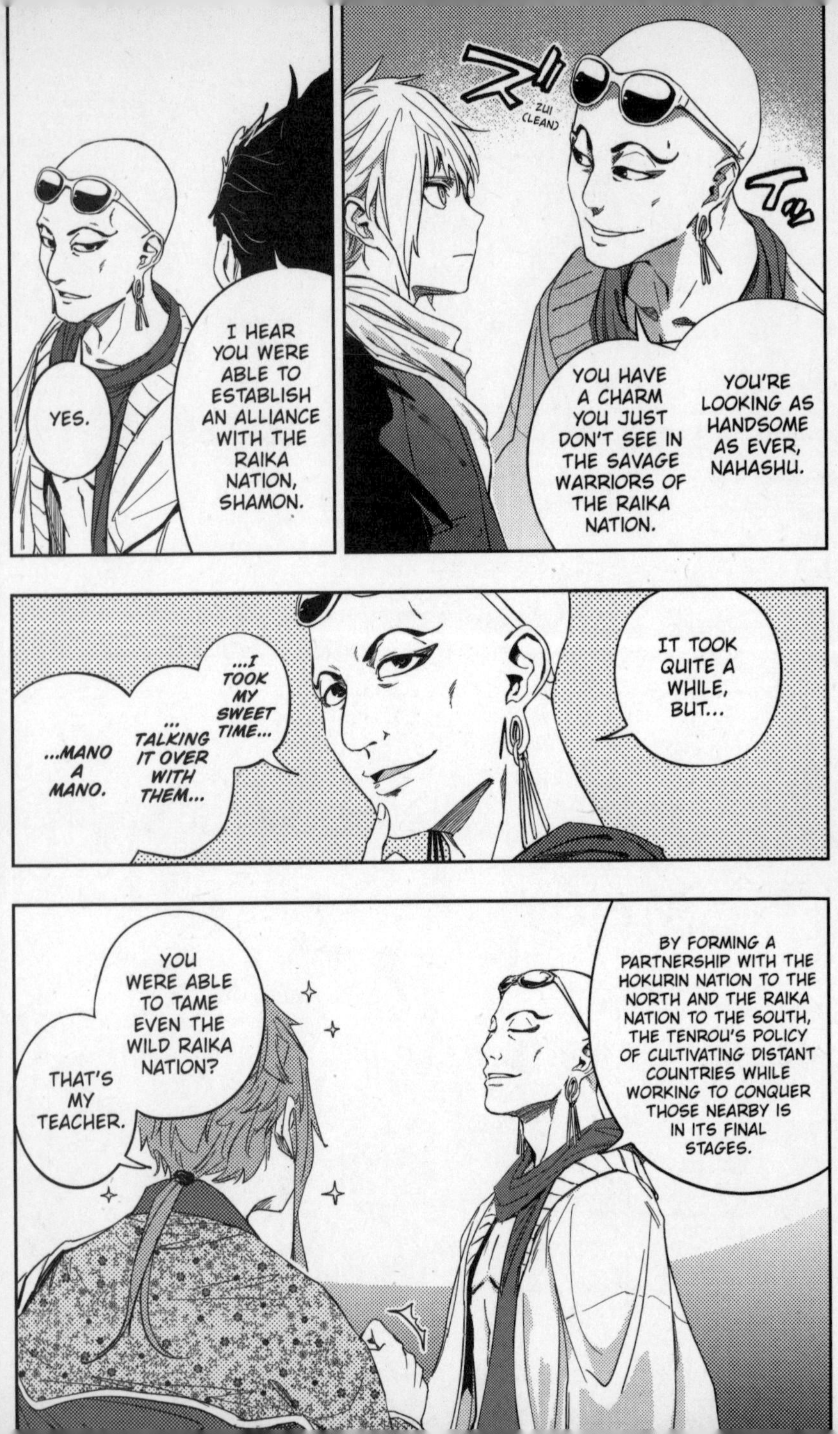
ZUI (LEAN)
YOU'RE LOOKING AS HANDSOME AS EVER, NAHASHU.
YOU HAVE A CHARM YOU JUST DON'T SEE IN THE SAVAGE WARRIORS OF THE RAIKA NATION.
I HEAR YOU WERE ABLE TO ESTABLISH AN ALLIANCE WITH THE RAIKA NATION, SHAMON.
YES.
IT TOOK QUITE A WHILE, BUT...
...I TOOK MY SWEET TIME...
...TALKING IT OVER WITH THEM...
...MANO A MANO.
BY FORMING A PARTNERSHIP WITH THE HOKURIN NATION TO THE NORTH AND THE RAIKA NATION TO THE SOUTH, THE TENROU'S POLICY OF CULTIVATING DISTANT COUNTRIES WHILE WORKING TO CONQUER THOSE NEARBY IS IN ITS FINAL STAGES.
YOU WERE ABLE TO TAME EVEN THE WILD RAIKA NATION?
THAT'S MY TEACHER.

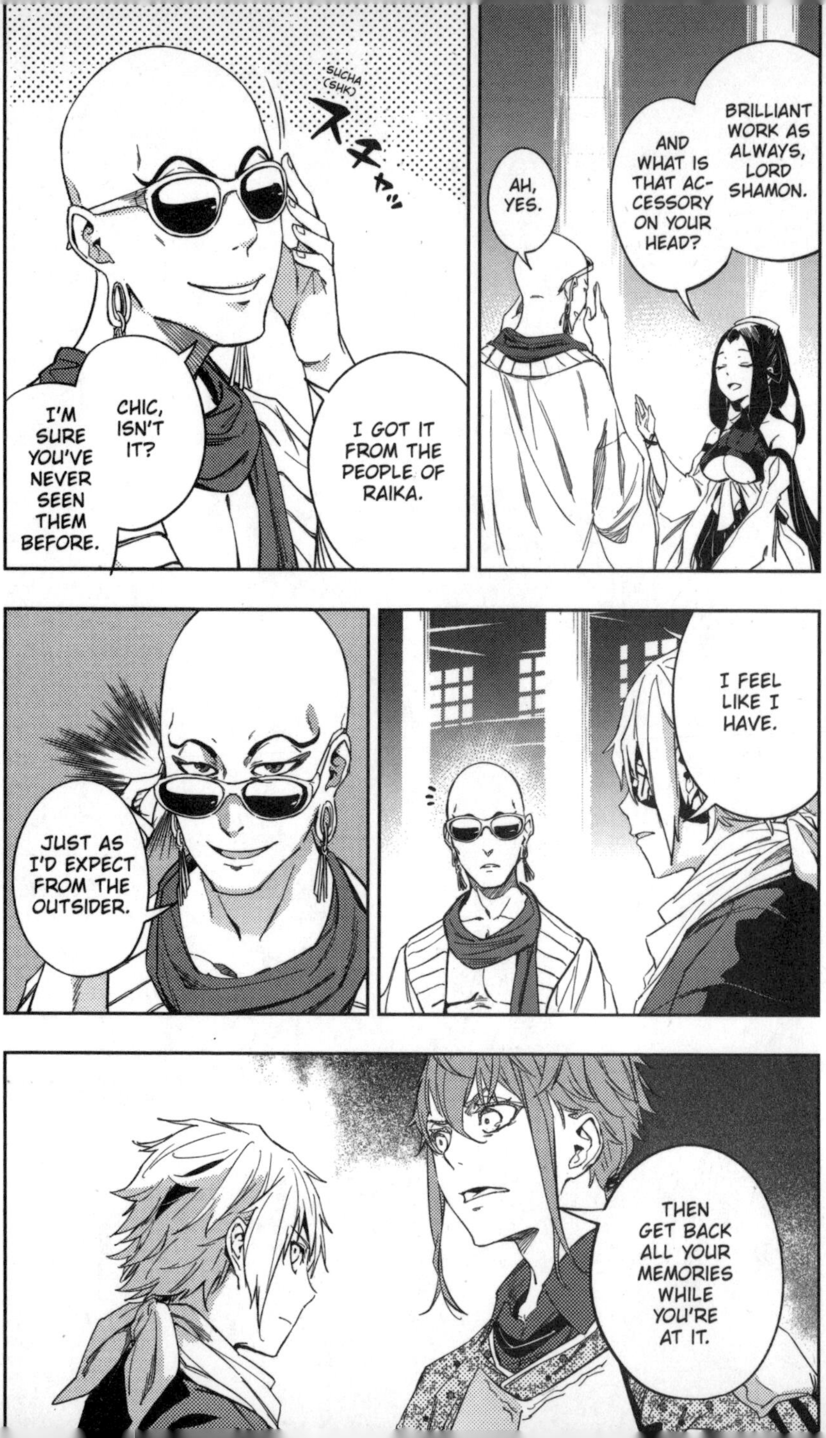
BRILLIANT WORK AS ALWAYS, LORD SHAMON.
AND WHAT IS THAT AC-CESSORY ON YOUR HEAD?
AH, YES.
SUCHA (SHK)
I GOT IT FROM THE PEOPLE OF RAIKA.
CHIC, ISN'T IT?
I'M SURE YOU'VE NEVER SEEN THEM BEFORE.
I FEEL LIKE I HAVE.
JUST AS I'D EXPECT FROM THE OUTSIDER.
THEN GET BACK ALL YOUR MEMORIES WHILE YOU'RE AT IT.

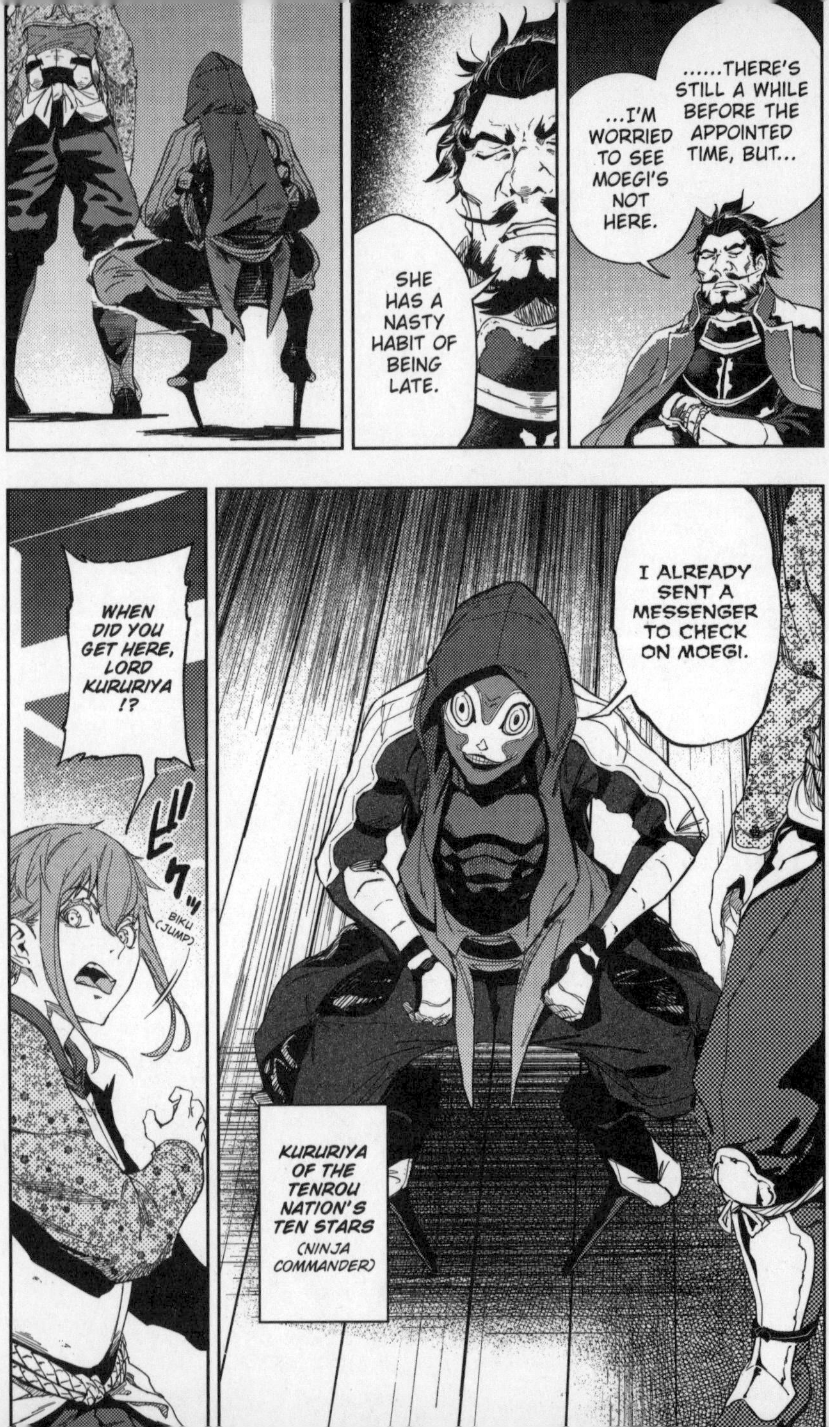
......THERE'S STILL A WHILE BEFORE THE APPOINTED TIME, BUT...
...I'M WORRIED TO SEE MOEGI'S NOT HERE.
SHE HAS A NASTY HABIT OF BEING LATE.
I ALREADY SENT A MESSENGER TO CHECK ON MOEGI.
KURURIYA OF THE TENROU NATION'S TEN STARS
(NINJA COMMANDER)
WHEN DID YOU GET HERE, LORD KURURIYA!?
ビクッ
BIKU (JUMP)

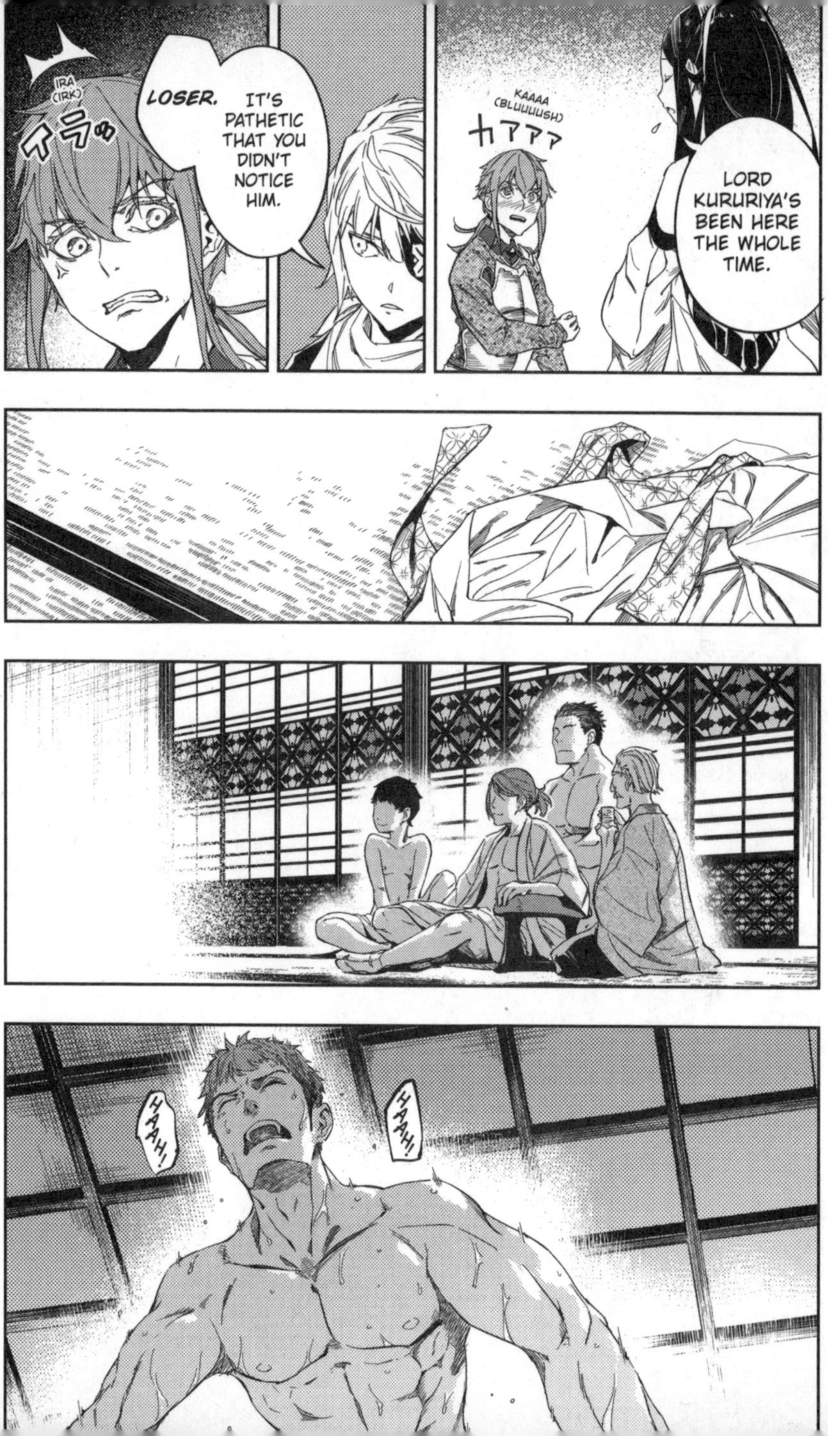
KAAAA (BLUUUUSH)
カァァァ
LORD KURURIYA'S BEEN HERE THE WHOLE TIME.
LOSER. IT'S PATHETIC THAT YOU DIDN'T NOTICE HIM.
IRA (IRK)
イラッ
HAAH!
HAAH!

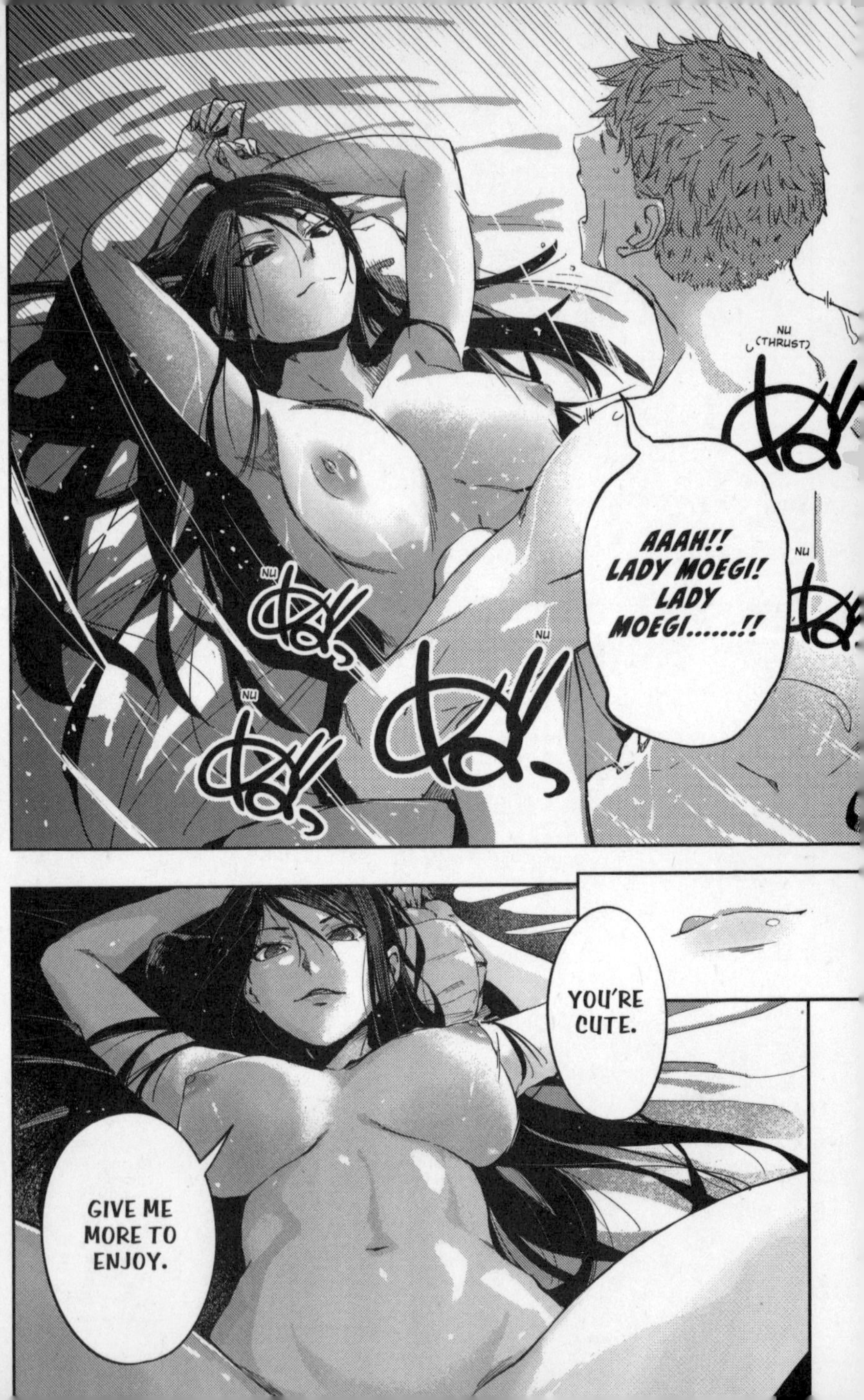
NU (THRUST)
NU
AAAH!! LADY MOEGI! LADY MOEGI......!!
NU
NU
NU
YOU'RE CUTE.
GIVE ME MORE TO ENJOY.

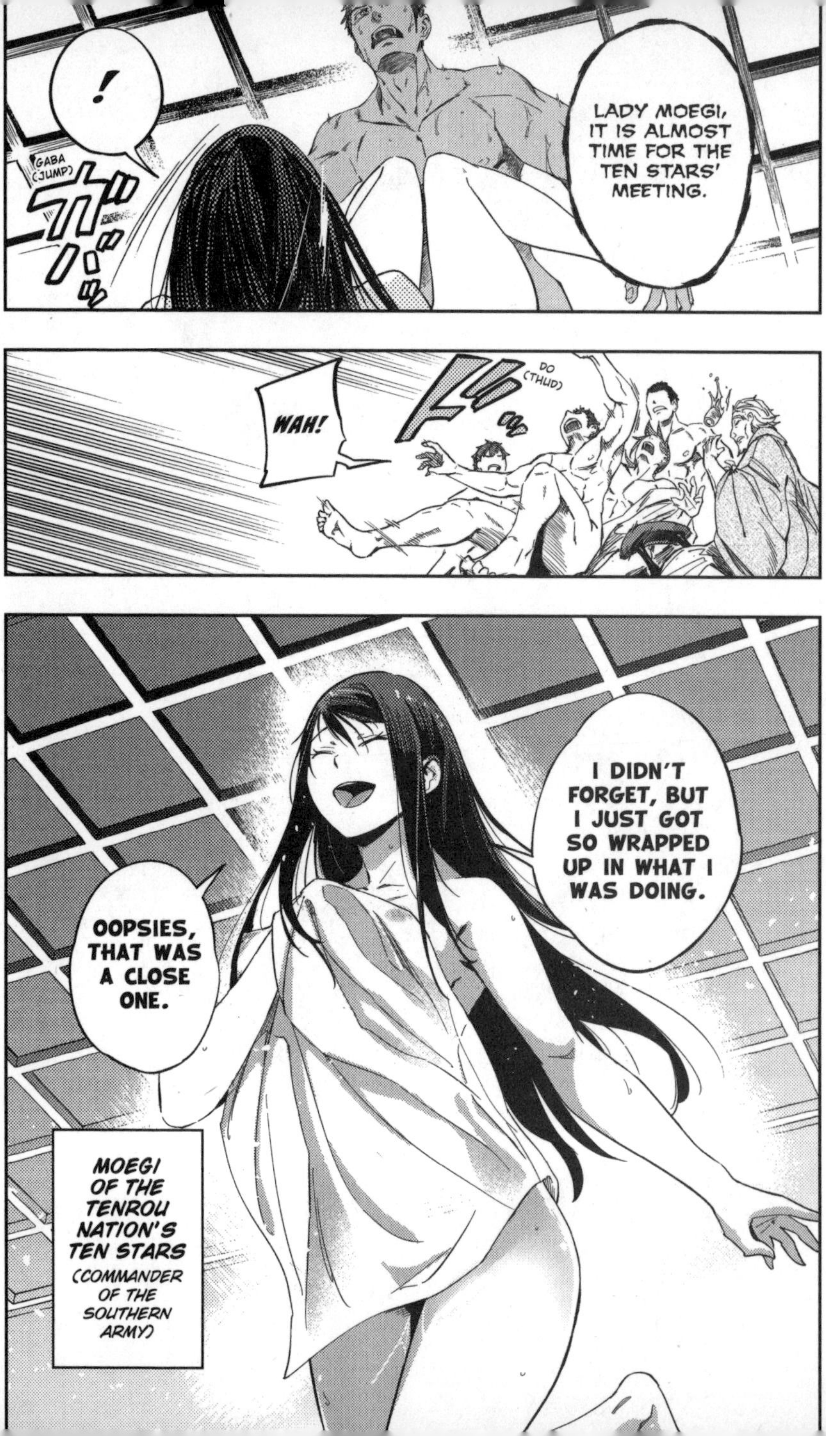
LADY MOEGI, IT IS ALMOST TIME FOR THE TEN STARS' MEETING.
!
GABA (JUMP)
DO (THUD)
WAH!
I DIDN'T FORGET, BUT I JUST GOT SO WRAPPED UP IN WHAT I WAS DOING.
OOPSIES, THAT WAS A CLOSE ONE.
MOEGI OF THE TENROU NATION'S TEN STARS (COMMANDER OF THE SOUTHERN ARMY)

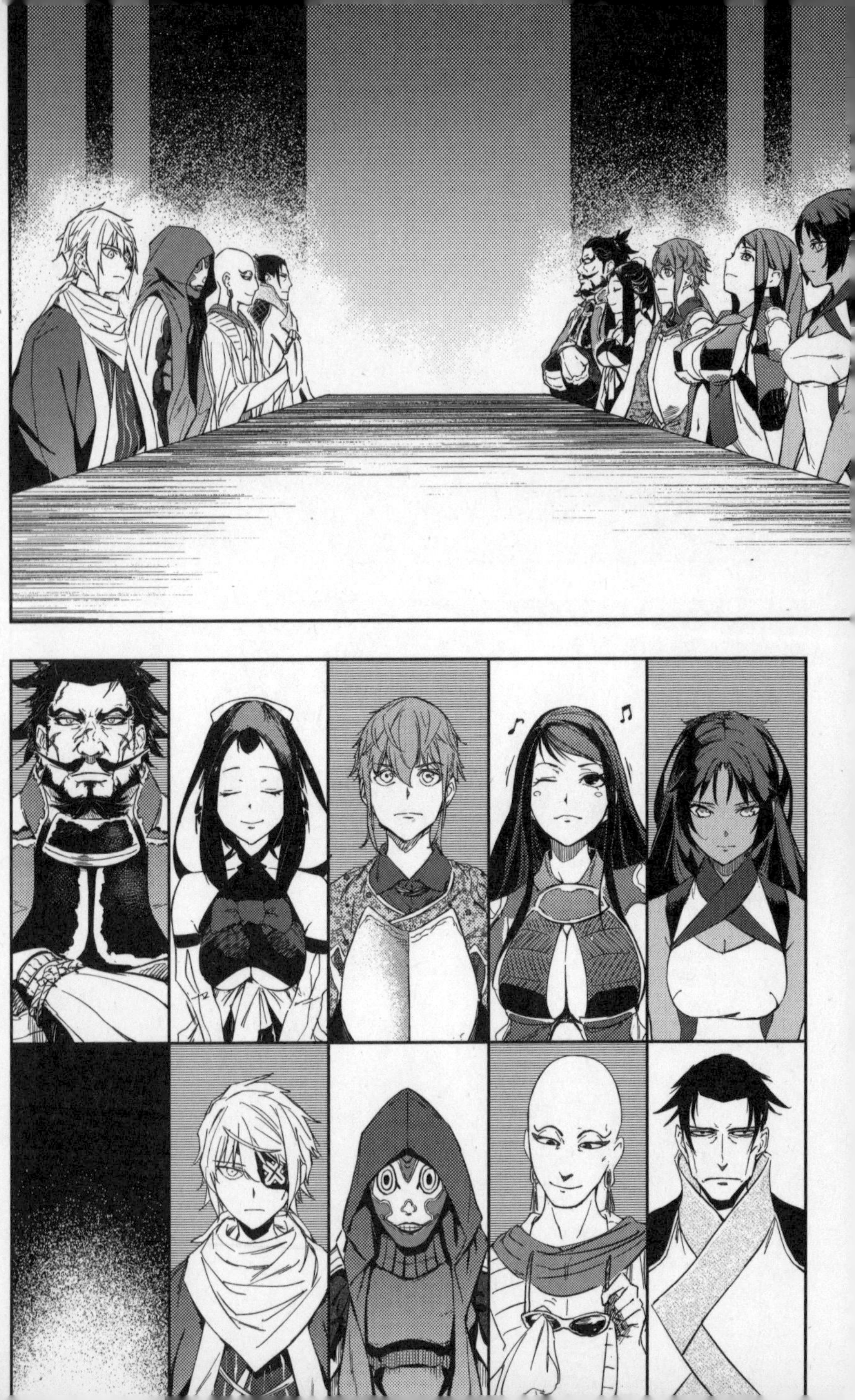

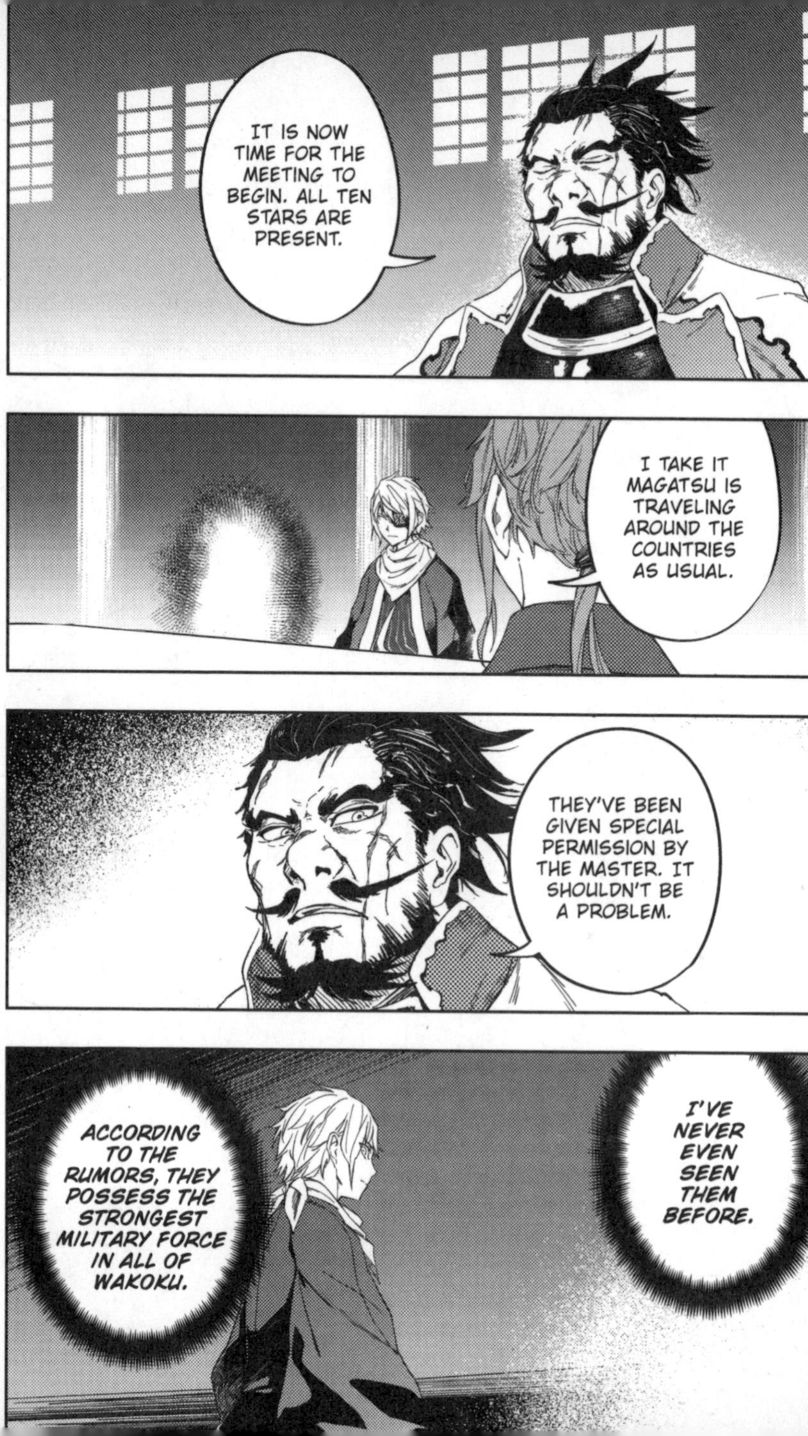
IT IS NOW TIME FOR THE MEETING TO BEGIN. ALL TEN STARS ARE PRESENT.
I TAKE IT MAGATSU IS TRAVELING AROUND THE COUNTRIES AS USUAL.
THEY'VE BEEN GIVEN SPECIAL PERMISSION BY THE MASTER. IT SHOULDN'T BE A PROBLEM.
I'VE NEVER EVEN SEEN THEM BEFORE.
ACCORDING TO THE RUMORS, THEY POSSESS THE STRONGEST MILITARY FORCE IN ALL OF WAKOKU.

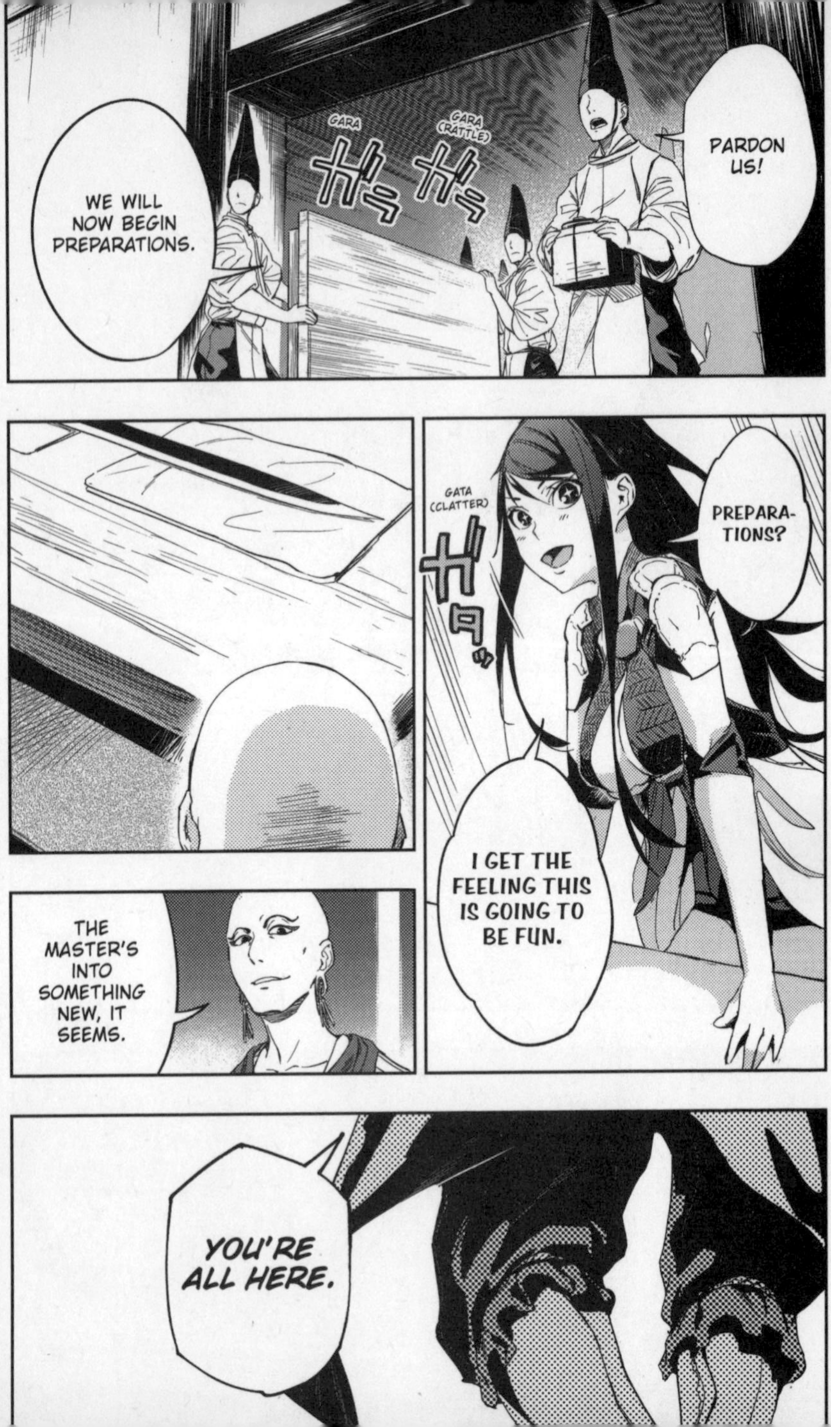
PARDON US!
GARA (RATTLE)
GARA
WE WILL NOW BEGIN PREPARATIONS.
PREPARATIONS?
GATA (CLATTER)
I GET THE FEELING THIS IS GOING TO BE FUN.
THE MASTER'S INTO SOMETHING NEW, IT SEEMS.
YOU'RE ALL HERE.

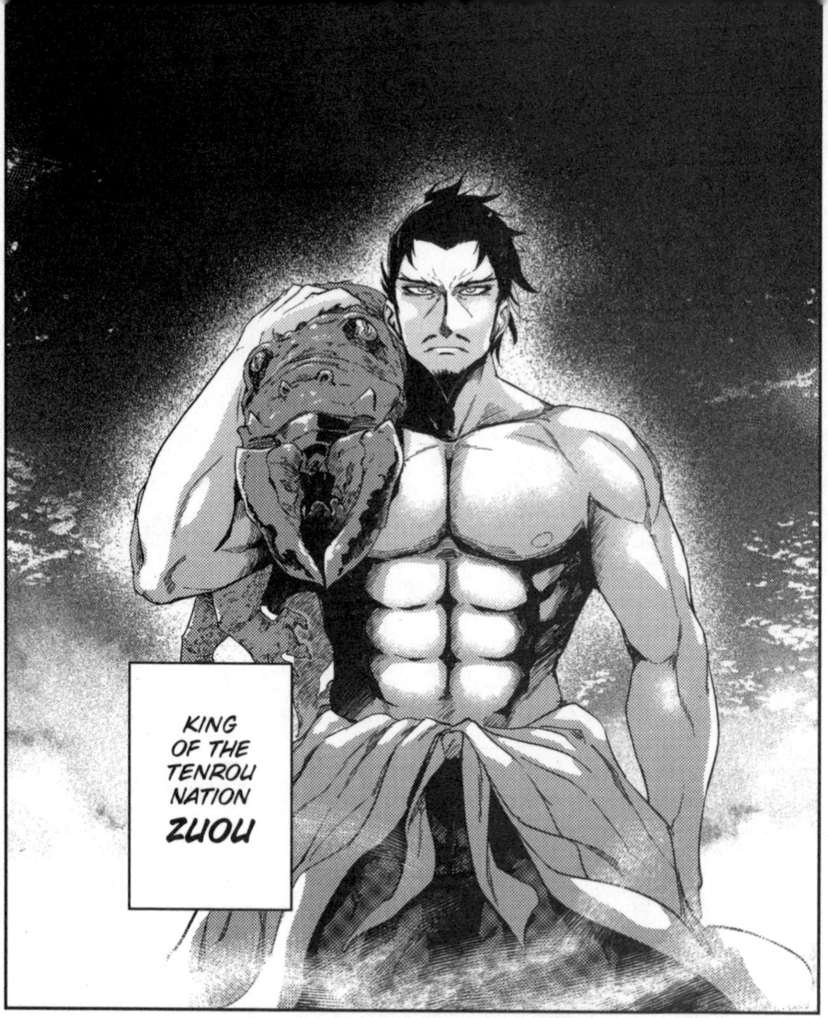
KING OF THE TENROU NATION ZUOU
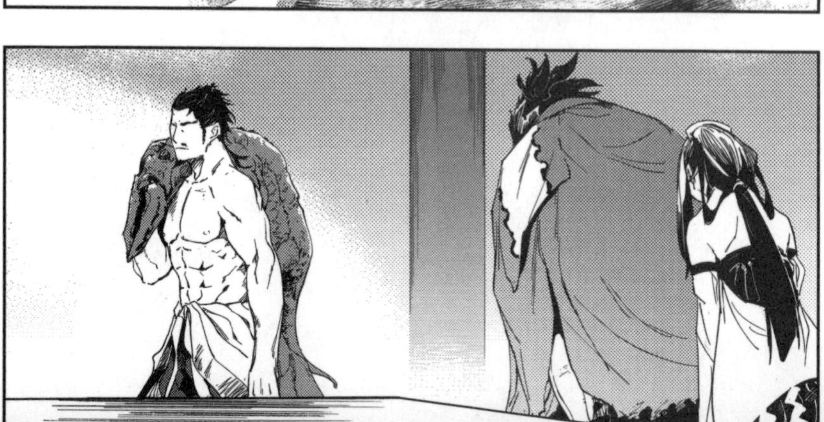

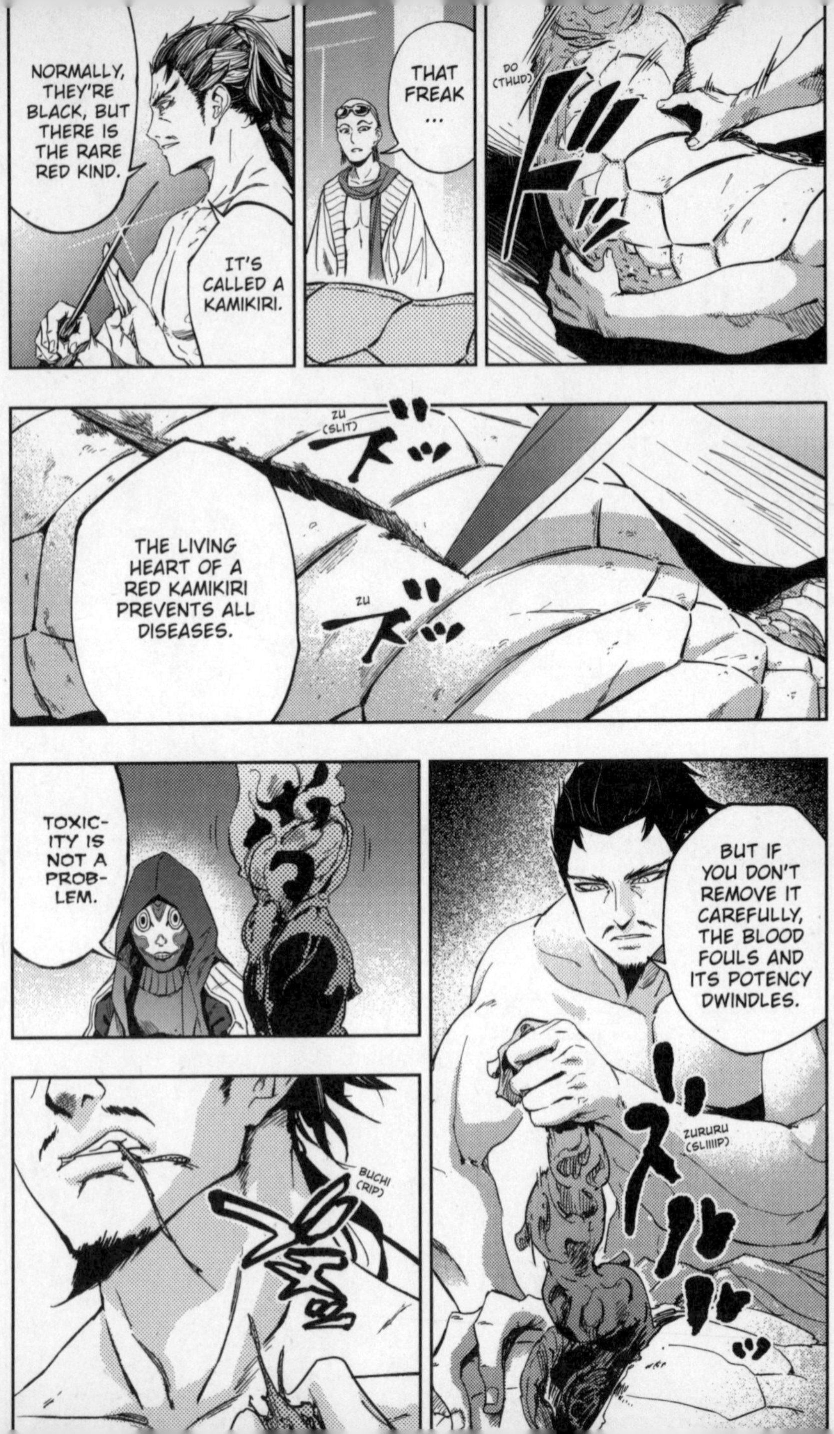
DO (THUD)
THAT FREAK ...
NORMALLY, THEY'RE BLACK, BUT THERE IS THE RARE RED KIND.
IT'S CALLED A KAMIKIRI.
ZU (SLIT)
THE LIVING HEART OF A RED KAMIKIRI PREVENTS ALL DISEASES.
ZU
BUT IF YOU DON'T REMOVE IT CAREFULLY, THE BLOOD FOULS AND ITS POTENCY DWINDLES.
ZURURU (SLIIIIP)
TOXIC-ITY IS NOT A PROB-LEM.
BUCHI (RIP)

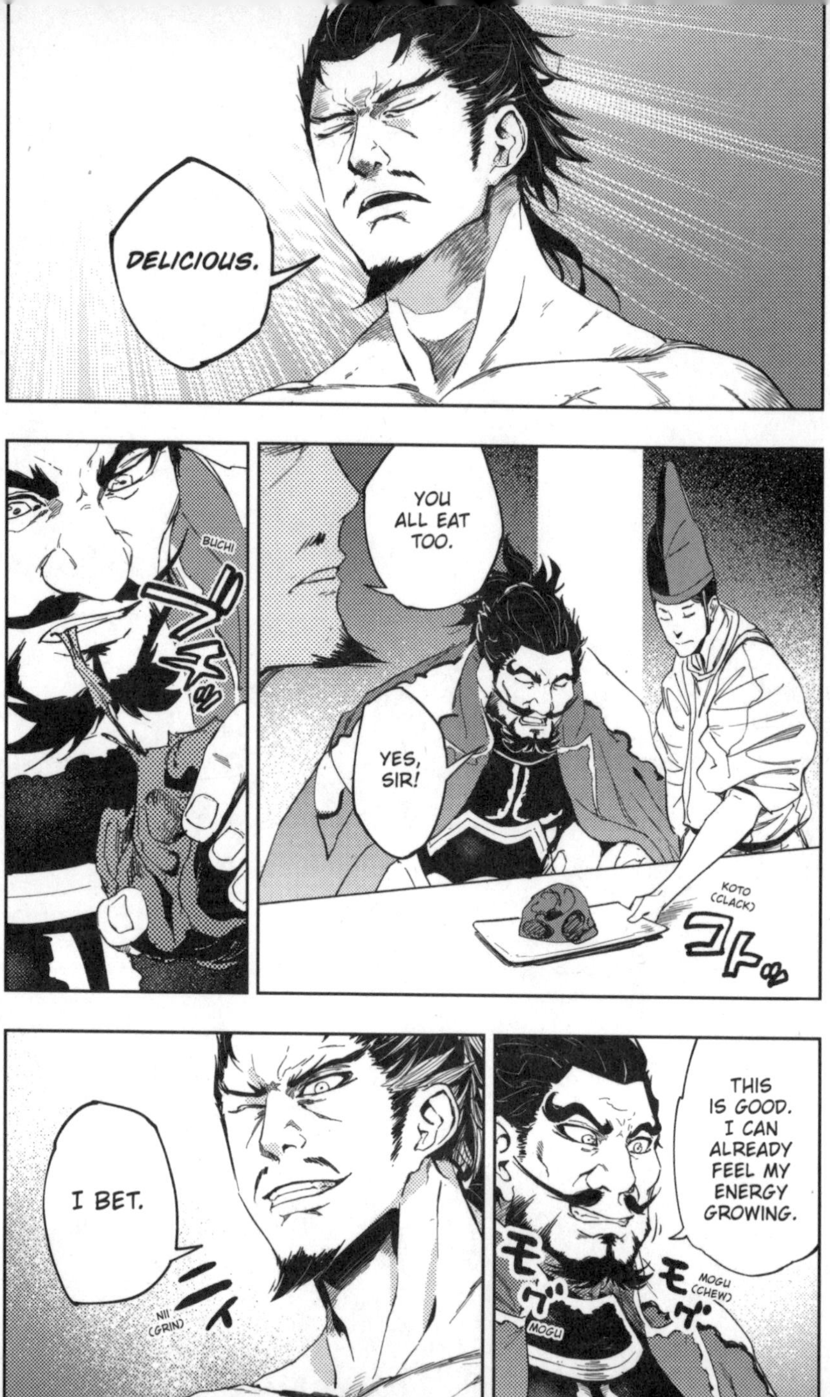
DELICIOUS.
YOU ALL EAT TOO.
YES, SIR!
KOTO (CLACK)
BUCHI
THIS IS GOOD. I CAN ALREADY FEEL MY ENERGY GROWING.
MOGU (CHEW)
MOGU
I BET.
NII (GRIN)

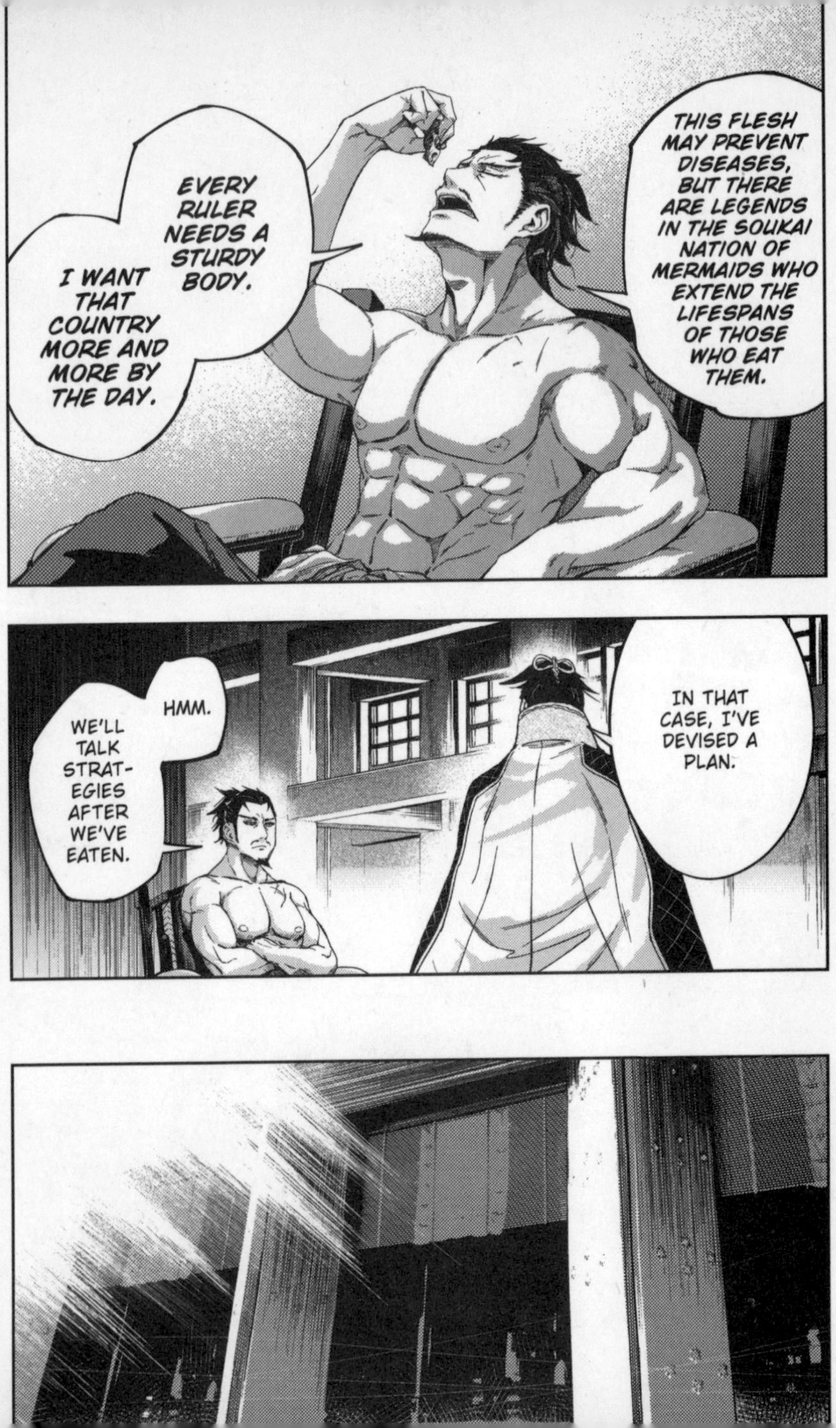
THIS FLESH MAY PREVENT DISEASES, BUT THERE ARE LEGENDS IN THE SOUKAI NATION OF MERMAIDS WHO EXTEND THE LIFESPANS OF THOSE WHO EAT THEM.
EVERY RULER NEEDS A STURDY BODY.
I WANT THAT COUNTRY MORE AND MORE BY THE DAY.
IN THAT CASE, I'VE DEVISED A PLAN.
HMM.
WE'LL TALK STRAT-EGIES AFTER WE'VE EATEN.

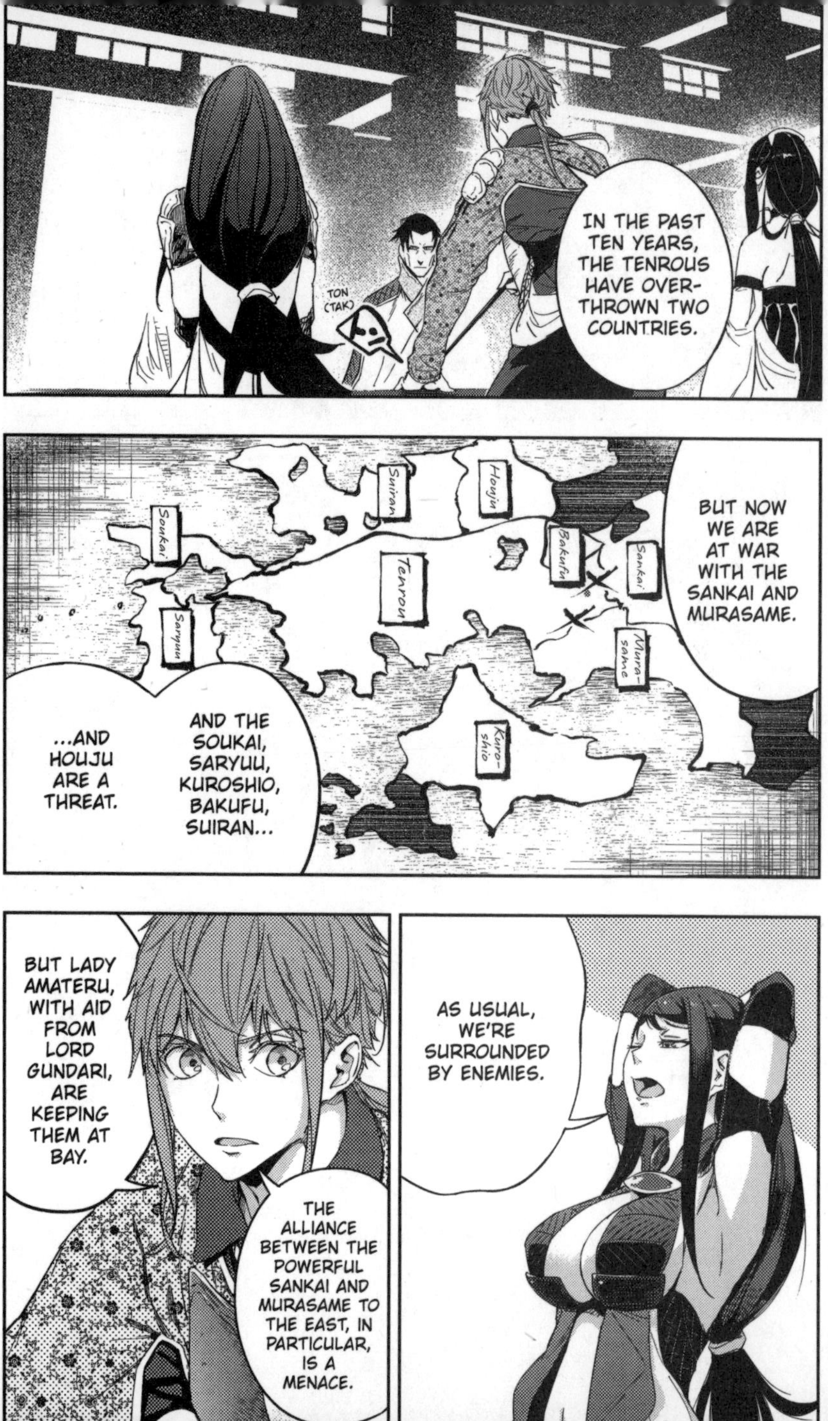
IN THE PAST TEN YEARS, THE TENROUS HAVE OVER-THROWN TWO COUNTRIES.
TON (TAK)
BUT NOW WE ARE AT WAR WITH THE SANKAI AND MURASAME.
Sankai
Bakufu
Houju
Suiran
Soukai
Tenrou
Mura-same
Saryuu
Kuro-shio
AND THE SOUKAI, SARYUU, KUROSHIO, BAKUFU, SUIRAN...
...AND HOUJU ARE A THREAT.
AS USUAL, WE'RE SURROUNDED BY ENEMIES.
BUT LADY AMATERU, WITH AID FROM LORD GUNDARI, ARE KEEPING THEM AT BAY.
THE ALLIANCE BETWEEN THE POWERFUL SANKAI AND MURASAME TO THE EAST, IN PARTICULAR, IS A MENACE.

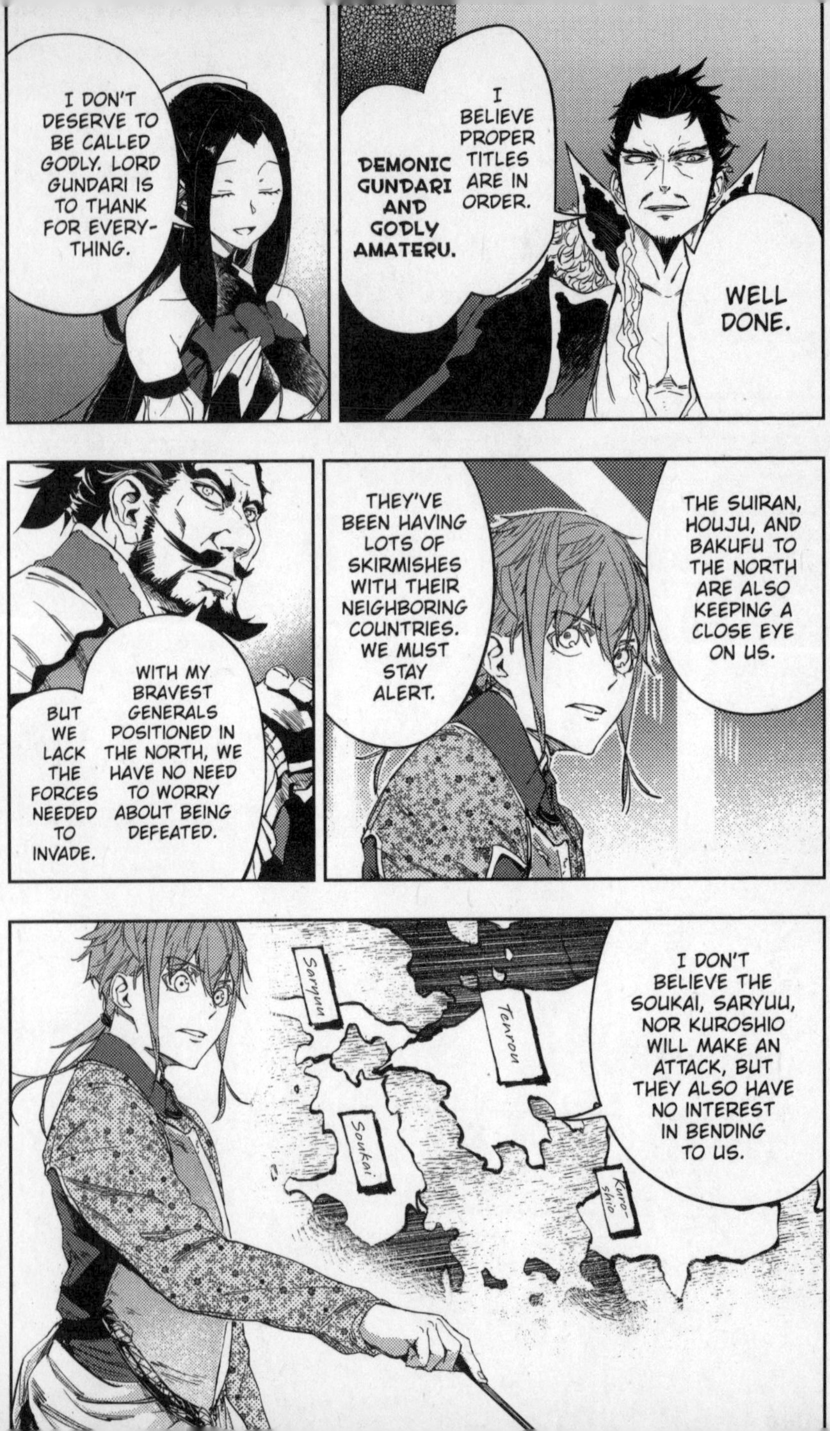

WELL DONE.
I BELIEVE PROPER TITLES ARE IN ORDER.
DEMONIC GUNDARI AND GODLY AMATERU.
I DON'T DESERVE TO BE CALLED GODLY. LORD GUNDARI IS TO THANK FOR EVERY-THING.
THE SUIRAN, HOUJU, AND BAKUFU TO THE NORTH ARE ALSO KEEPING A CLOSE EYE ON US.
THEY'VE BEEN HAVING LOTS OF SKIRMISHES WITH THEIR NEIGHBORING COUNTRIES. WE MUST STAY ALERT.
WITH MY BRAVEST GENERALS POSITIONED IN THE NORTH, WE HAVE NO NEED TO WORRY ABOUT BEING DEFEATED.
BUT WE LACK THE FORCES NEEDED TO INVADE.
I DON'T BELIEVE THE SOUKAI, SARYUU, NOR KUROSHIO WILL MAKE AN ATTACK, BUT THEY ALSO HAVE NO INTEREST IN BENDING TO US.
Tenrou
Saryuu
Kuro-shio
Soukai

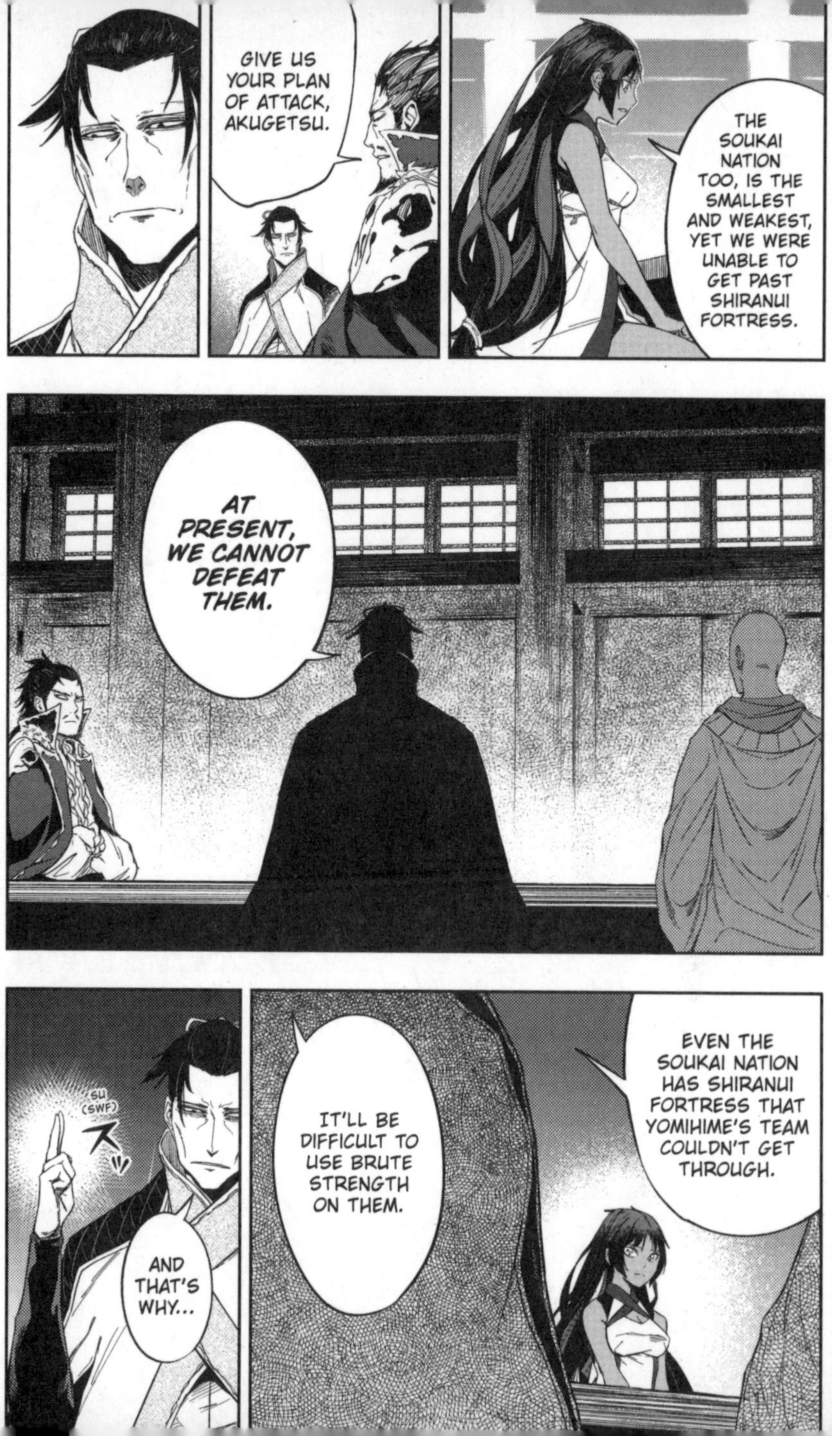
THE SOUKAI NATION TOO, IS THE SMALLEST AND WEAKEST, YET WE WERE UNABLE TO GET PAST SHIRANUI FORTRESS.
GIVE US YOUR PLAN OF ATTACK, AKUGETSU.
AT PRESENT, WE CANNOT DEFEAT THEM.
EVEN THE SOUKAI NATION HAS SHIRANUI FORTRESS THAT YOMIHIME'S TEAM COULDN'T GET THROUGH.
IT'LL BE DIFFICULT TO USE BRUTE STRENGTH ON THEM.
SU (SWF)
ス
AND THAT'S WHY...

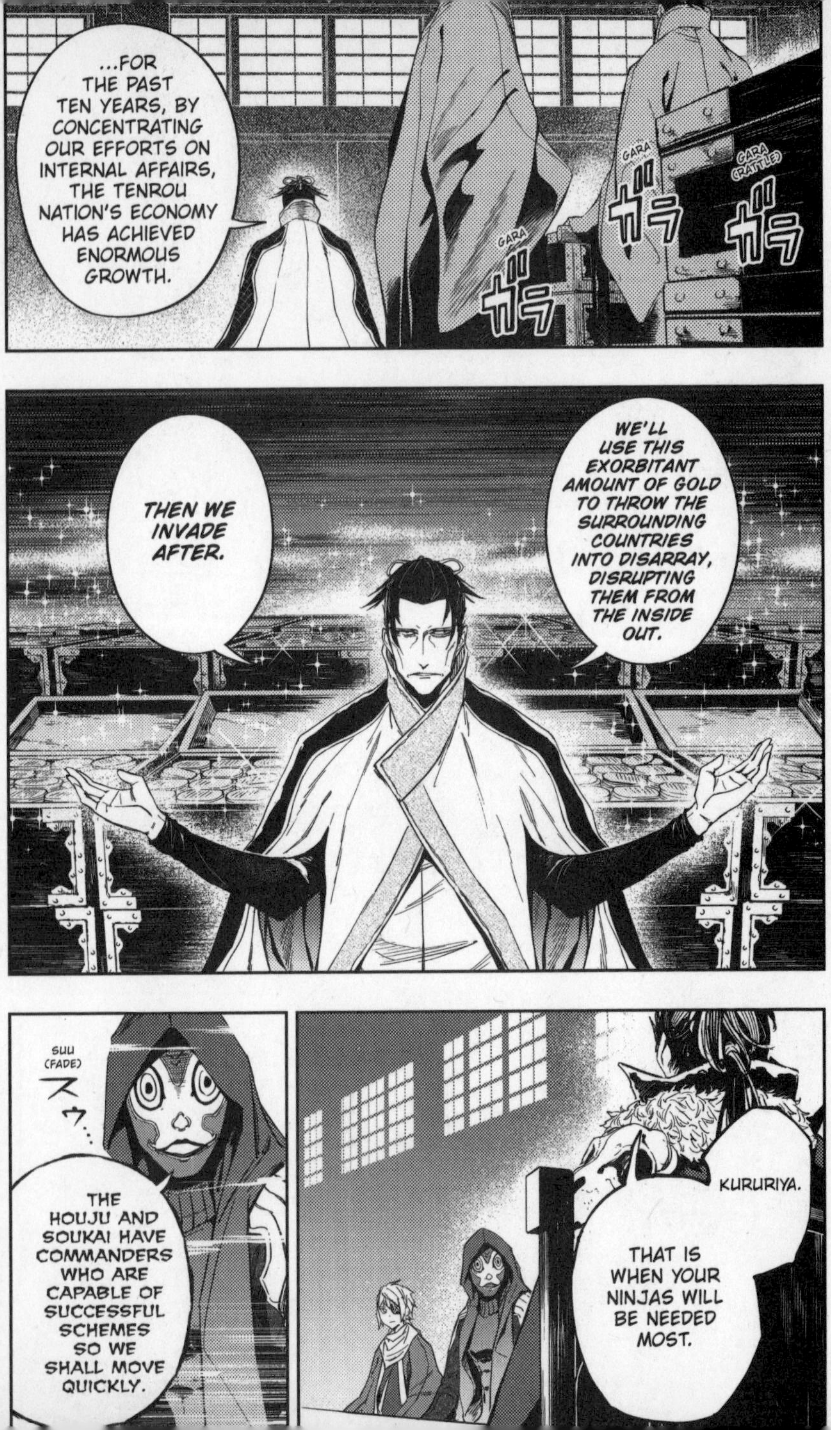
GARA (RATTLE)
GARA
GARA
...FOR THE PAST TEN YEARS, BY CONCENTRATING OUR EFFORTS ON INTERNAL AFFAIRS, THE TENROU NATION'S ECONOMY HAS ACHIEVED ENORMOUS GROWTH.
WE'LL USE THIS EXORBITANT AMOUNT OF GOLD TO THROW THE SURROUNDING COUNTRIES INTO DISARRAY, DISRUPTING THEM FROM THE INSIDE OUT.
THEN WE INVADE AFTER.
KURURIYA.
THAT IS WHEN YOUR NINJAS WILL BE NEEDED MOST.
SUU (FADE)
THE HOUJU AND SOUKAI HAVE COMMANDERS WHO ARE CAPABLE OF SUCCESSFUL SCHEMES SO WE SHALL MOVE QUICKLY.

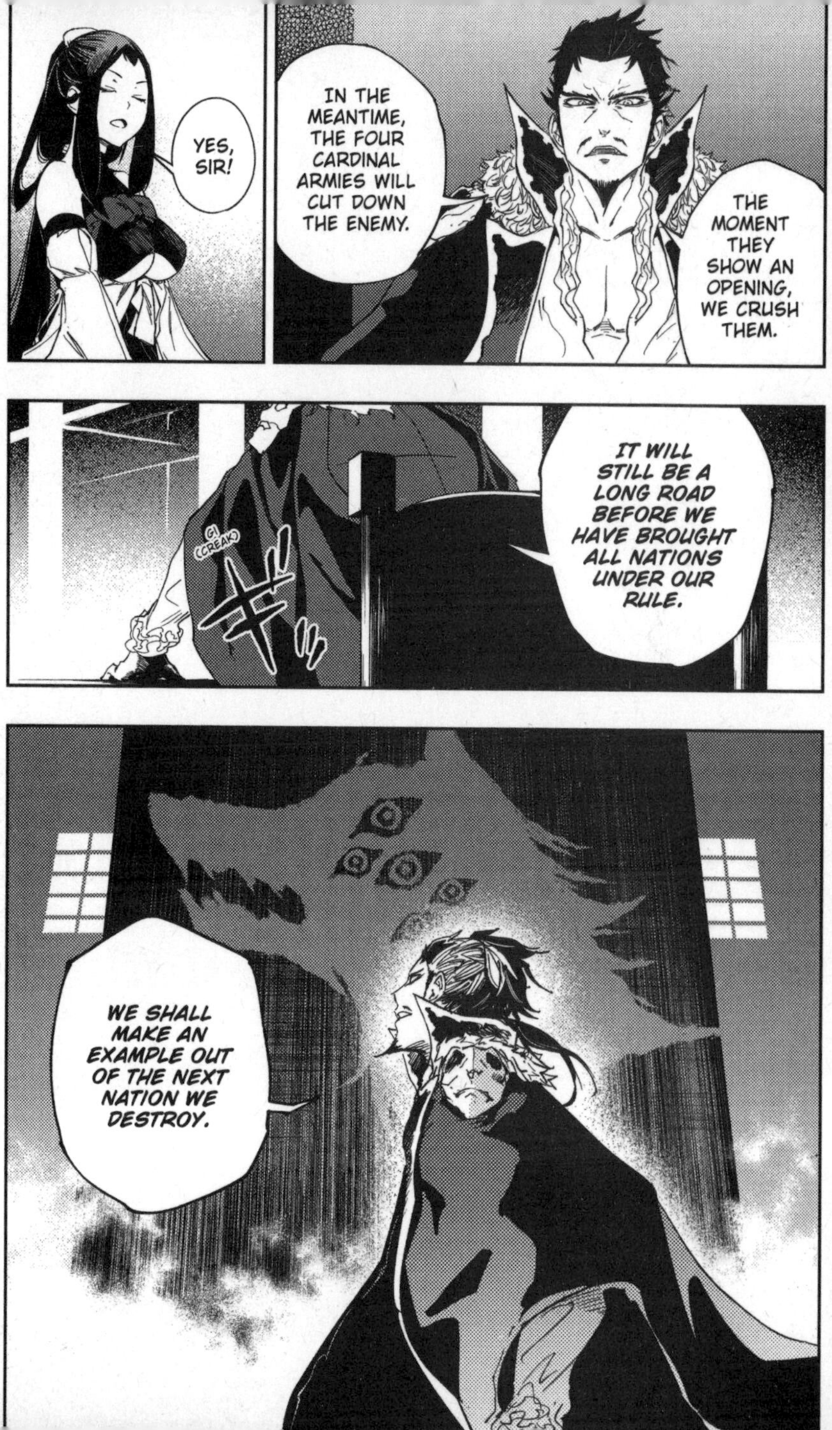
THE MOMENT THEY SHOW AN OPENING, WE CRUSH THEM.
IN THE MEANTIME, THE FOUR CARDINAL ARMIES WILL CUT DOWN THE ENEMY.
YES, SIR!
IT WILL STILL BE A LONG ROAD BEFORE WE HAVE BROUGHT ALL NATIONS UNDER OUR RULE.
GI (CREAK)
WE SHALL MAKE AN EXAMPLE OUT OF THE NEXT NATION WE DESTROY.

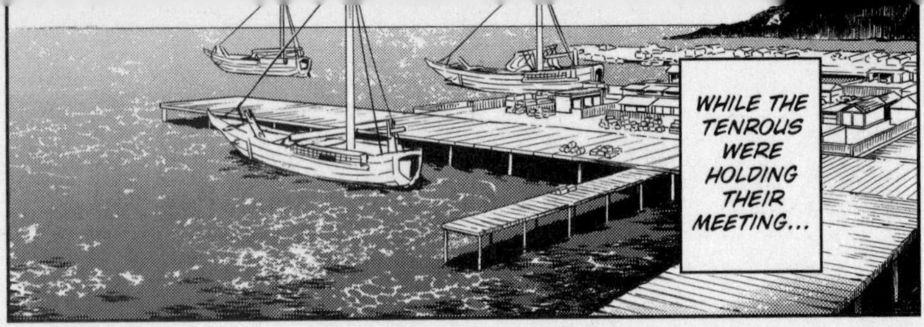
WHILE THE TENROUS WERE HOLDING THEIR MEETING...
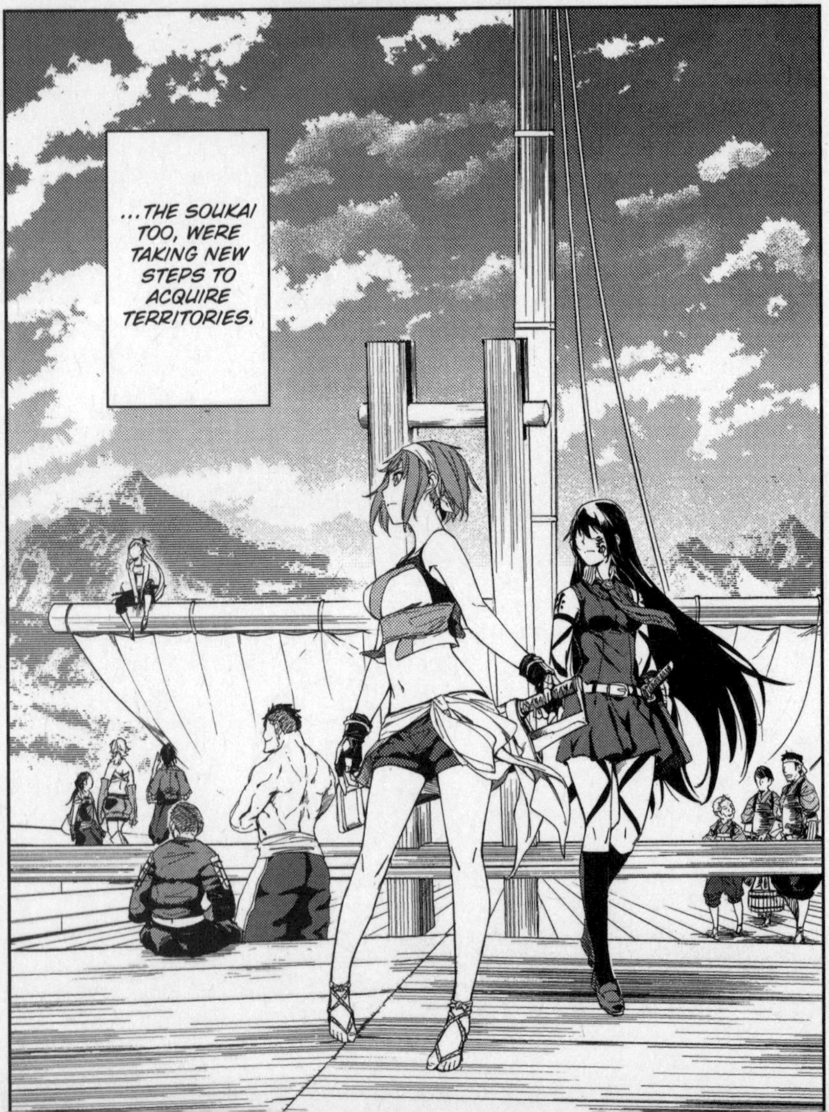
...THE SOUKAI TOO, WERE TAKING NEW STEPS TO ACQUIRE TERRITORIES.

Hinowa ga CRUSH!

Hijnowa ga CRUSH!

Design Drafts ①

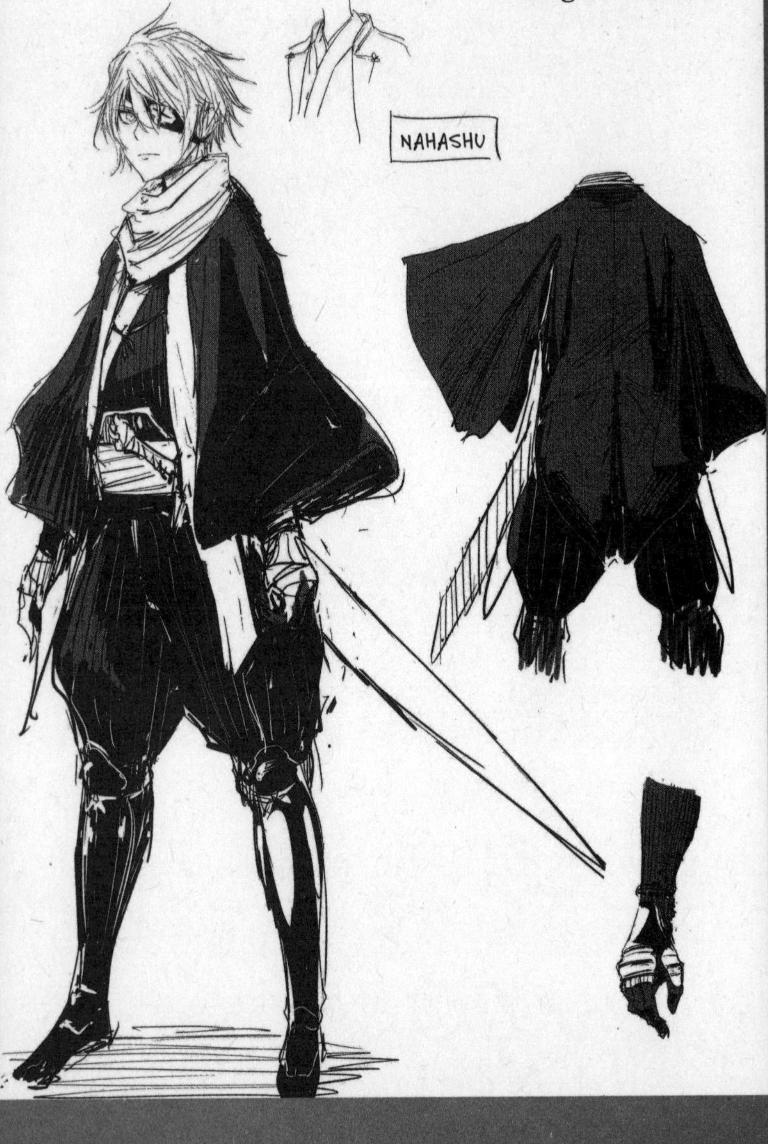
NAHASHU

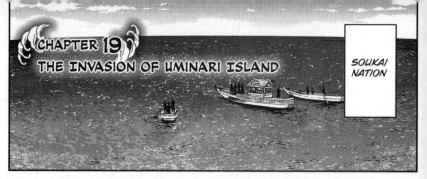

CHAPTER 19
THE INVASION OF UMINARI ISLAND

SOUKAI
NATION

SOUKAI
NATION
KING
SOTETSU

THE
EMBRACE OF
THE SEA IS
EVEN BETTER
THAN THE
EMBRACE OF
A WOMAN.

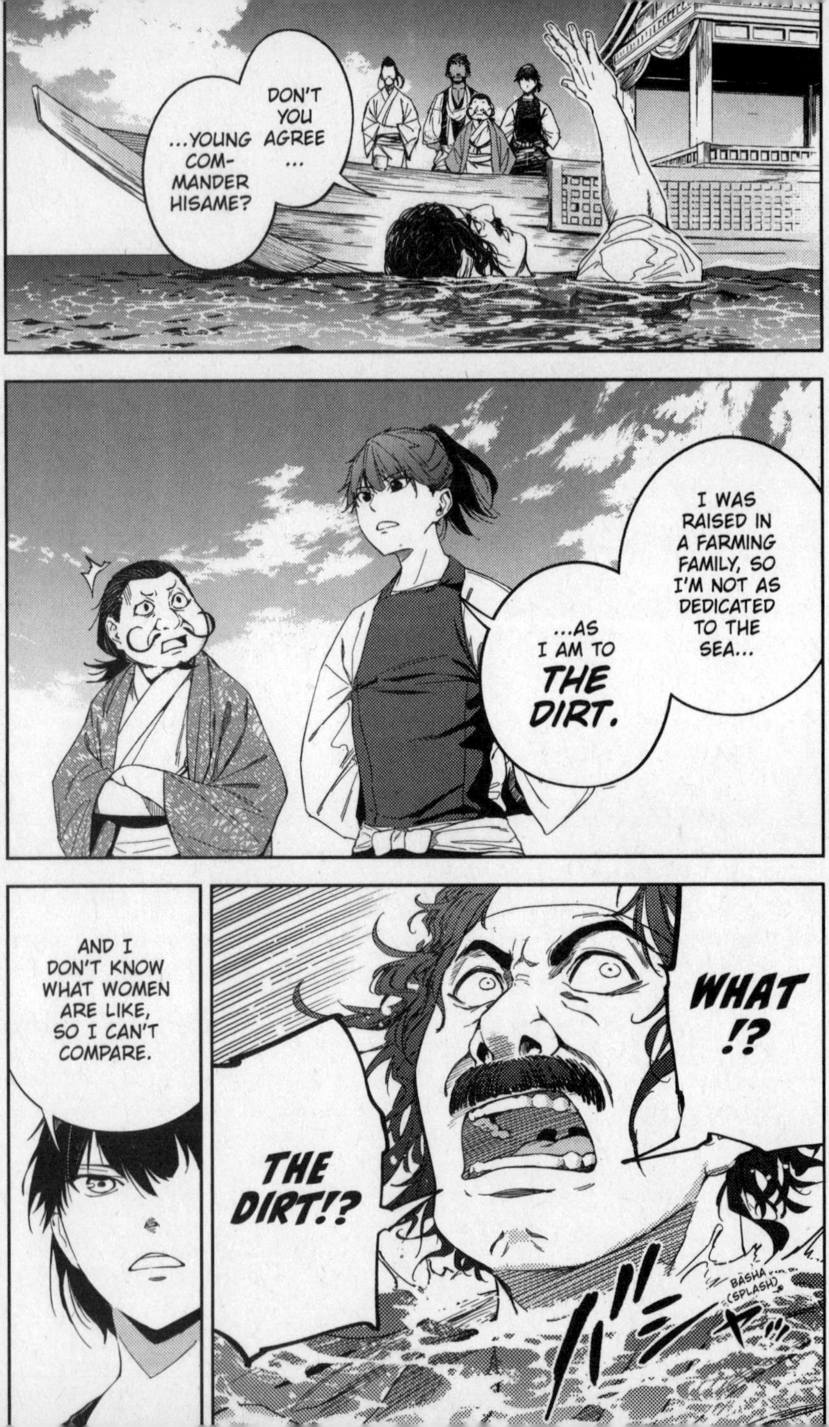
DON'T YOU AGREE...
...YOUNG COMMANDER HISAME?
I WAS RAISED IN A FARMING FAMILY, SO I'M NOT AS DEDICATED TO THE SEA...
...AS I AM TO THE DIRT.
WHAT!?
THE DIRT!?
BĀSHA (SPLASH)
AND I DON'T KNOW WHAT WOMEN ARE LIKE, SO I CAN'T COMPARE.

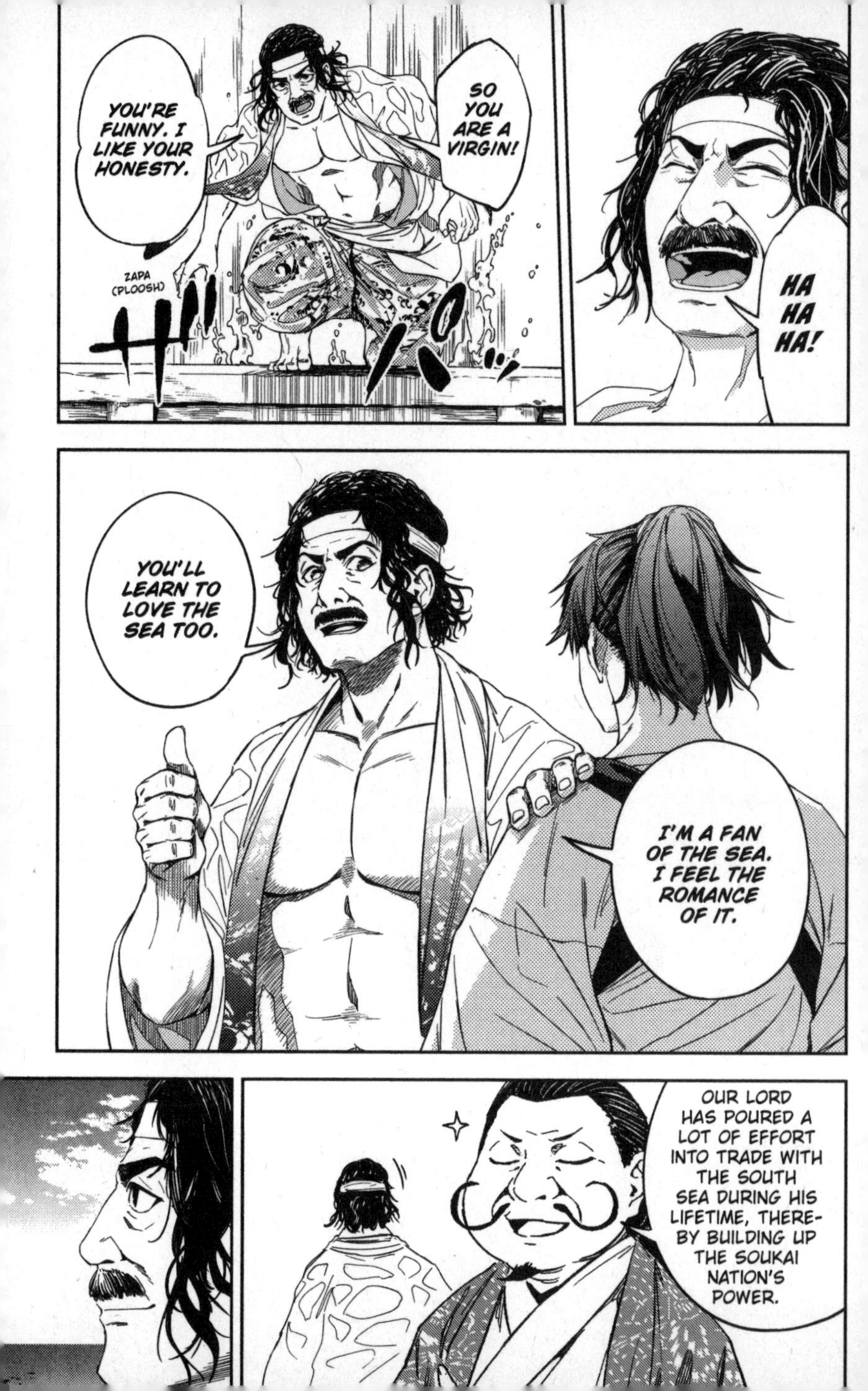
HA HA HA!
SO YOU ARE A VIRGIN!
YOU'RE FUNNY. I LIKE YOUR HONESTY.
ZAPA (PLOOSH)
I'M A FAN OF THE SEA. I FEEL THE ROMANCE OF IT.
YOU'LL LEARN TO LOVE THE SEA TOO.
OUR LORD HAS POURED A LOT OF EFFORT INTO TRADE WITH THE SOUTH SEA DURING HIS LIFETIME, THEREBY BUILDING UP THE SOUKAI NATION'S POWER.

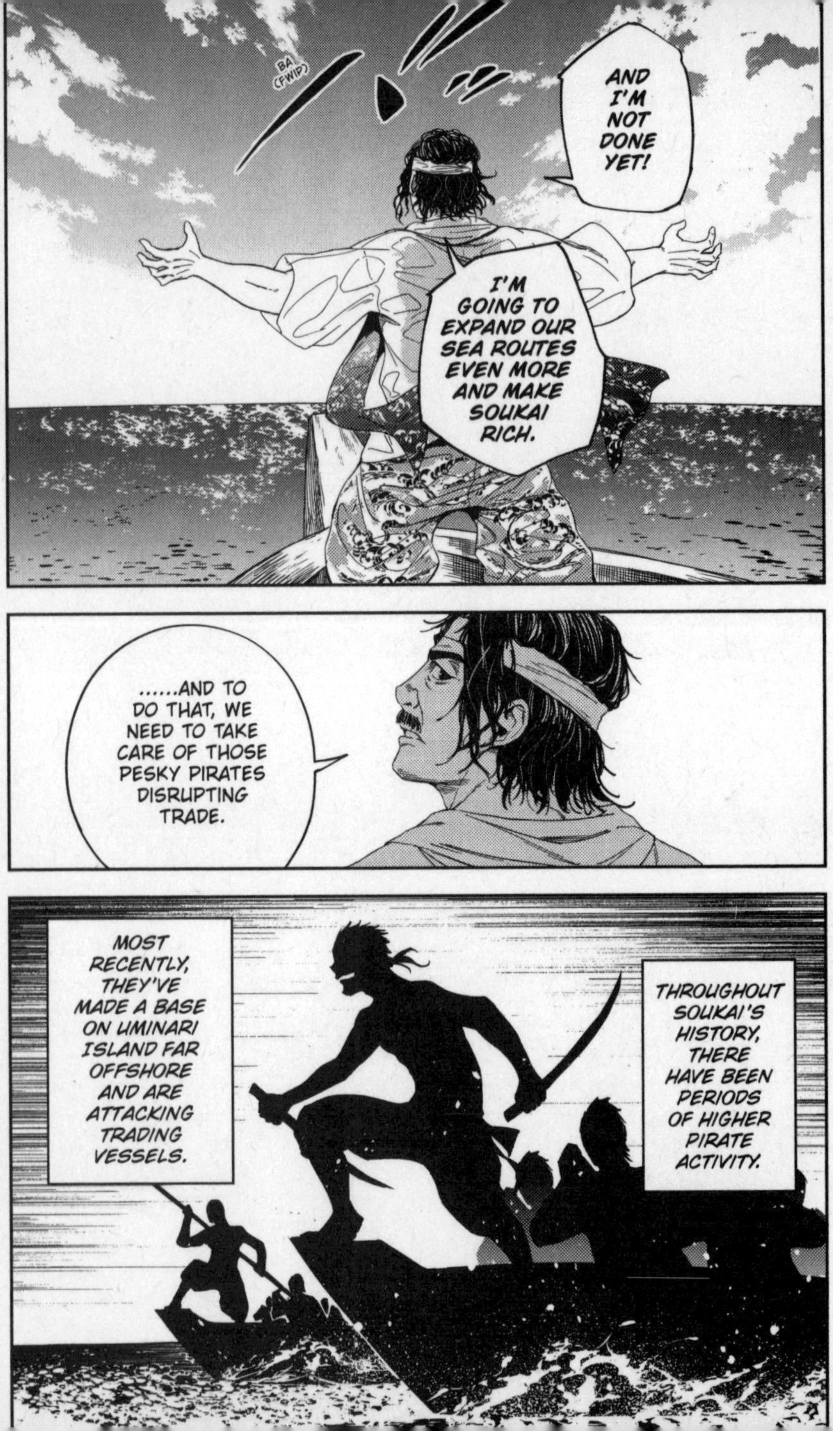
BA (FWIP)
AND I'M NOT DONE YET!
I'M GOING TO EXPAND OUR SEA ROUTES EVEN MORE AND MAKE SOUKAI RICH.
......AND TO DO THAT, WE NEED TO TAKE CARE OF THOSE PESKY PIRATES DISRUPTING TRADE.
THROUGHOUT SOUKAI'S HISTORY, THERE HAVE BEEN PERIODS OF HIGHER PIRATE ACTIVITY.
MOST RECENTLY, THEY'VE MADE A BASE ON UMINARI ISLAND FAR OFFSHORE AND ARE ATTACKING TRADING VESSELS.

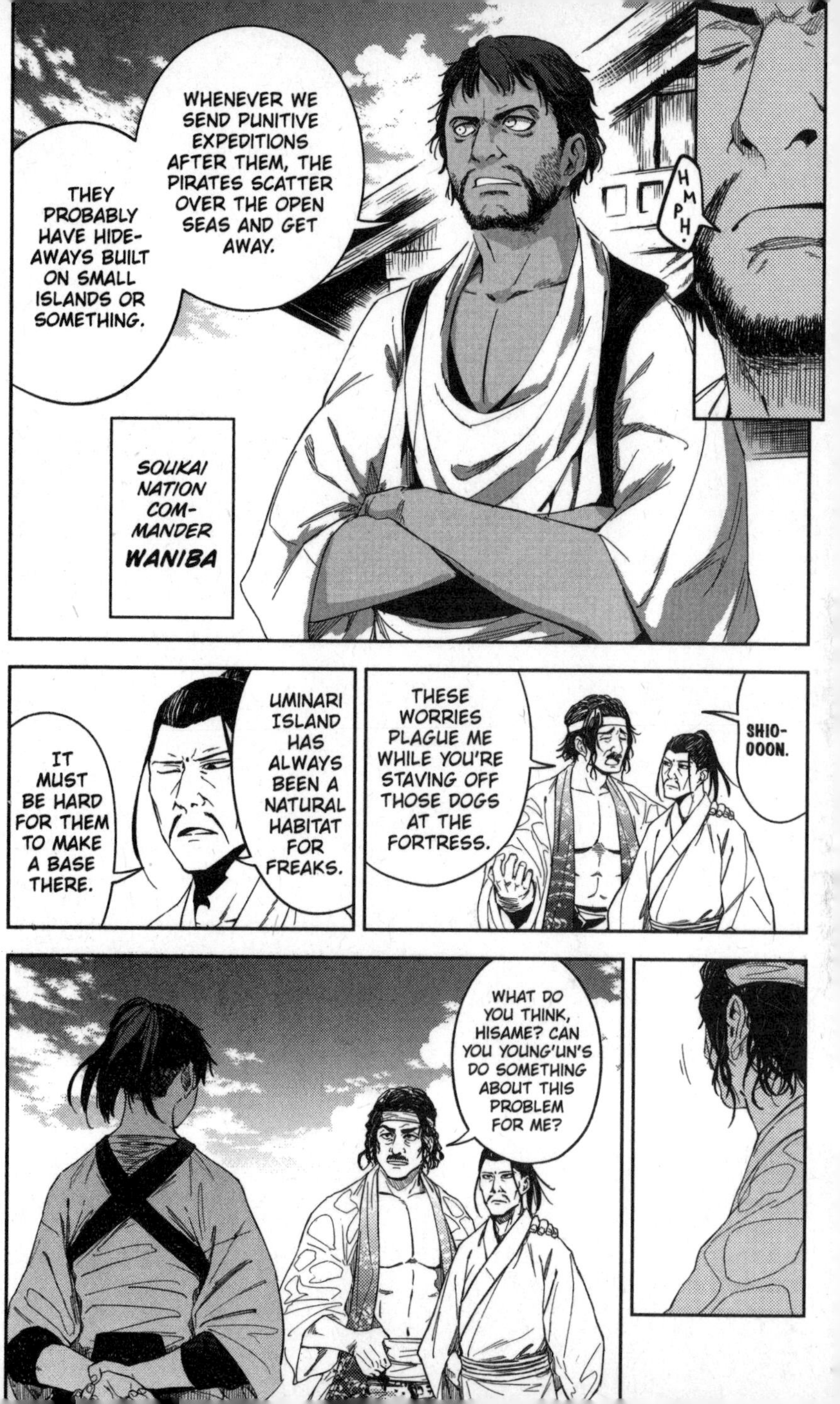
HMPH.
WHENEVER WE SEND PUNITIVE EXPEDITIONS AFTER THEM, THE PIRATES SCATTER OVER THE OPEN SEAS AND GET AWAY.
THEY PROBABLY HAVE HIDE-AWAYS BUILT ON SMALL ISLANDS OR SOMETHING.
SOUKAI NATION COM-MANDER WANIBA
SHIO-OOON.
THESE WORRIES PLAGUE ME WHILE YOU'RE STAVING OFF THOSE DOGS AT THE FORTRESS.
UMINARI ISLAND HAS ALWAYS BEEN A NATURAL HABITAT FOR FREAKS.
IT MUST BE HARD FOR THEM TO MAKE A BASE THERE.
WHAT DO YOU THINK, HISAME? CAN YOU YOUNG'UN'S DO SOMETHING ABOUT THIS PROBLEM FOR ME?

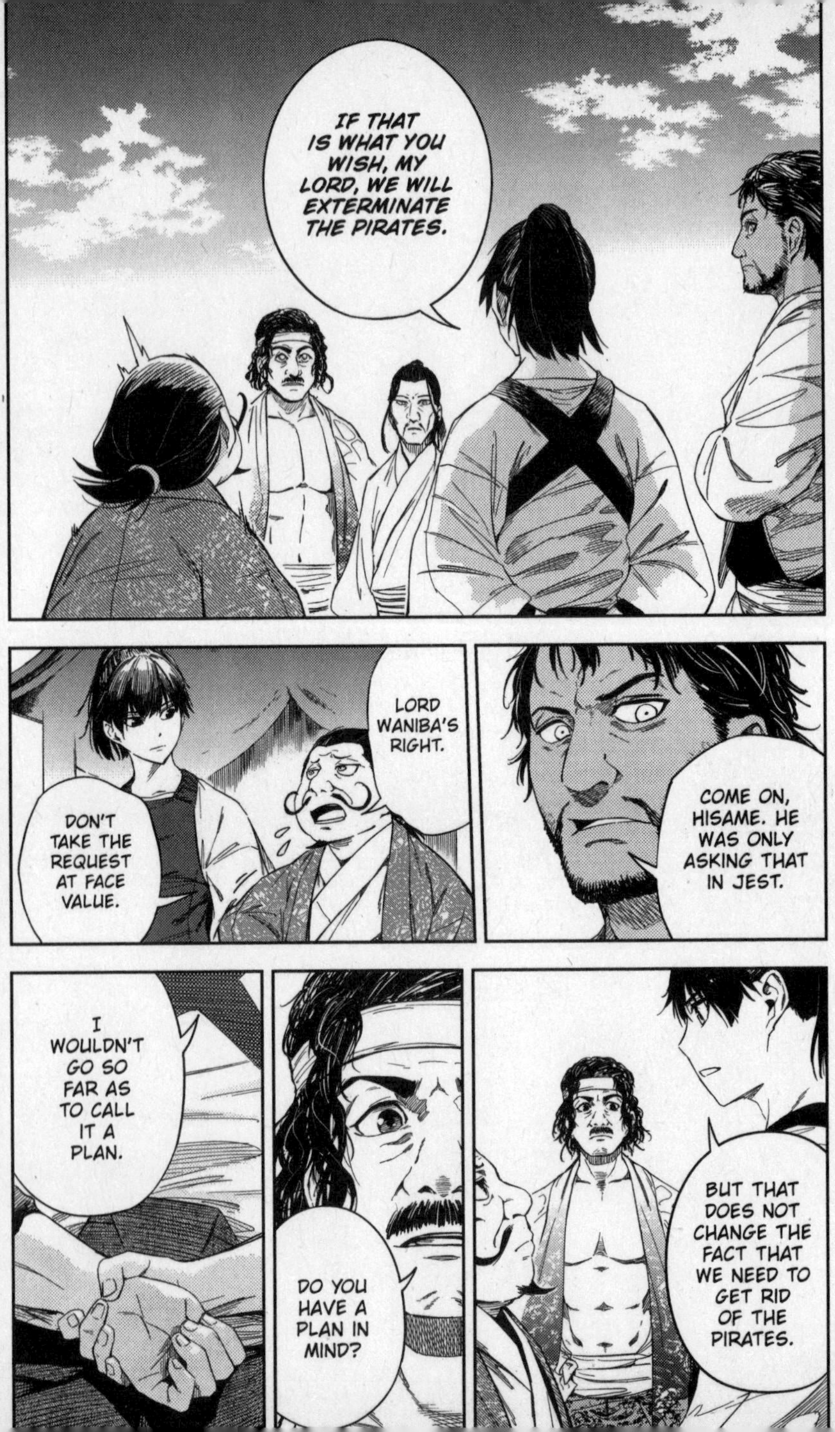
IF THAT IS WHAT YOU WISH, MY LORD, WE WILL EXTERMINATE THE PIRATES.
COME ON, HISAME. HE WAS ONLY ASKING THAT IN JEST.
LORD WANIBA'S RIGHT.
DON'T TAKE THE REQUEST AT FACE VALUE.
BUT THAT DOES NOT CHANGE THE FACT THAT WE NEED TO GET RID OF THE PIRATES.
DO YOU HAVE A PLAN IN MIND?
I WOULDN'T GO SO FAR AS TO CALL IT A PLAN.

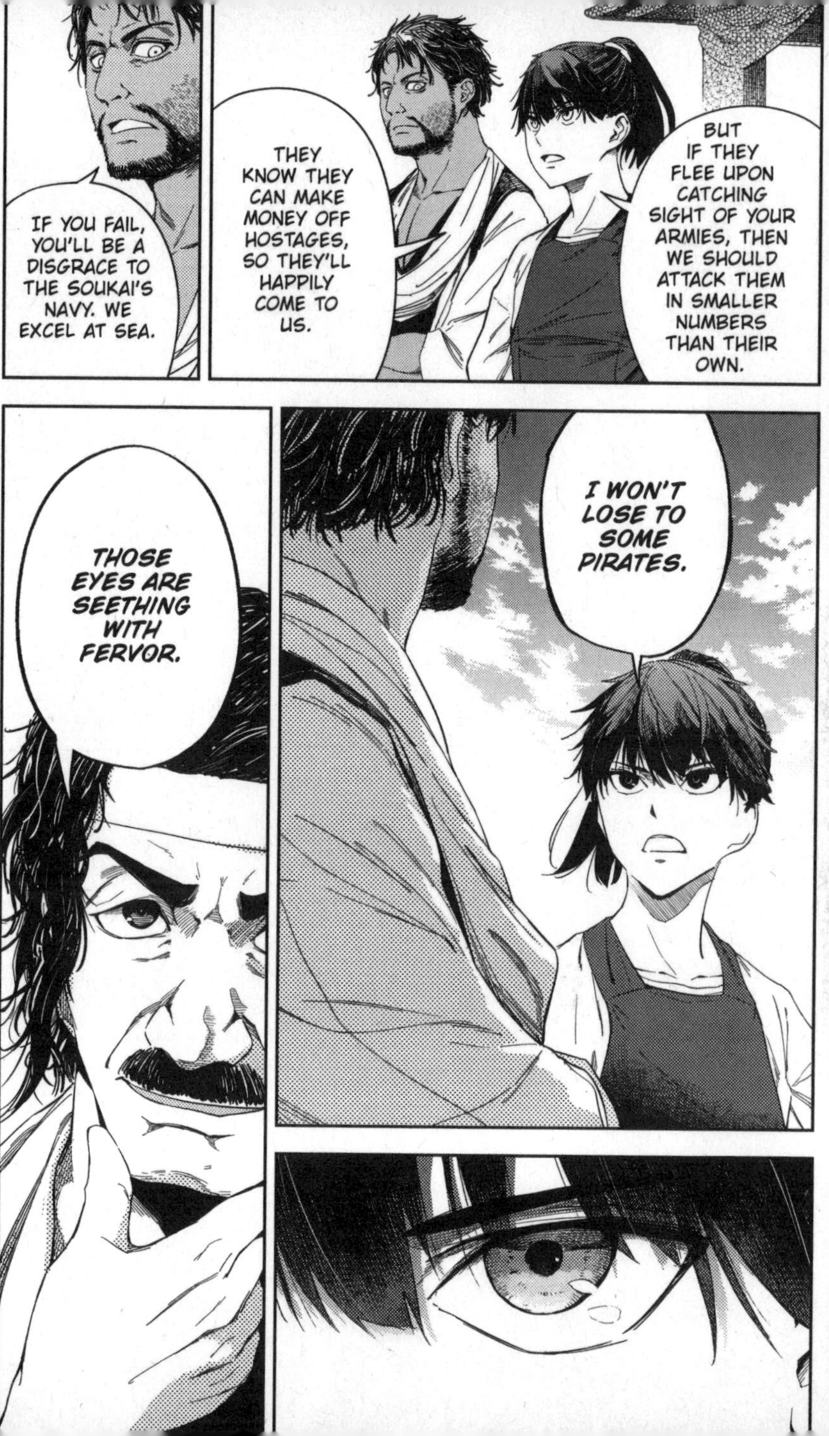
BUT IF THEY FLEE UPON CATCHING SIGHT OF YOUR ARMIES, THEN WE SHOULD ATTACK THEM IN SMALLER NUMBERS THAN THEIR OWN.
THEY KNOW THEY CAN MAKE MONEY OFF HOSTAGES, SO THEY'LL HAPPILY COME TO US.
IF YOU FAIL, YOU'LL BE A DISGRACE TO THE SOUKAI'S NAVY. WE EXCEL AT SEA.
I WON'T LOSE TO SOME PIRATES.
THOSE EYES ARE SEETHING WITH FERVOR.

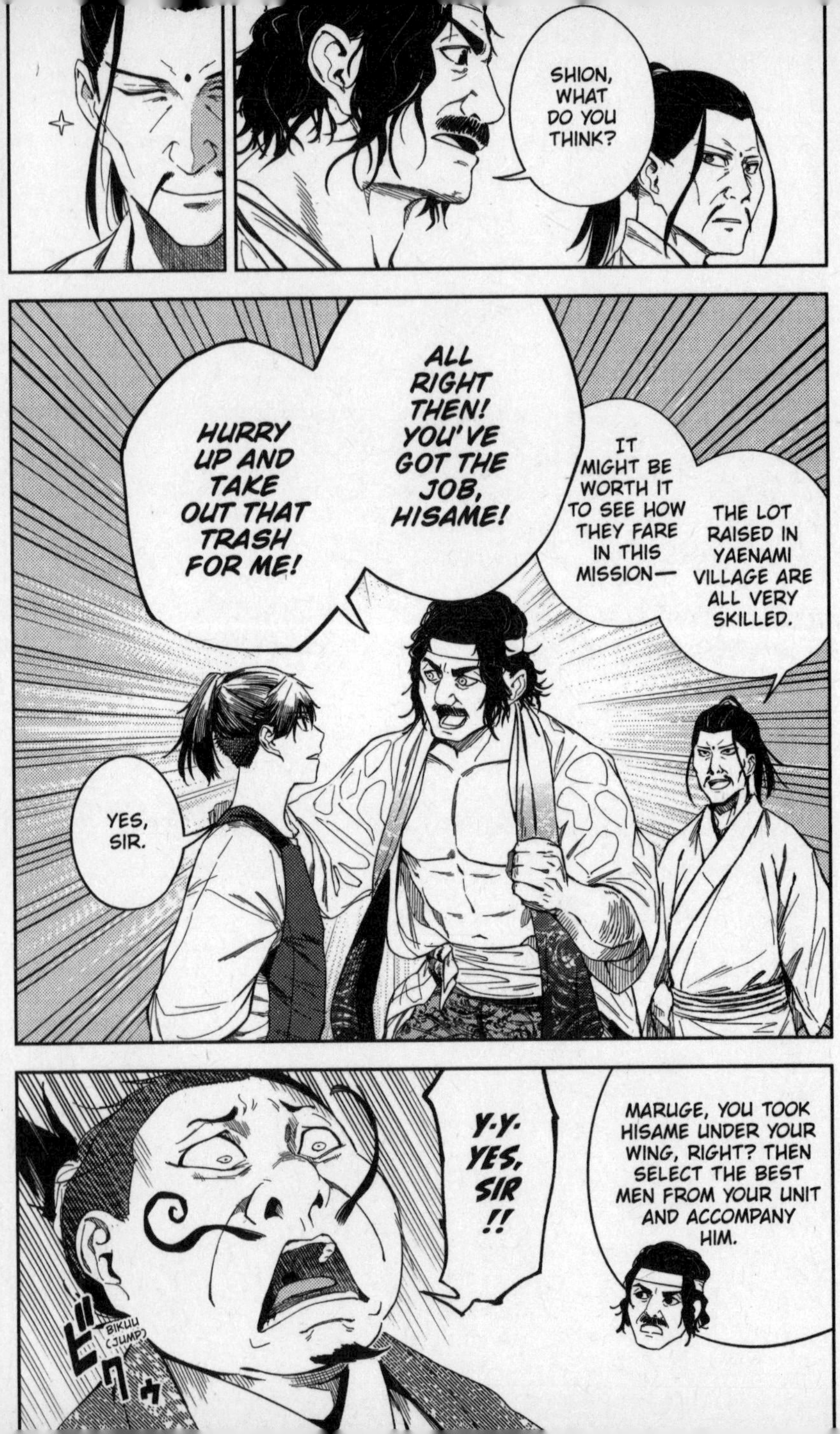
SHION, WHAT DO YOU THINK?
THE LOT RAISED IN YAENAMI VILLAGE ARE ALL VERY SKILLED.
IT MIGHT BE WORTH IT TO SEE HOW THEY FARE IN THIS MISSION—
ALL RIGHT THEN! YOU'VE GOT THE JOB, HISAME!
HURRY UP AND TAKE OUT THAT TRASH FOR ME!
YES, SIR.
MARUGE, YOU TOOK HISAME UNDER YOUR WING, RIGHT? THEN SELECT THE BEST MEN FROM YOUR UNIT AND ACCOMPANY HIM.
Y-Y-YES, SIR!!
BIKUU (JUMP)

IF THIS IS A SUCCESS, THE REWARDS WILL BE GREAT.

... ME...?

WHY...

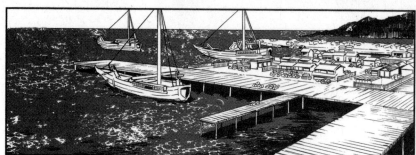

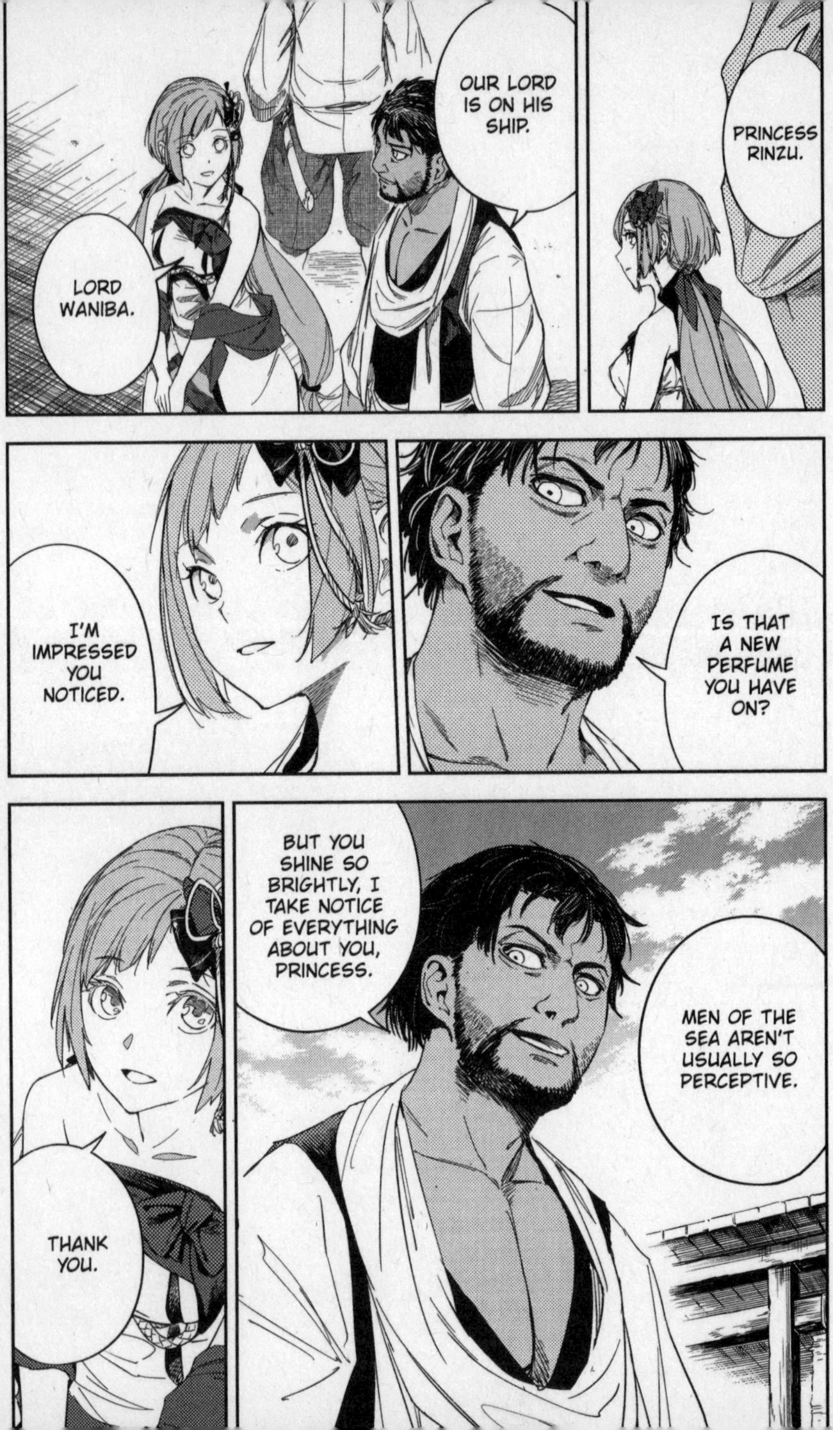
PRINCESS RINZU.
OUR LORD IS ON HIS SHIP.
LORD WANIBA.
IS THAT A NEW PERFUME YOU HAVE ON?
I'M IMPRESSED YOU NOTICED.
MEN OF THE SEA AREN'T USUALLY SO PERCEPTIVE.
BUT YOU SHINE SO BRIGHTLY, I TAKE NOTICE OF EVERYTHING ABOUT YOU, PRINCESS.
THANK YOU.

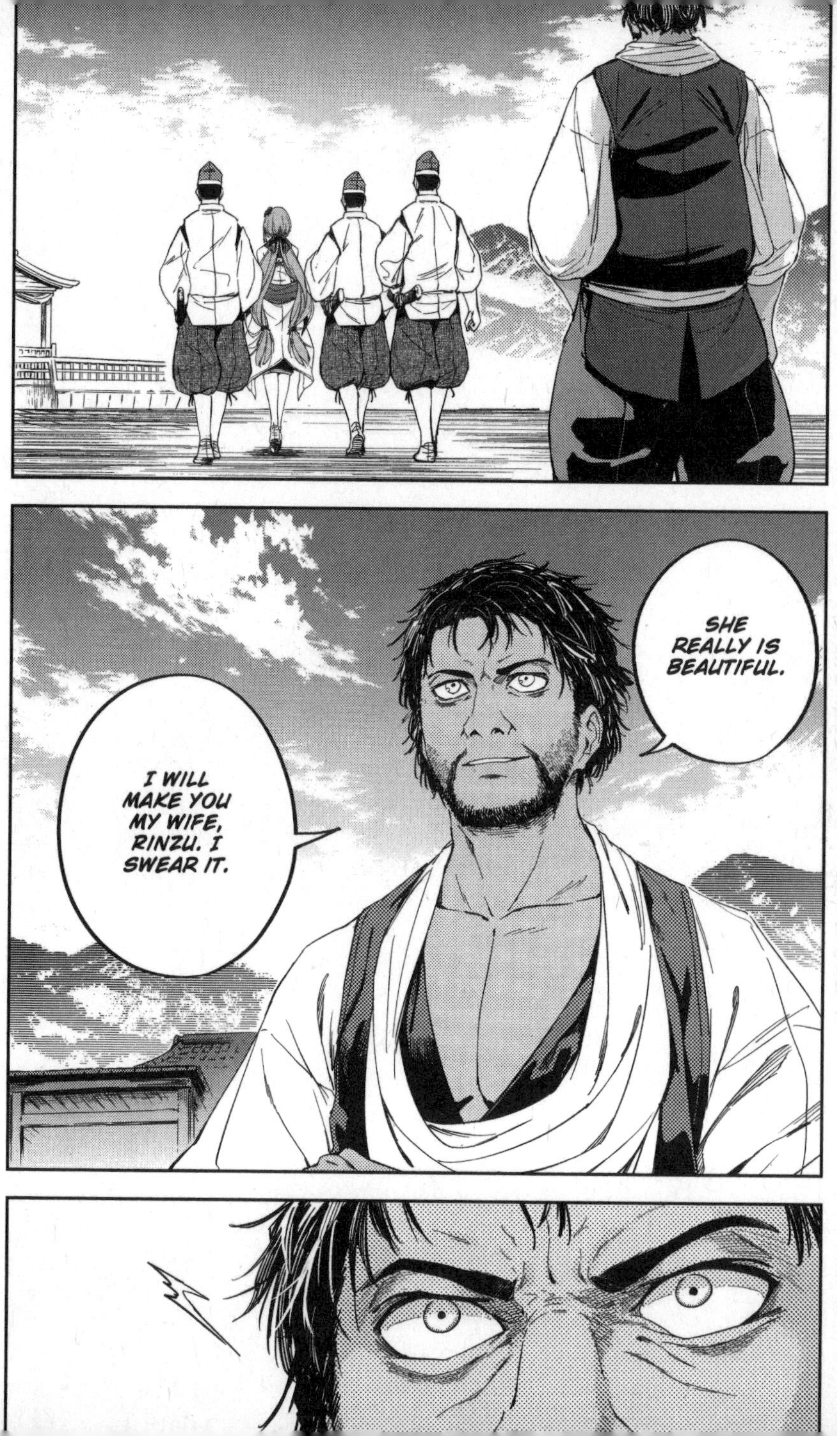
SHE REALLY IS BEAUTIFUL.
I WILL MAKE YOU MY WIFE, RINZU. I SWEAR IT.

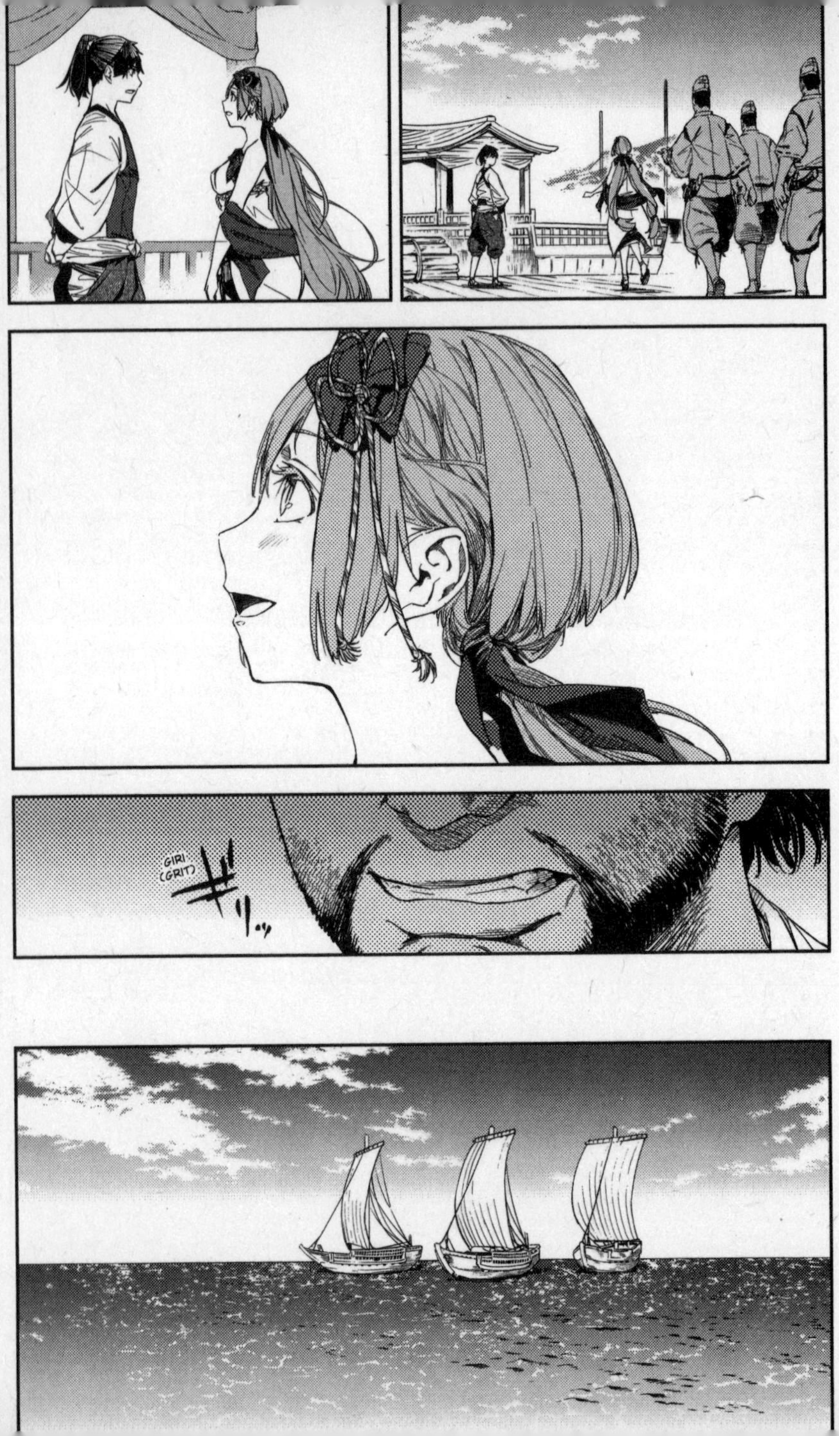
GIRI
(GRIT)

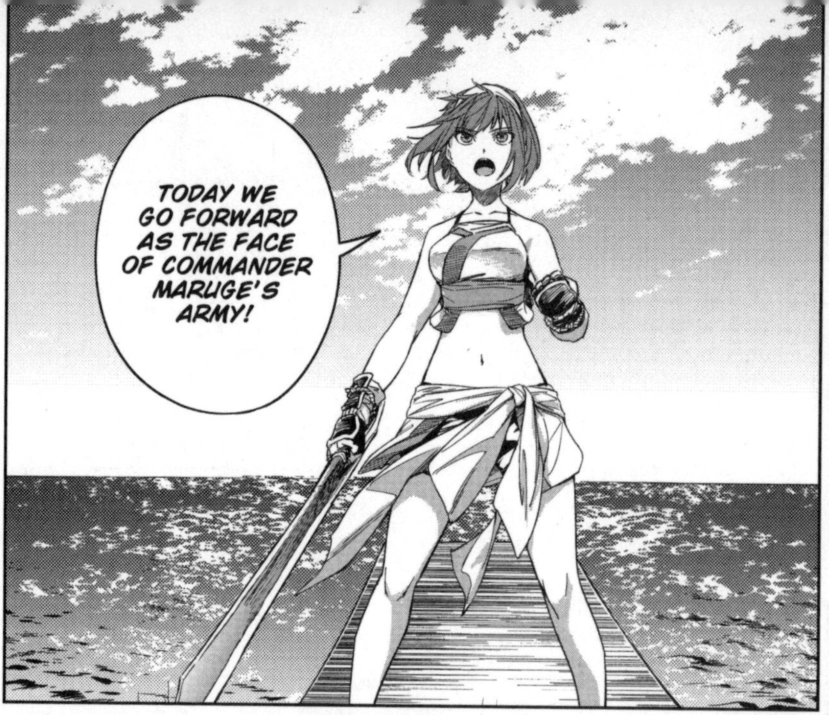
TODAY WE GO FORWARD AS THE FACE OF COMMANDER MARUGE'S ARMY!
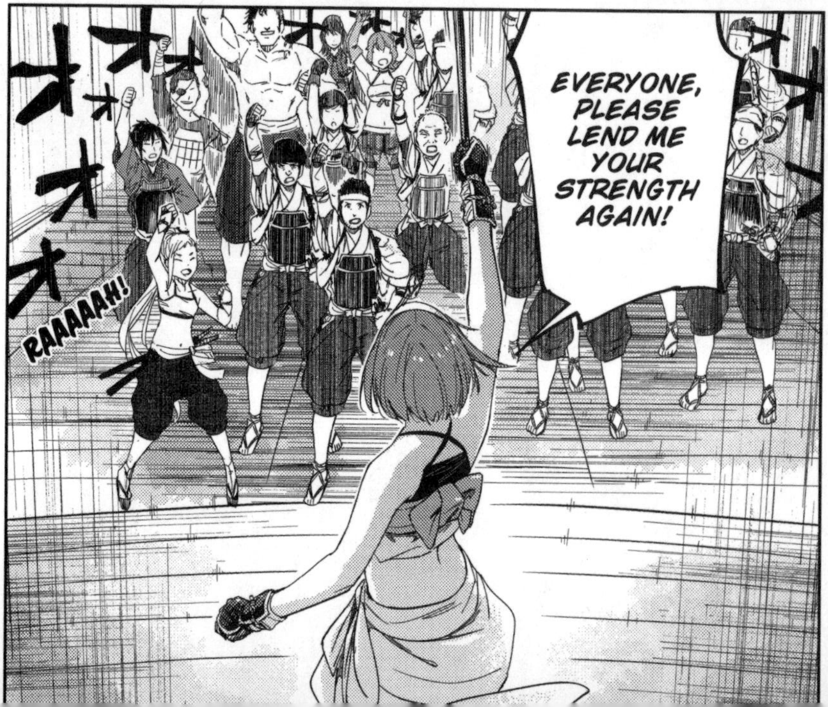
EVERYONE, PLEASE LEND ME YOUR STRENGTH AGAIN!
RAAAAAH!

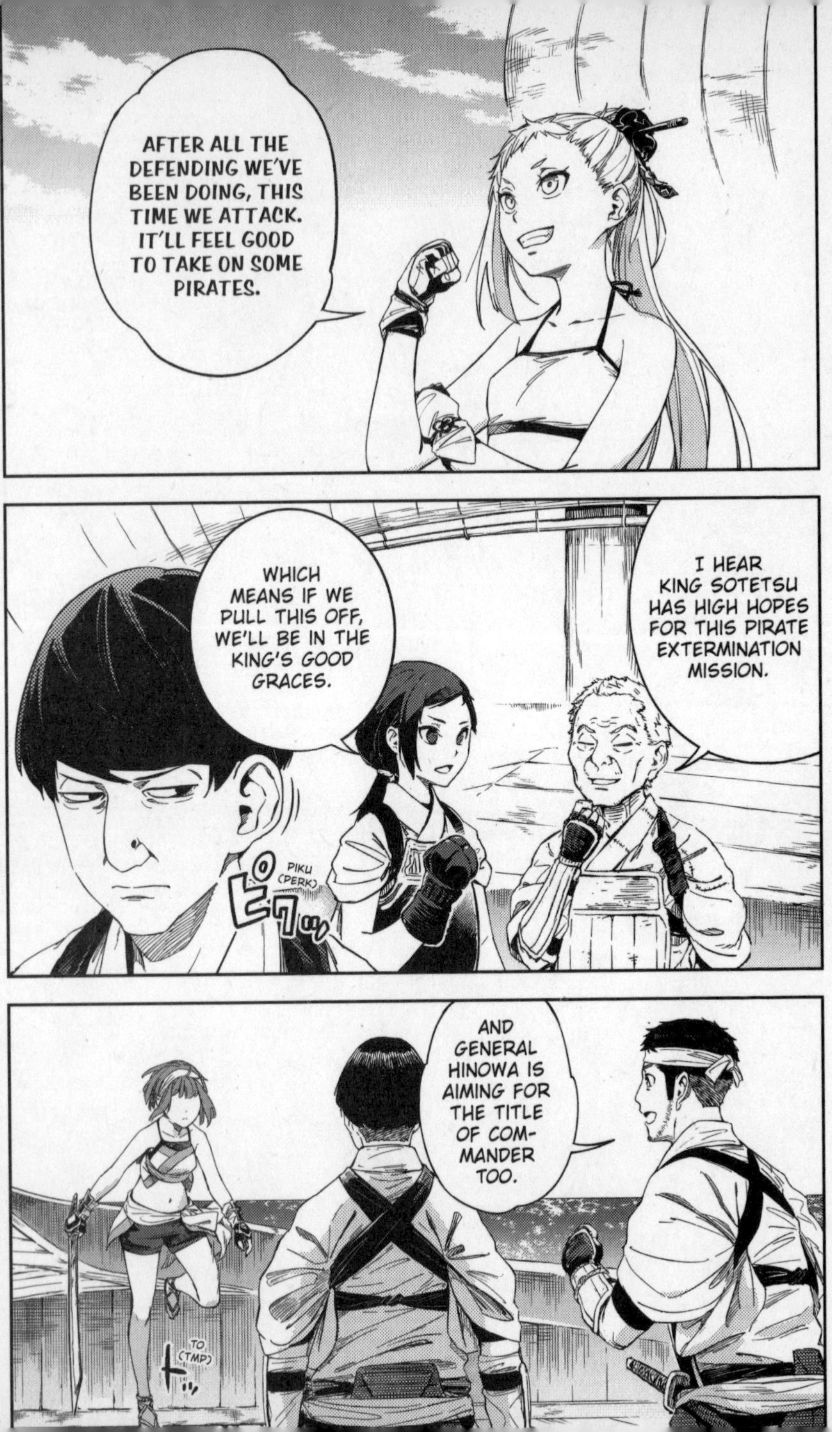
AFTER ALL THE DEFENDING WE'VE BEEN DOING, THIS TIME WE ATTACK. IT'LL FEEL GOOD TO TAKE ON SOME PIRATES.
I HEAR KING SOTETSU HAS HIGH HOPES FOR THIS PIRATE EXTERMINATION MISSION.
WHICH MEANS IF WE PULL THIS OFF, WE'LL BE IN THE KING'S GOOD GRACES.
PIKU (PERK)
AND GENERAL HINOWA IS AIMING FOR THE TITLE OF COM-MANDER TOO.
TO (TMP)

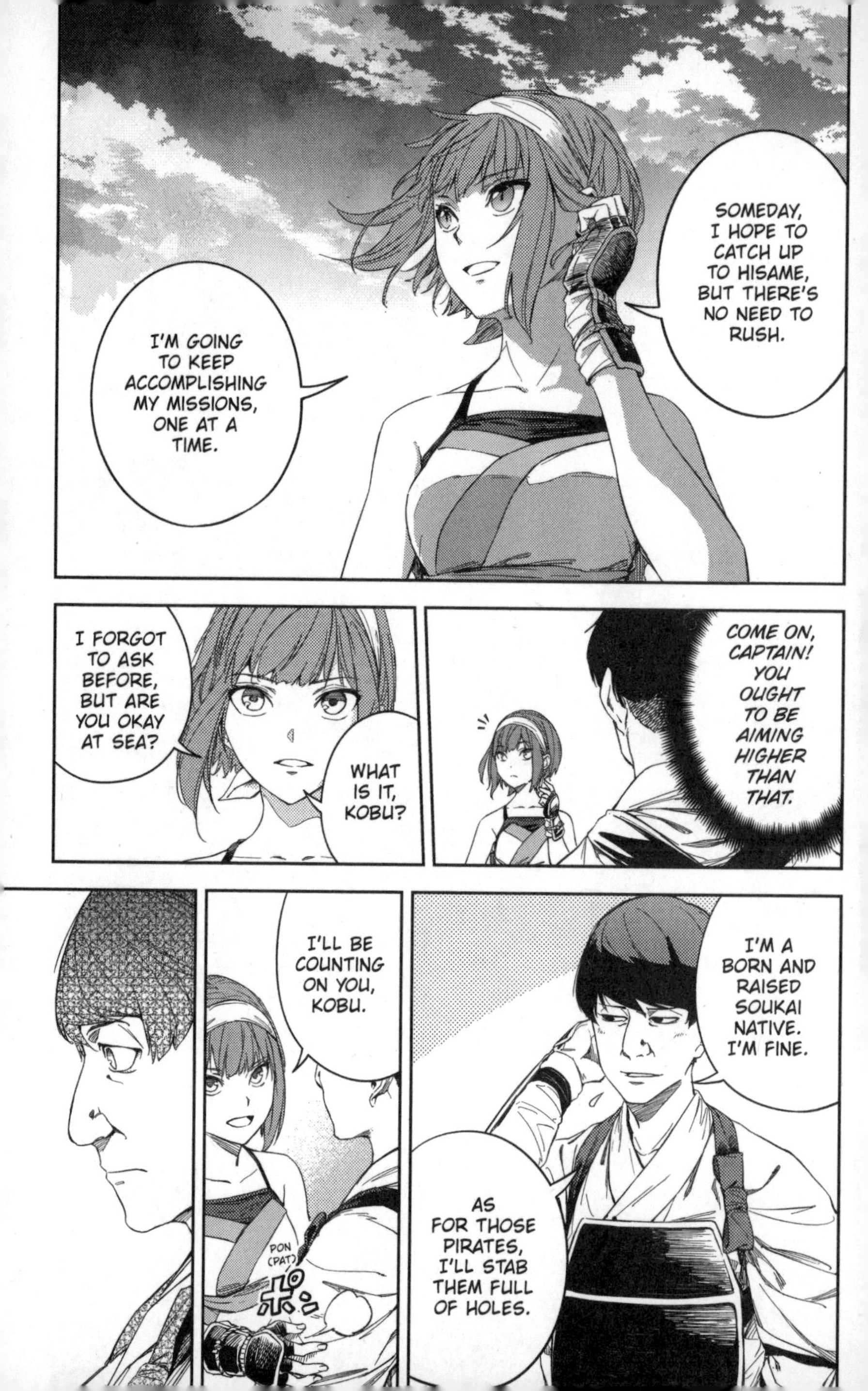
SOMEDAY, I HOPE TO CATCH UP TO HISAME, BUT THERE'S NO NEED TO RUSH.
I'M GOING TO KEEP ACCOMPLISHING MY MISSIONS, ONE AT A TIME.
COME ON, CAPTAIN! YOU OUGHT TO BE AIMING HIGHER THAN THAT.
WHAT IS IT, KOBU?
I FORGOT TO ASK BEFORE, BUT ARE YOU OKAY AT SEA?
I'M A BORN AND RAISED SOUKAI NATIVE. I'M FINE.
AS FOR THOSE PIRATES, I'LL STAB THEM FULL OF HOLES.
I'LL BE COUNTING ON YOU, KOBU.
PON (PAT)

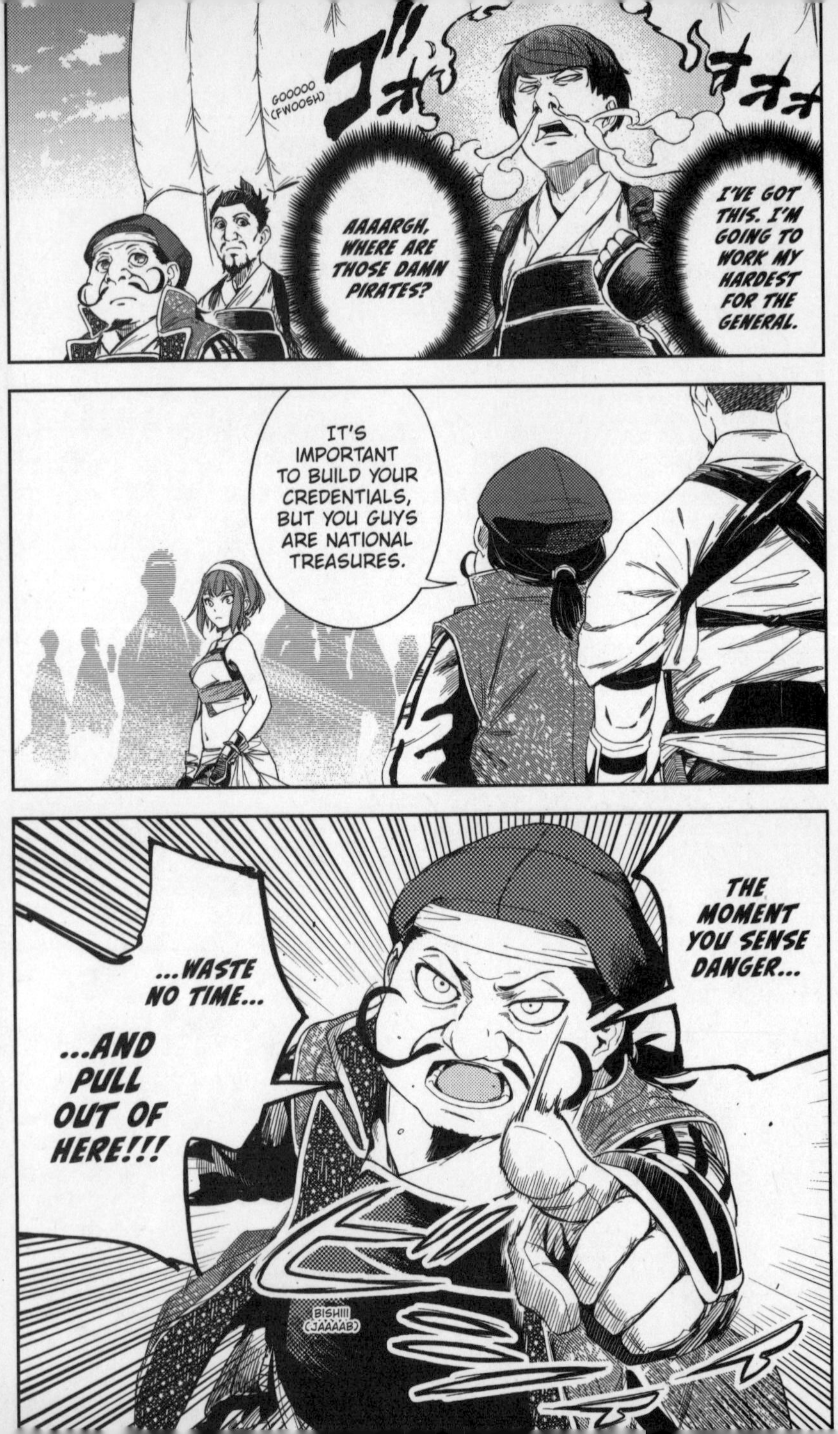
GOOOOO (FWOOSH)
I'VE GOT THIS. I'M GOING TO WORK MY HARDEST FOR THE GENERAL.
AAAARGH, WHERE ARE THOSE DAMN PIRATES?
IT'S IMPORTANT TO BUILD YOUR CREDENTIALS, BUT YOU GUYS ARE NATIONAL TREASURES.
THE MOMENT YOU SENSE DANGER...
...WASTE NO TIME...
...AND PULL OUT OF HERE!!!
BISHIII (JAAAAB)

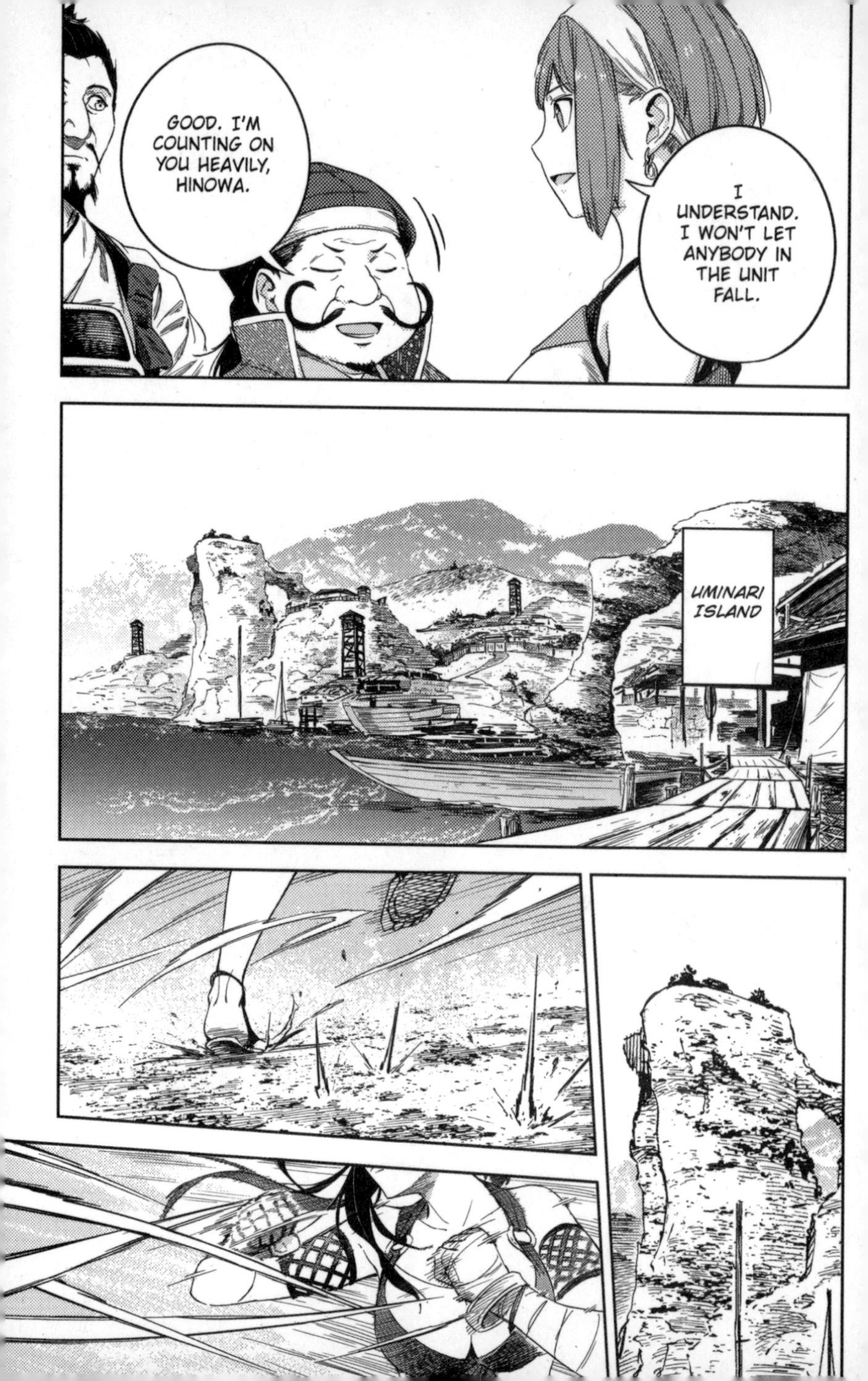
I UNDERSTAND. I WON'T LET ANYBODY IN THE UNIT FALL.
GOOD. I'M COUNTING ON YOU HEAVILY, HINOWA.
UMINARI ISLAND

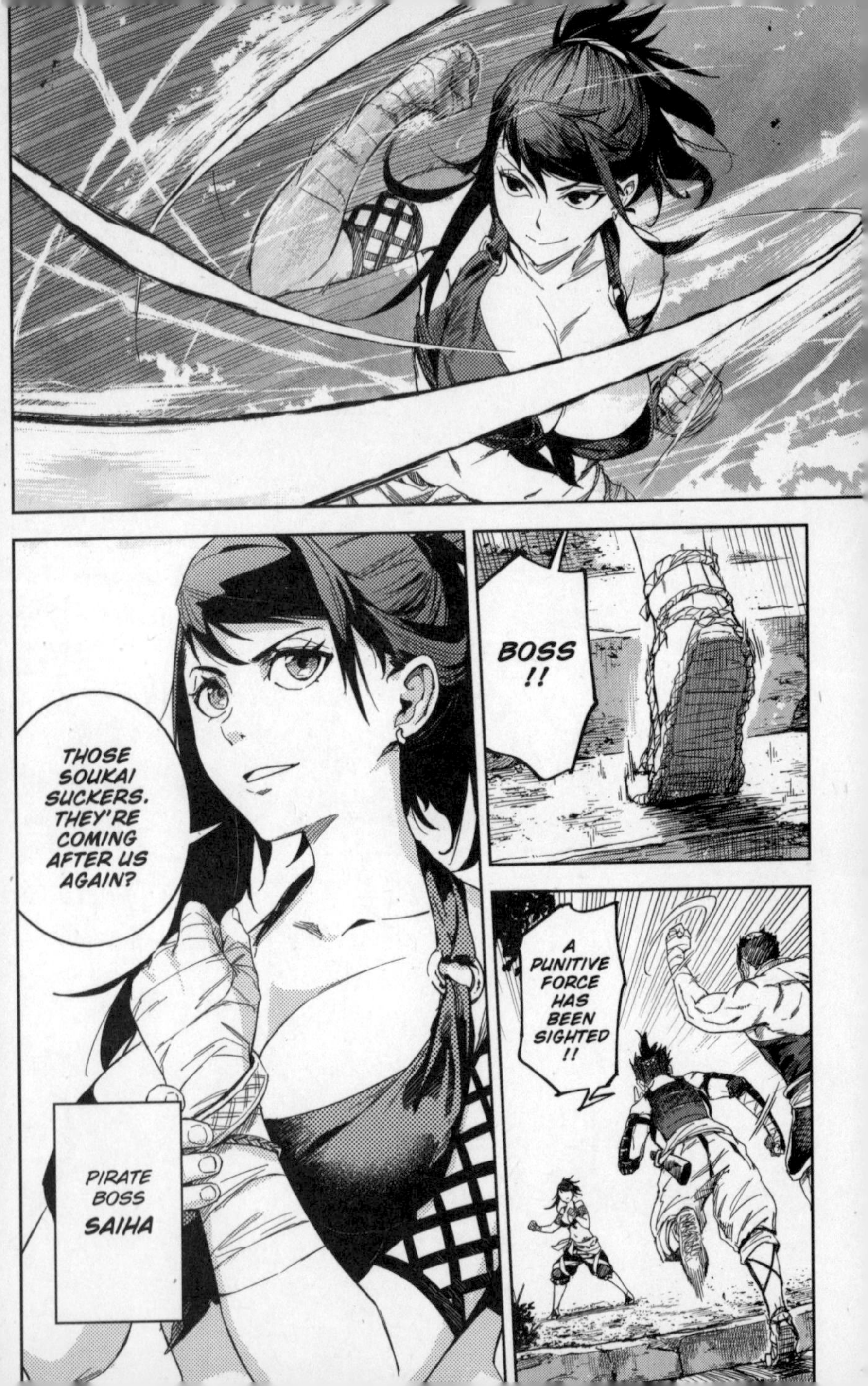
BOSS!!
A PUNITIVE FORCE HAS BEEN SIGHTED!!
THOSE SOUKAI SUCKERS. THEY'RE COMING AFTER US AGAIN?
PIRATE BOSS SAIHA

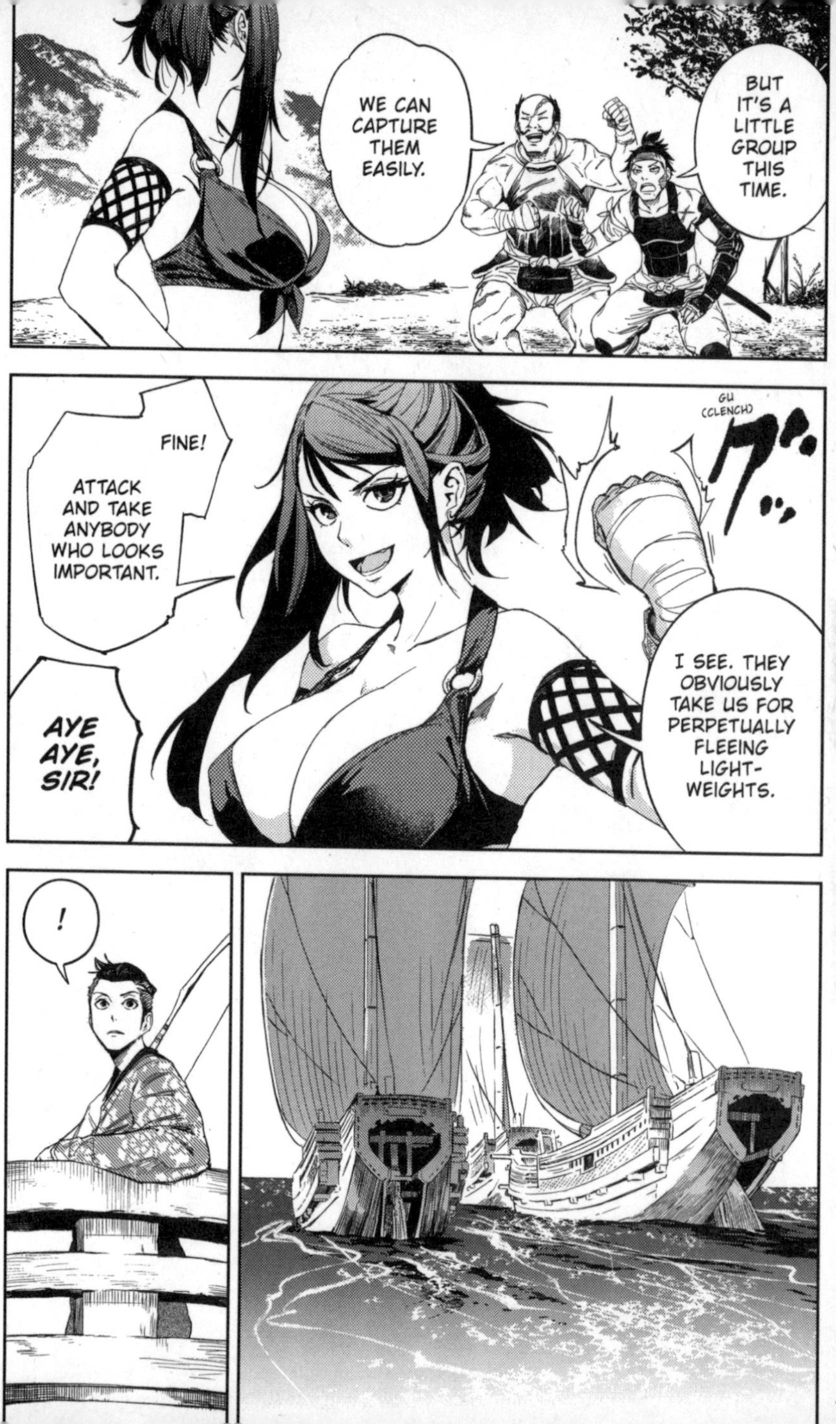
BUT IT'S A LITTLE GROUP THIS TIME.
WE CAN CAPTURE THEM EASILY.
GU (CLENCH)
I SEE. THEY OBVIOUSLY TAKE US FOR PERPETUALLY FLEEING LIGHT-WEIGHTS.
FINE!
ATTACK AND TAKE ANYBODY WHO LOOKS IMPORTANT.
AYE AYE, SIR!
!

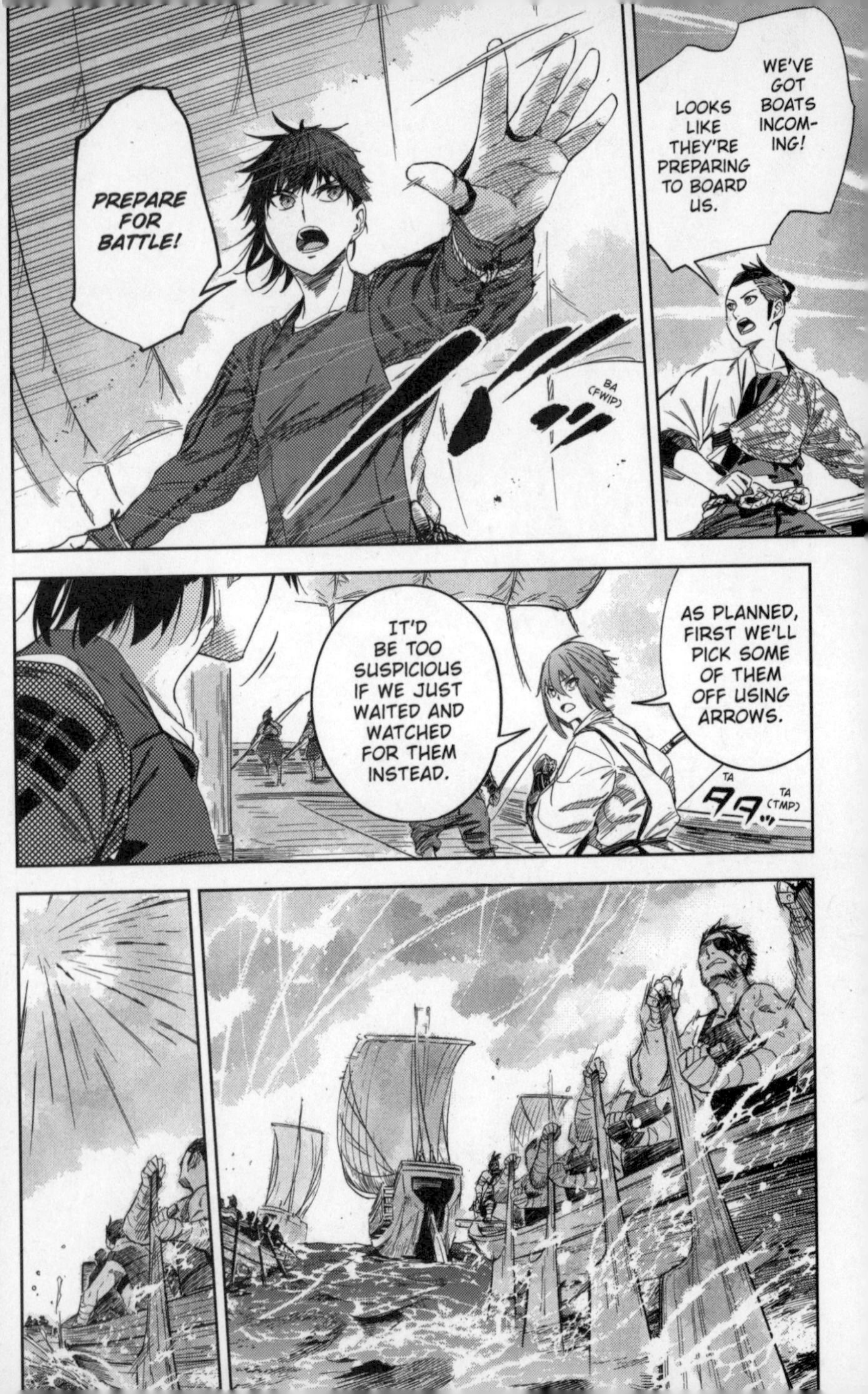
WE'VE GOT BOATS INCOMING!
LOOKS LIKE THEY'RE PREPARING TO BOARD US.
PREPARE FOR BATTLE!
BA (FWIP)
AS PLANNED, FIRST WE'LL PICK SOME OF THEM OFF USING ARROWS.
IT'D BE TOO SUSPICIOUS IF WE JUST WAITED AND WATCHED FOR THEM INSTEAD.
TA TA (TMP)

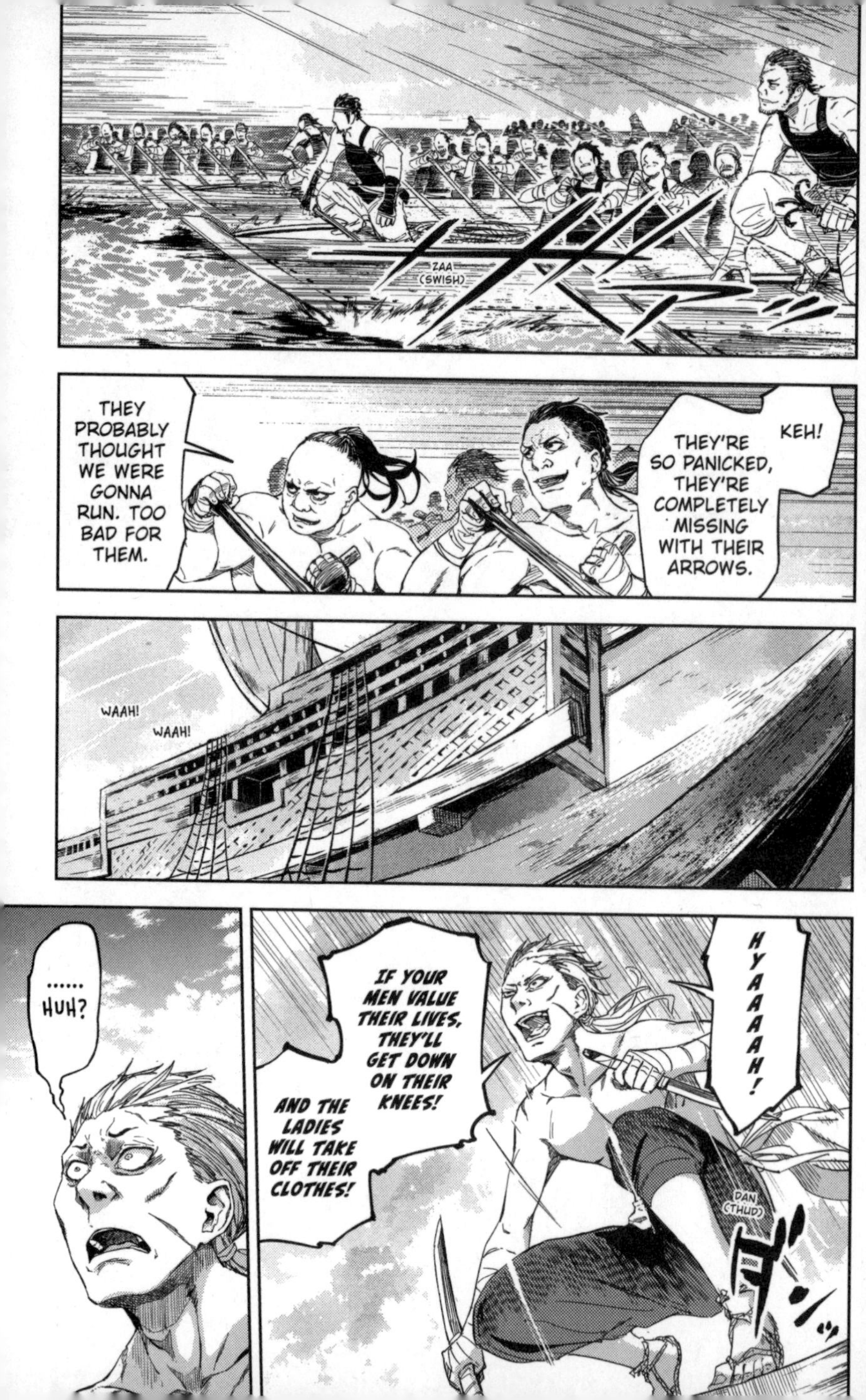
ZAA (SWISH)
KEH!
THEY'RE SO PANICKED, THEY'RE COMPLETELY MISSING WITH THEIR ARROWS.
THEY PROBABLY THOUGHT WE WERE GONNA RUN. TOO BAD FOR THEM.
WAAH!
WAAH!
HYAAAAAH!
IF YOUR MEN VALUE THEIR LIVES, THEY'LL GET DOWN ON THEIR KNEES!
AND THE LADIES WILL TAKE OFF THEIR CLOTHES!
DAN (THUD)
......HUH?

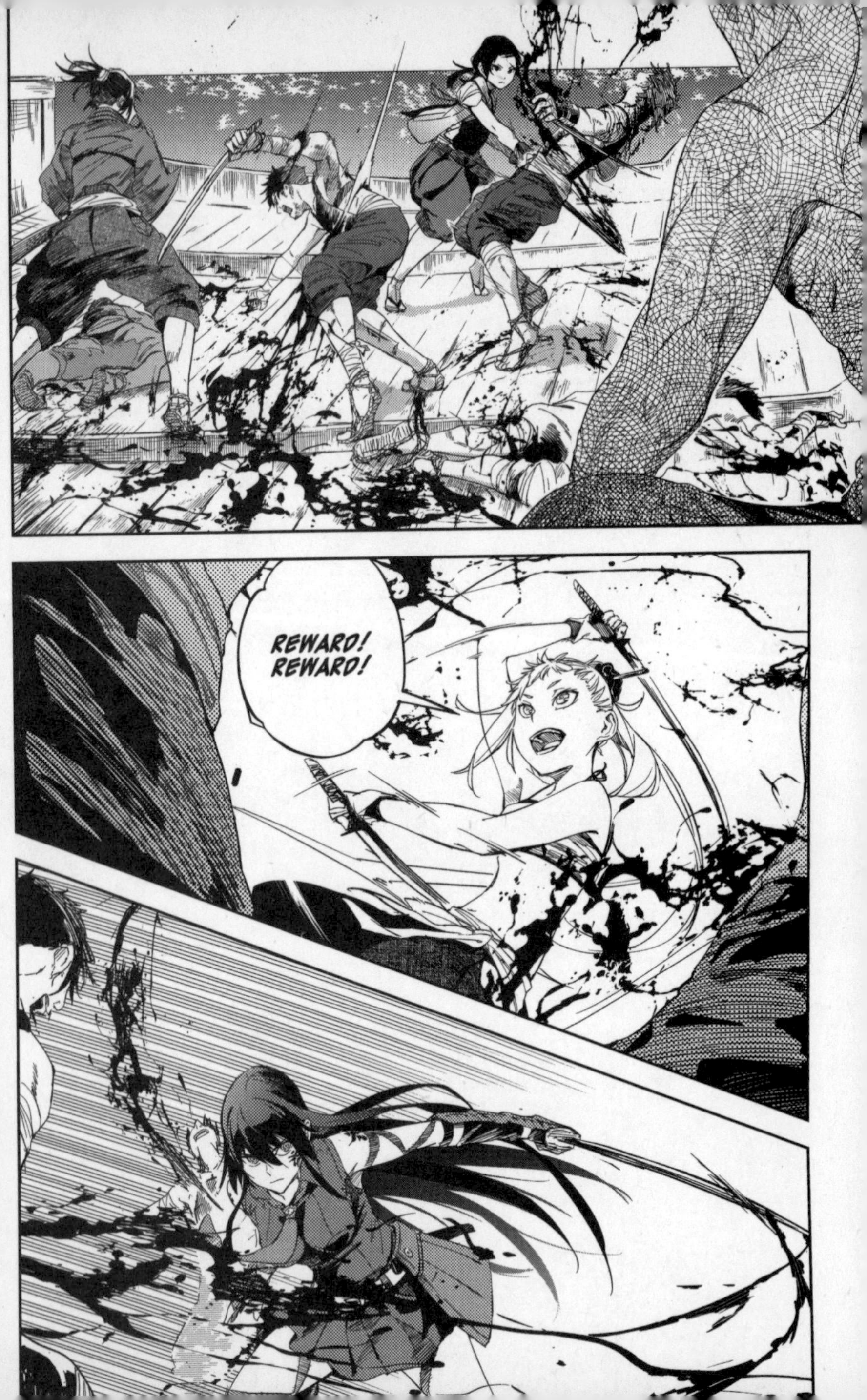
REWARD! REWARD!

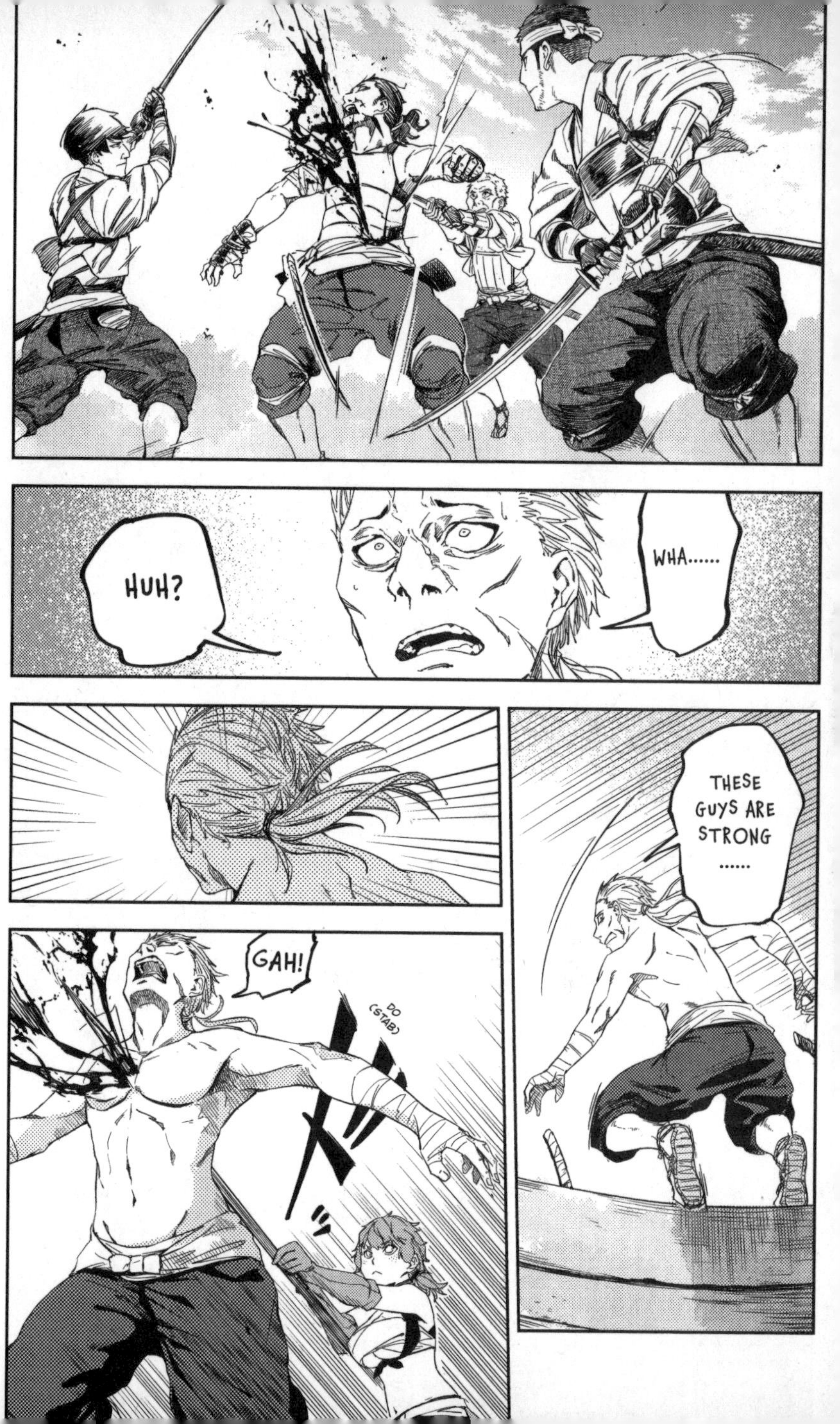
WHA......
HUH?
THESE GUYS ARE STRONG ......
GAH!
DO (STAB)

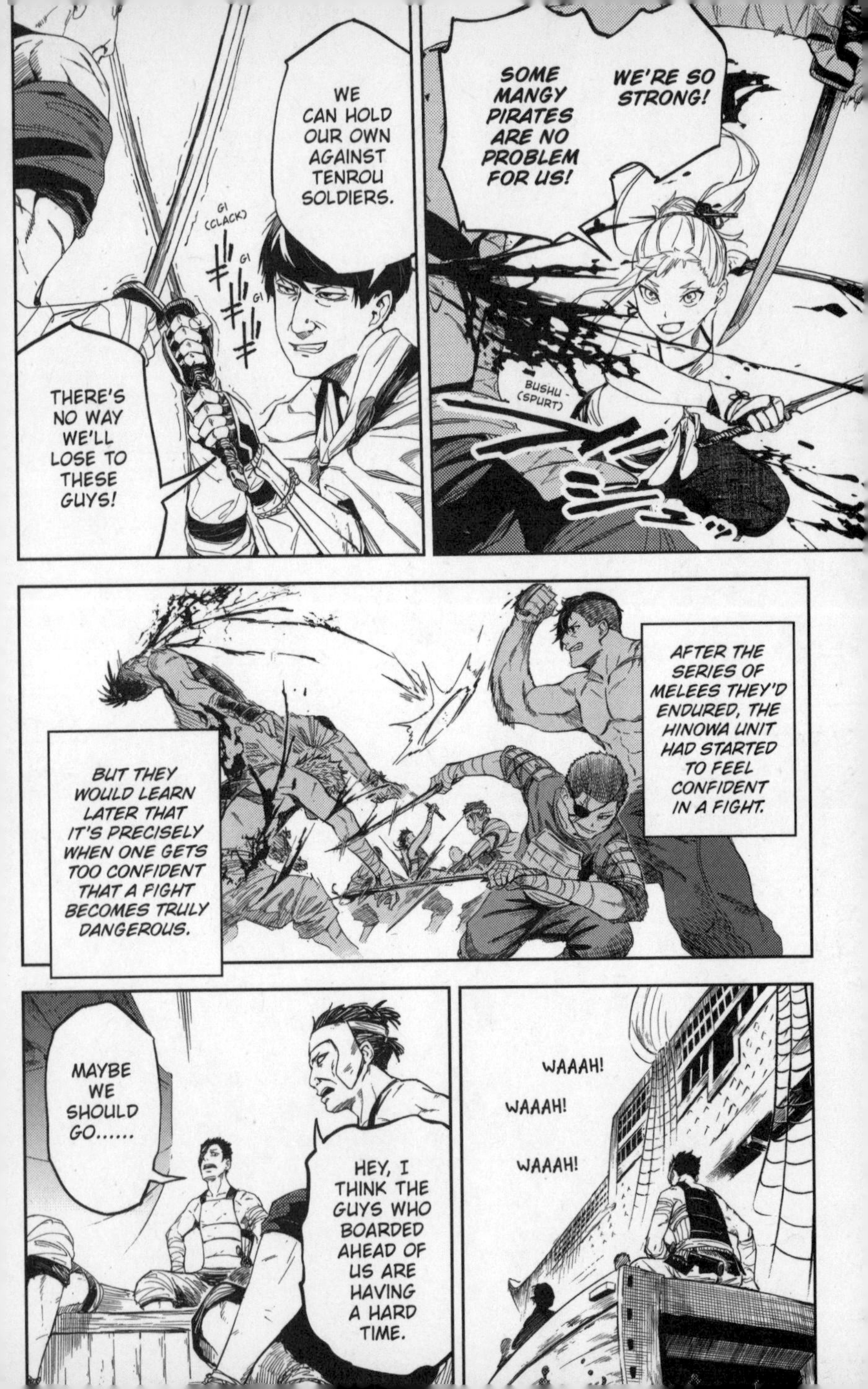
WE'RE SO STRONG!
SOME MANGY PIRATES ARE NO PROBLEM FOR US!
BUSHU (SPURT)
WE CAN HOLD OUR OWN AGAINST TENROU SOLDIERS.
GI (CLACK)
GI
GI
THERE'S NO WAY WE'LL LOSE TO THESE GUYS!
AFTER THE SERIES OF MELEES THEY'D ENDURED, THE HINOWA UNIT HAD STARTED TO FEEL CONFIDENT IN A FIGHT.
BUT THEY WOULD LEARN LATER THAT IT'S PRECISELY WHEN ONE GETS TOO CONFIDENT THAT A FIGHT BECOMES TRULY DANGEROUS.
WAAAH!
WAAAH!
WAAAH!
HEY, I THINK THE GUYS WHO BOARDED AHEAD OF US ARE HAVING A HARD TIME.
MAYBE WE SHOULD GO......

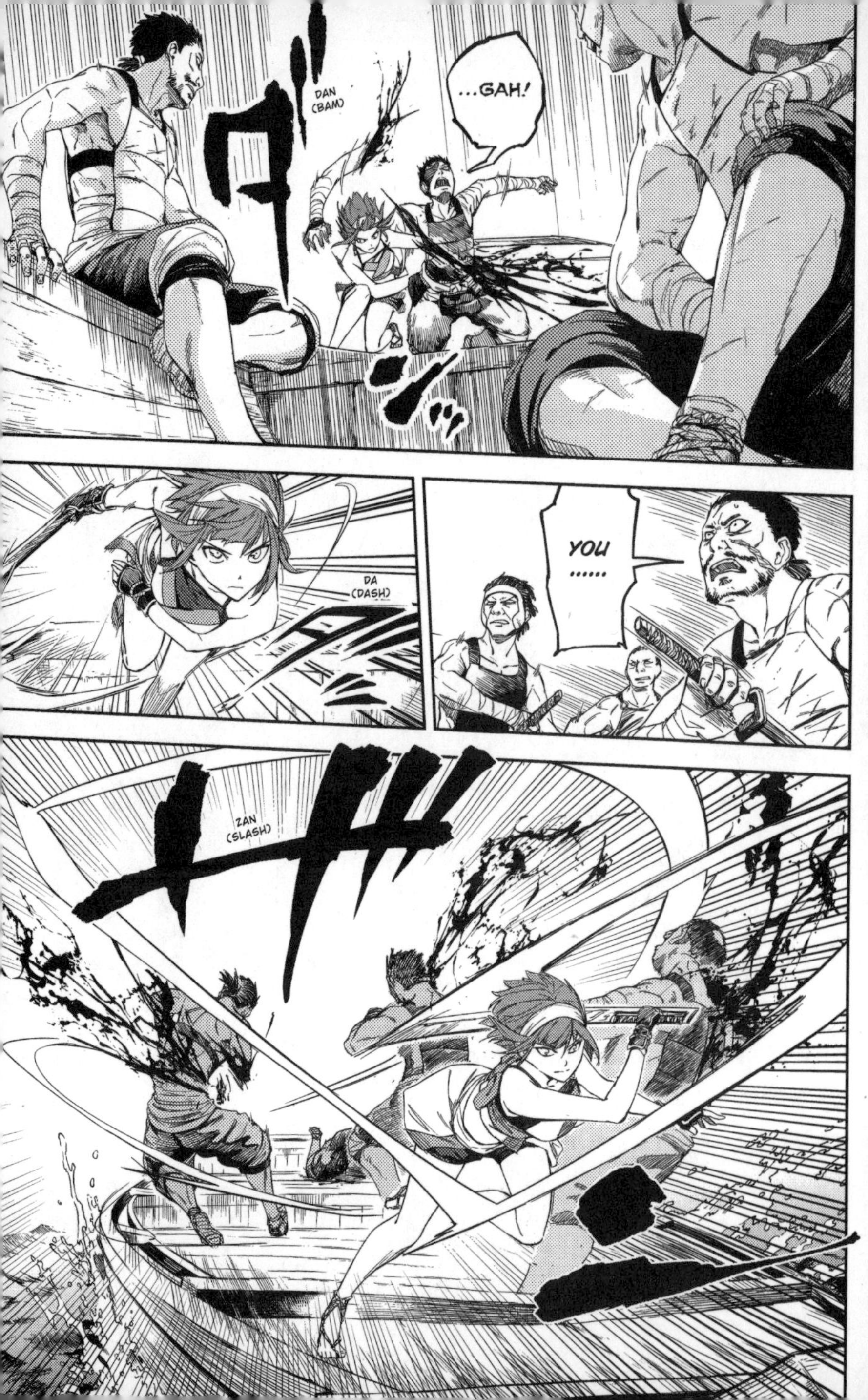
...GAH!
DAN
(BAM)
YOU
......
DA
(DASH)
ZAN
(SLASH)

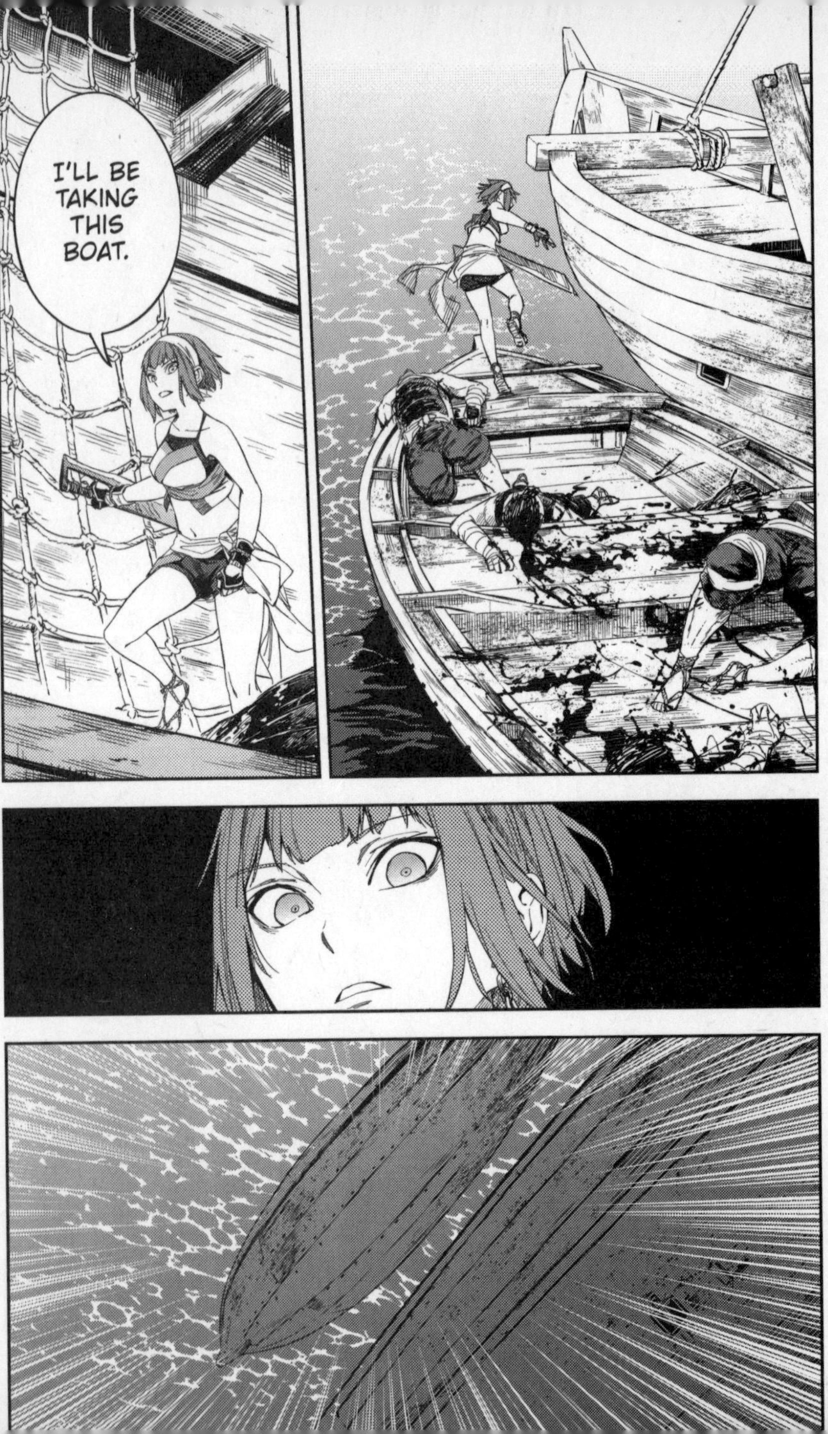
I'LL BE TAKING THIS BOAT.

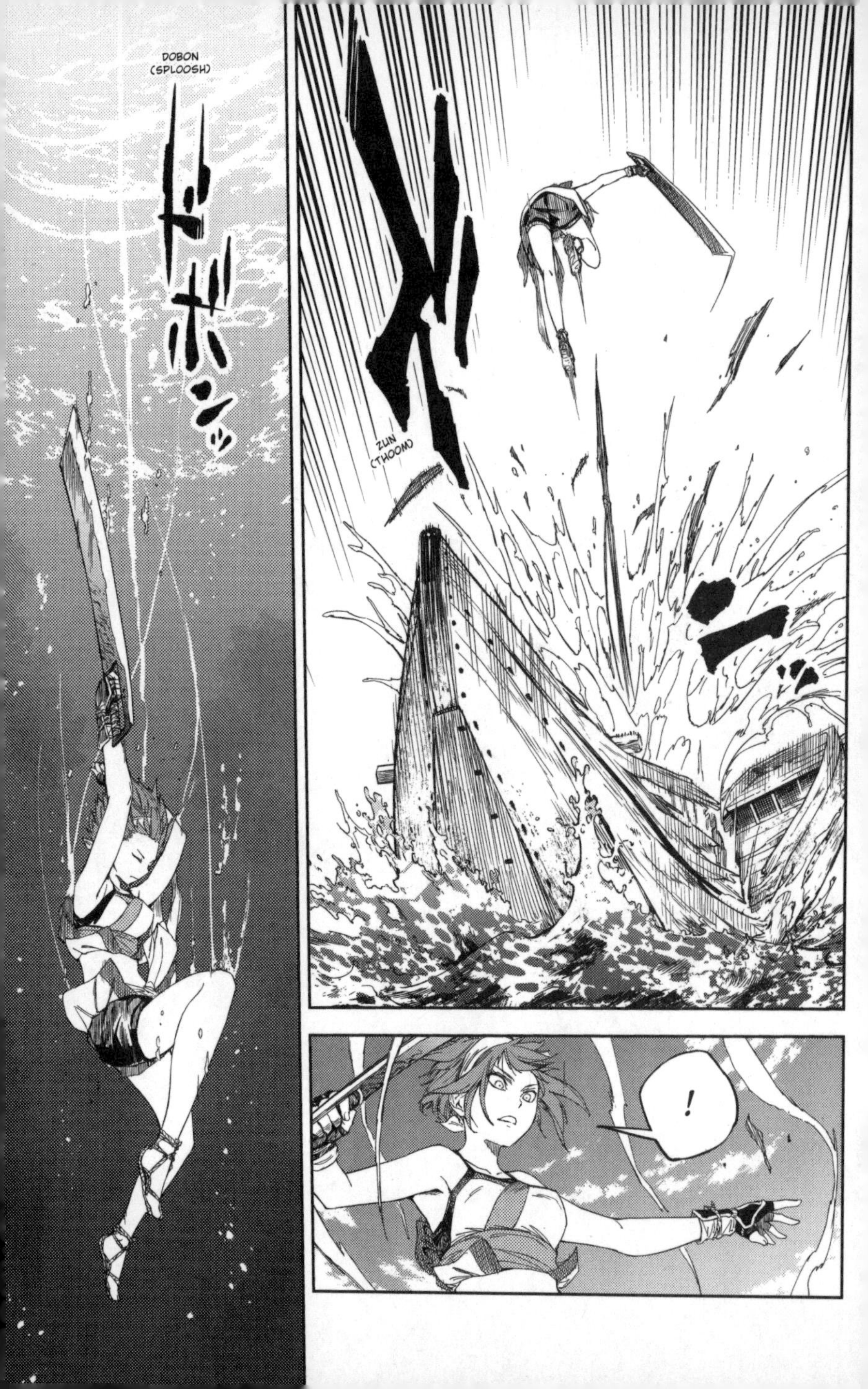
ZUN (THOOM)
!
DOBON (SPLOOSH)

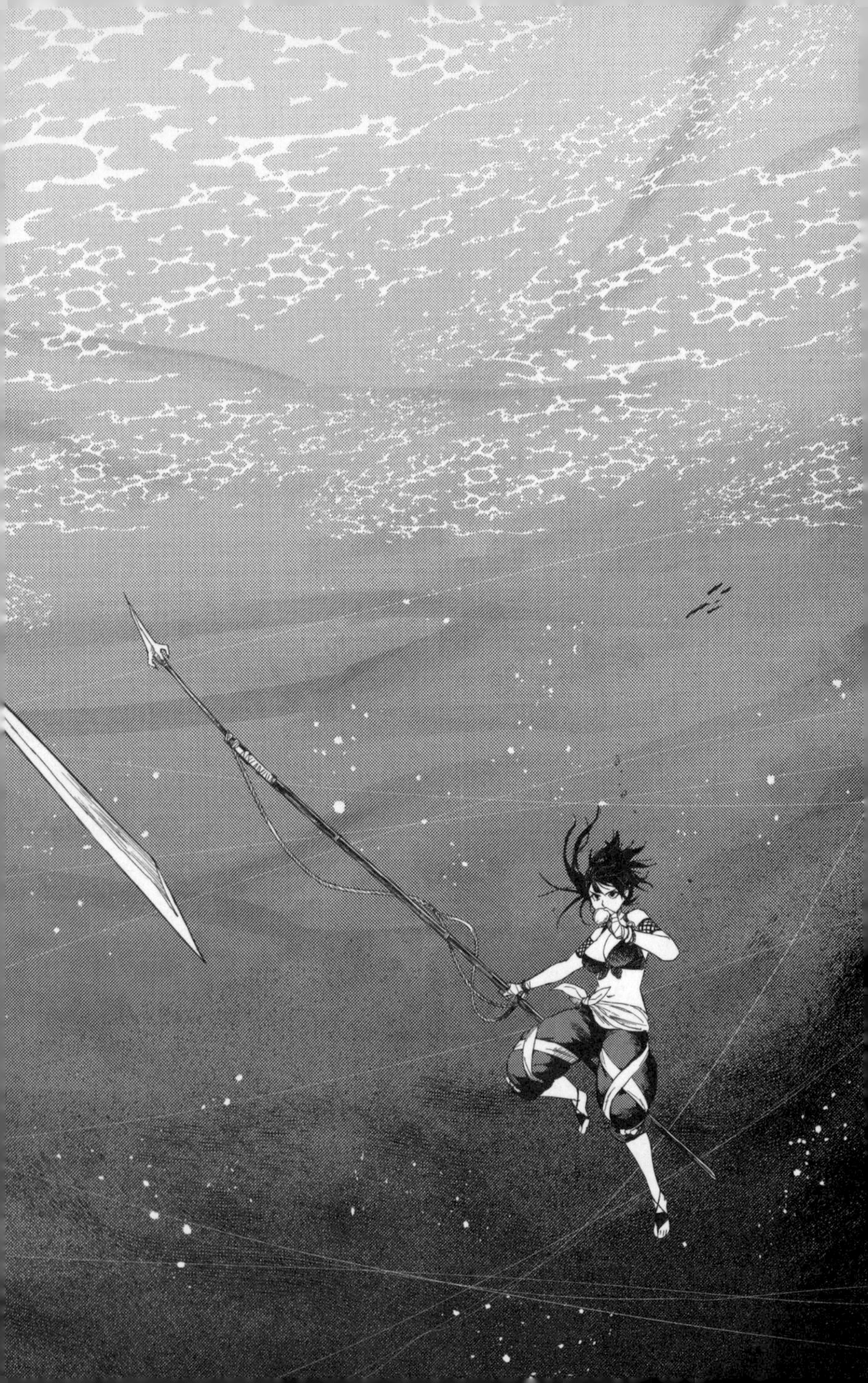

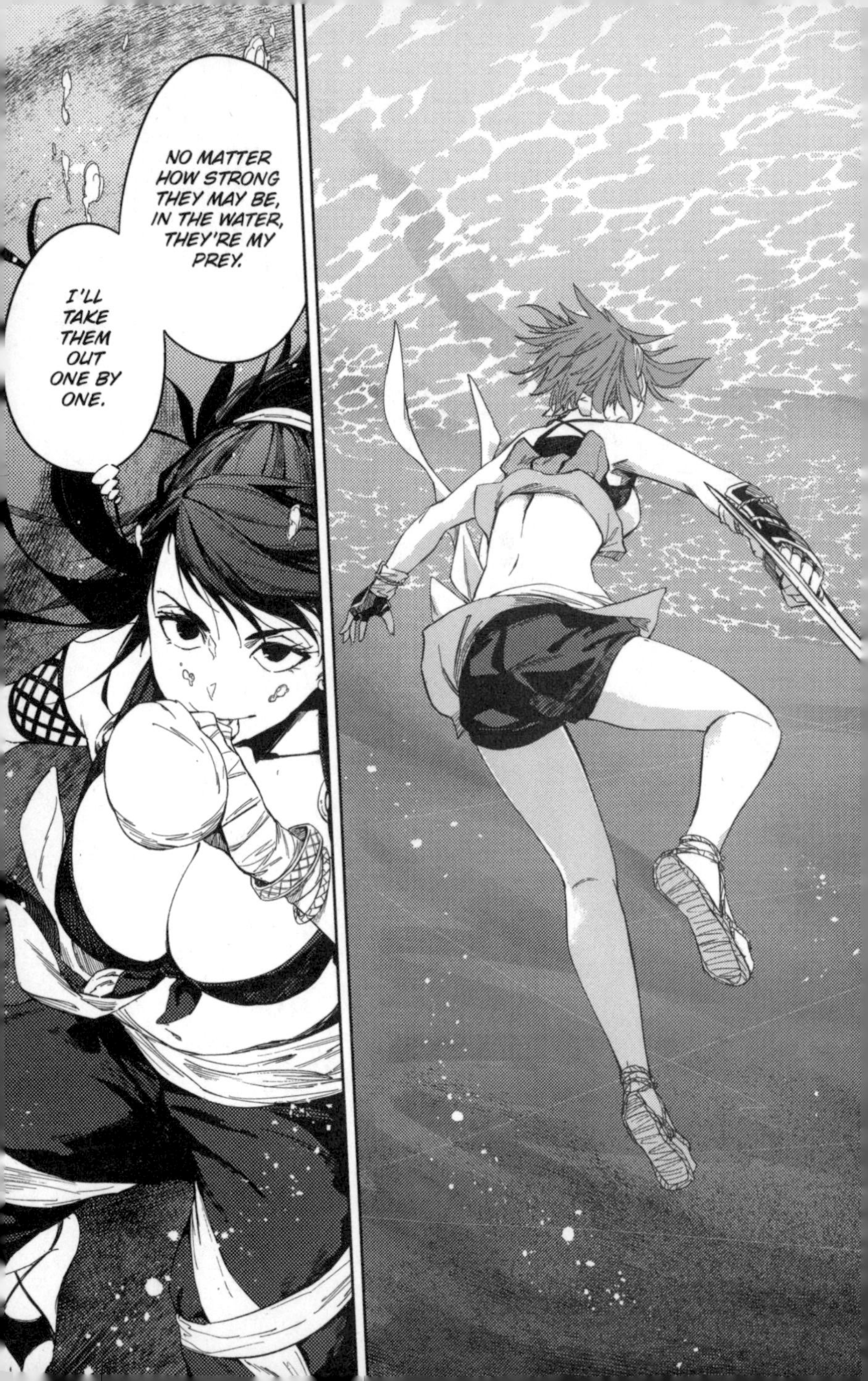
NO MATTER HOW STRONG THEY MAY BE, IN THE WATER, THEY'RE MY PREY.
I'LL TAKE THEM OUT ONE BY ONE.

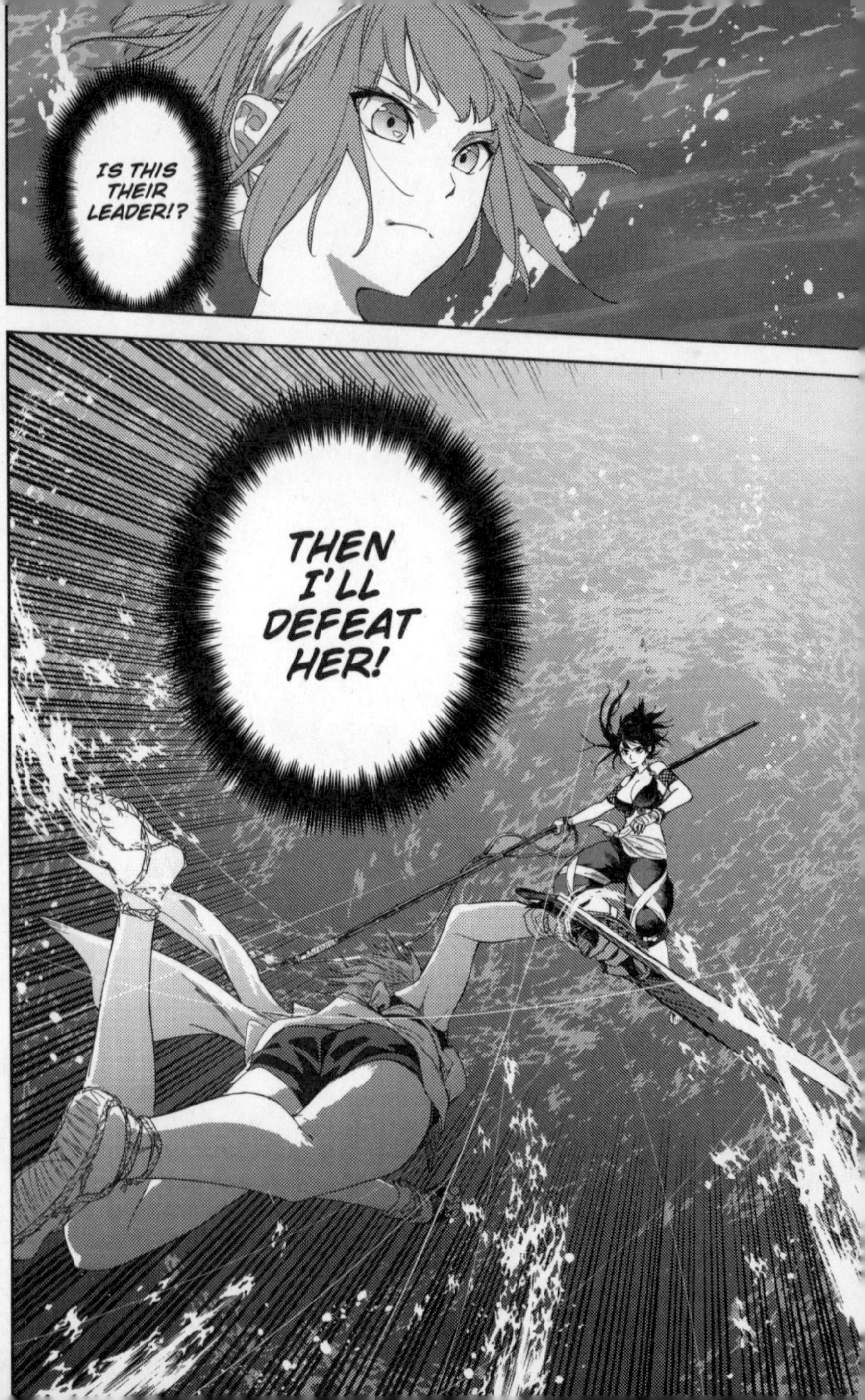
IS THIS THEIR LEADER!?
THEN I'LL DEFEAT HER!

Hinowa ga CRUSH!

Hijnowa ga CRUSH!

Design Drafts ②

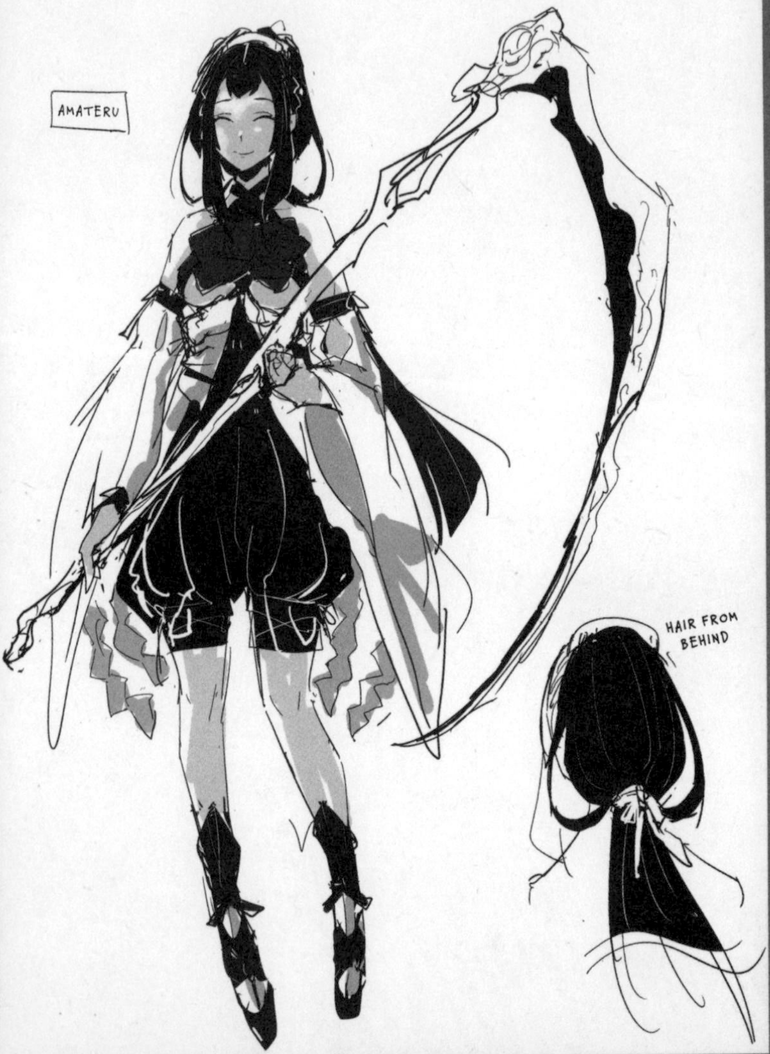
AMATERU
HAIR FROM BEHIND

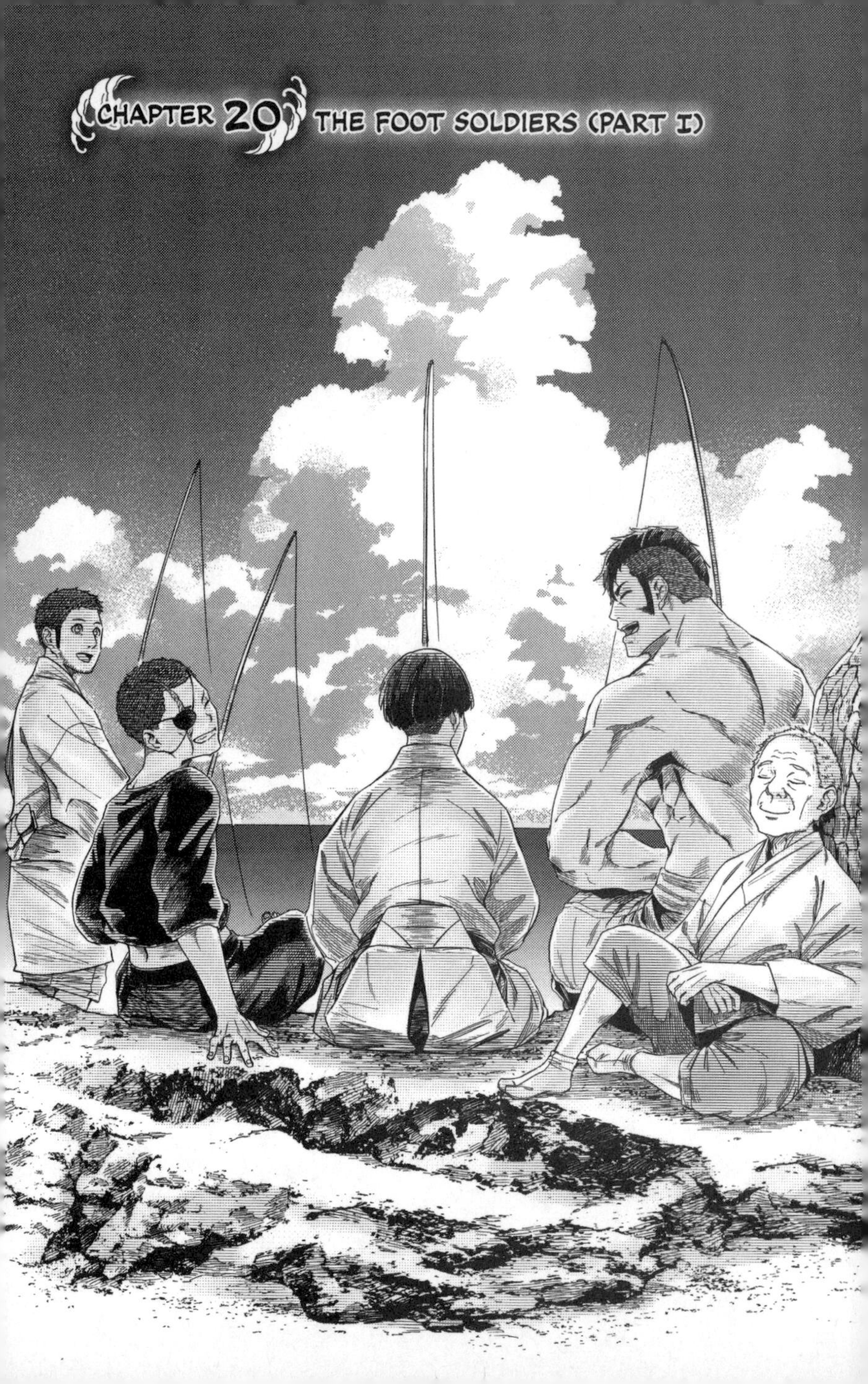
CHAPTER 20
THE FOOT SOLDIERS (PART I)

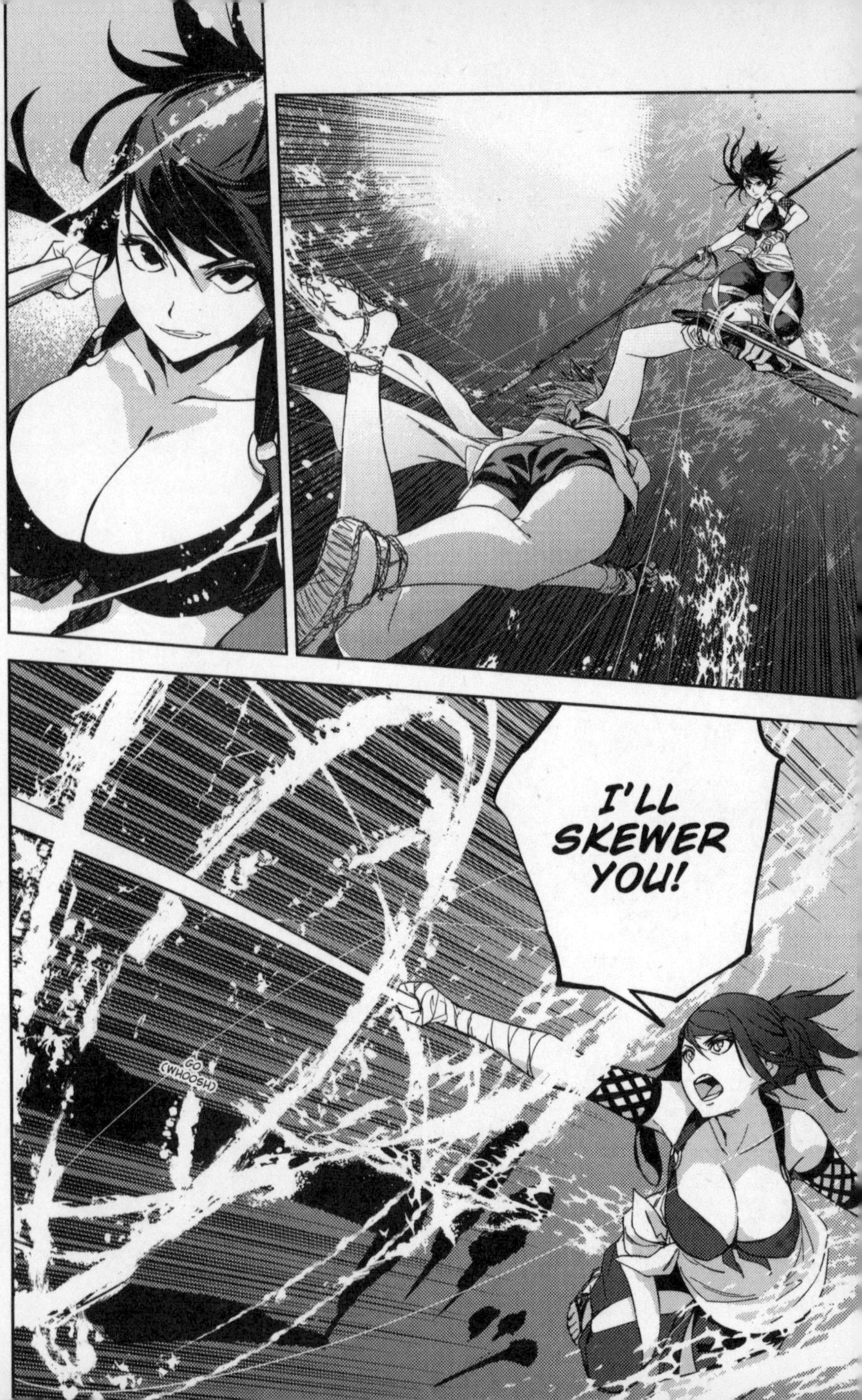
I'LL SKEWER YOU!
GO (WHOOSH)

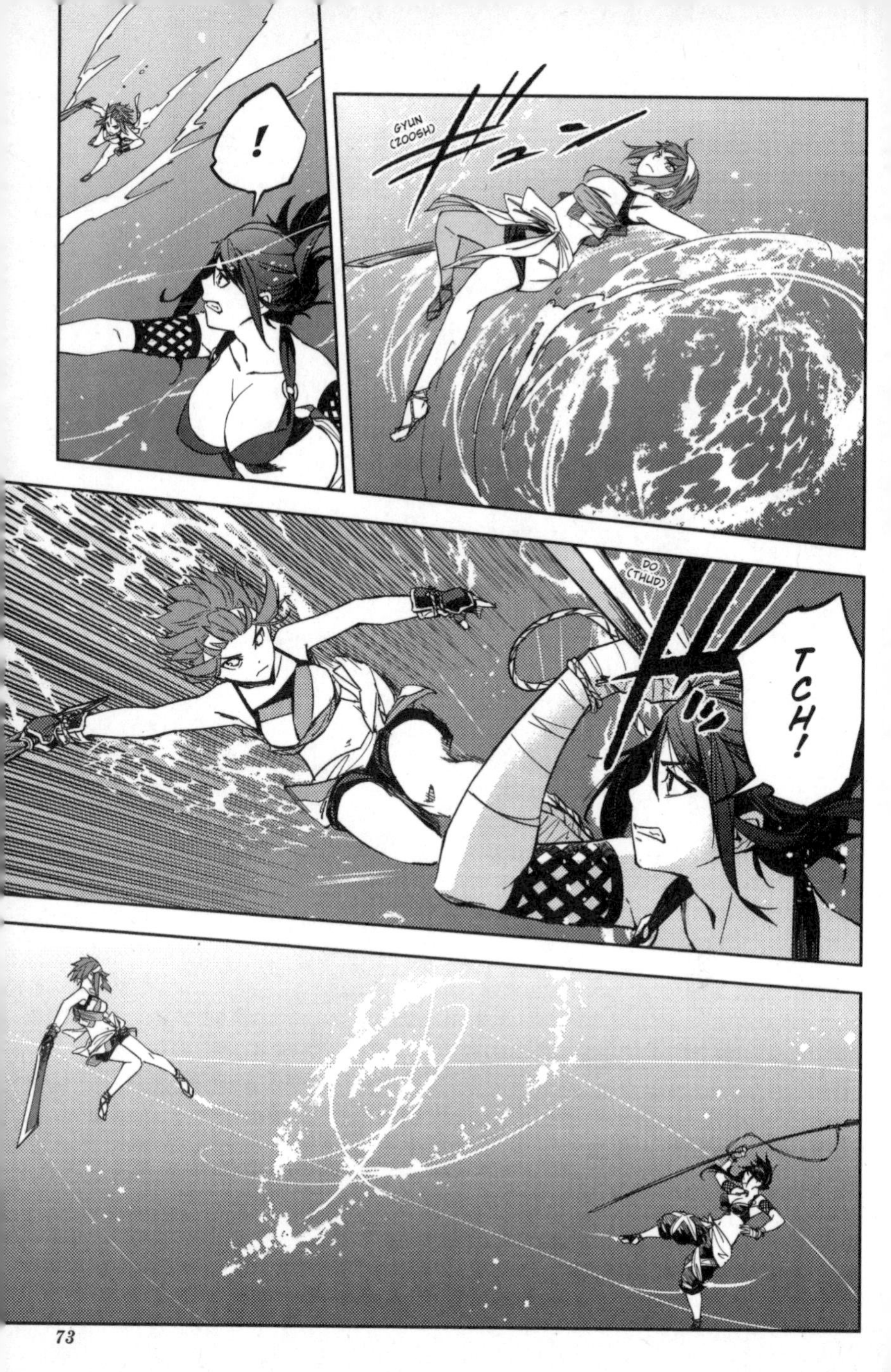
GYUN (ZOOSH)
!
DO (THUD)
TCH!

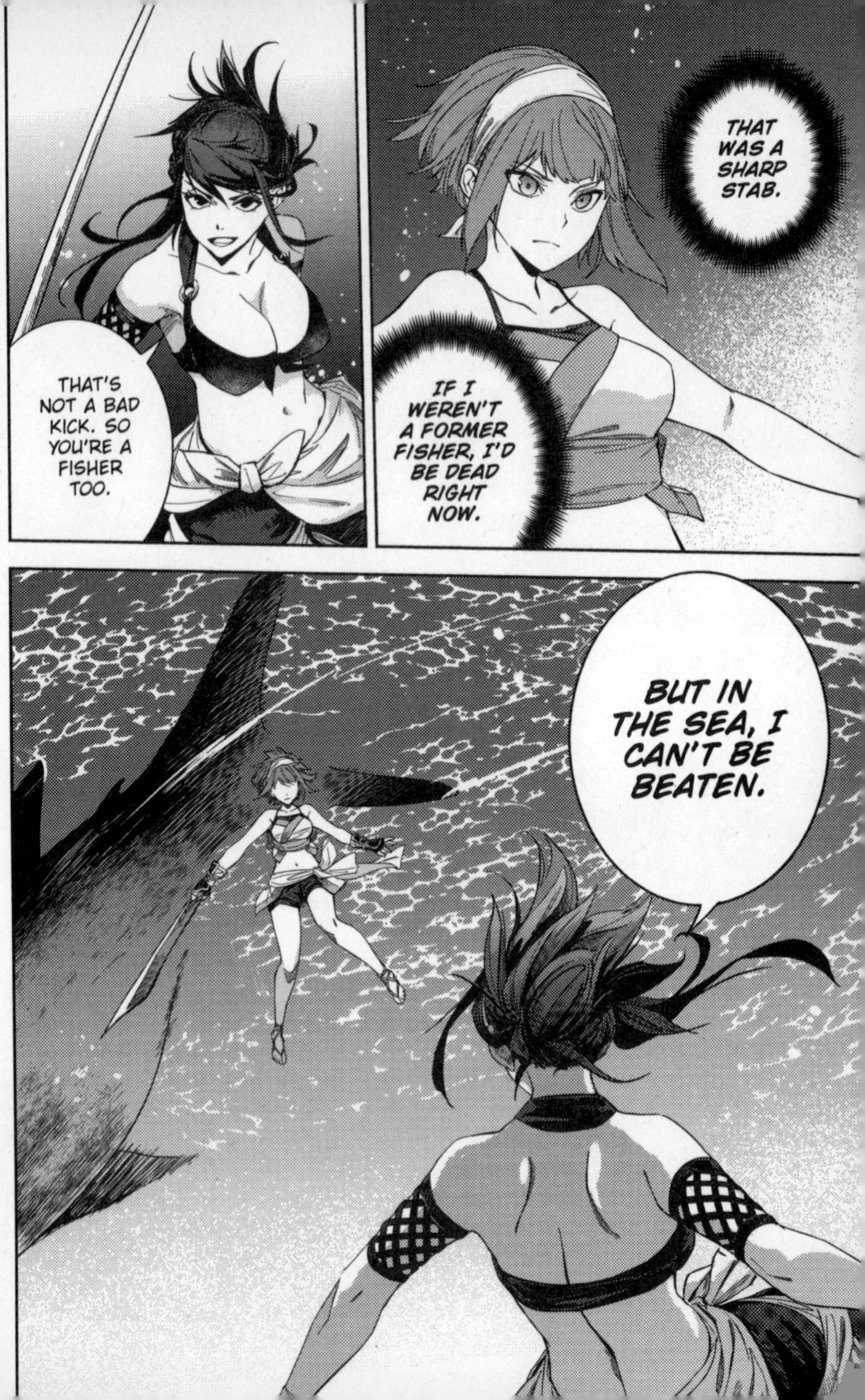
THAT WAS A SHARP STAB.
IF I WEREN'T A FORMER FISHER, I'D BE DEAD RIGHT NOW.
THAT'S NOT A BAD KICK. SO YOU'RE A FISHER TOO.
BUT IN THE SEA, I CAN'T BE BEATEN.

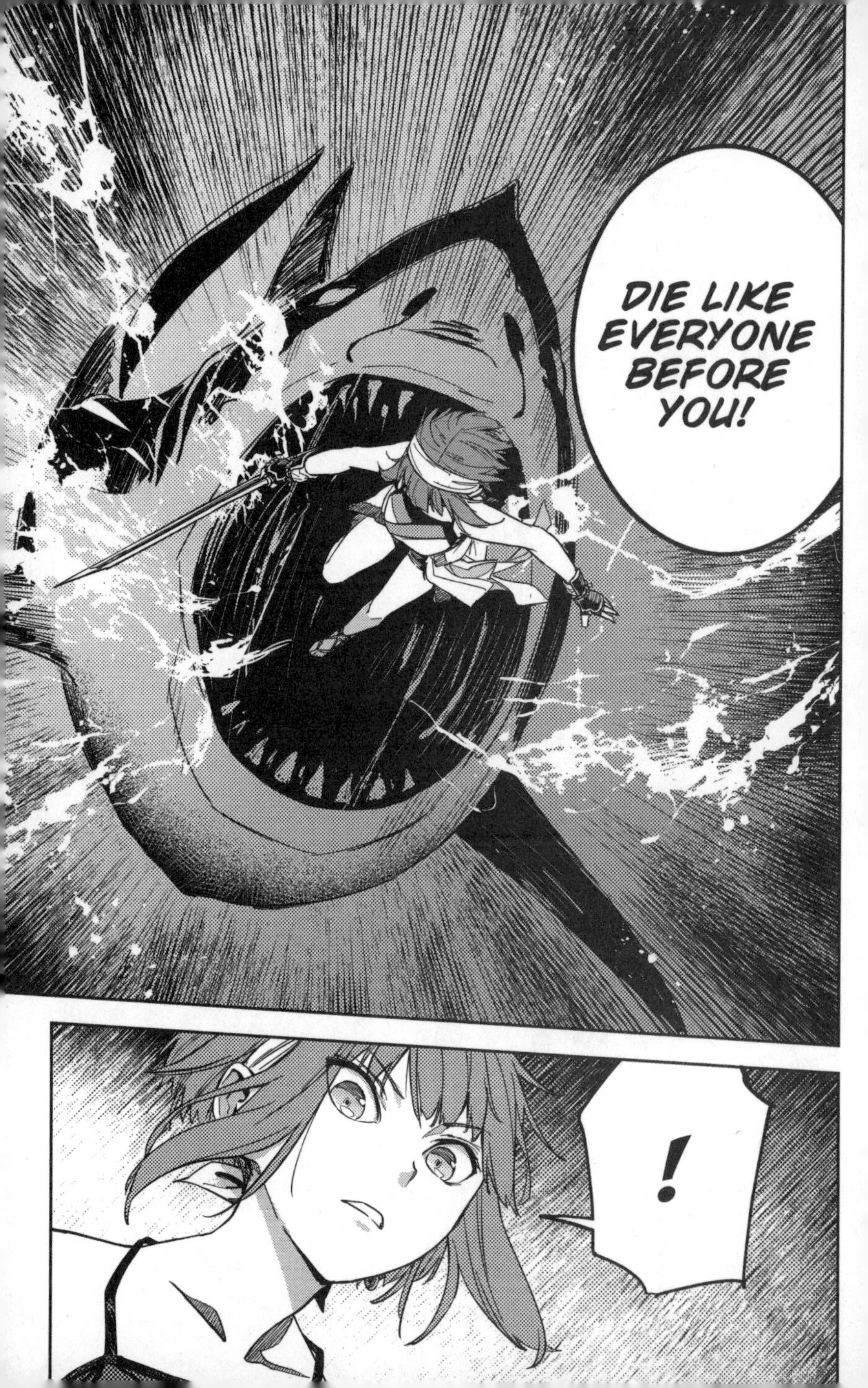
DIE LIKE EVERYONE BEFORE YOU!
!

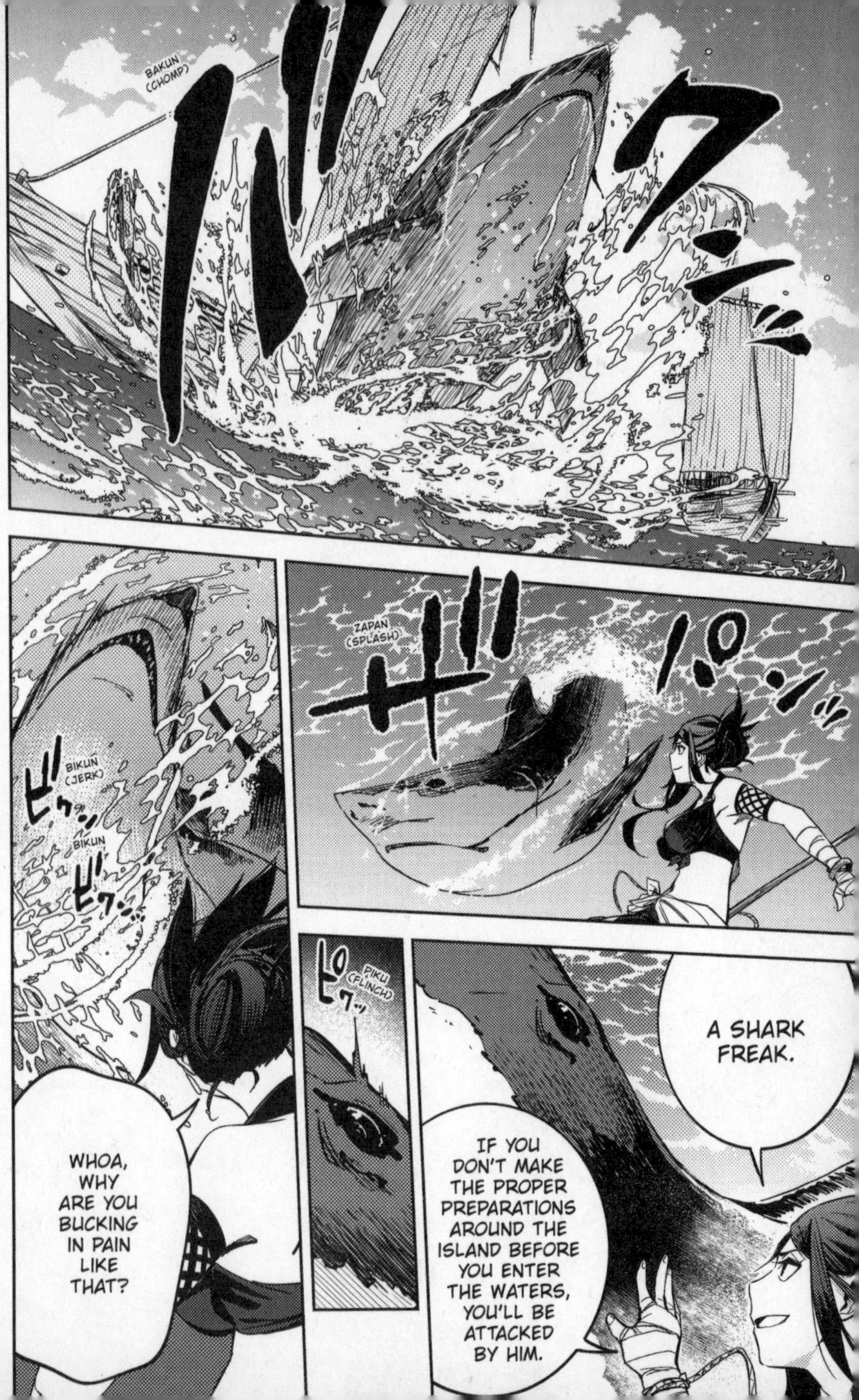
BAKUN (CHOMP)
ZAPAN (SPLASH)
A SHARK FREAK.
IF YOU DON'T MAKE THE PROPER PREPARATIONS AROUND THE ISLAND BEFORE YOU ENTER THE WATERS, YOU'LL BE ATTACKED BY HIM.
PIKU (FLINCH)
BIKUN (JERK)
BIKUN
WHOA, WHY ARE YOU BUCKING IN PAIN LIKE THAT?

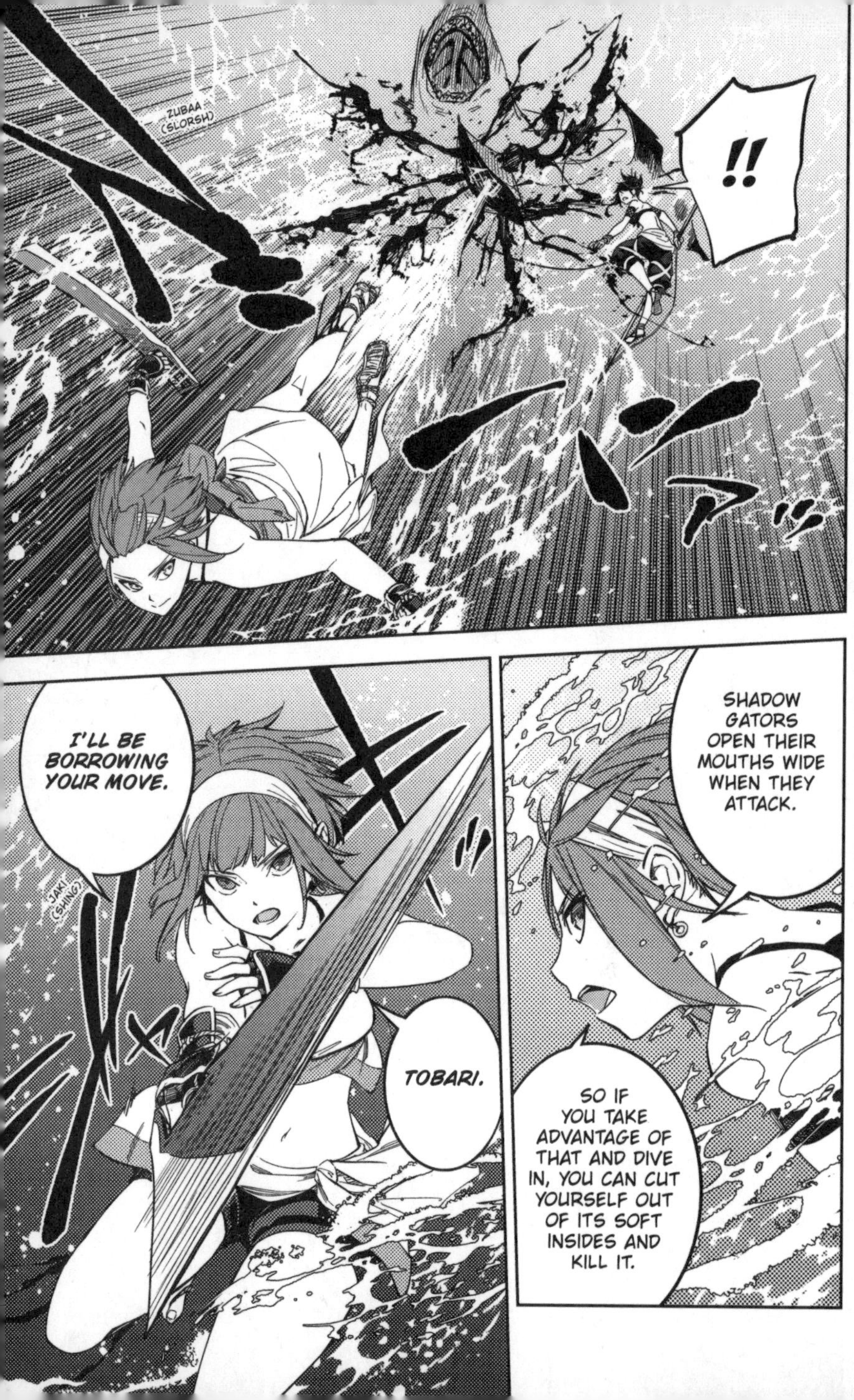
!!
ZUBAA
(SLORSH)
SHADOW GATORS OPEN THEIR MOUTHS WIDE WHEN THEY ATTACK.
SO IF YOU TAKE ADVANTAGE OF THAT AND DIVE IN, YOU CAN CUT YOURSELF OUT OF ITS SOFT INSIDES AND KILL IT.
I'LL BE BORROWING YOUR MOVE.
TOBARI.
JAKI
(SHING)

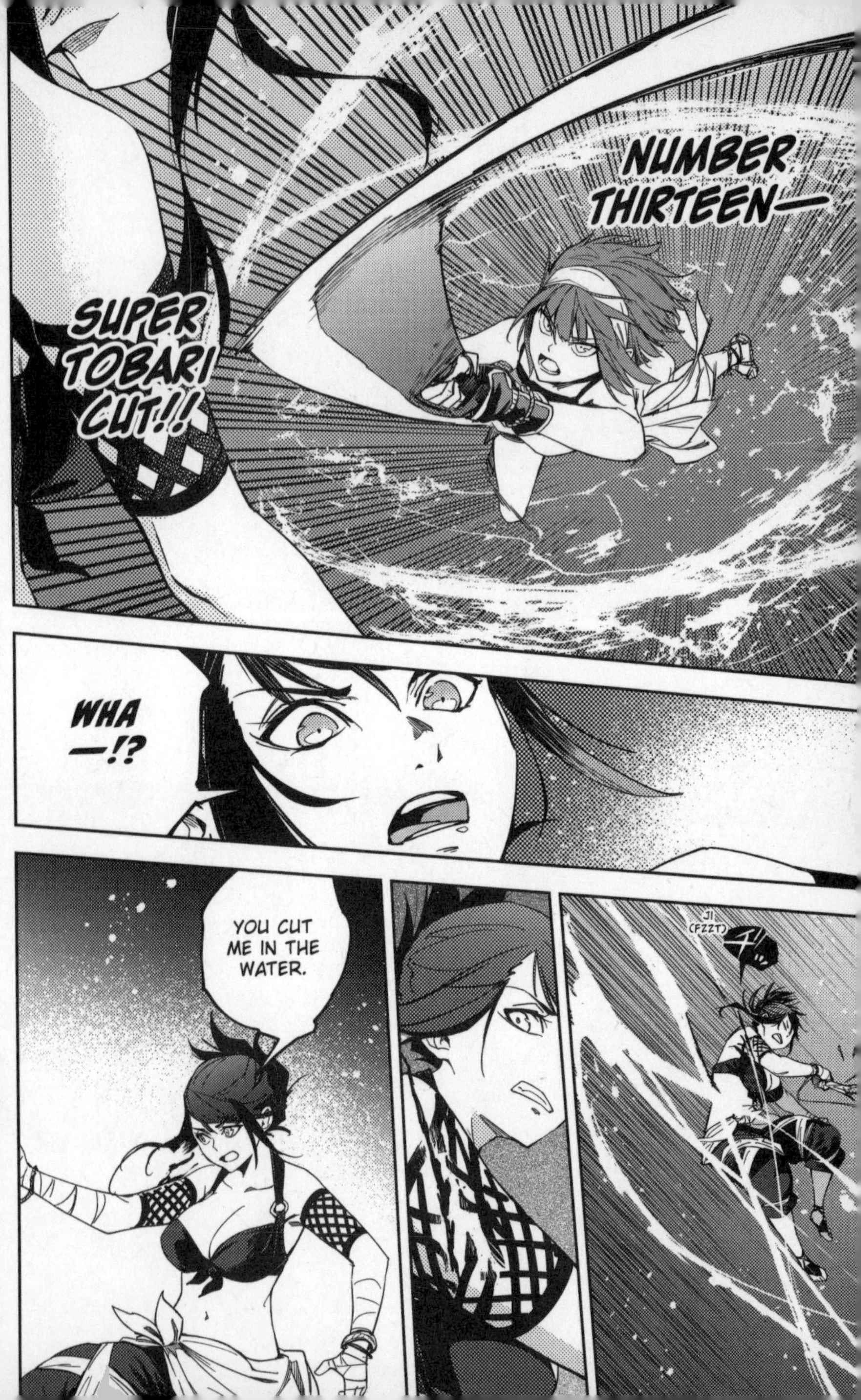
NUMBER THIRTEEN—
SUPER TOBARI CUT!!
WHA—!?
JI (FZZT)
YOU CUT ME IN THE WATER.

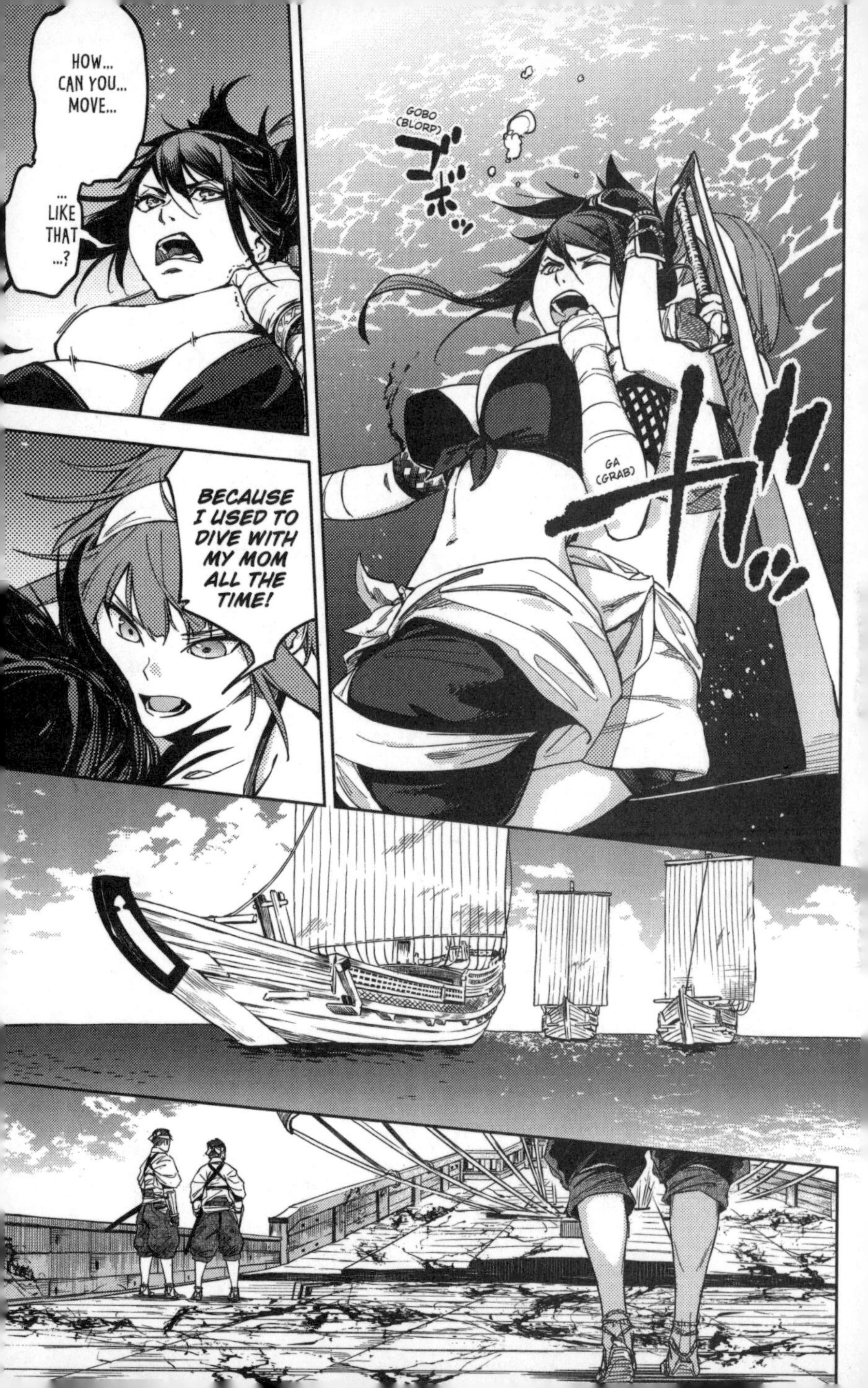
GOBO (BLORP)
ゴボッ
GA (GRAB)
HOW... CAN YOU... MOVE...
... LIKE THAT ...?
BECAUSE I USED TO DIVE WITH MY MOM ALL THE TIME!

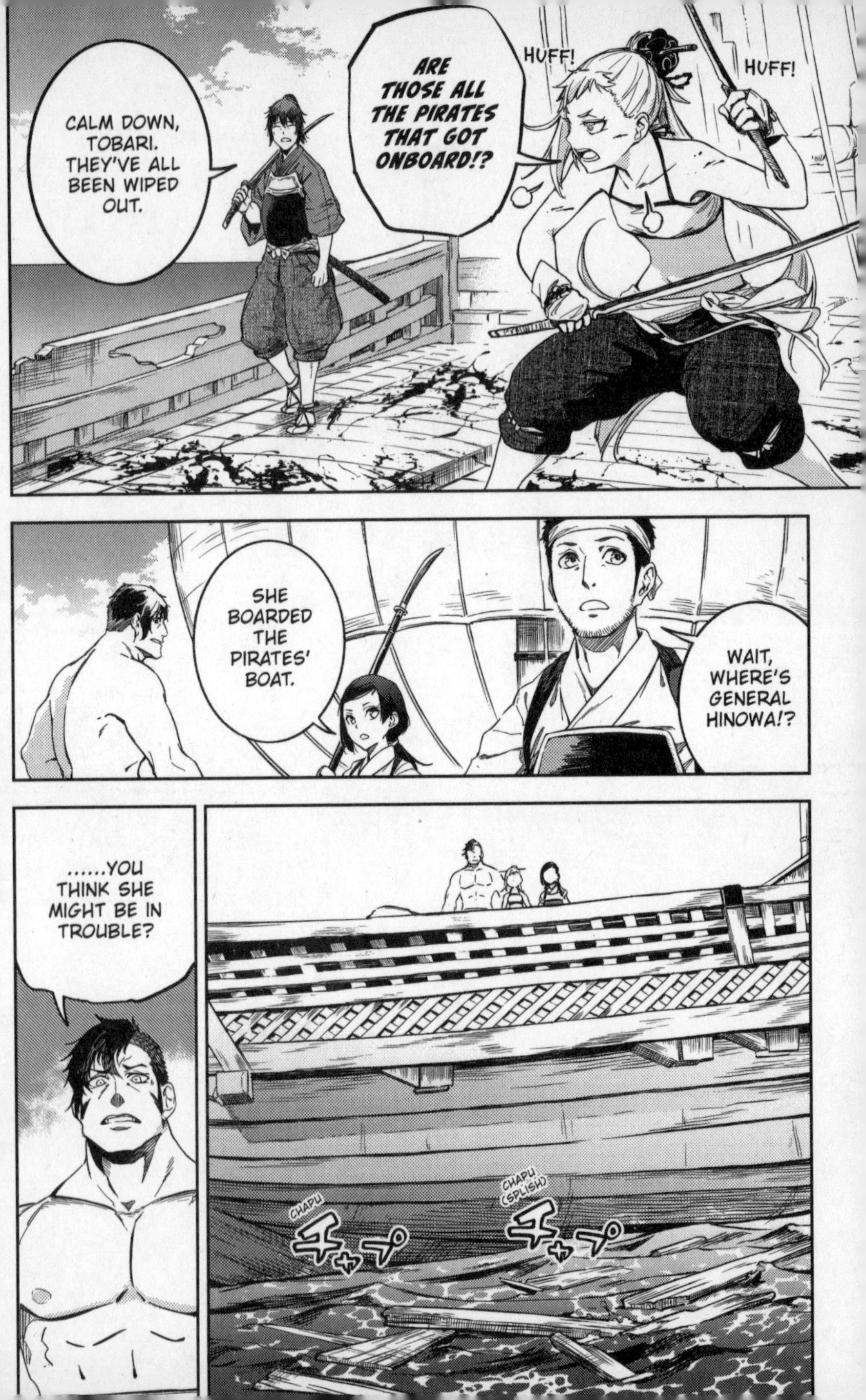
HUFF!
HUFF!
ARE THOSE ALL THE PIRATES THAT GOT ONBOARD!?
CALM DOWN, TOBARI. THEY'VE ALL BEEN WIPED OUT.
WAIT, WHERE'S GENERAL HINOWA!?
SHE BOARDED THE PIRATES' BOAT.
CHAPU (SPLISH)
チャプ
CHAPU
チャプ
......YOU THINK SHE MIGHT BE IN TROUBLE?

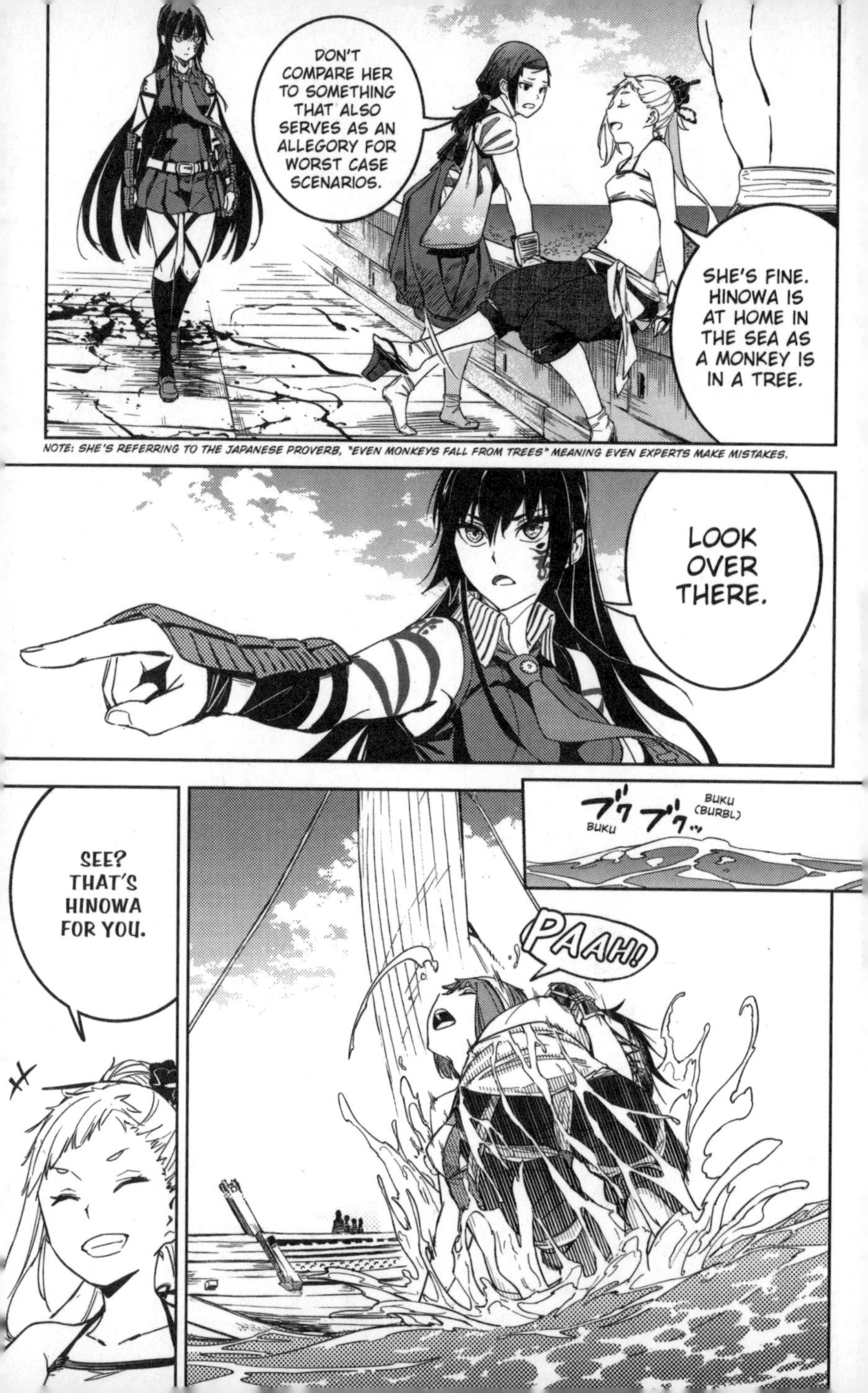
SHE'S FINE. HINOWA IS AT HOME IN THE SEA AS A MONKEY IS IN A TREE.
DON'T COMPARE HER TO SOMETHING THAT ALSO SERVES AS AN ALLEGORY FOR WORST CASE SCENARIOS.
NOTE: SHE'S REFERRING TO THE JAPANESE PROVERB, "EVEN MONKEYS FALL FROM TREES" MEANING EVEN EXPERTS MAKE MISTAKES.
LOOK OVER THERE.
ブク BUKU ブクッ BUKU (BURBL)
PAAH!
SEE? THAT'S HINOWA FOR YOU.

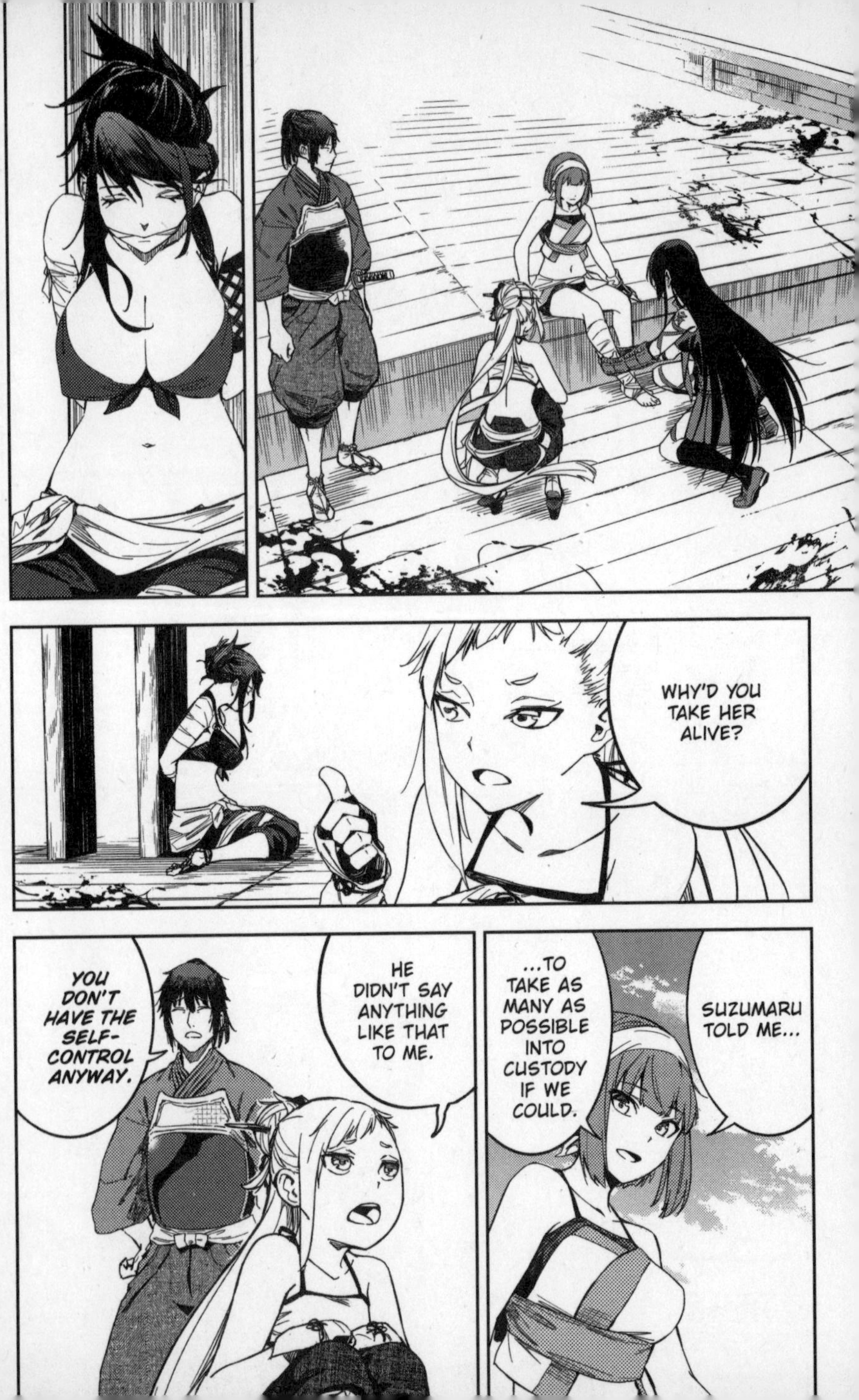
WHY'D YOU TAKE HER ALIVE?
SUZUMARU TOLD ME...
...TO TAKE AS MANY AS POSSIBLE INTO CUSTODY IF WE COULD.
HE DIDN'T SAY ANYTHING LIKE THAT TO ME.
YOU DON'T HAVE THE SELF-CONTROL ANYWAY.

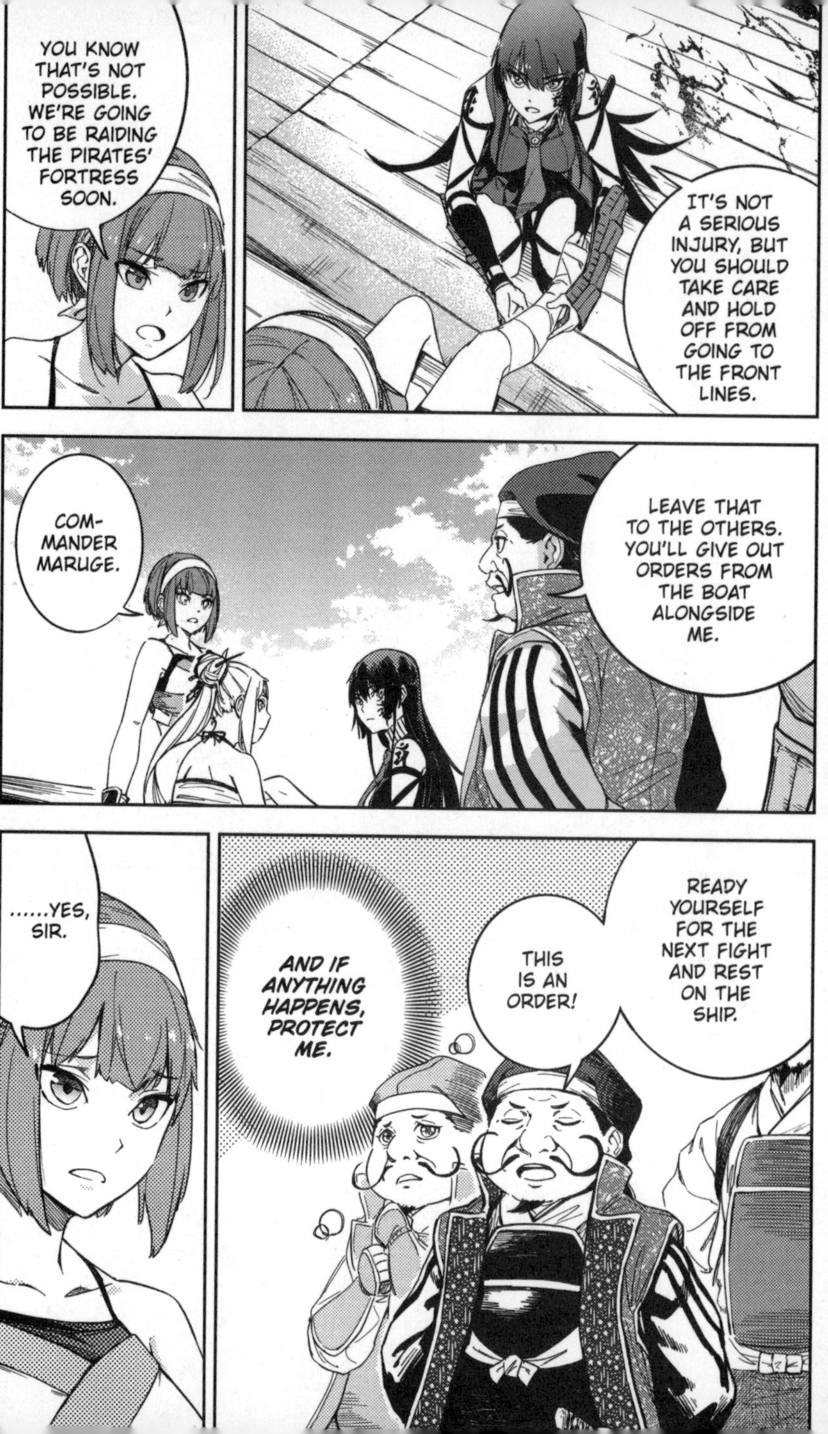

IT'S NOT A SERIOUS INJURY, BUT YOU SHOULD TAKE CARE AND HOLD OFF FROM GOING TO THE FRONT LINES.
YOU KNOW THAT'S NOT POSSIBLE. WE'RE GOING TO BE RAIDING THE PIRATES' FORTRESS SOON.
LEAVE THAT TO THE OTHERS. YOU'LL GIVE OUT ORDERS FROM THE BOAT ALONGSIDE ME.
COM-MANDER MARUGE.
READY YOURSELF FOR THE NEXT FIGHT AND REST ON THE SHIP.
THIS IS AN ORDER!
AND IF ANYTHING HAPPENS, PROTECT ME.
......YES, SIR.

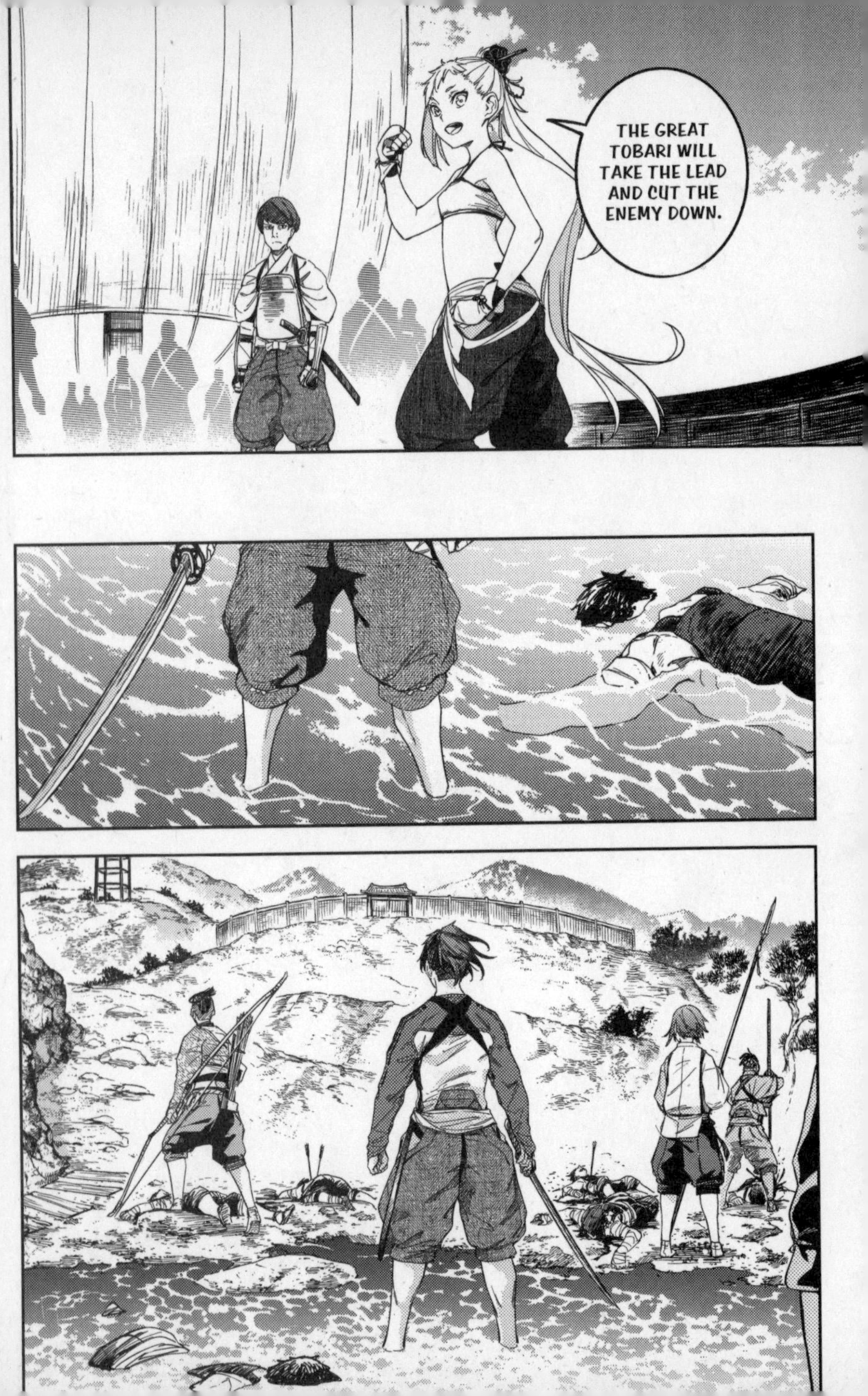
THE GREAT TOBARI WILL TAKE THE LEAD AND CUT THE ENEMY DOWN.

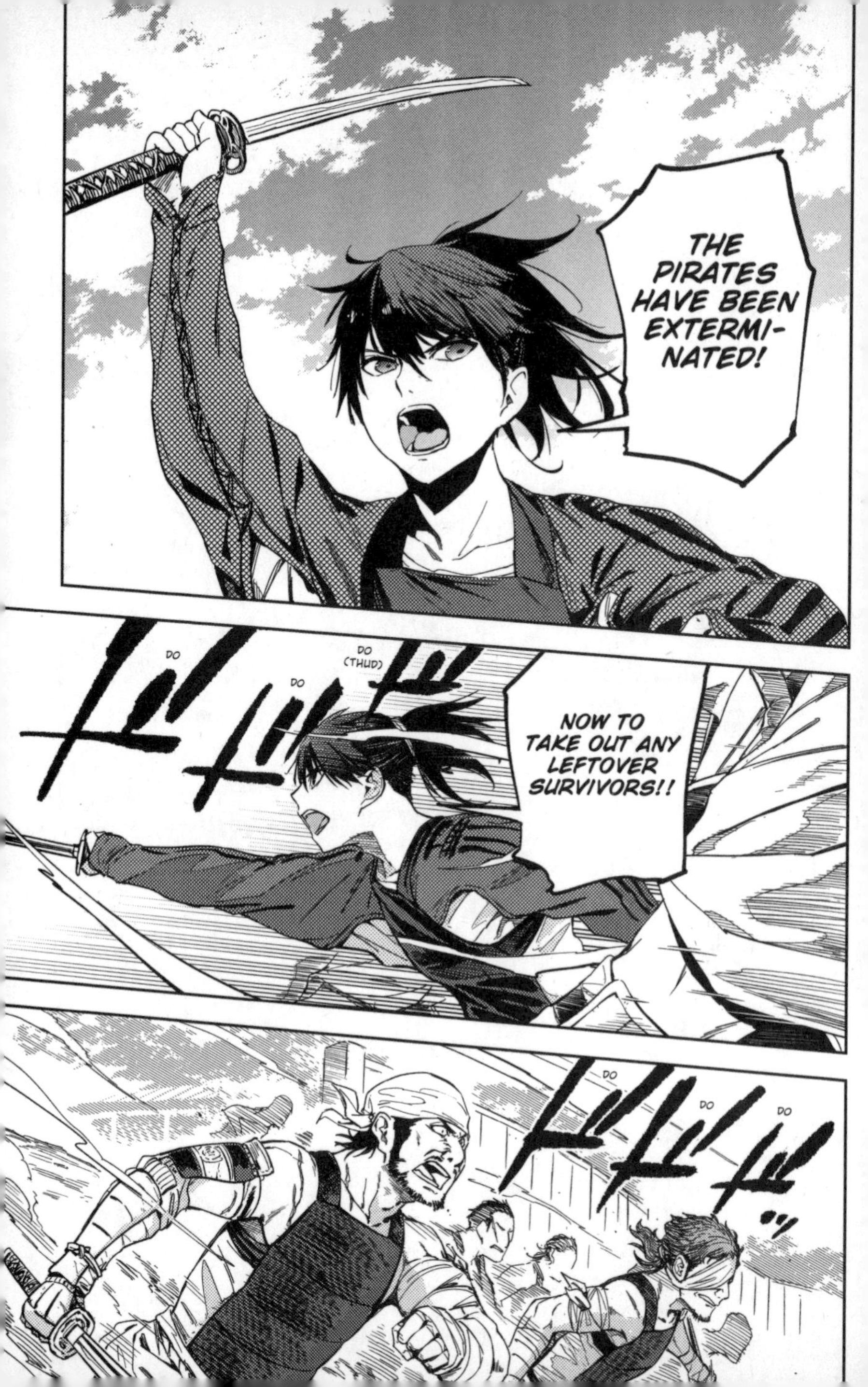
THE PIRATES HAVE BEEN EXTERMI-NATED!
DO (THUD)
DO
DO
NOW TO TAKE OUT ANY LEFTOVER SURVIVORS!!
DO
DO
DO

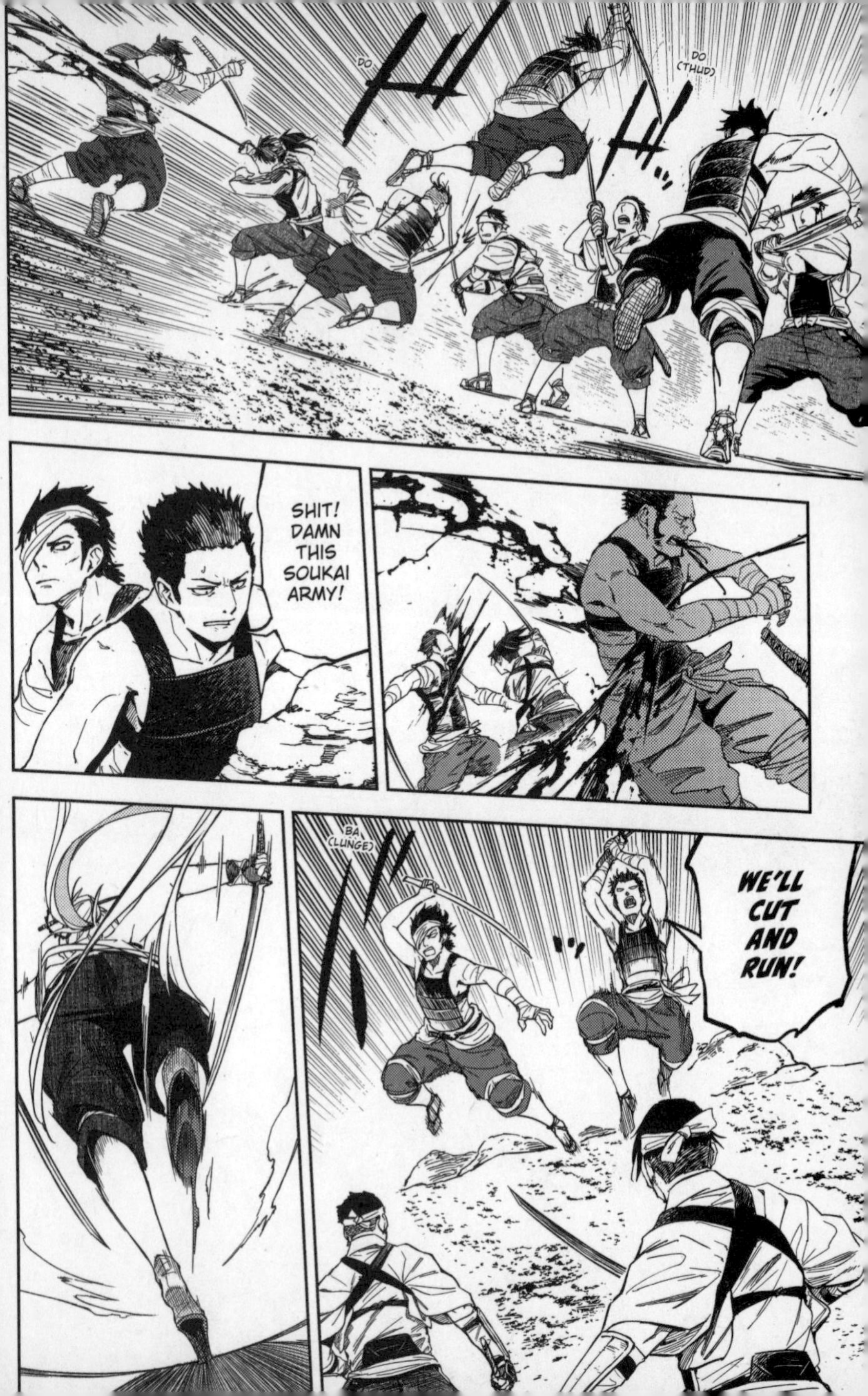
DO (THUD)
DO
SHIT! DAMN THIS SOUKAI ARMY!
WE'LL CUT AND RUN!
BA (LUNGE)

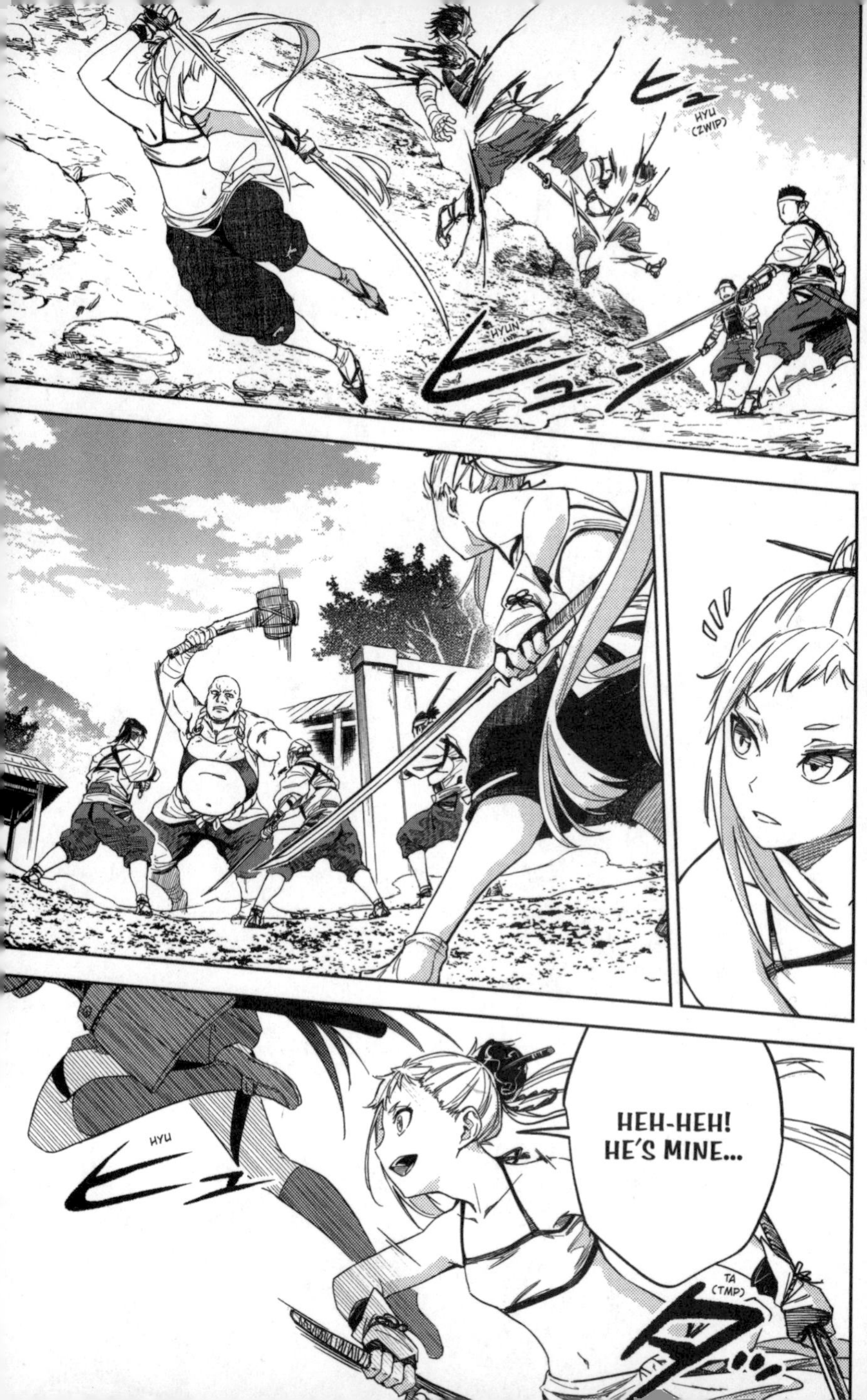
HYU (ZWIP)
HYUN
HEH-HEH! HE'S MINE...
HYU
TA (TMP)

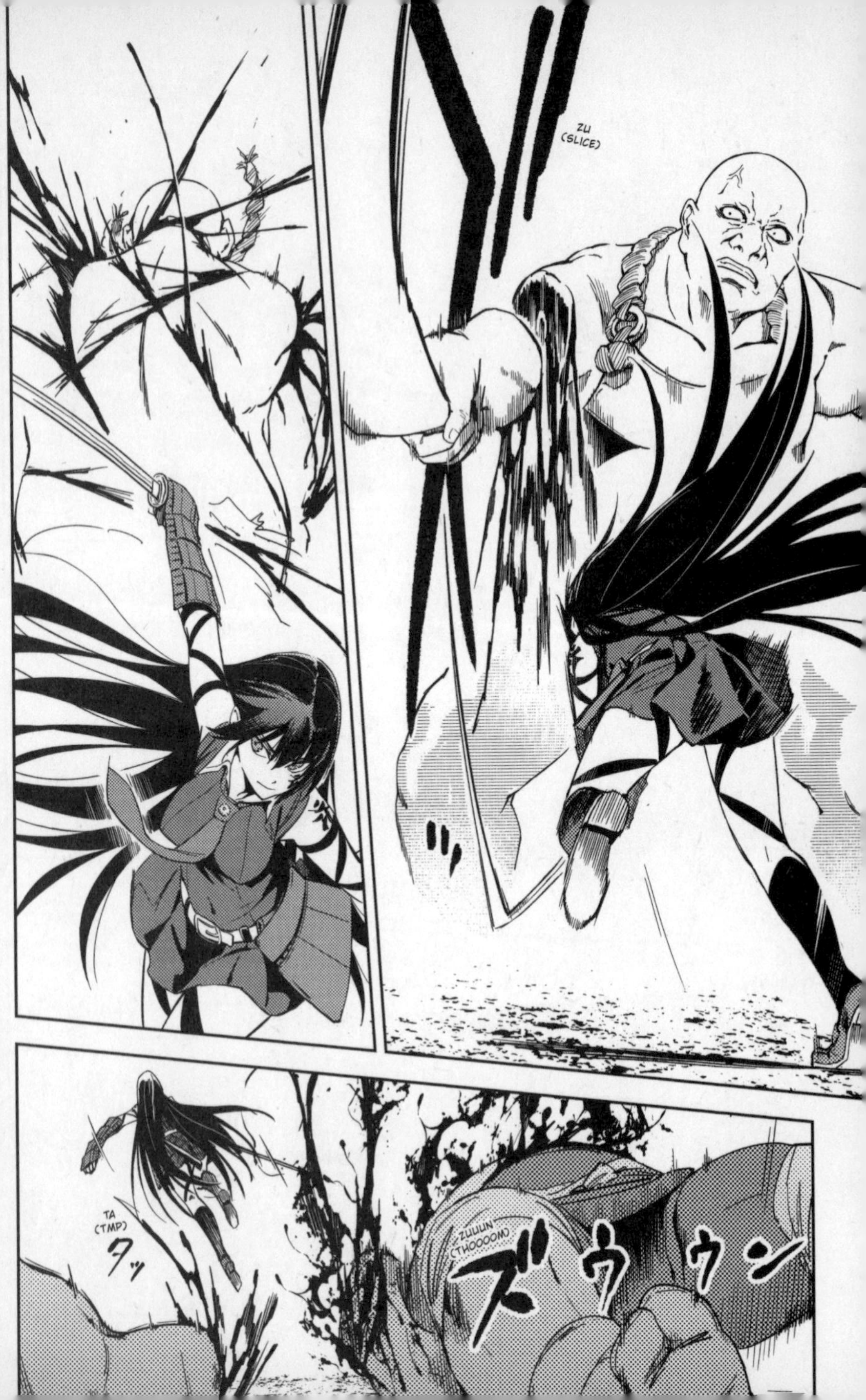
ZU
(SLICE)
ZUUUN
(THOOOOM)
ズウウン
TA
(TMP)
タッ

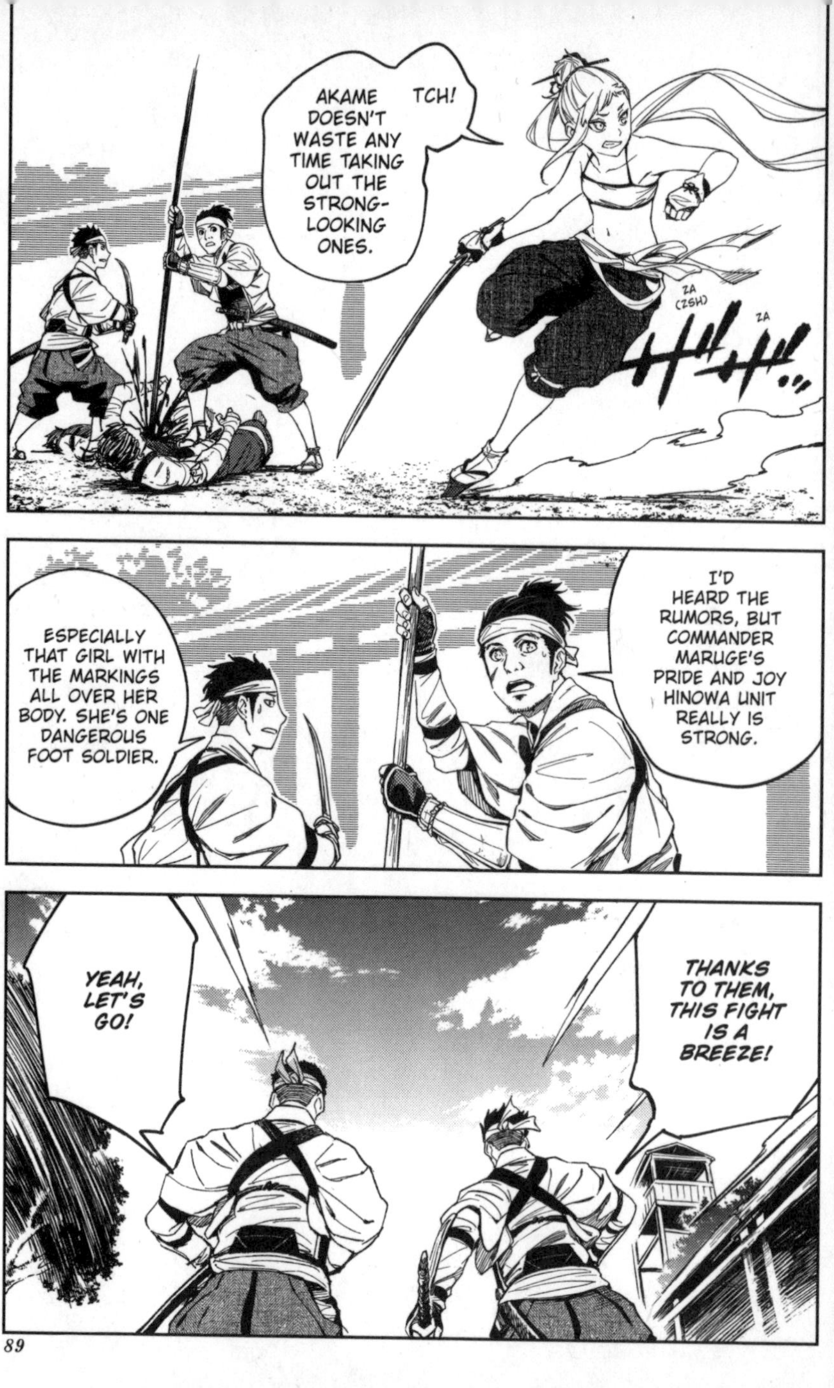
TCH!
AKAME DOESN'T WASTE ANY TIME TAKING OUT THE STRONG-LOOKING ONES.
ZA (ZSH)
ZA
I'D HEARD THE RUMORS, BUT COMMANDER MARUGE'S PRIDE AND JOY HINOWA UNIT REALLY IS STRONG.
ESPECIALLY THAT GIRL WITH THE MARKINGS ALL OVER HER BODY. SHE'S ONE DANGEROUS FOOT SOLDIER.
THANKS TO THEM, THIS FIGHT IS A BREEZE!
YEAH, LET'S GO!

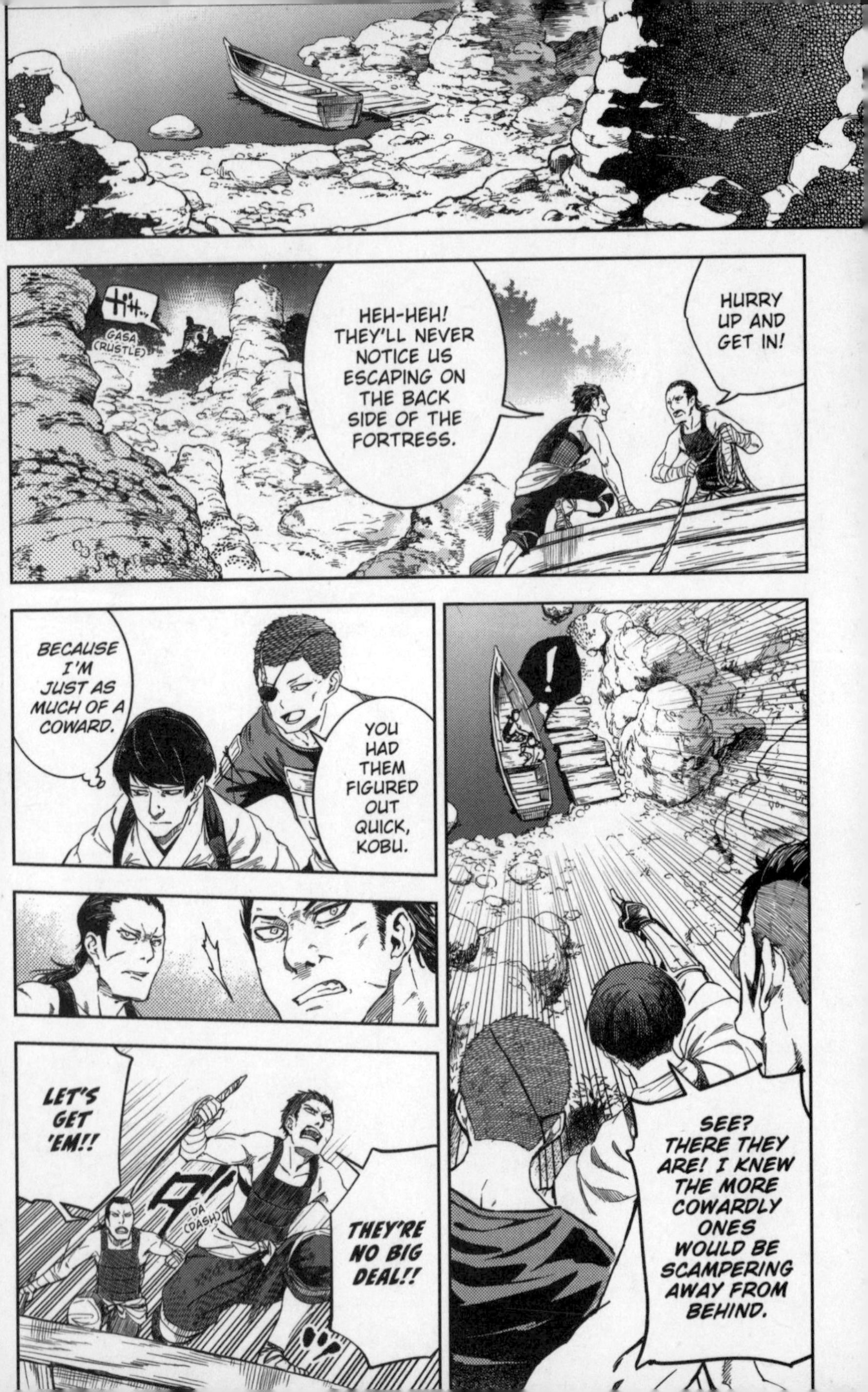
HURRY UP AND GET IN!
HEH-HEH! THEY'LL NEVER NOTICE US ESCAPING ON THE BACK SIDE OF THE FORTRESS.
GASA (RUSTLE)
SEE? THERE THEY ARE! I KNEW THE MORE COWARDLY ONES WOULD BE SCAMPERING AWAY FROM BEHIND.
YOU HAD THEM FIGURED OUT QUICK, KOBU.
BECAUSE I'M JUST AS MUCH OF A COWARD.
THEY'RE NO BIG DEAL!!
LET'S GET 'EM!!
DA (DASH)

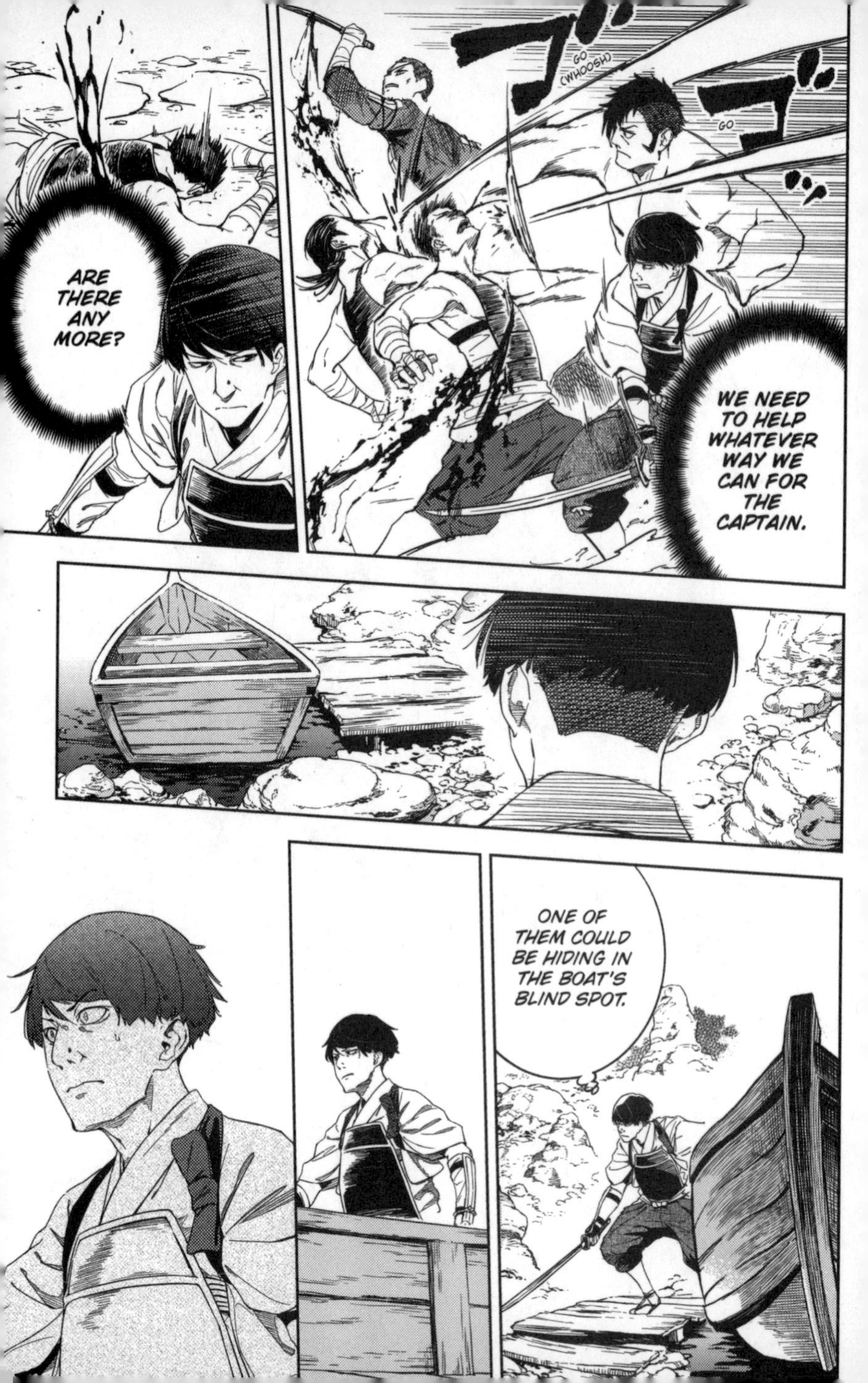

GO (WHOOSH)
GO
WE NEED TO HELP WHATEVER WAY WE CAN FOR THE CAPTAIN.
ARE THERE ANY MORE?
ONE OF THEM COULD BE HIDING IN THE BOAT'S BLIND SPOT.

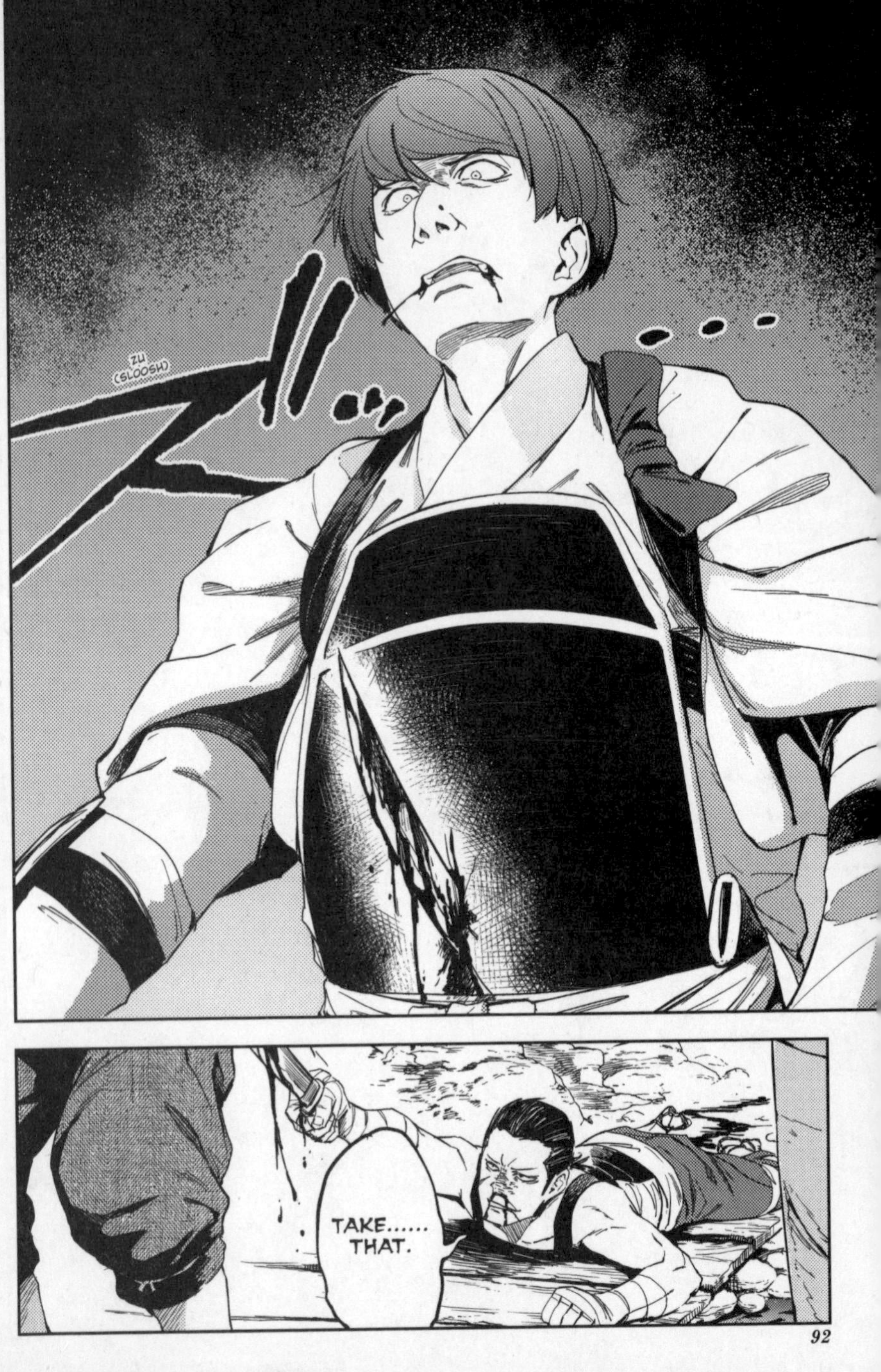
ZU (SLOOSH)
......
TAKE...... THAT.

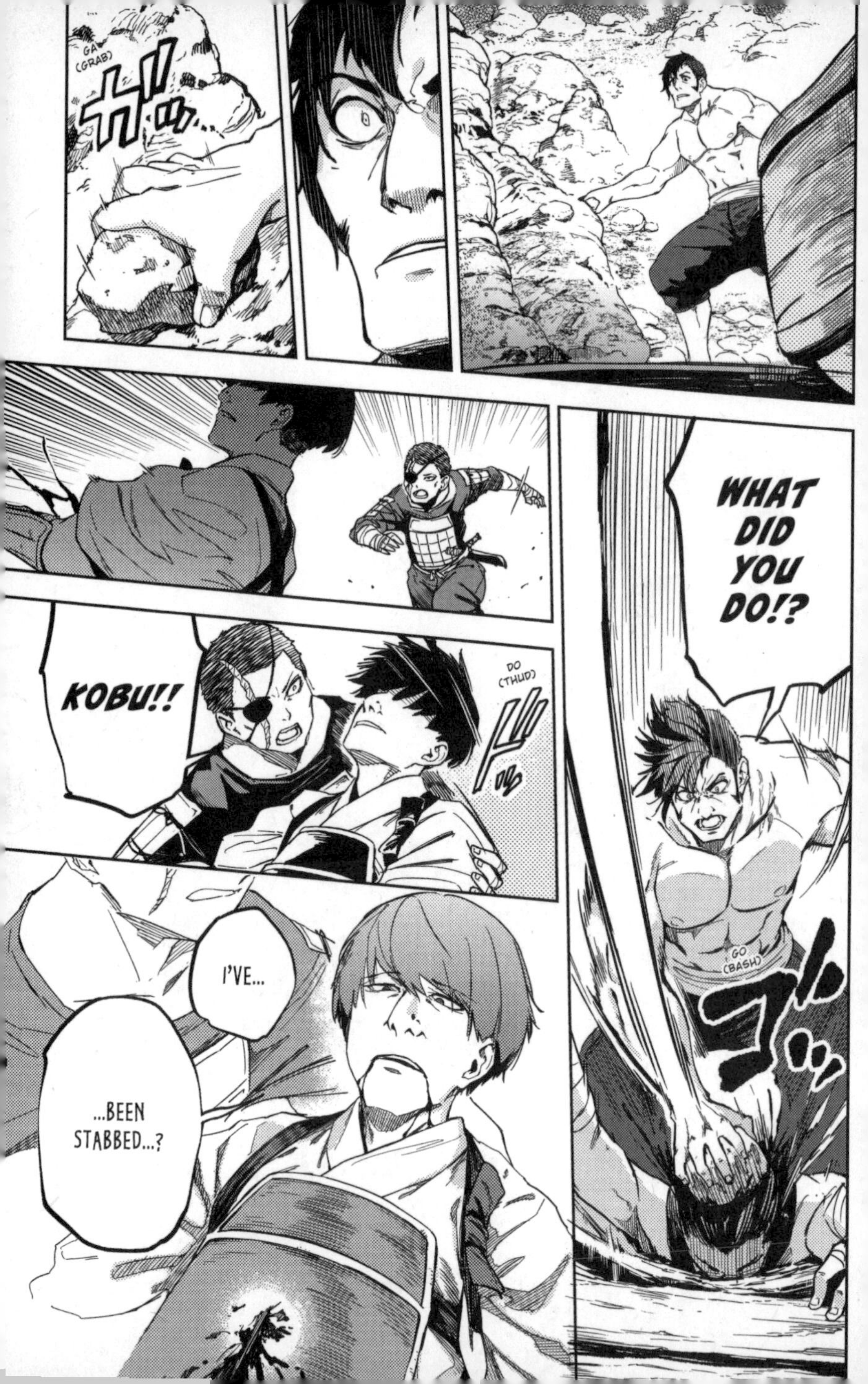
GA (GRAB)
WHAT DID YOU DO!?
GO (BASH)
KOBU!!
DO (THUD)
I'VE...
...BEEN STABBED...?

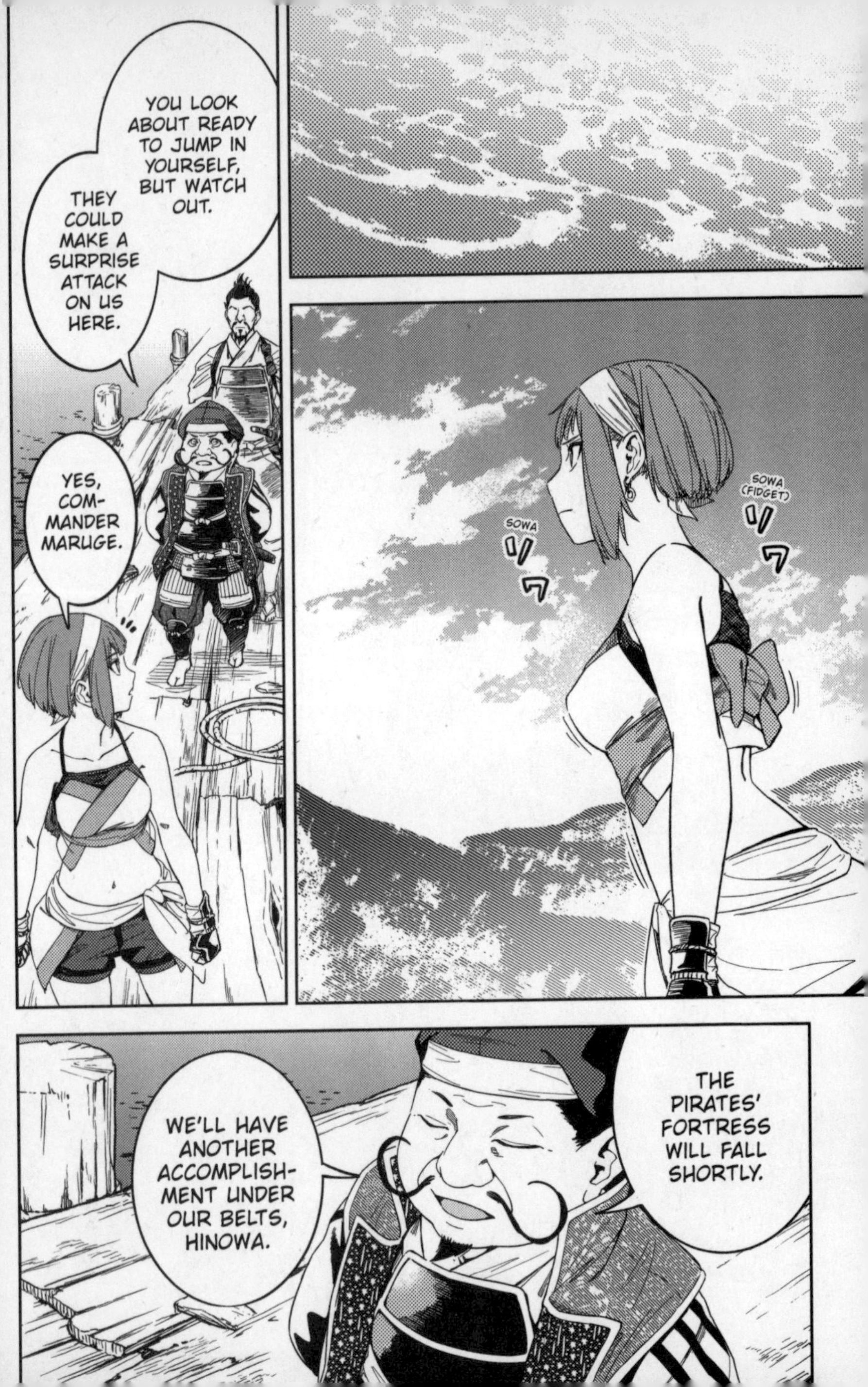
SOWA (FIDGET)
SOWA
YOU LOOK ABOUT READY TO JUMP IN YOURSELF, BUT WATCH OUT.
THEY COULD MAKE A SURPRISE ATTACK ON US HERE.
YES, COMMANDER MARUGE.
THE PIRATES' FORTRESS WILL FALL SHORTLY.
WE'LL HAVE ANOTHER ACCOMPLISHMENT UNDER OUR BELTS, HINOWA.

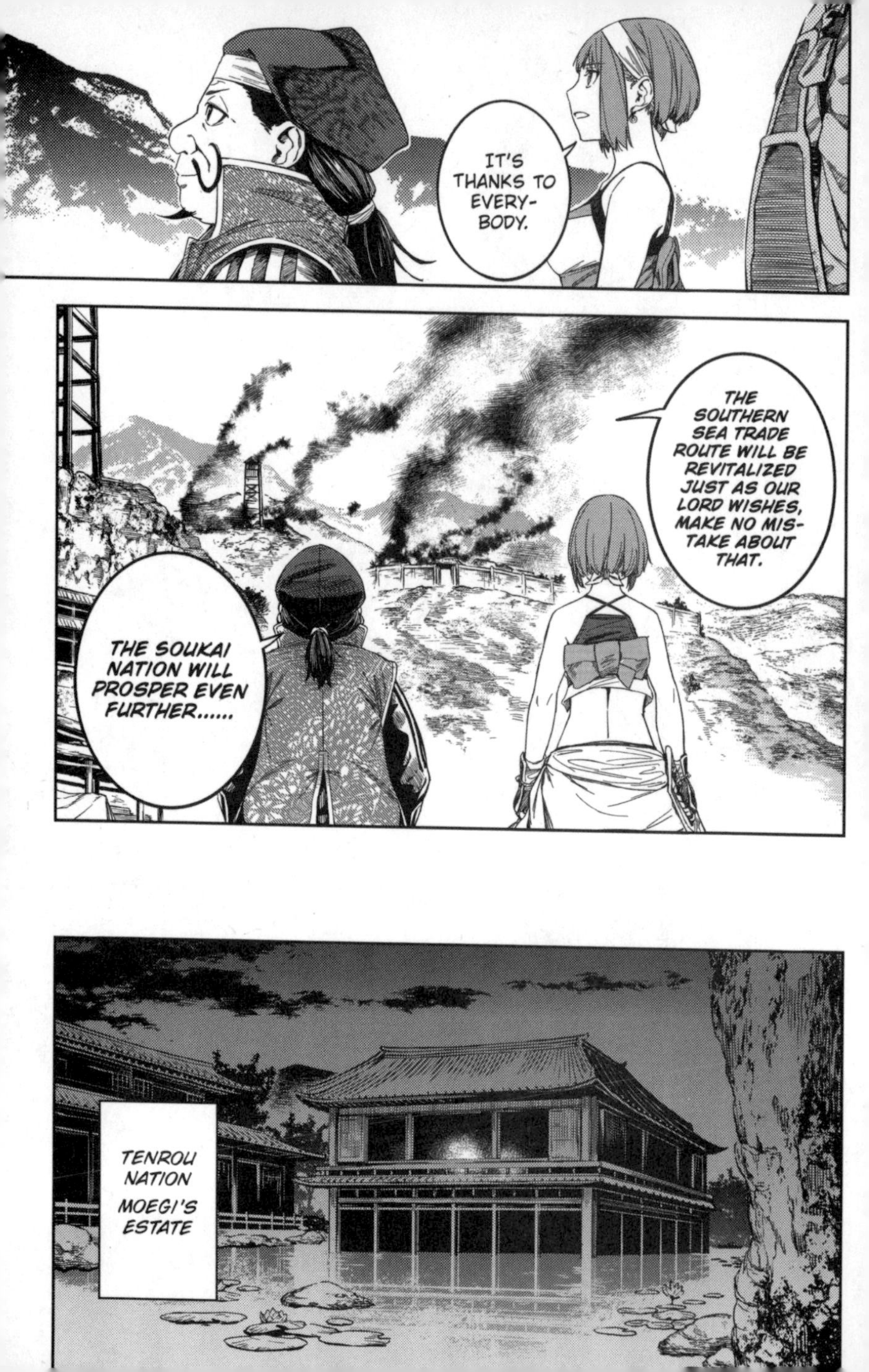
IT'S THANKS TO EVERY-BODY.
THE SOUTHERN SEA TRADE ROUTE WILL BE REVITALIZED JUST AS OUR LORD WISHES, MAKE NO MIS-TAKE ABOUT THAT.
THE SOUKAI NATION WILL PROSPER EVEN FURTHER......
TENROU NATION
MOEGI'S ESTATE

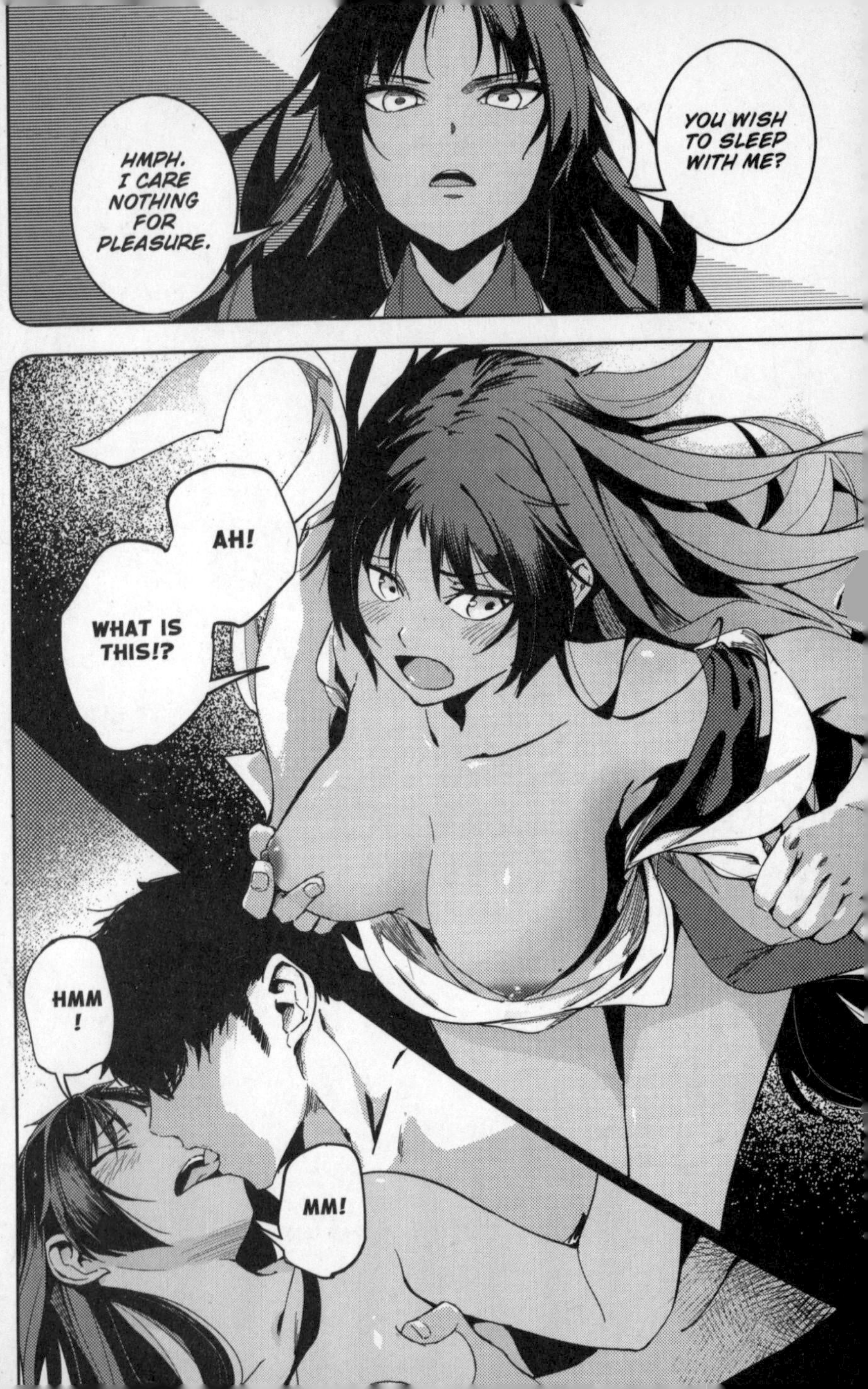
YOU WISH TO SLEEP WITH ME?
HMPH. I CARE NOTHING FOR PLEASURE.
AH!
WHAT IS THIS!?
HMM !
MM!

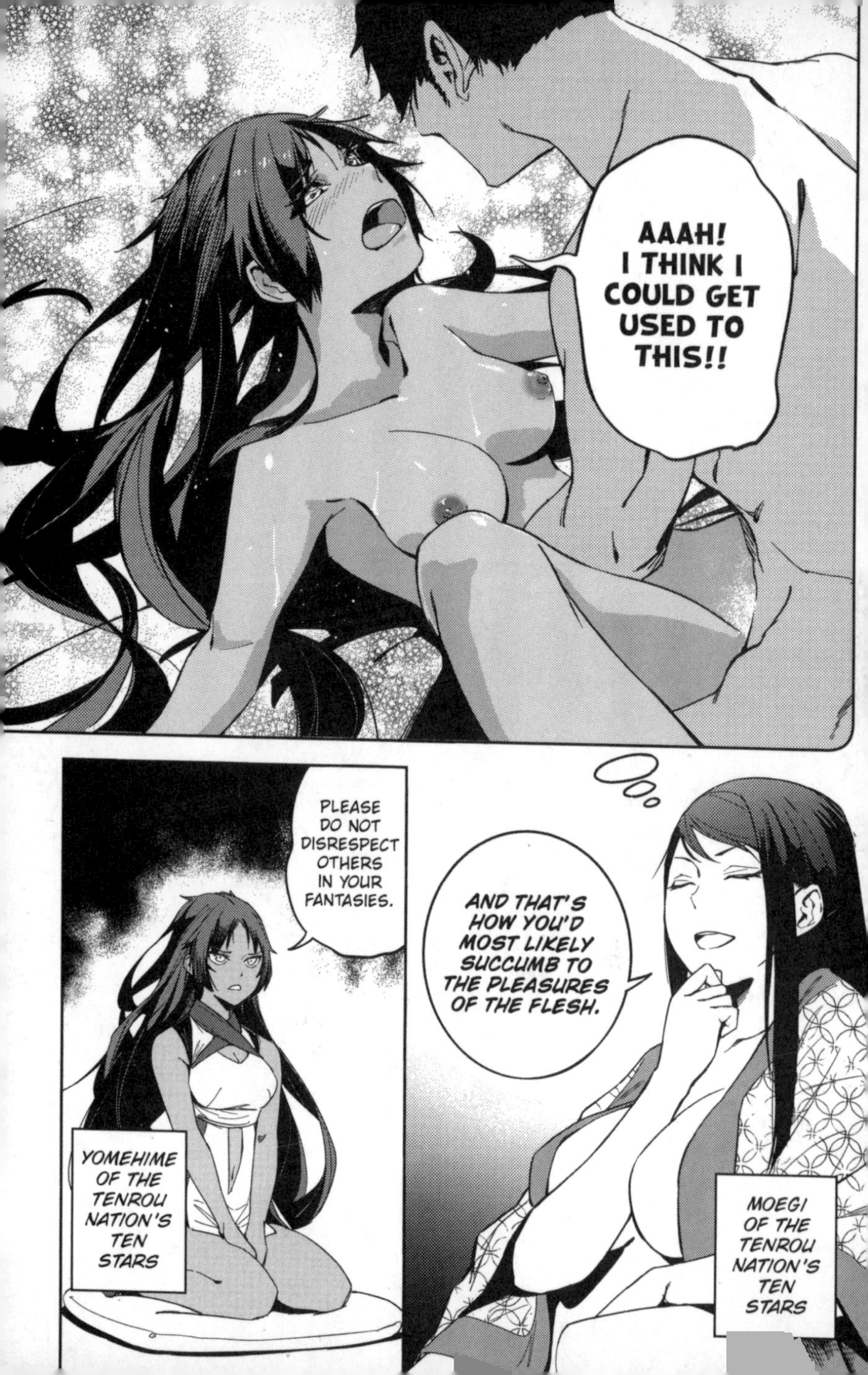
AAAH! I THINK I COULD GET USED TO THIS!!
AND THAT'S HOW YOU'D MOST LIKELY SUCCUMB TO THE PLEASURES OF THE FLESH.
MOEGI OF THE TENROU NATION'S TEN STARS
PLEASE DO NOT DISRESPECT OTHERS IN YOUR FANTASIES.
YOMEHIME OF THE TENROU NATION'S TEN STARS

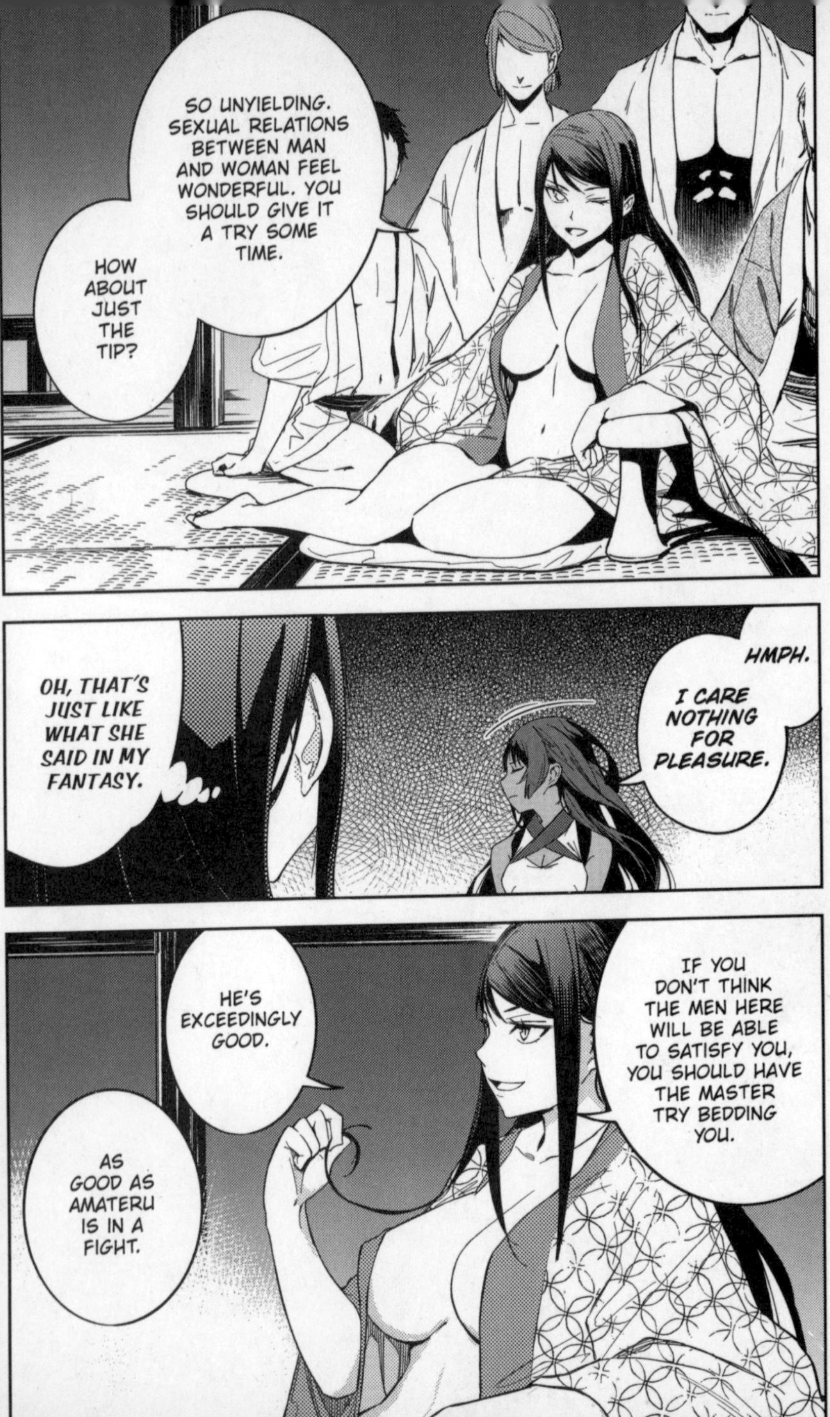
SO UNYIELDING. SEXUAL RELATIONS BETWEEN MAN AND WOMAN FEEL WONDERFUL. YOU SHOULD GIVE IT A TRY SOME TIME.
HOW ABOUT JUST THE TIP?
HMPH.
I CARE NOTHING FOR PLEASURE.
OH, THAT'S JUST LIKE WHAT SHE SAID IN MY FANTASY.
IF YOU DON'T THINK THE MEN HERE WILL BE ABLE TO SATISFY YOU, YOU SHOULD HAVE THE MASTER TRY BEDDING YOU.
HE'S EXCEEDINGLY GOOD.
AS GOOD AS AMATERU IS IN A FIGHT.

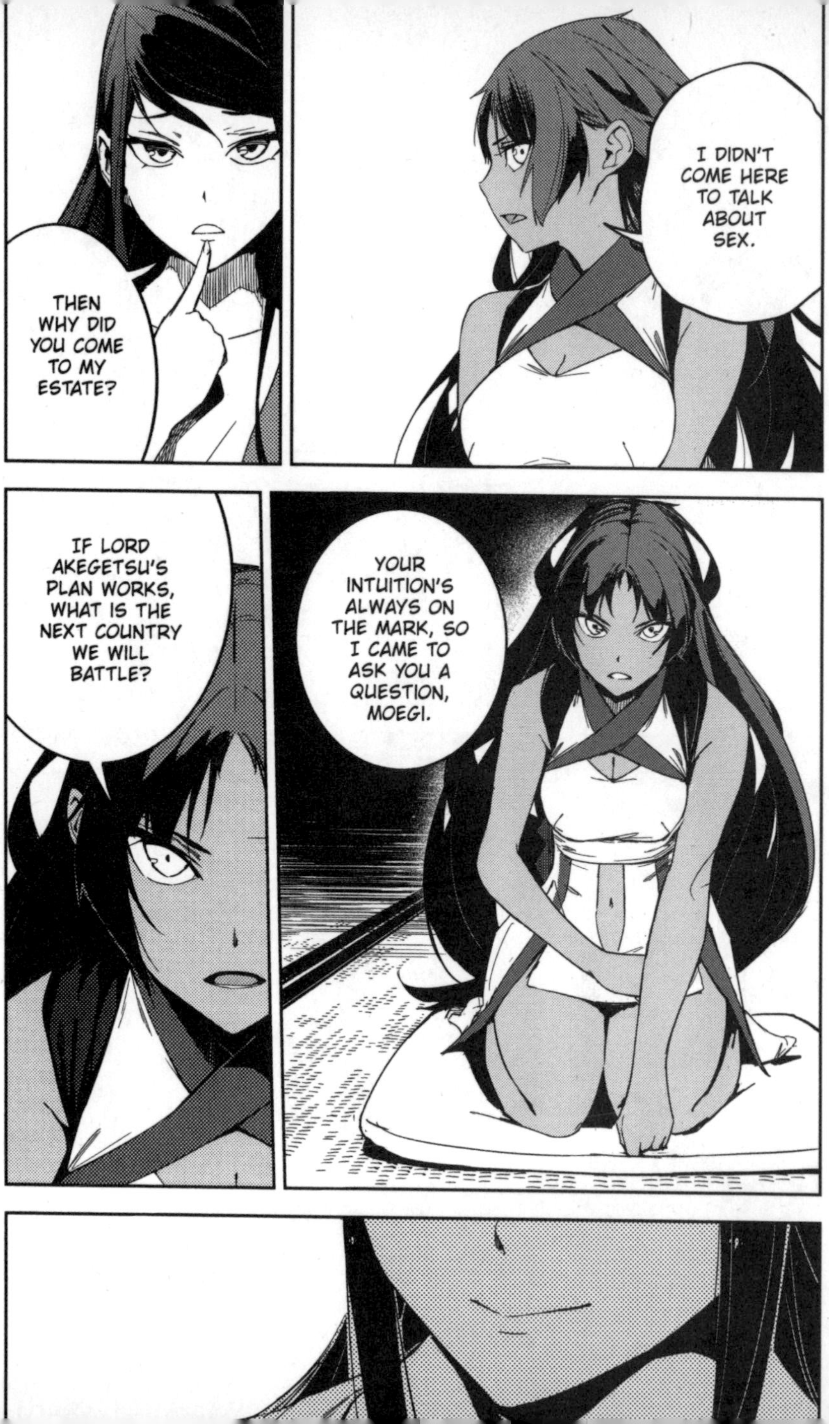
I DIDN'T COME HERE TO TALK ABOUT SEX.
THEN WHY DID YOU COME TO MY ESTATE?
YOUR INTUITION'S ALWAYS ON THE MARK, SO I CAME TO ASK YOU A QUESTION, MOEGI.
IF LORD AKEGETSU'S PLAN WORKS, WHAT IS THE NEXT COUNTRY WE WILL BATTLE?

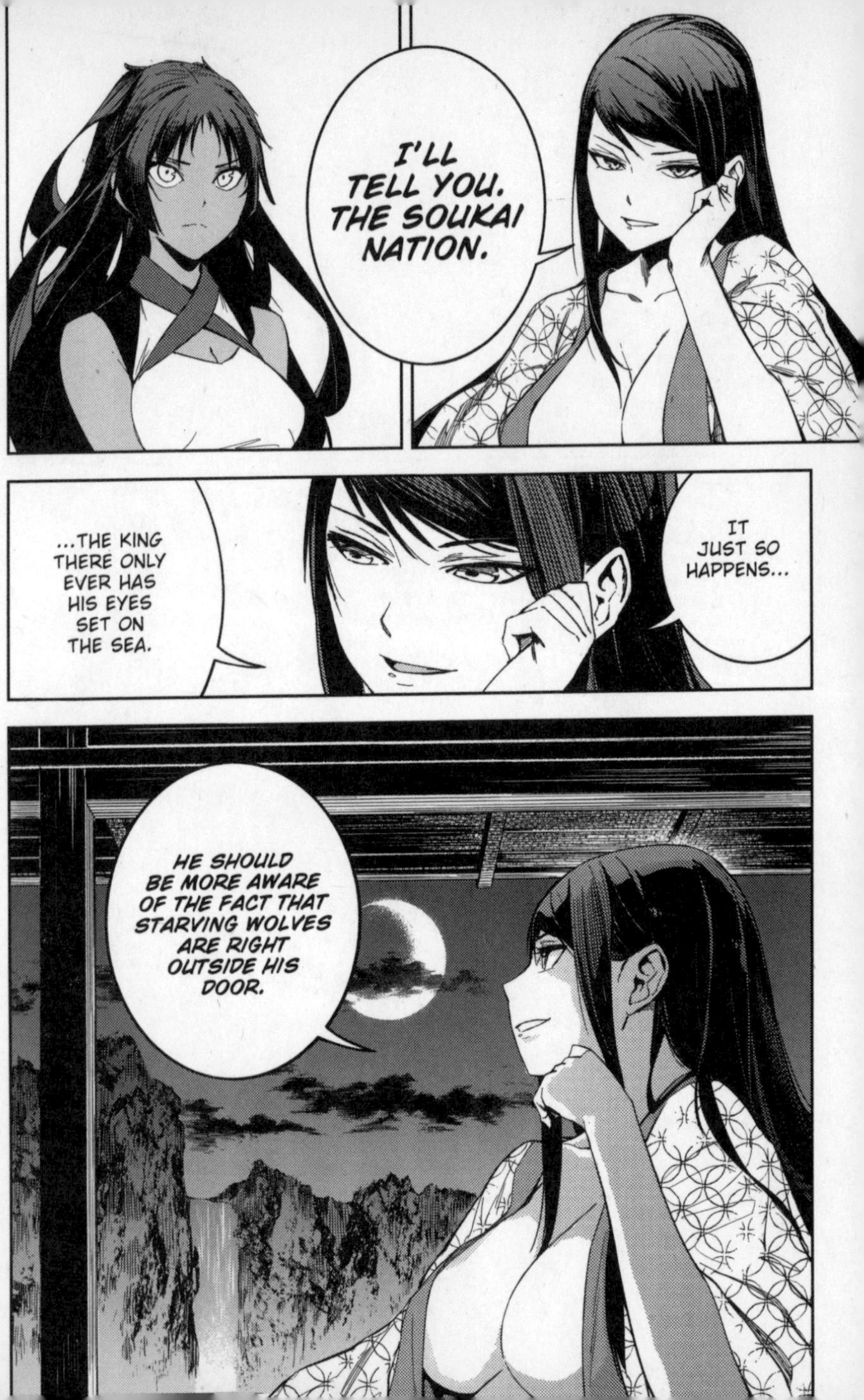
I'LL TELL YOU. THE SOUKAI NATION.
IT JUST SO HAPPENS...
...THE KING THERE ONLY EVER HAS HIS EYES SET ON THE SEA.
HE SHOULD BE MORE AWARE OF THE FACT THAT STARVING WOLVES ARE RIGHT OUTSIDE HIS DOOR.

Hjnowa ga CRUSH!

Hijowa ga CRUSH!

Design Drafts ③

MOEGI

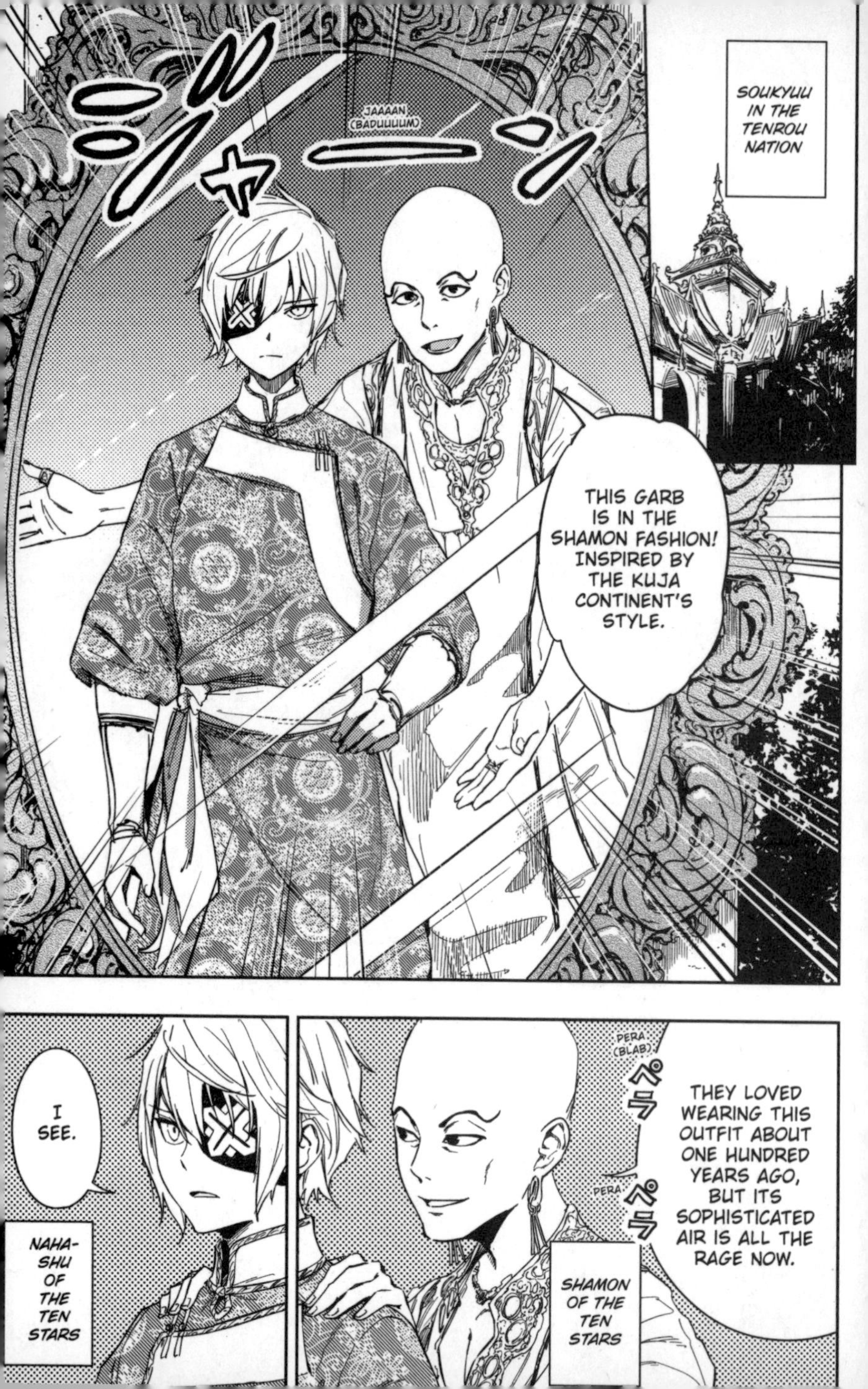
SOUKYUU IN THE TENROU NATION
JAAAAN (BADUUUUM)
THIS GARB IS IN THE SHAMON FASHION! INSPIRED BY THE KUJA CONTINENT'S STYLE.
PERA (BLAB)
PERA
THEY LOVED WEARING THIS OUTFIT ABOUT ONE HUNDRED YEARS AGO, BUT ITS SOPHISTICATED AIR IS ALL THE RAGE NOW.
SHAMON OF THE TEN STARS
I SEE.
NAHA-SHU OF THE TEN STARS

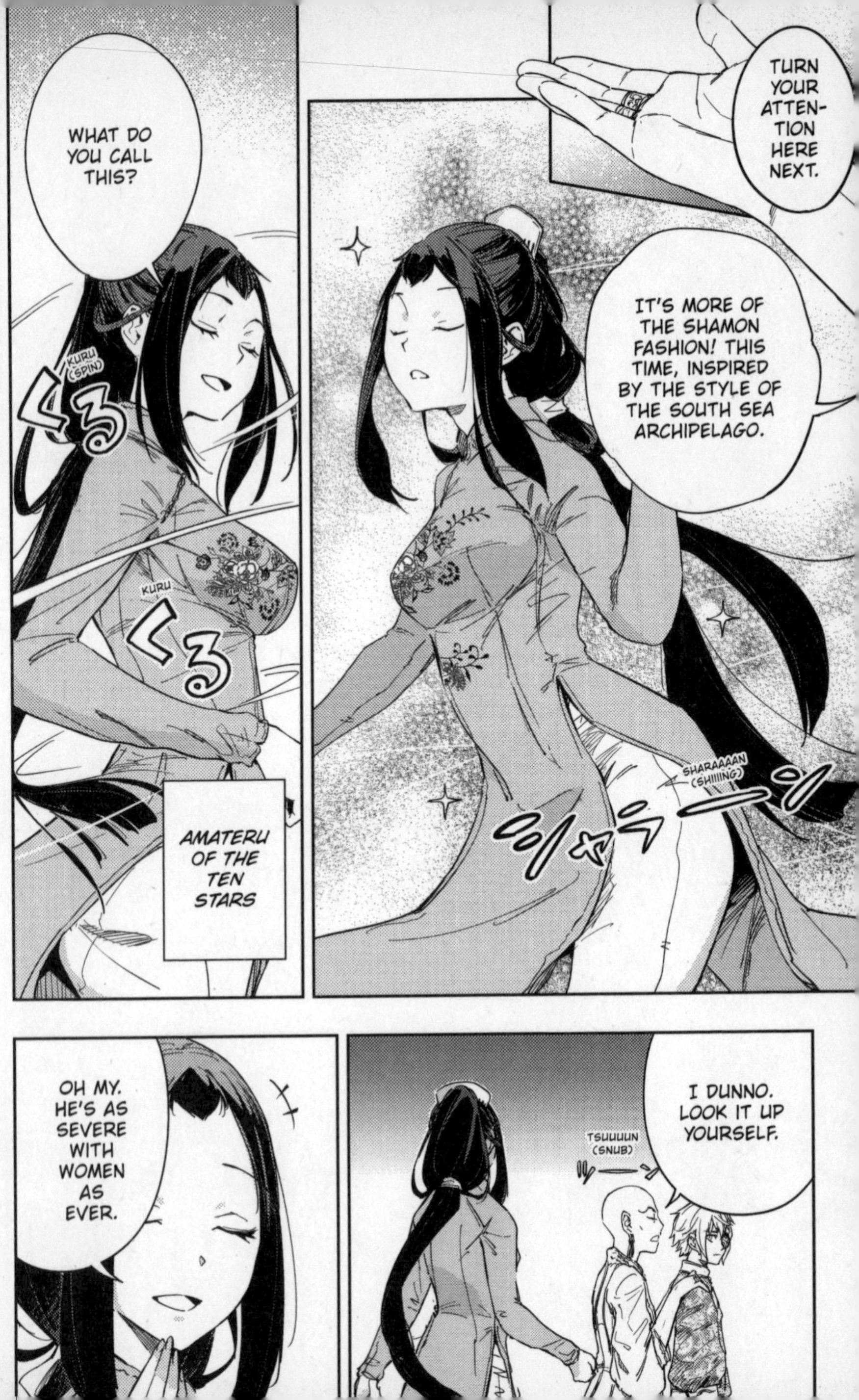
TURN YOUR ATTEN-TION HERE NEXT.
IT'S MORE OF THE SHAMON FASHION! THIS TIME, INSPIRED BY THE STYLE OF THE SOUTH SEA ARCHIPELAGO.
SHARAAAAN (SHIIIING)
WHAT DO YOU CALL THIS?
KURU (SPIN)
くる
KURU
くる
AMATERU OF THE TEN STARS
I DUNNO. LOOK IT UP YOURSELF.
TSUUUUN (SNUB)
OH MY. HE'S AS SEVERE WITH WOMEN AS EVER.

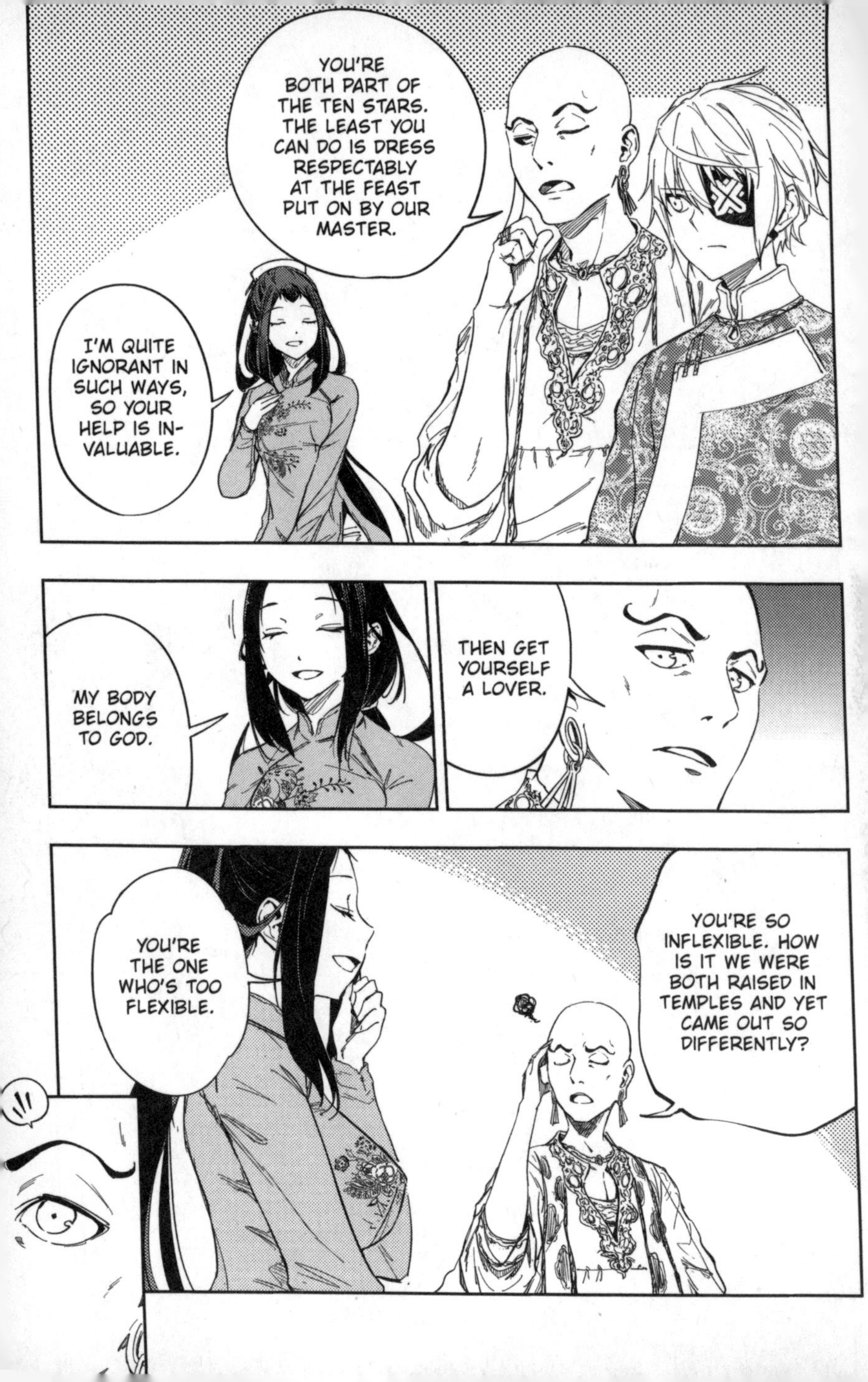
YOU'RE BOTH PART OF THE TEN STARS. THE LEAST YOU CAN DO IS DRESS RESPECTABLY AT THE FEAST PUT ON BY OUR MASTER.
I'M QUITE IGNORANT IN SUCH WAYS, SO YOUR HELP IS IN-VALUABLE.
THEN GET YOURSELF A LOVER.
MY BODY BELONGS TO GOD.
YOU'RE SO INFLEXIBLE. HOW IS IT WE WERE BOTH RAISED IN TEMPLES AND YET CAME OUT SO DIFFERENTLY?
YOU'RE THE ONE WHO'S TOO FLEXIBLE.

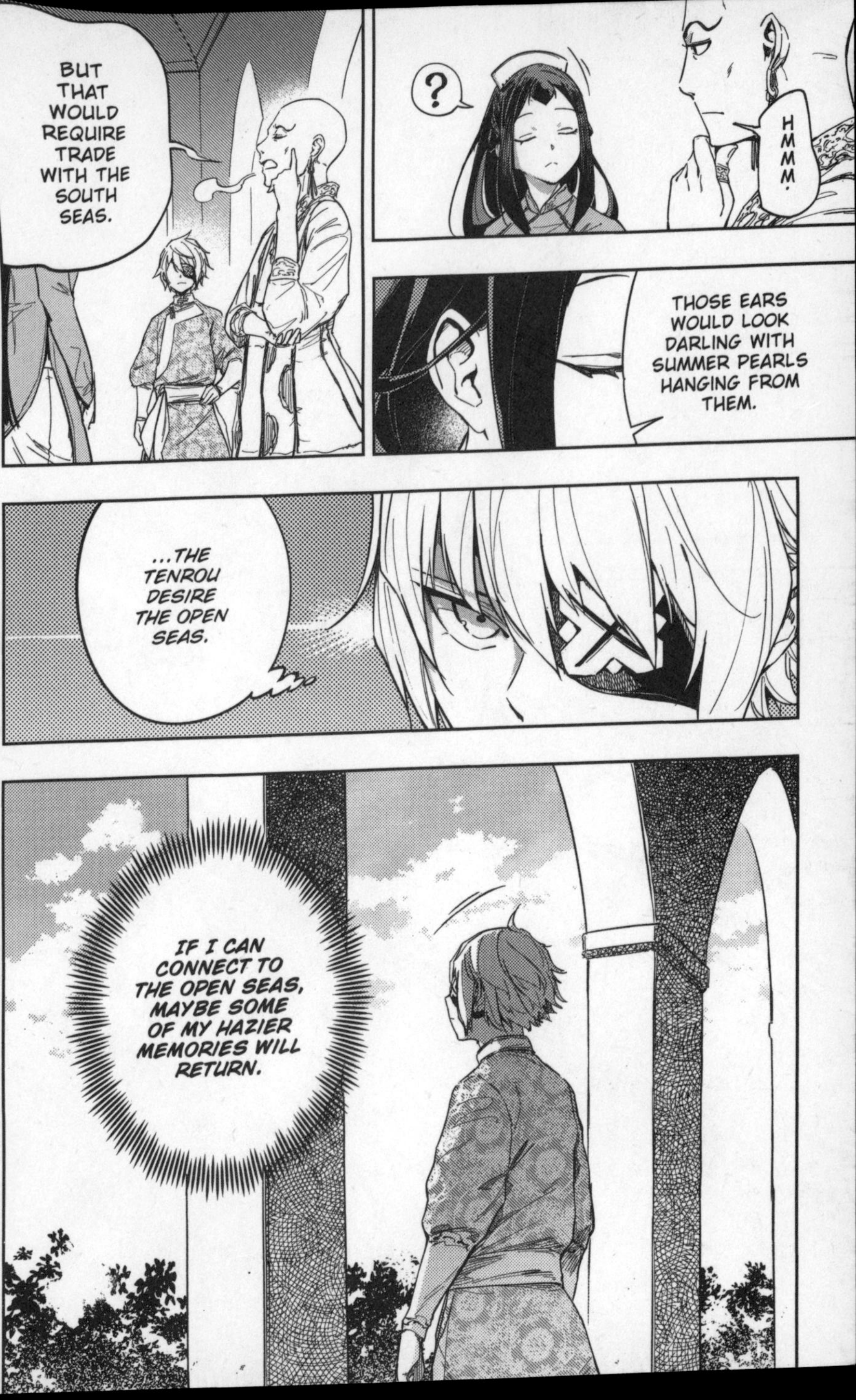
HMMM.
?
THOSE EARS WOULD LOOK DARLING WITH SUMMER PEARLS HANGING FROM THEM.
BUT THAT WOULD REQUIRE TRADE WITH THE SOUTH SEAS.
...THE TENROU DESIRE THE OPEN SEAS.
IF I CAN CONNECT TO THE OPEN SEAS, MAYBE SOME OF MY HAZIER MEMORIES WILL RETURN.

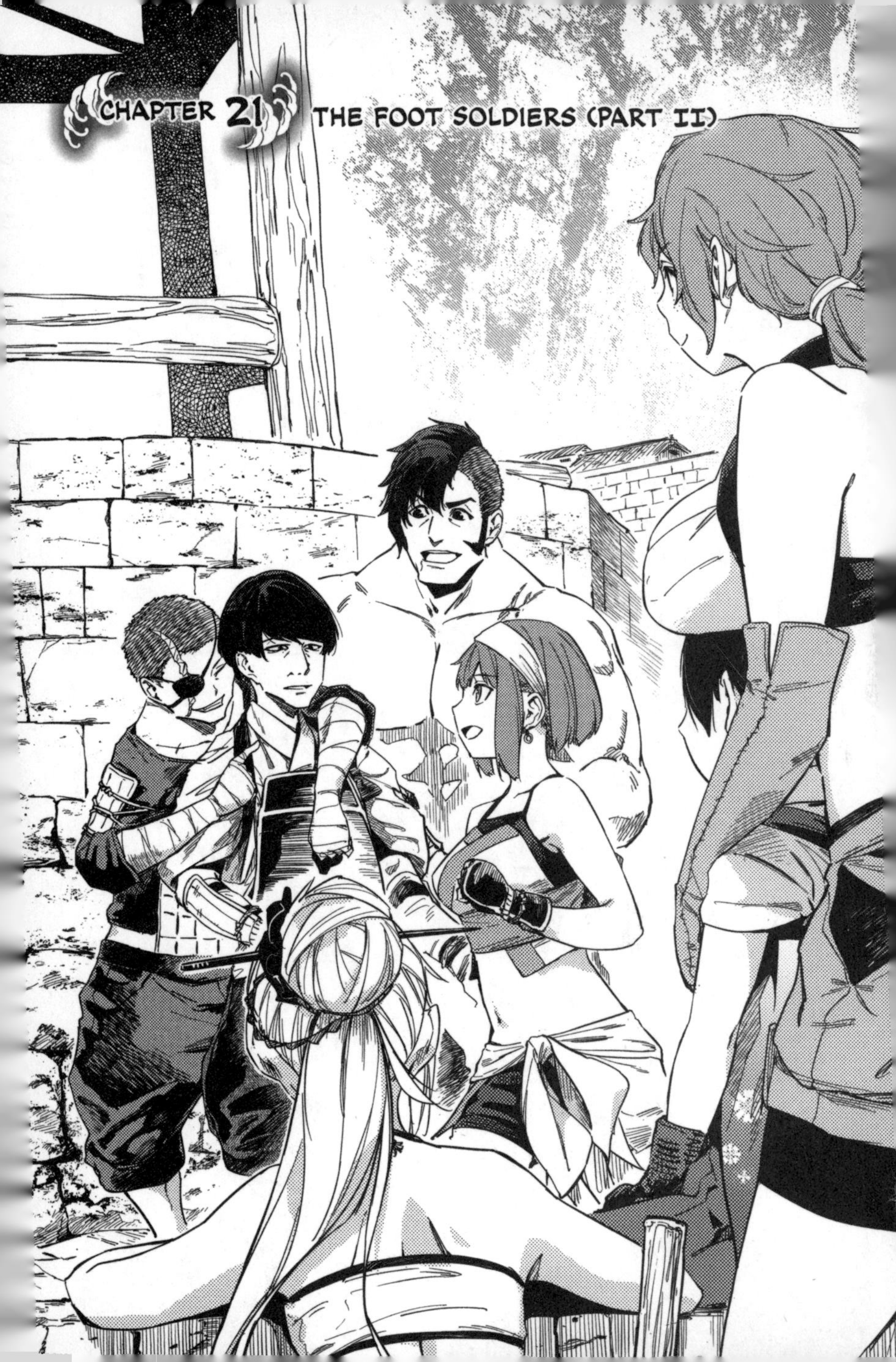
CHAPTER 21
THE FOOT SOLDIERS (PART II)

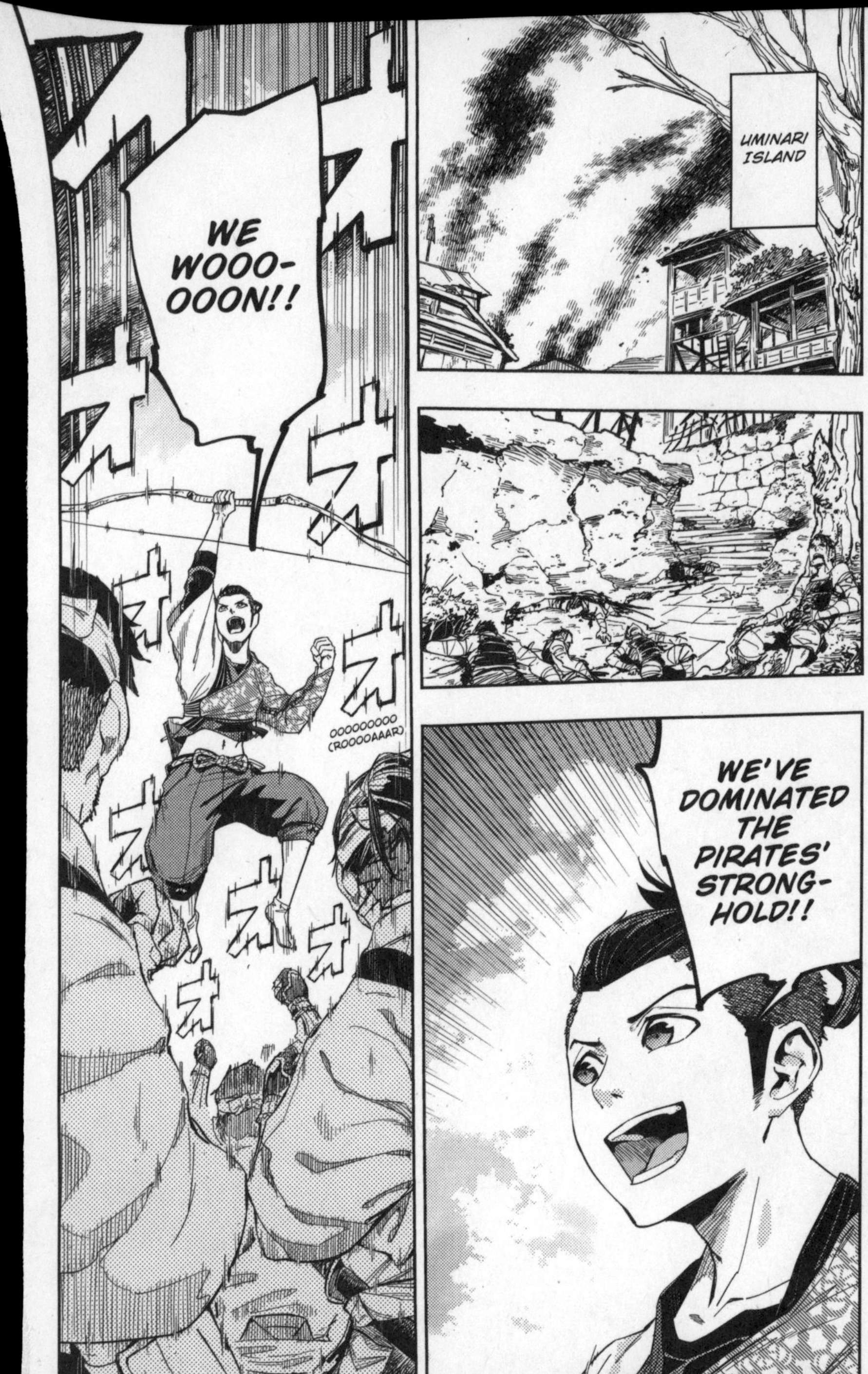
UMINARI ISLAND
WE'VE DOMINATED THE PIRATES' STRONG-HOLD!!
WE WOOOO-OOON!!
OOOOOOOOO (ROOOOAAAR)

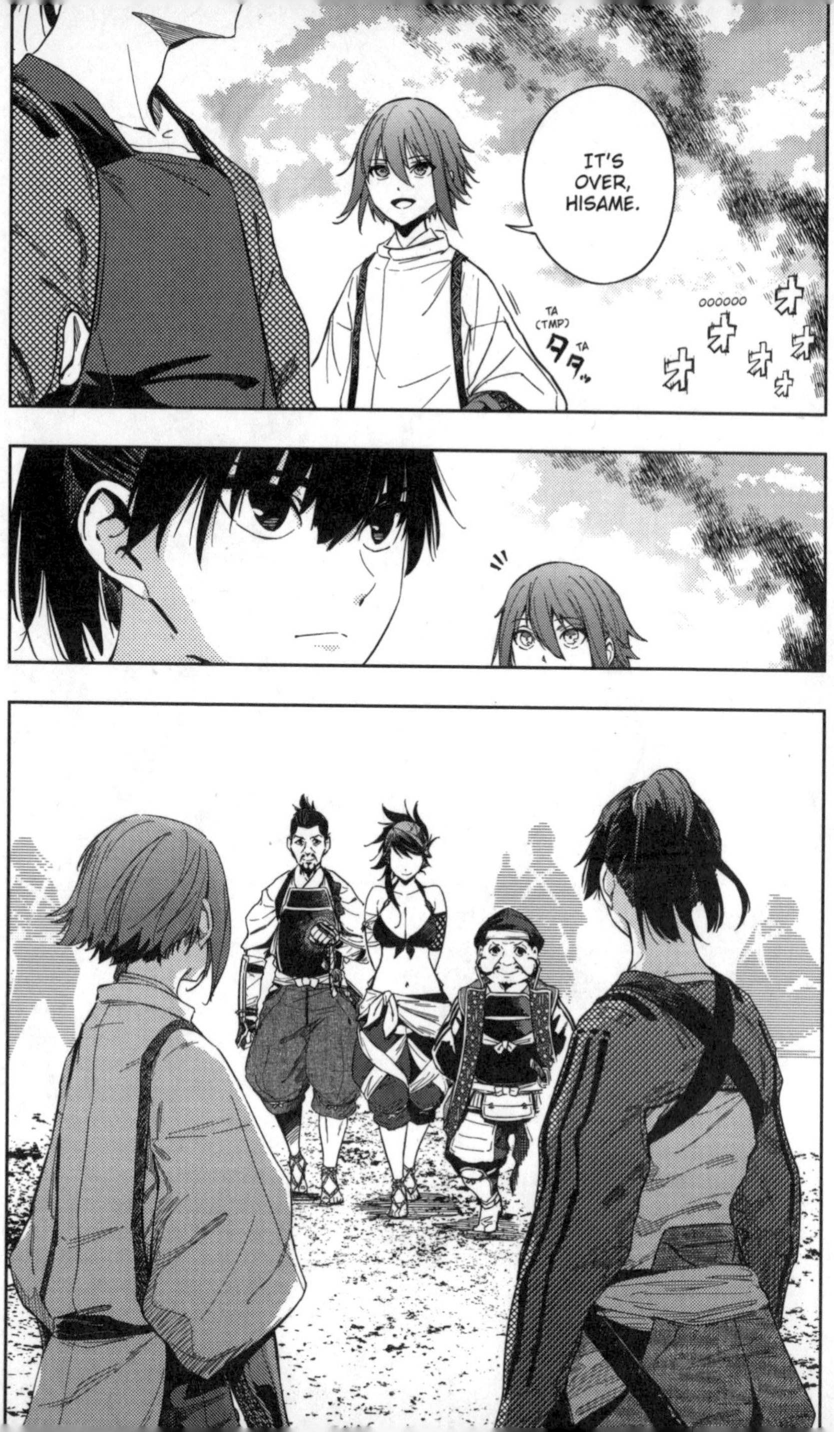

OOOOOO
オオオオオオ
IT'S OVER, HISAME.
TA (TMP) TA
タタッ

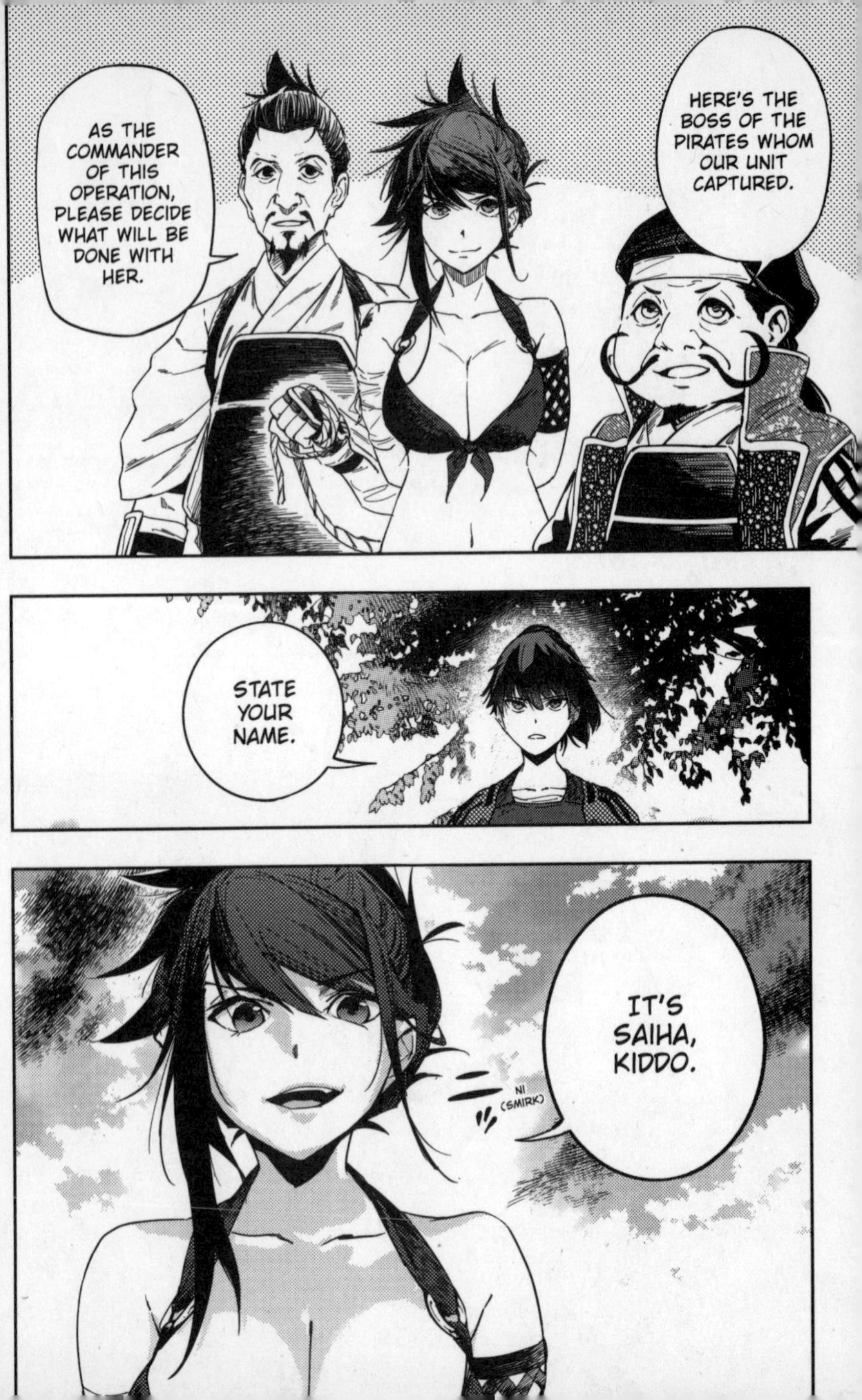
HERE'S THE BOSS OF THE PIRATES WHOM OUR UNIT CAPTURED.
AS THE COMMANDER OF THIS OPERATION, PLEASE DECIDE WHAT WILL BE DONE WITH HER.
STATE YOUR NAME.
IT'S SAIHA, KIDDO.
NI (SMIRK)

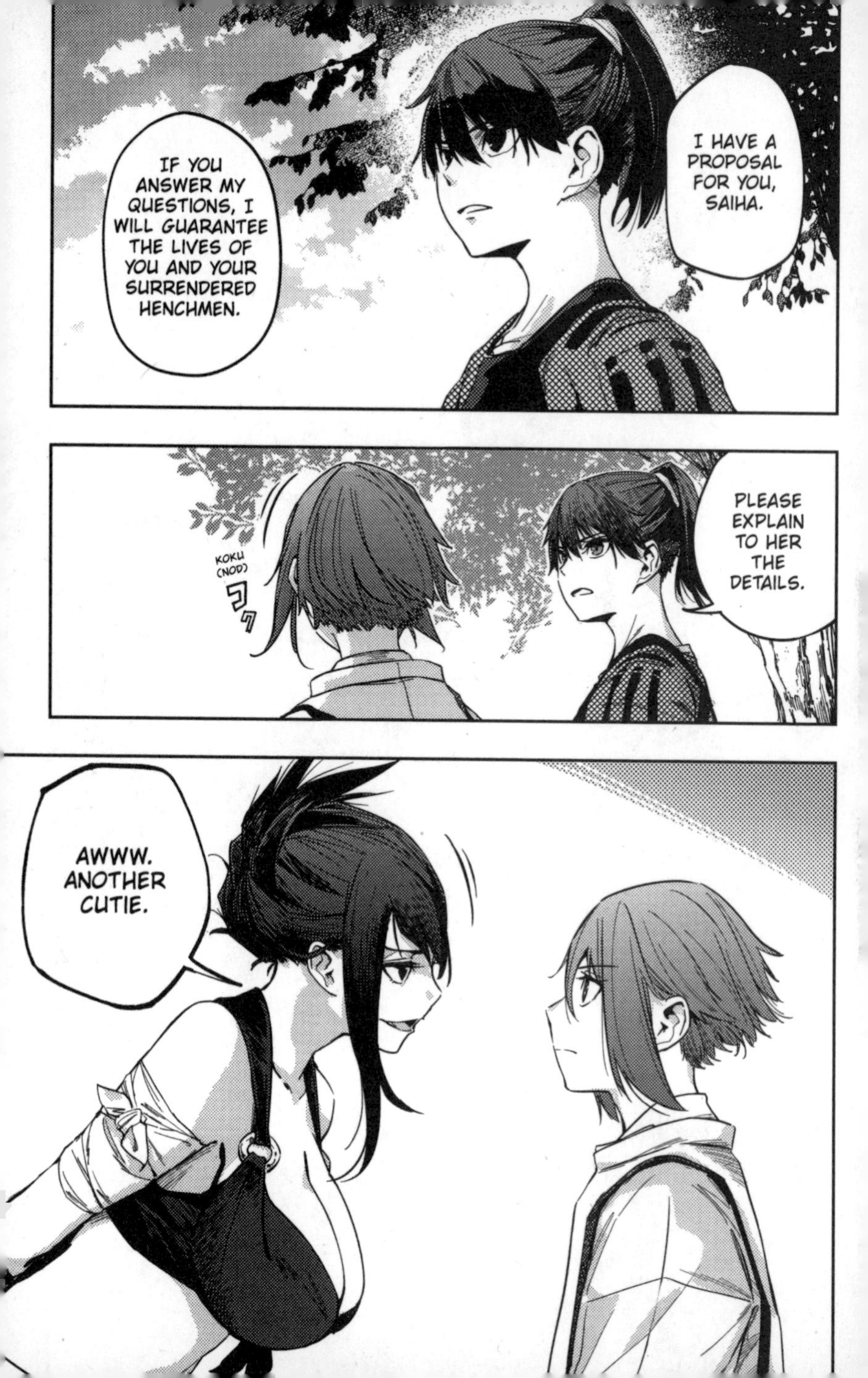
I HAVE A PROPOSAL FOR YOU, SAIHA.
IF YOU ANSWER MY QUESTIONS, I WILL GUARANTEE THE LIVES OF YOU AND YOUR SURRENDERED HENCHMEN.
PLEASE EXPLAIN TO HER THE DETAILS.
KOKU (NOD)
AWWW. ANOTHER CUTIE.

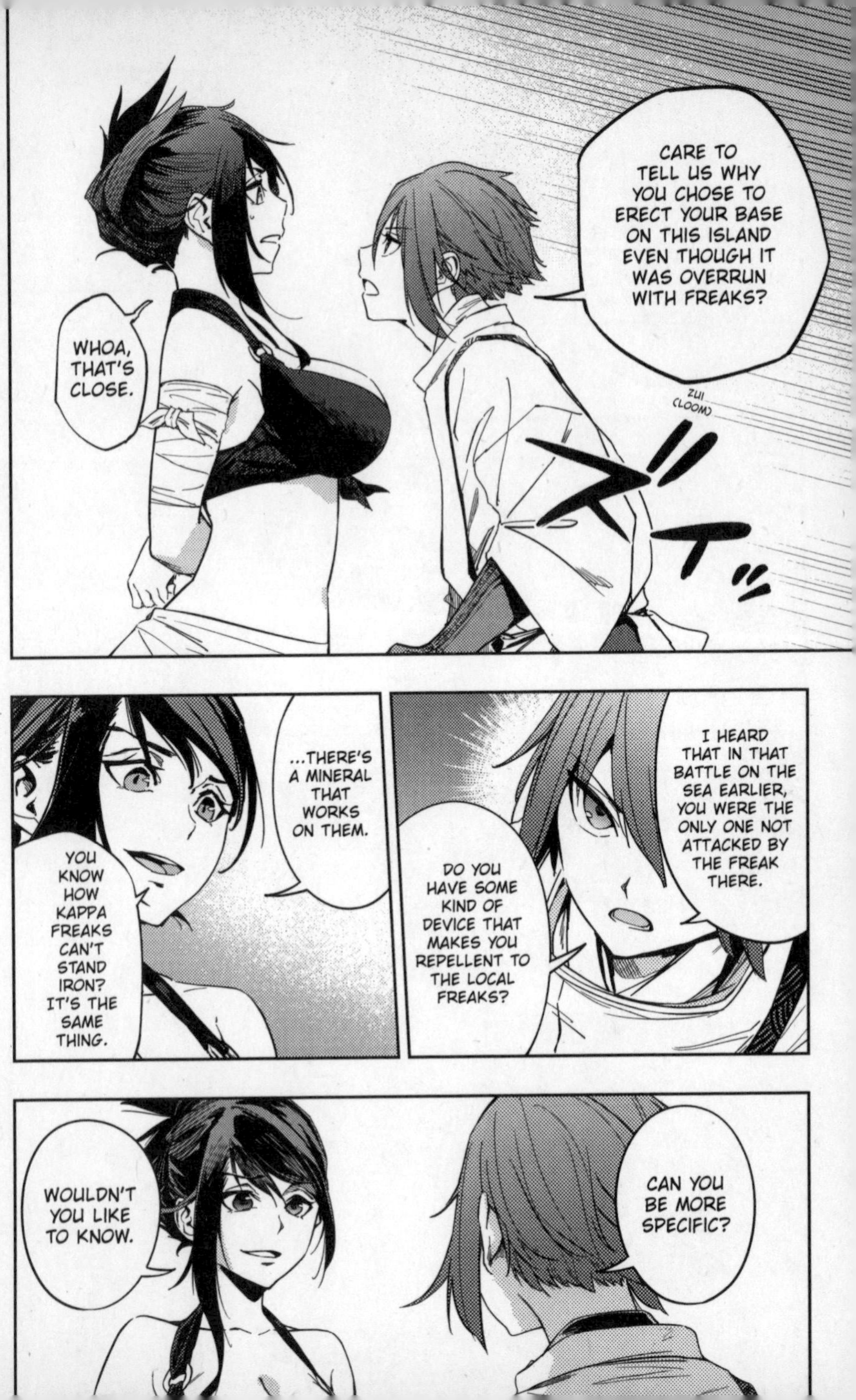
CARE TO TELL US WHY YOU CHOSE TO ERECT YOUR BASE ON THIS ISLAND EVEN THOUGH IT WAS OVERRUN WITH FREAKS?
ZUI (LOOM)
WHOA, THAT'S CLOSE.
I HEARD THAT IN THAT BATTLE ON THE SEA EARLIER, YOU WERE THE ONLY ONE NOT ATTACKED BY THE FREAK THERE.
DO YOU HAVE SOME KIND OF DEVICE THAT MAKES YOU REPELLENT TO THE LOCAL FREAKS?
...THERE'S A MINERAL THAT WORKS ON THEM.
YOU KNOW HOW KAPPA FREAKS CAN'T STAND IRON? IT'S THE SAME THING.
CAN YOU BE MORE SPECIFIC?
WOULDN'T YOU LIKE TO KNOW.

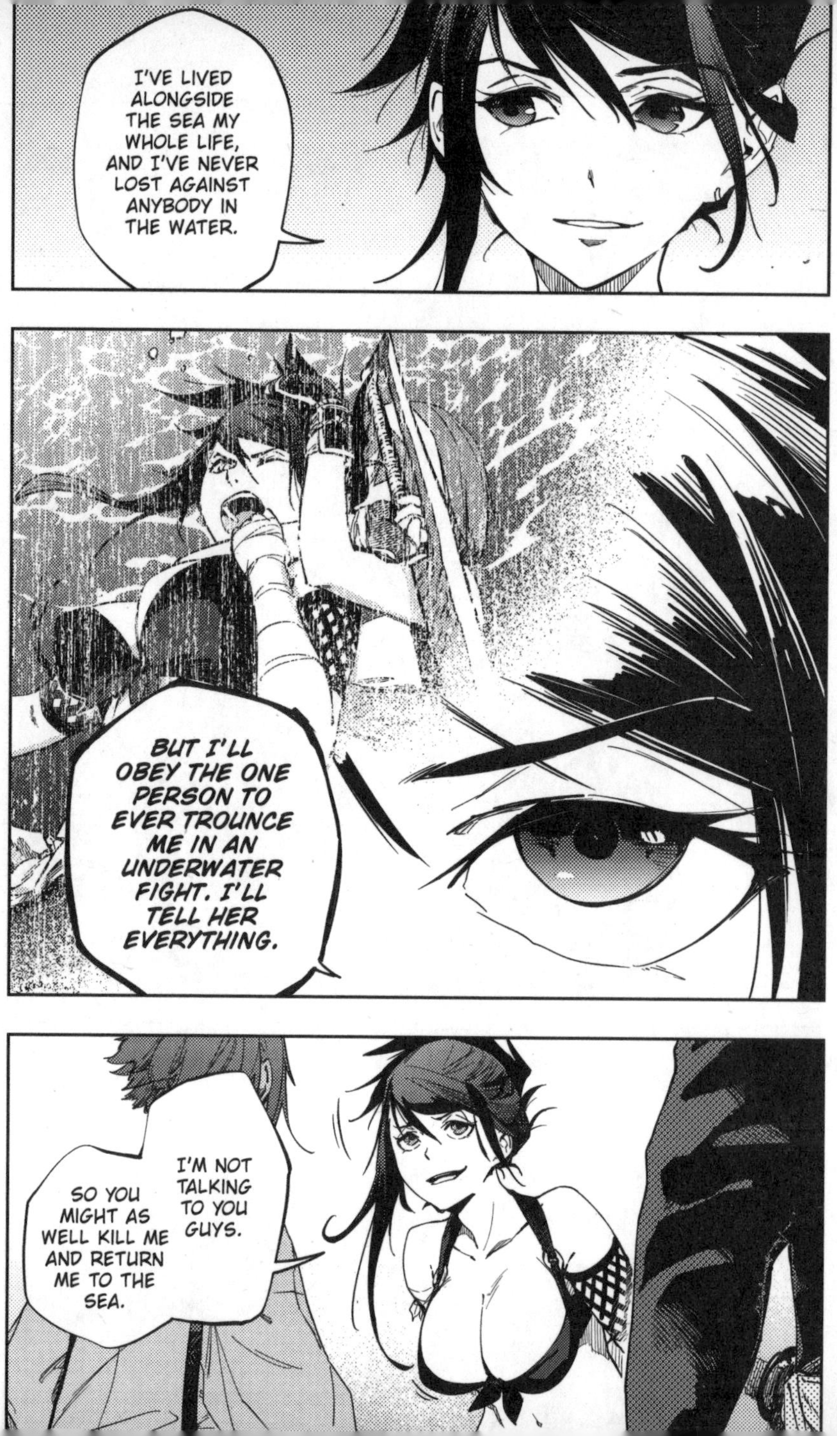
I'VE LIVED ALONGSIDE THE SEA MY WHOLE LIFE, AND I'VE NEVER LOST AGAINST ANYBODY IN THE WATER.
BUT I'LL OBEY THE ONE PERSON TO EVER TROUNCE ME IN AN UNDERWATER FIGHT. I'LL TELL HER EVERYTHING.
I'M NOT TALKING TO YOU GUYS.
SO YOU MIGHT AS WELL KILL ME AND RETURN ME TO THE SEA.

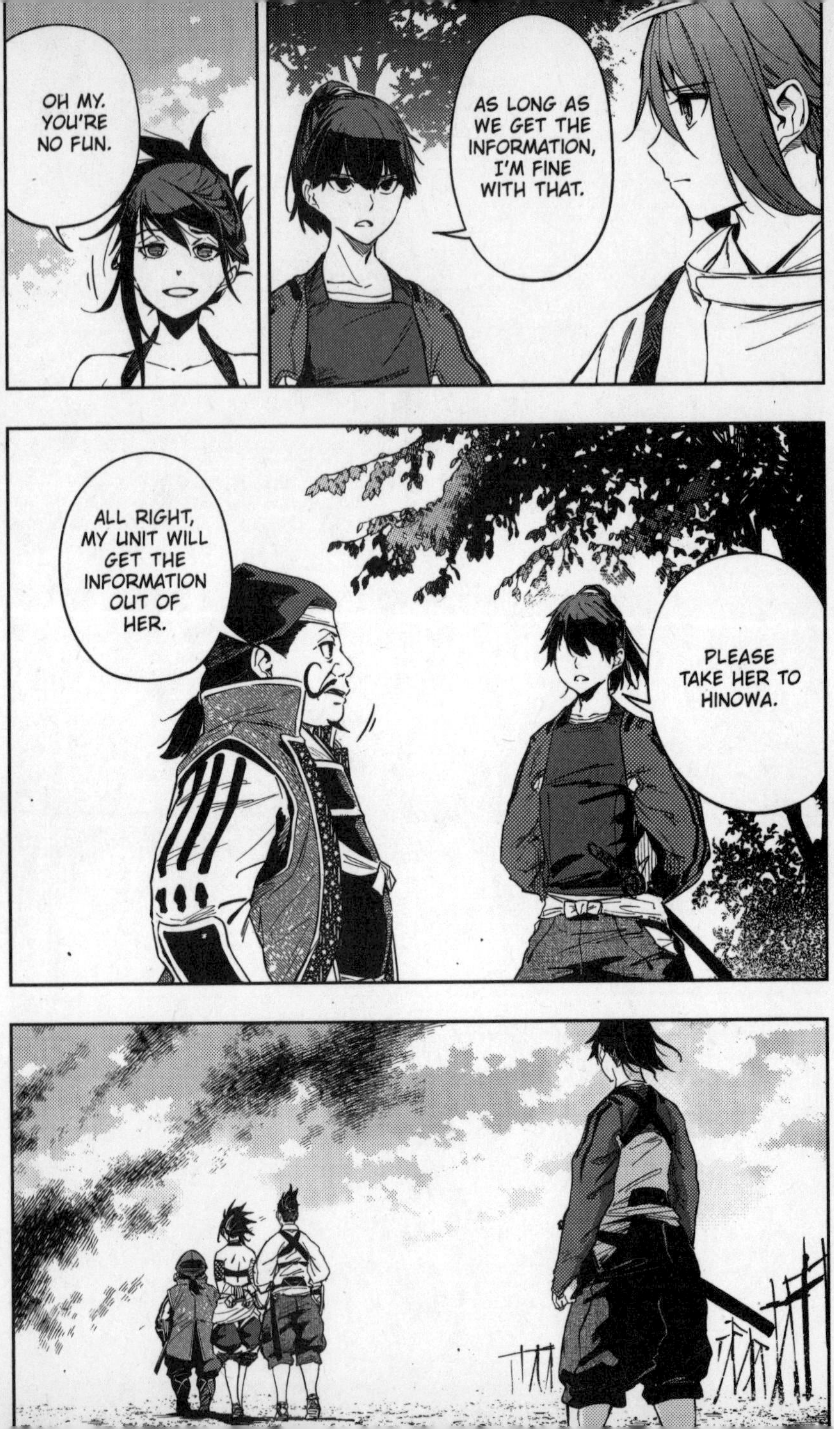
AS LONG AS WE GET THE INFORMATION, I'M FINE WITH THAT.
OH MY. YOU'RE NO FUN.
PLEASE TAKE HER TO HINOWA.
ALL RIGHT, MY UNIT WILL GET THE INFORMATION OUT OF HER.

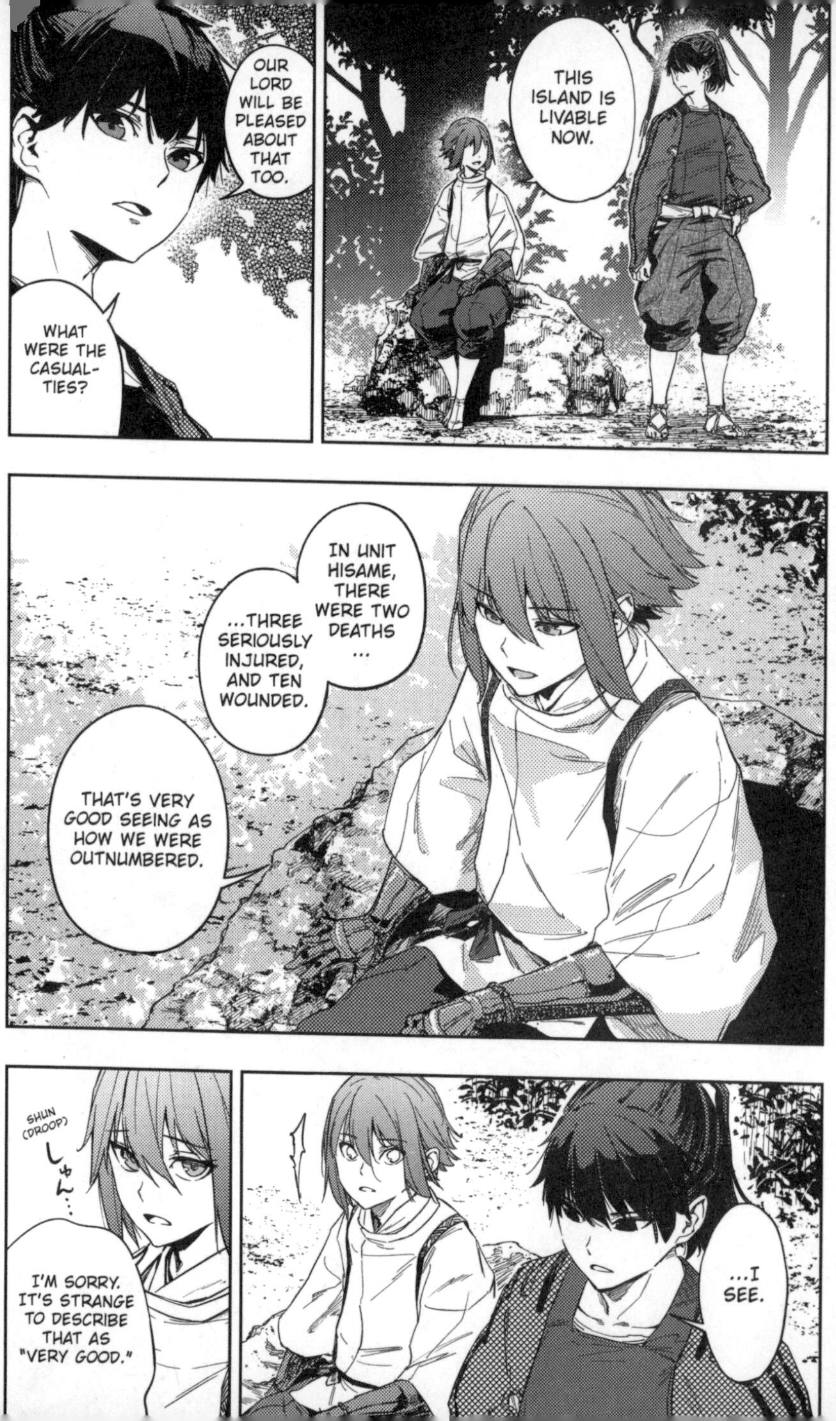
THIS ISLAND IS LIVABLE NOW.
OUR LORD WILL BE PLEASED ABOUT THAT TOO.
WHAT WERE THE CASUAL-TIES?
IN UNIT HISAME, THERE WERE TWO DEATHS ...
...THREE SERIOUSLY INJURED, AND TEN WOUNDED.
THAT'S VERY GOOD SEEING AS HOW WE WERE OUTNUMBERED.
...I SEE.
SHUN (DROOP)
しゅん…
I'M SORRY. IT'S STRANGE TO DESCRIBE THAT AS "VERY GOOD."

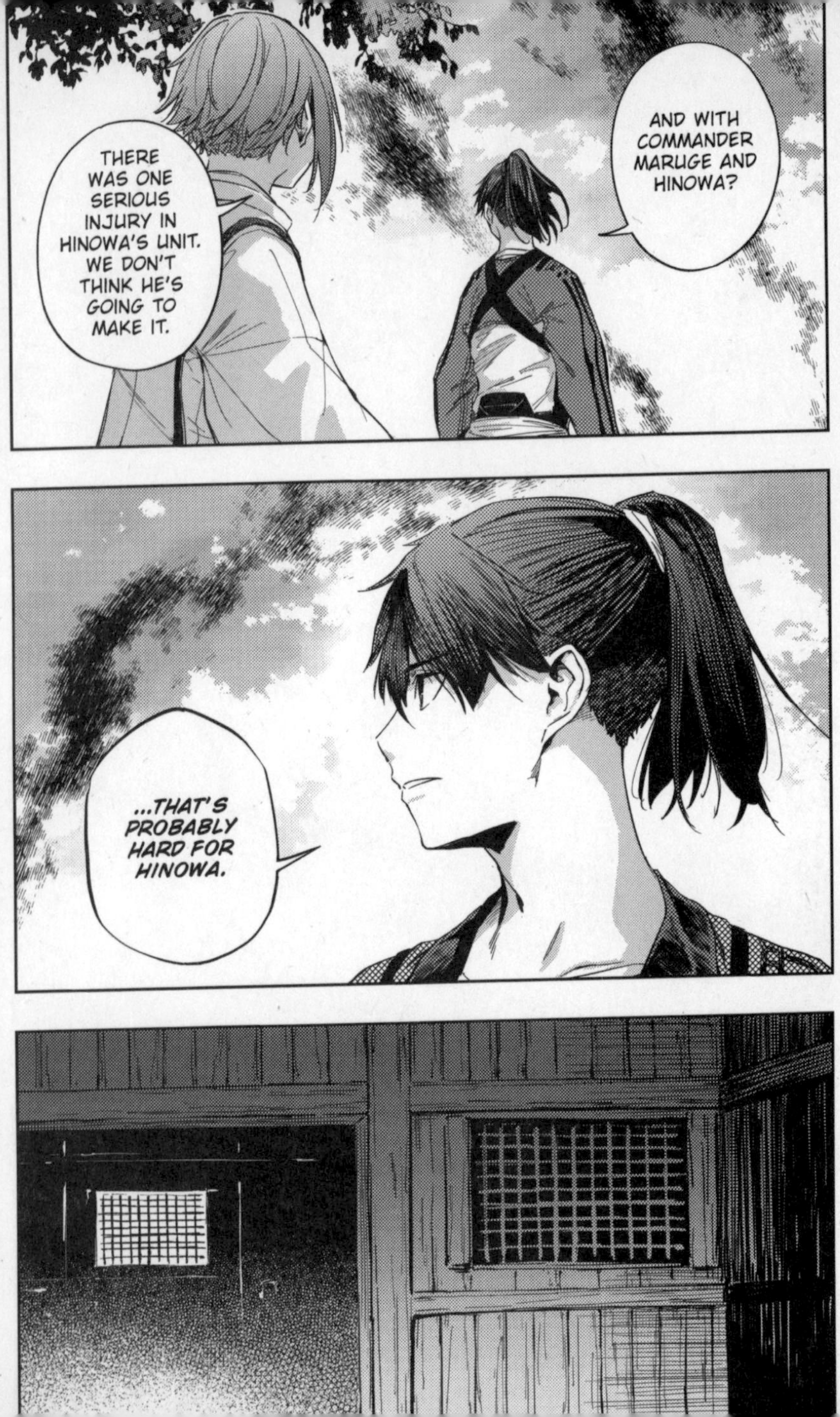
AND WITH COMMANDER MARUGE AND HINOWA?
THERE WAS ONE SERIOUS INJURY IN HINOWA'S UNIT. WE DON'T THINK HE'S GOING TO MAKE IT.
...THAT'S PROBABLY HARD FOR HINOWA.

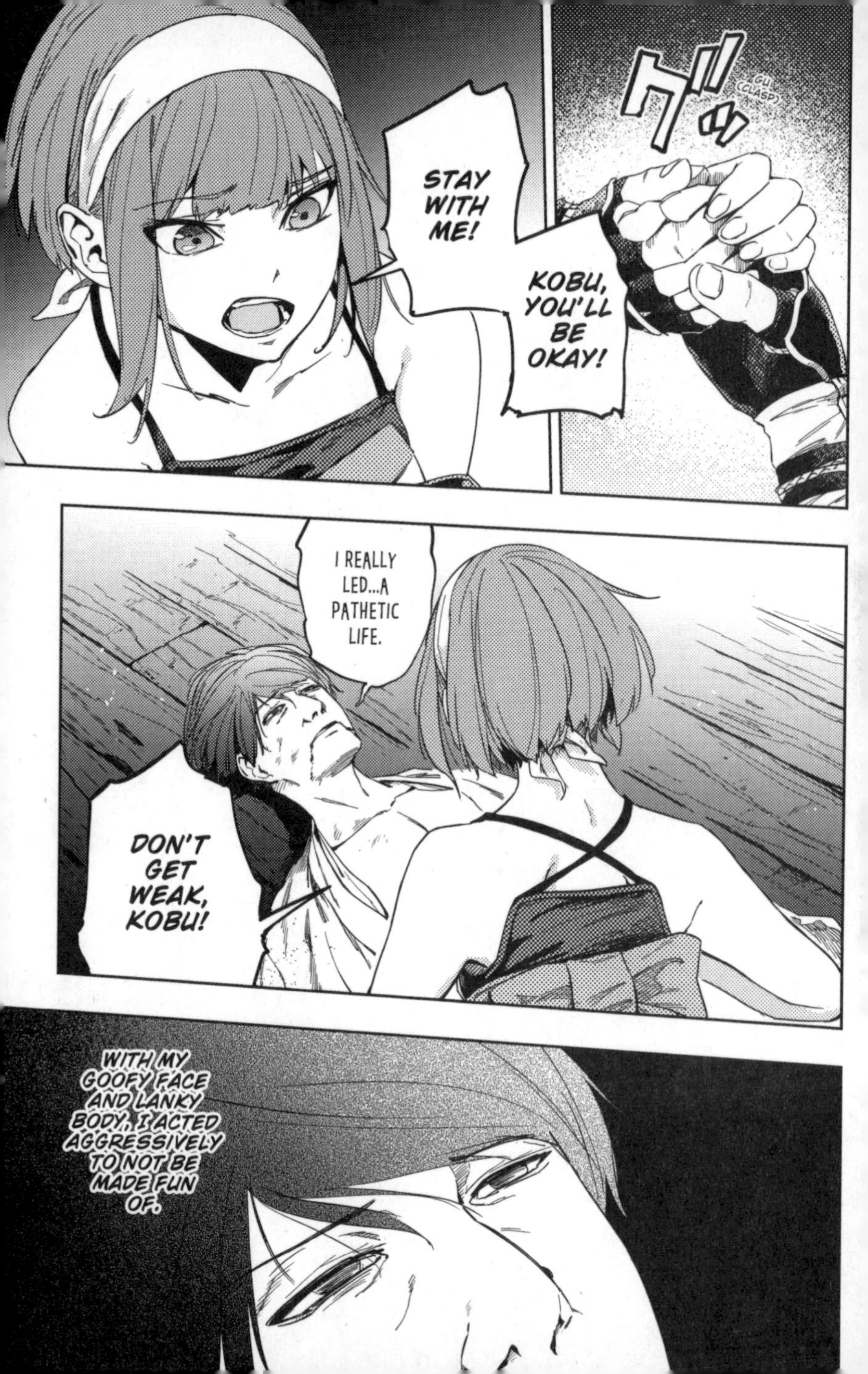
GU (CLASP)
KOBU, YOU'LL BE OKAY!
STAY WITH ME!
I REALLY LED...A PATHETIC LIFE.
DON'T GET WEAK, KOBU!
WITH MY GOOFY FACE AND LANKY BODY, I ACTED AGGRESSIVELY TO NOT BE MADE FUN OF.

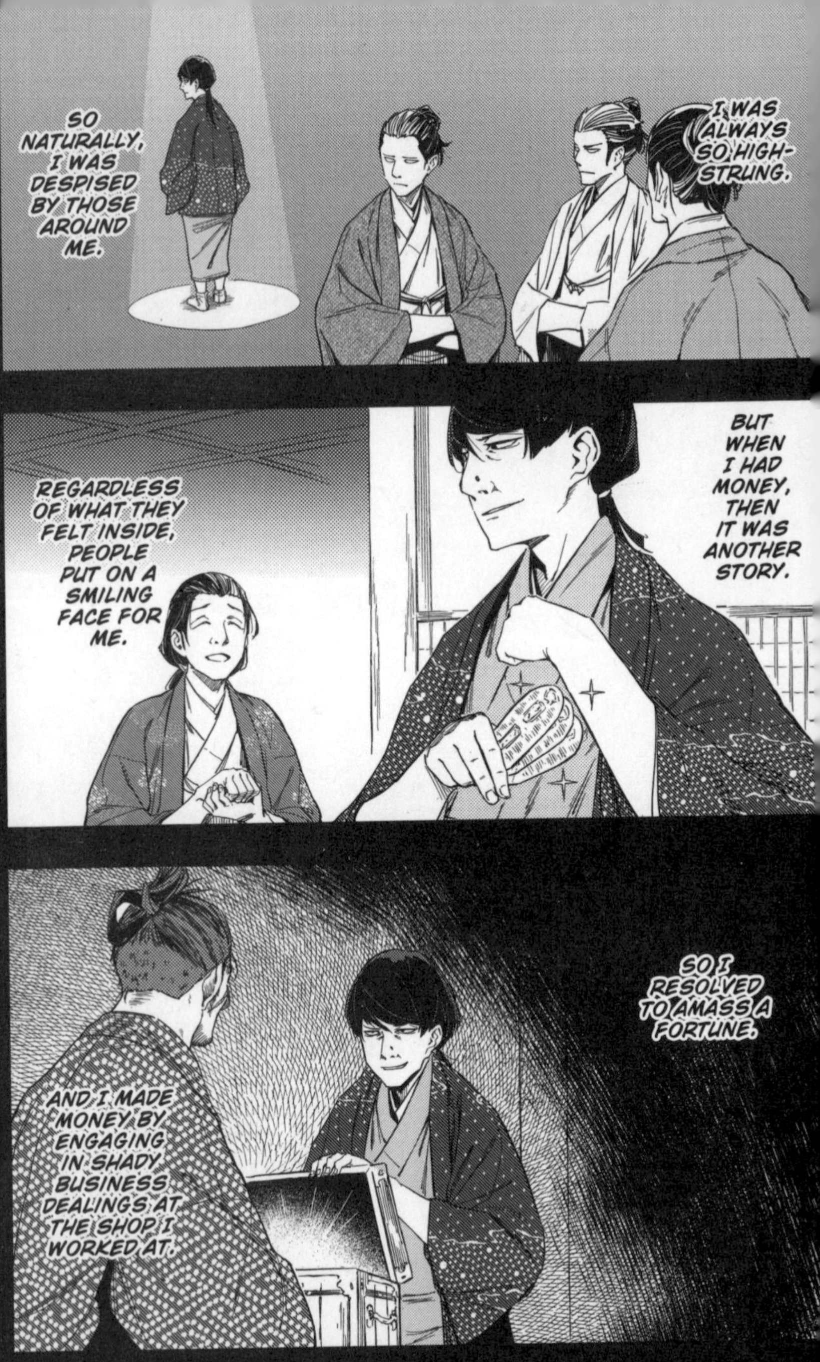
I WAS ALWAYS SO HIGH-STRUNG.
SO NATURALLY, I WAS DESPISED BY THOSE AROUND ME.
BUT WHEN I HAD MONEY, THEN IT WAS ANOTHER STORY.
REGARDLESS OF WHAT THEY FELT INSIDE, PEOPLE PUT ON A SMILING FACE FOR ME.
SO I RESOLVED TO AMASS A FORTUNE.
AND I MADE MONEY BY ENGAGING IN SHADY BUSINESS DEALINGS AT THE SHOP I WORKED AT.

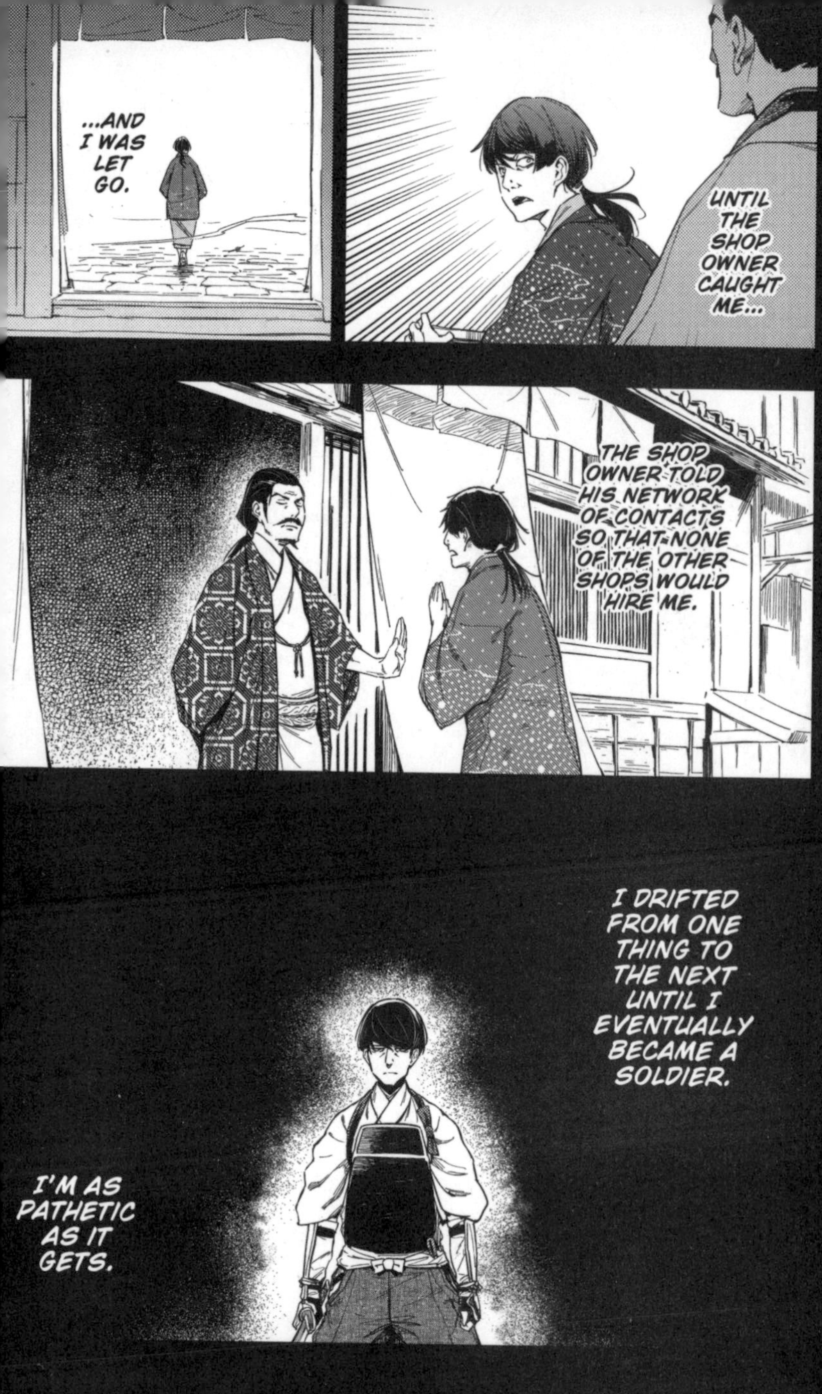
UNTIL THE SHOP OWNER CAUGHT ME...
...AND I WAS LET GO.
THE SHOP OWNER TOLD HIS NETWORK OF CONTACTS SO THAT NONE OF THE OTHER SHOPS WOULD HIRE ME.
I DRIFTED FROM ONE THING TO THE NEXT UNTIL I EVENTUALLY BECAME A SOLDIER.
I'M AS PATHETIC AS IT GETS.

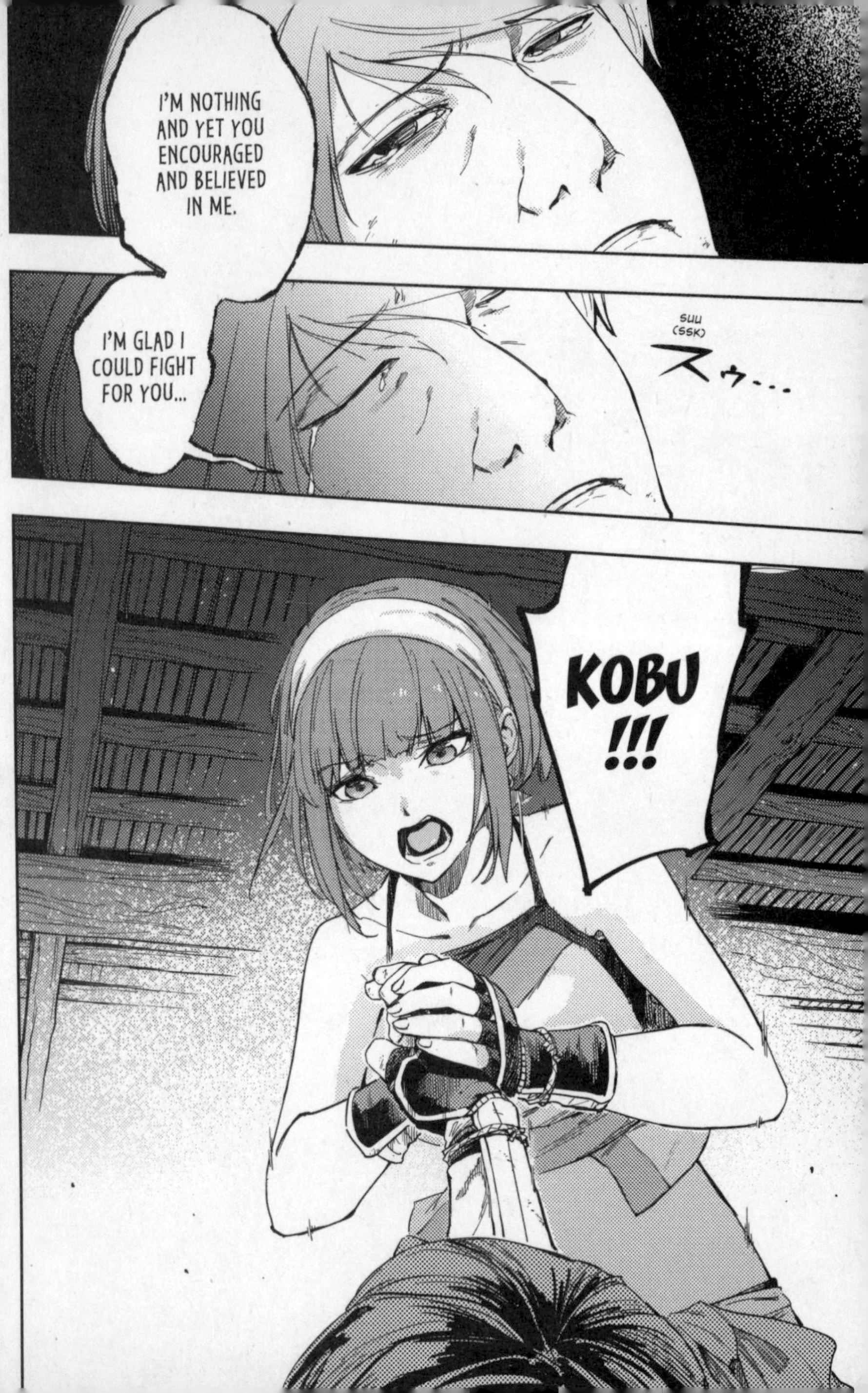
I'M NOTHING AND YET YOU ENCOURAGED AND BELIEVED IN ME.
SUU (SSK)
スゥ…
I'M GLAD I COULD FIGHT FOR YOU...
KOBU!!!

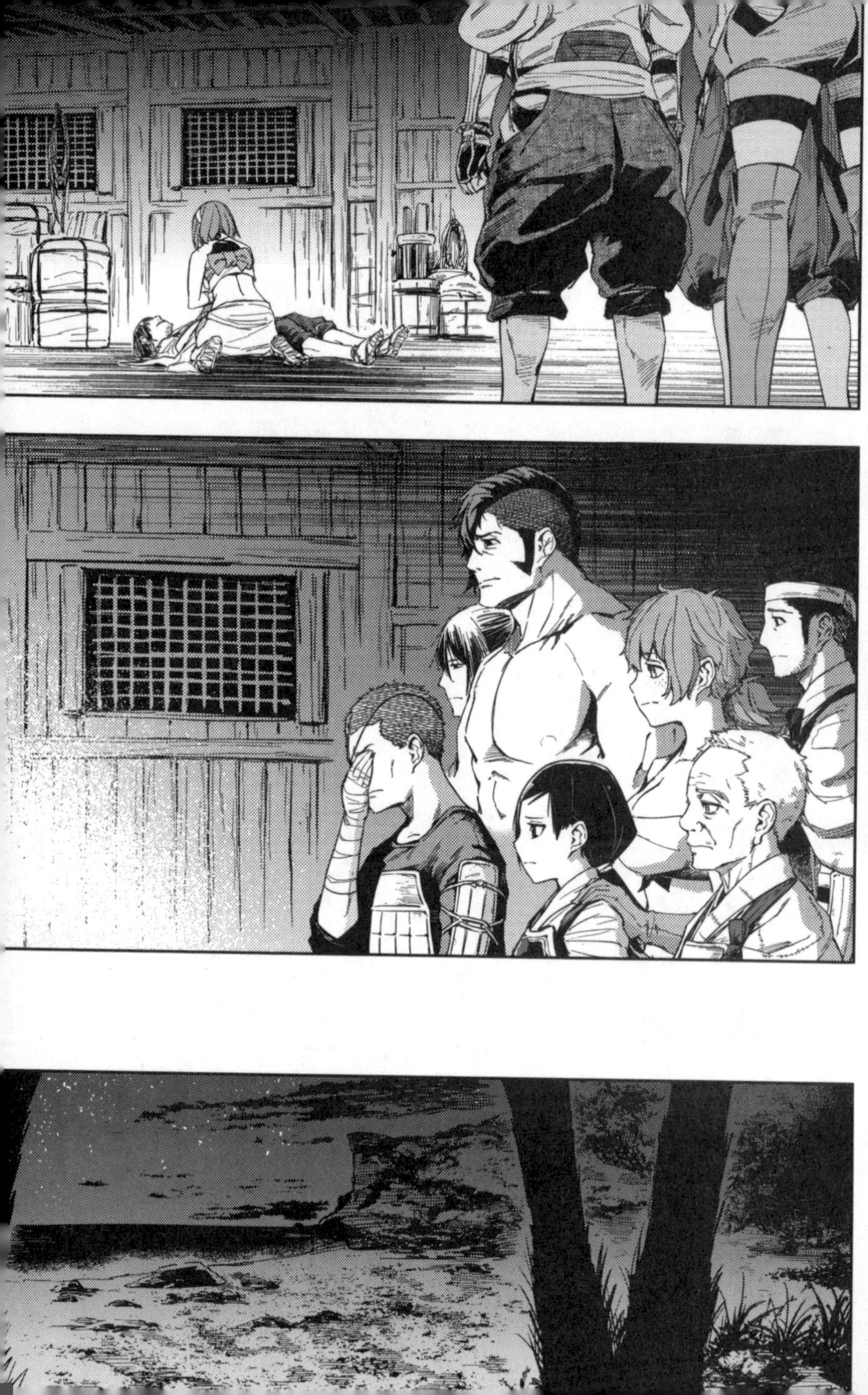

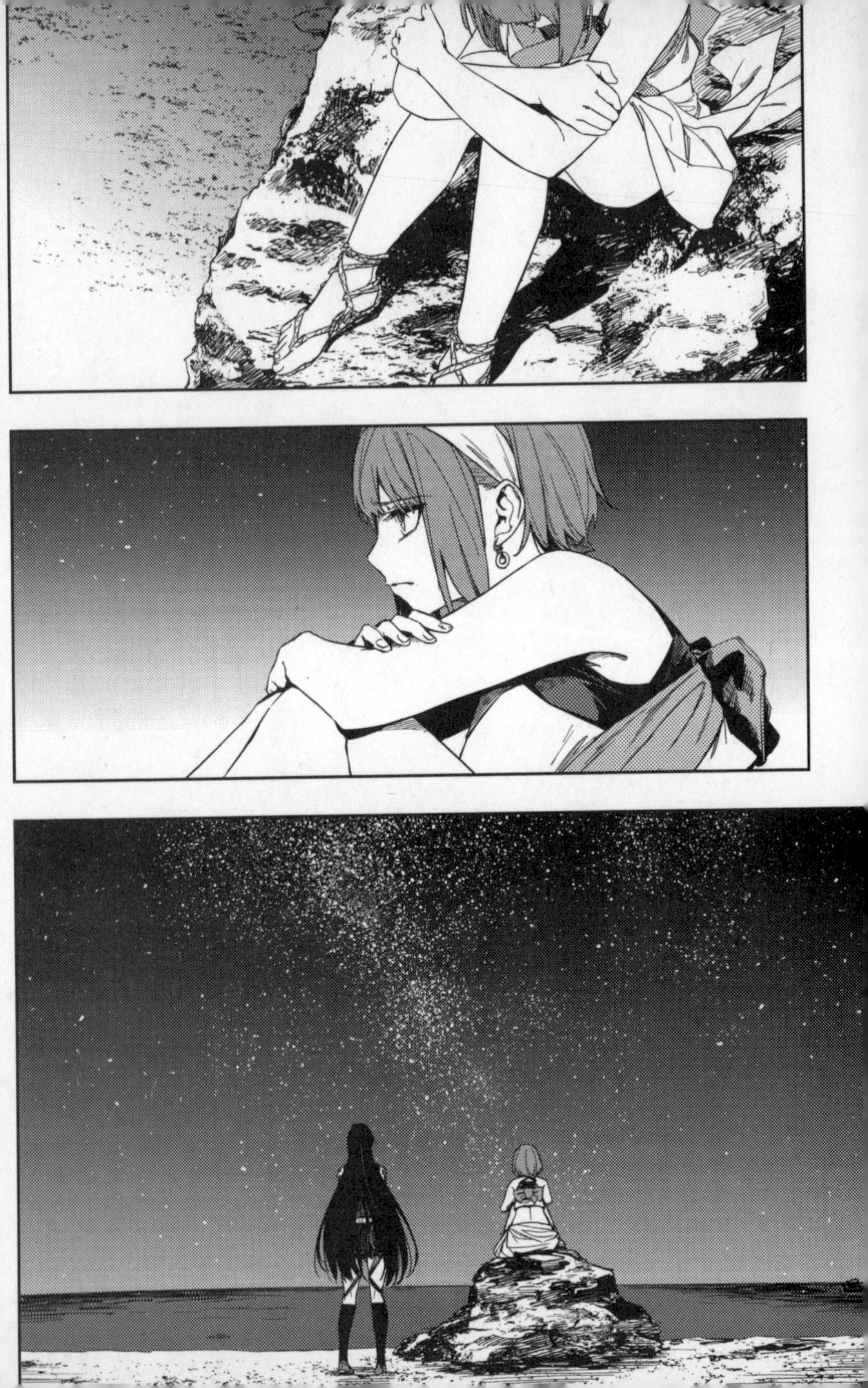

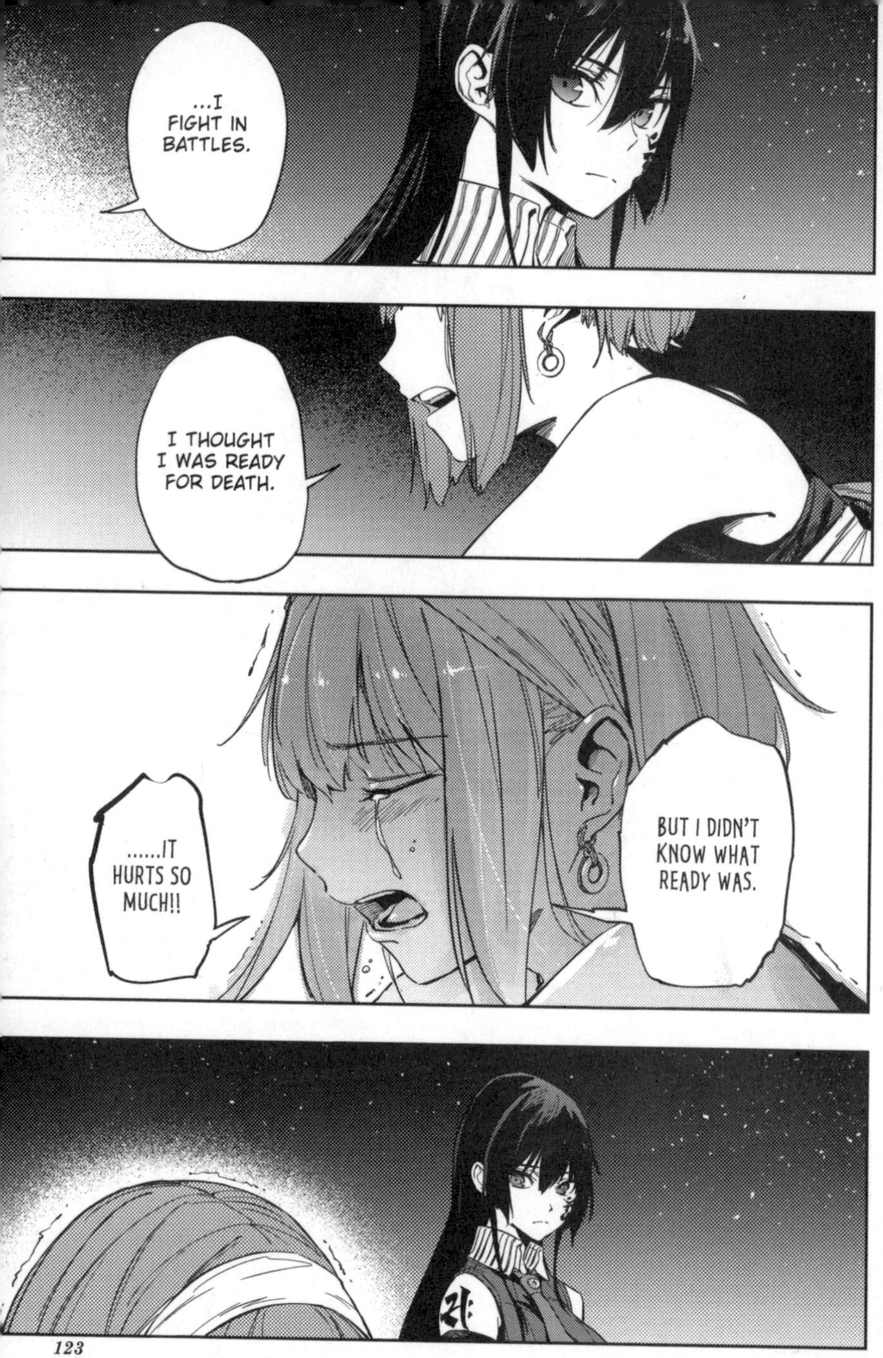
...I FIGHT IN BATTLES.
I THOUGHT I WAS READY FOR DEATH.
BUT I DIDN'T KNOW WHAT READY WAS.
......IT HURTS SO MUCH!!

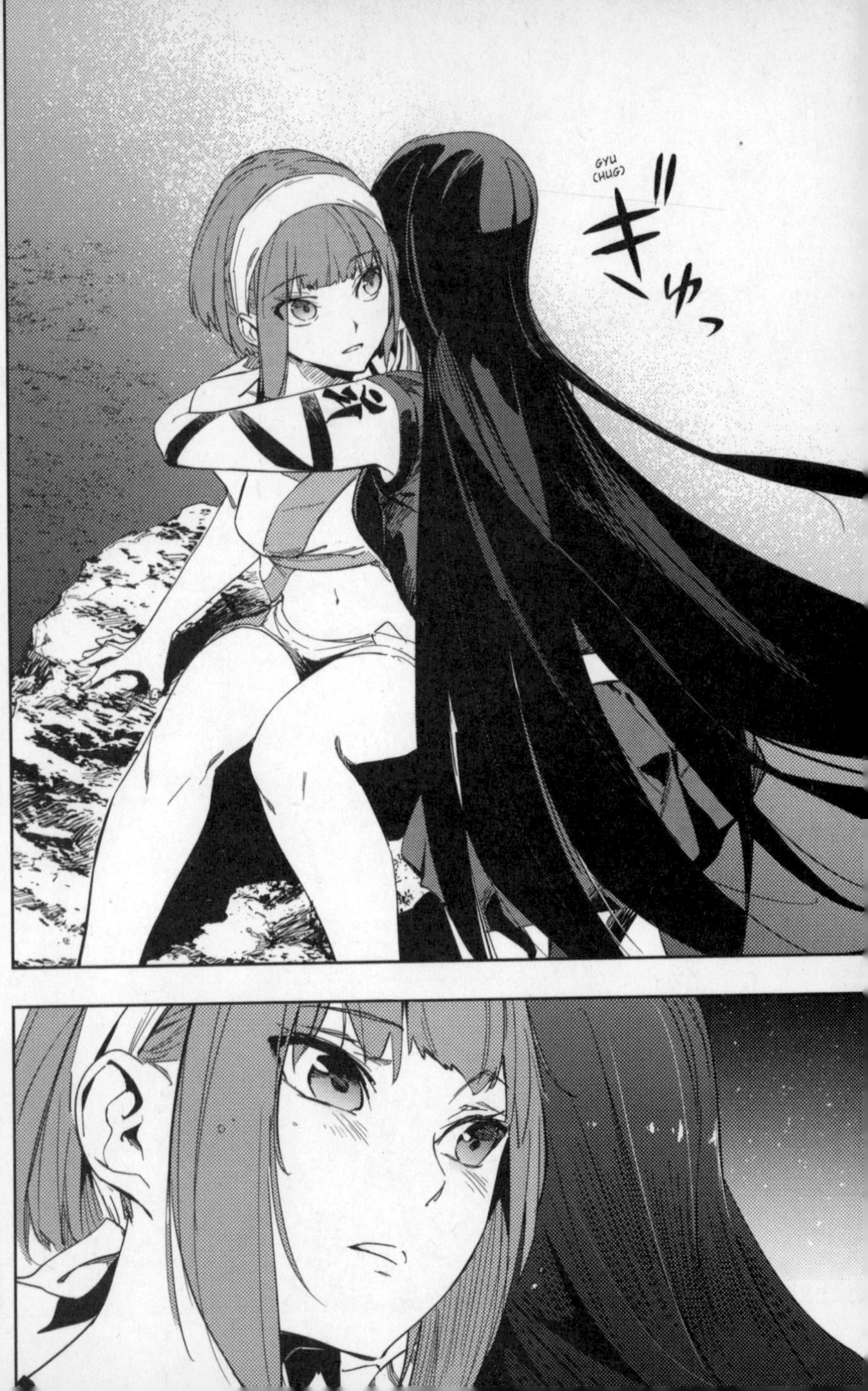
GYU (HUG)
ぎゅっ

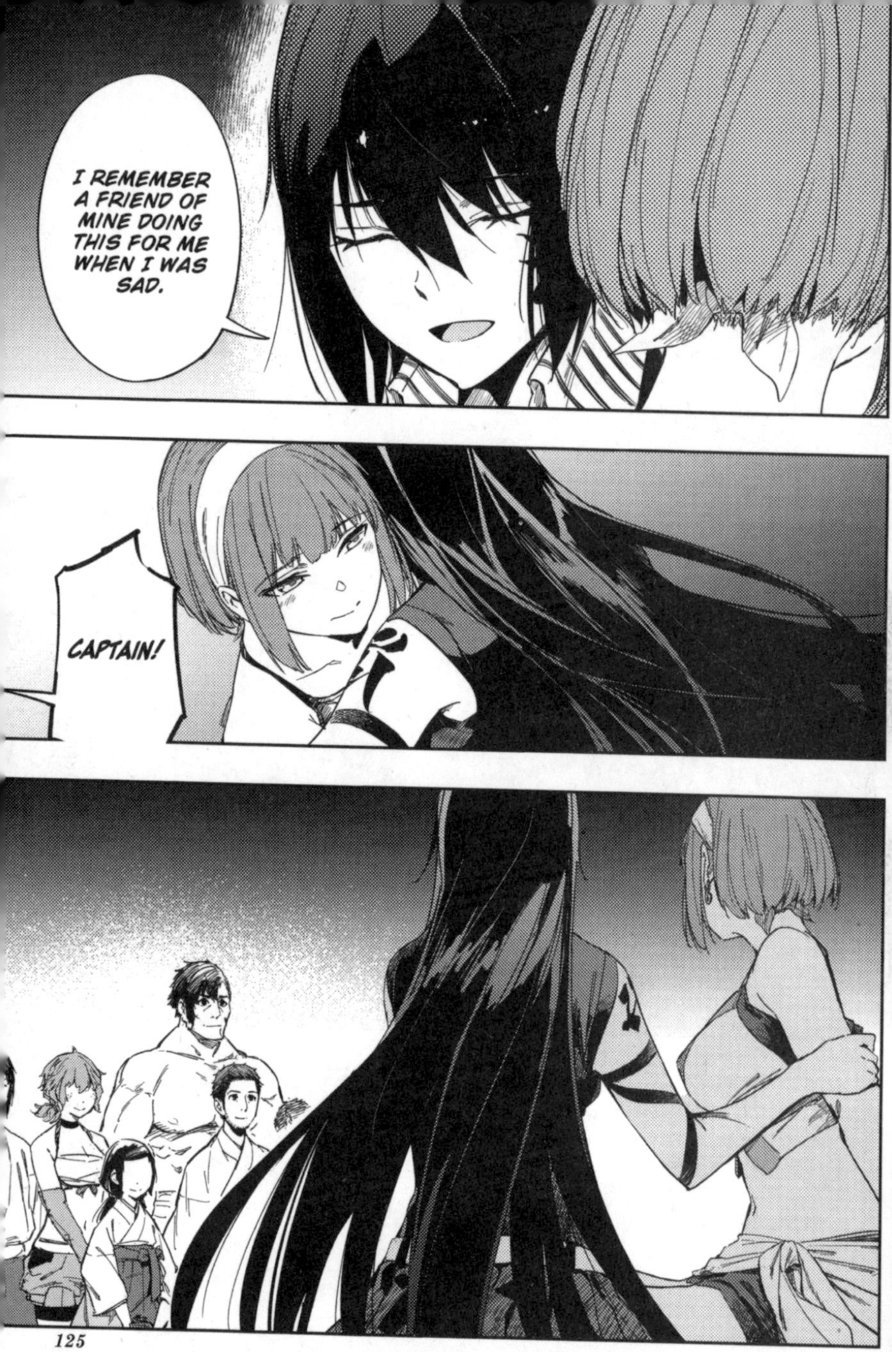
I REMEMBER A FRIEND OF MINE DOING THIS FOR ME WHEN I WAS SAD.
CAPTAIN!

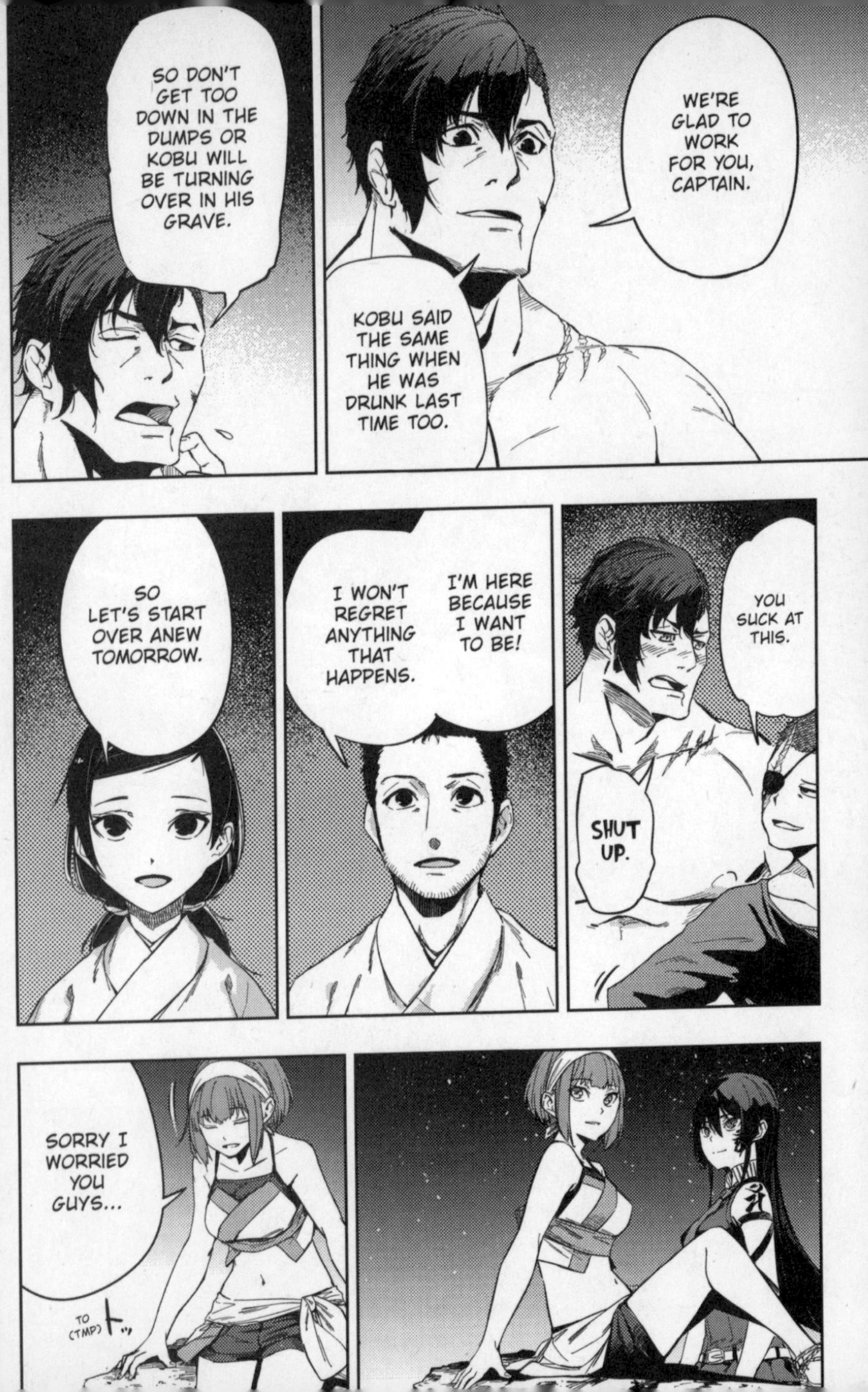
WE'RE GLAD TO WORK FOR YOU, CAPTAIN.
KOBU SAID THE SAME THING WHEN HE WAS DRUNK LAST TIME TOO.
SO DON'T GET TOO DOWN IN THE DUMPS OR KOBU WILL BE TURNING OVER IN HIS GRAVE.
YOU SUCK AT THIS.
SHUT UP.
I'M HERE BECAUSE I WANT TO BE!
I WON'T REGRET ANYTHING THAT HAPPENS.
SO LET'S START OVER ANEW TOMORROW.
SORRY I WORRIED YOU GUYS...
TO (TMP)

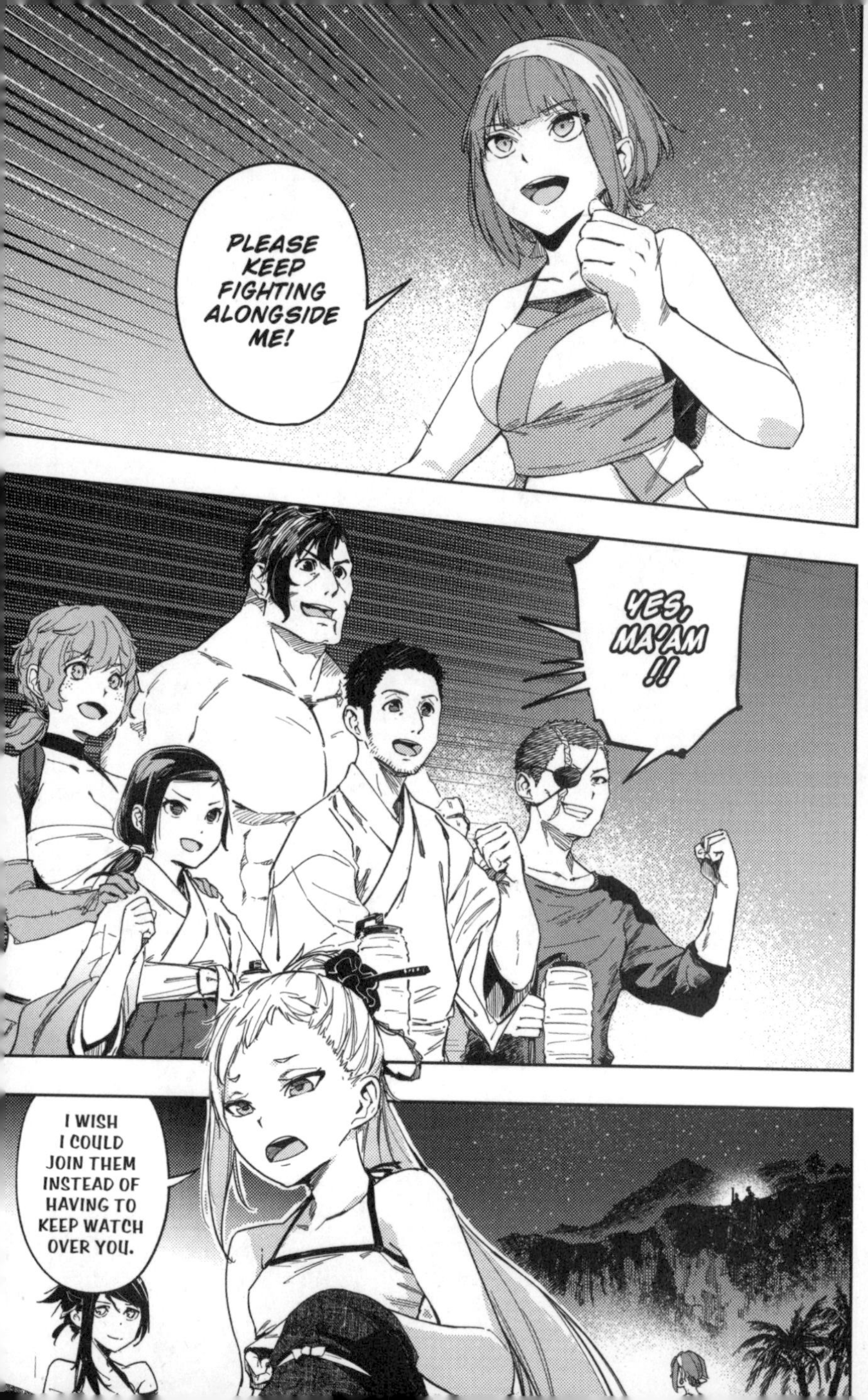
PLEASE KEEP FIGHTING ALONGSIDE ME!
YES, MA'AM!!
I WISH I COULD JOIN THEM INSTEAD OF HAVING TO KEEP WATCH OVER YOU.

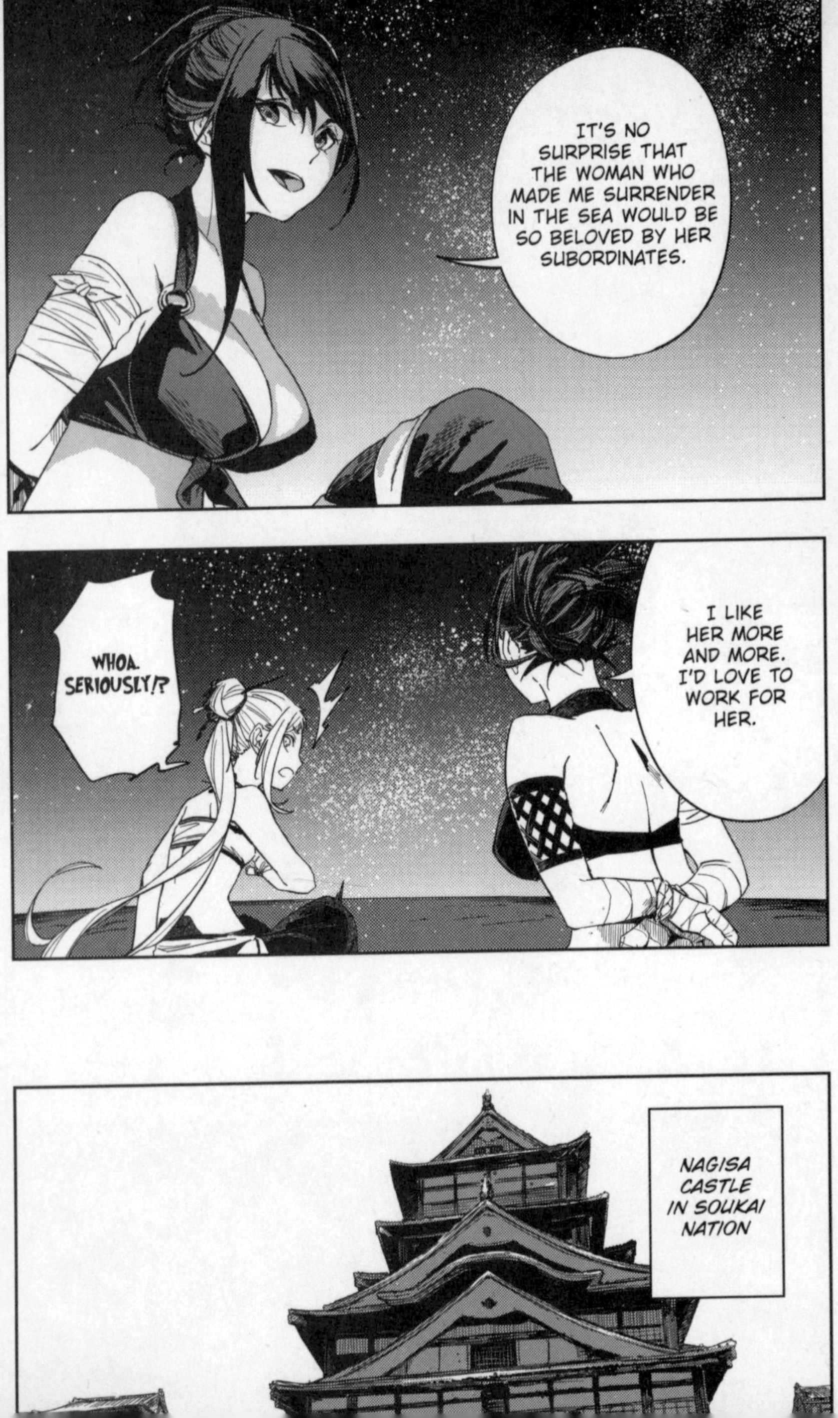
IT'S NO SURPRISE THAT THE WOMAN WHO MADE ME SURRENDER IN THE SEA WOULD BE SO BELOVED BY HER SUBORDINATES.
I LIKE HER MORE AND MORE. I'D LOVE TO WORK FOR HER.
WHOA. SERIOUSLY!?
NAGISA CASTLE IN SOUKAI NATION

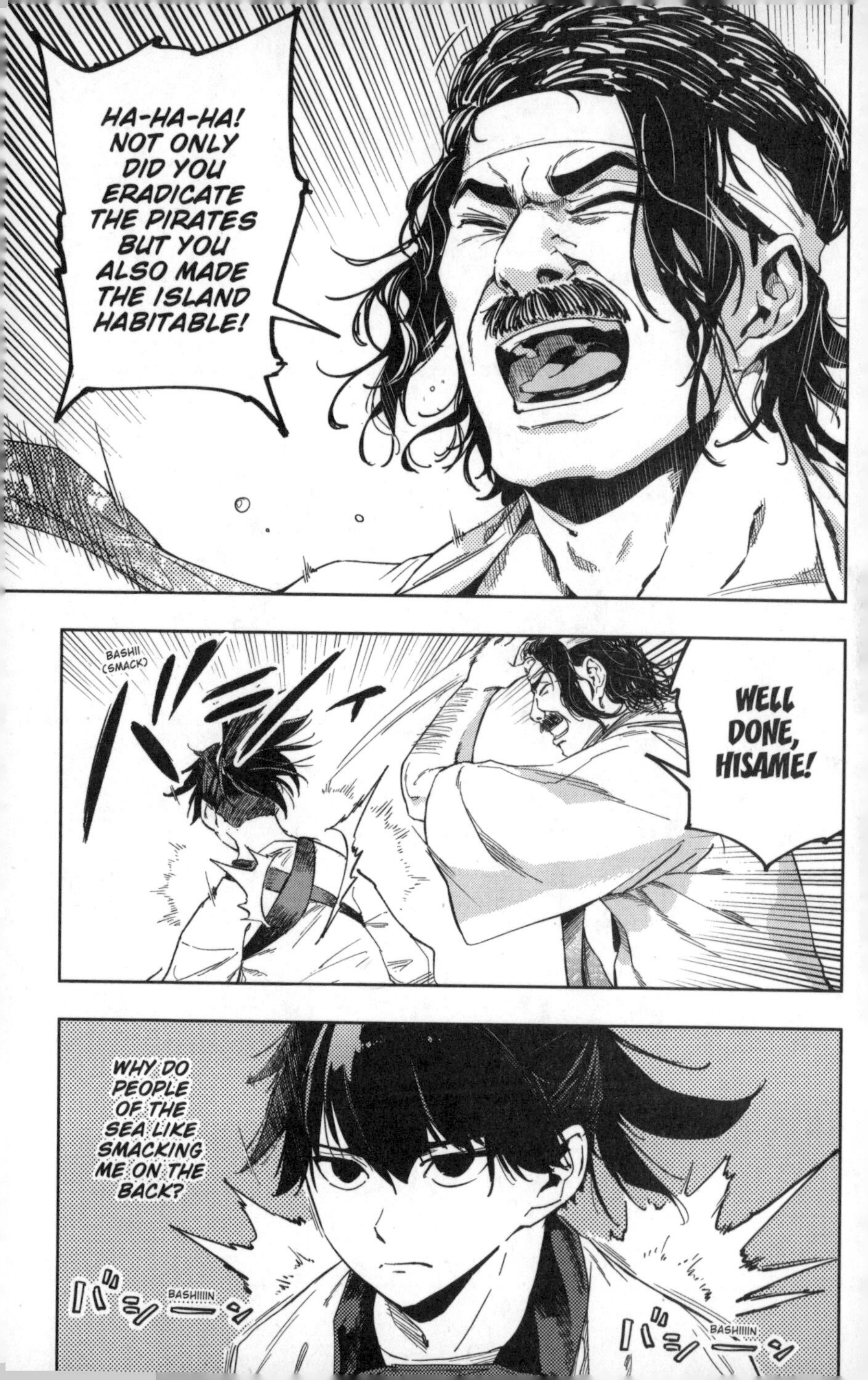
HA-HA-HA! NOT ONLY DID YOU ERADICATE THE PIRATES BUT YOU ALSO MADE THE ISLAND HABITABLE!
WELL DONE, HISAME!
BASHII (SMACK)
WHY DO PEOPLE OF THE SEA LIKE SMACKING ME ON THE BACK?
BASHIIIIN
BASHIIIIN

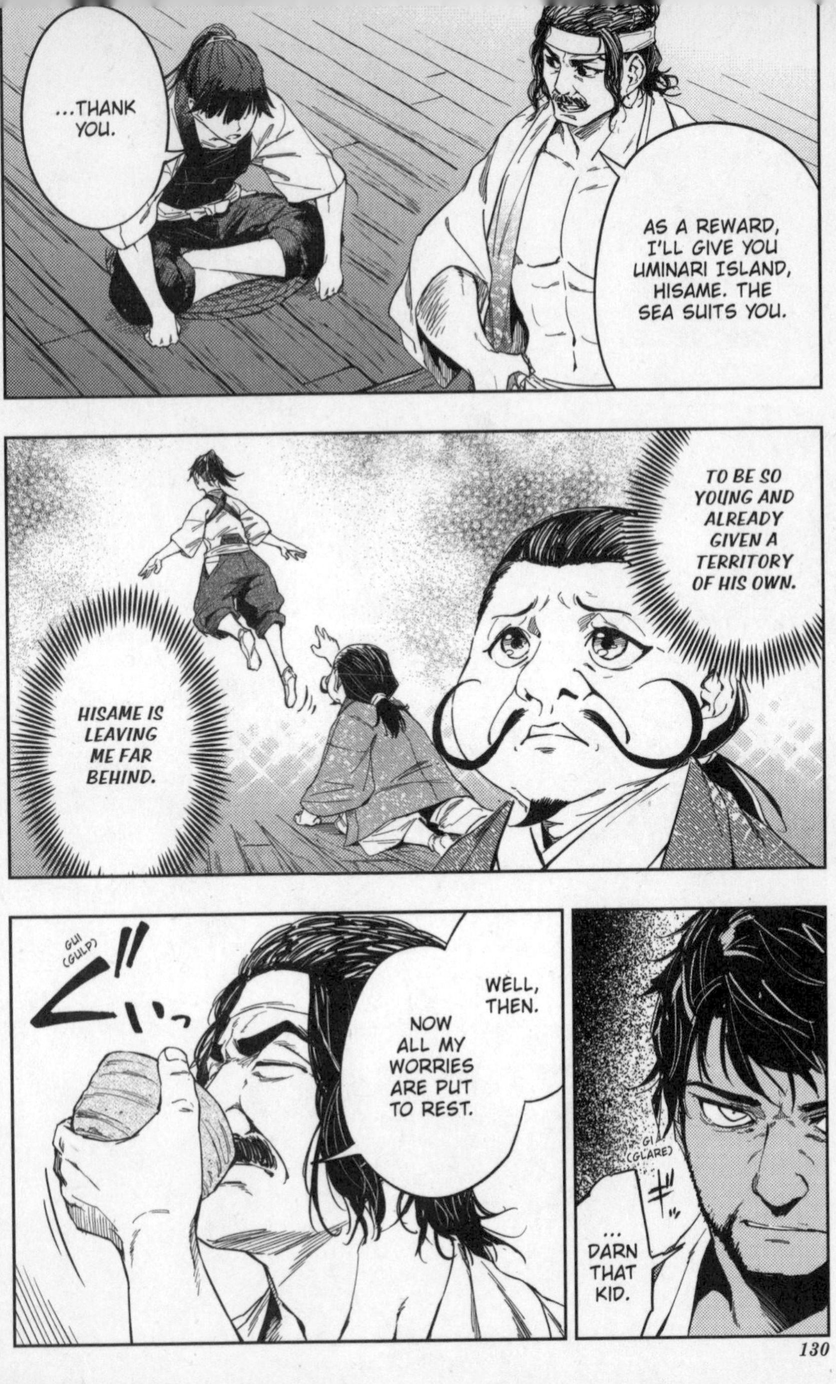
AS A REWARD, I'LL GIVE YOU UMINARI ISLAND, HISAME. THE SEA SUITS YOU.
...THANK YOU.
TO BE SO YOUNG AND ALREADY GIVEN A TERRITORY OF HIS OWN.
HISAME IS LEAVING ME FAR BEHIND.
GI (GLARE)
... DARN THAT KID.
WELL, THEN.
NOW ALL MY WORRIES ARE PUT TO REST.
GUI (GULP)

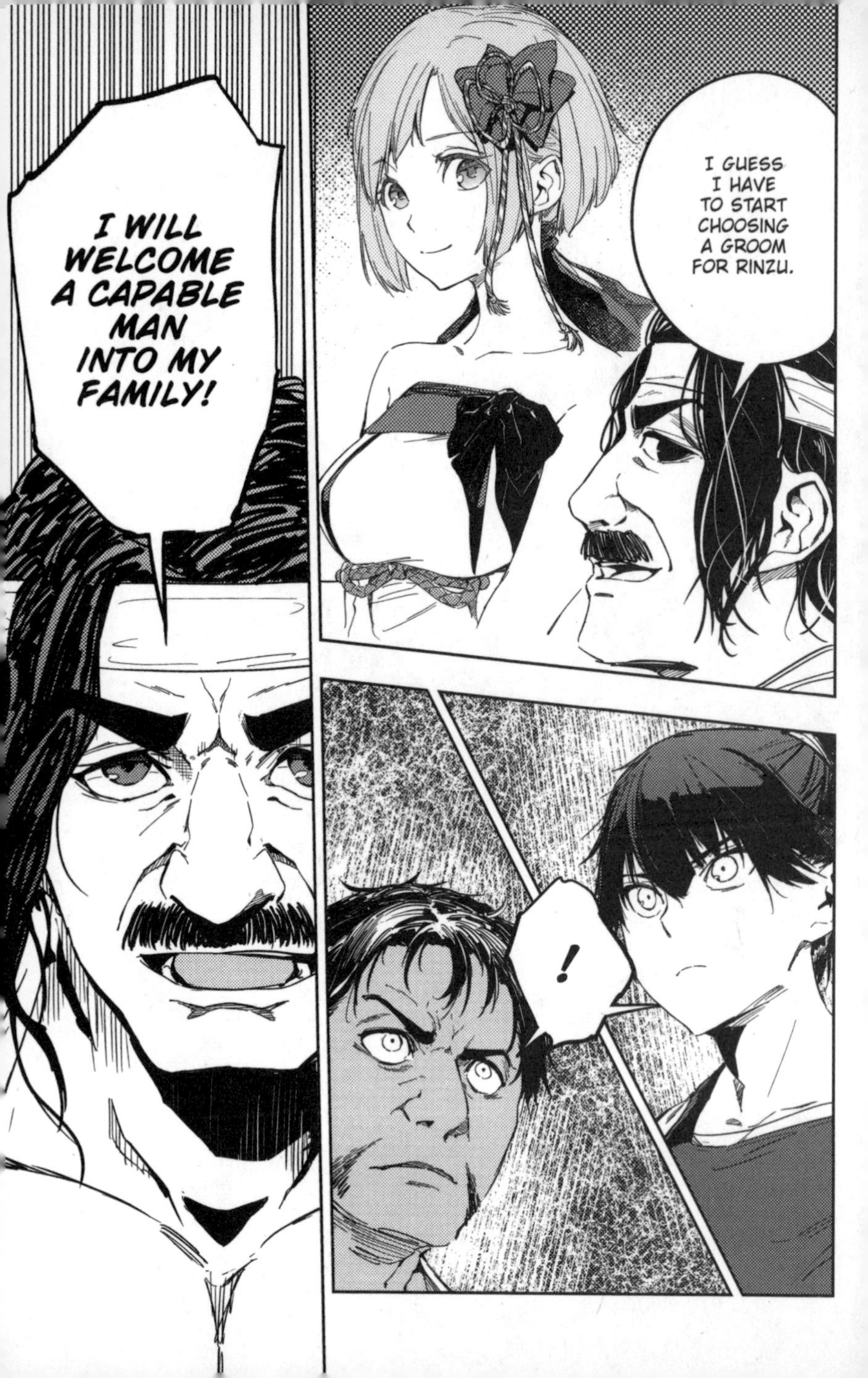
I GUESS I HAVE TO START CHOOSING A GROOM FOR RINZU.
I WILL WELCOME A CAPABLE MAN INTO MY FAMILY!
!

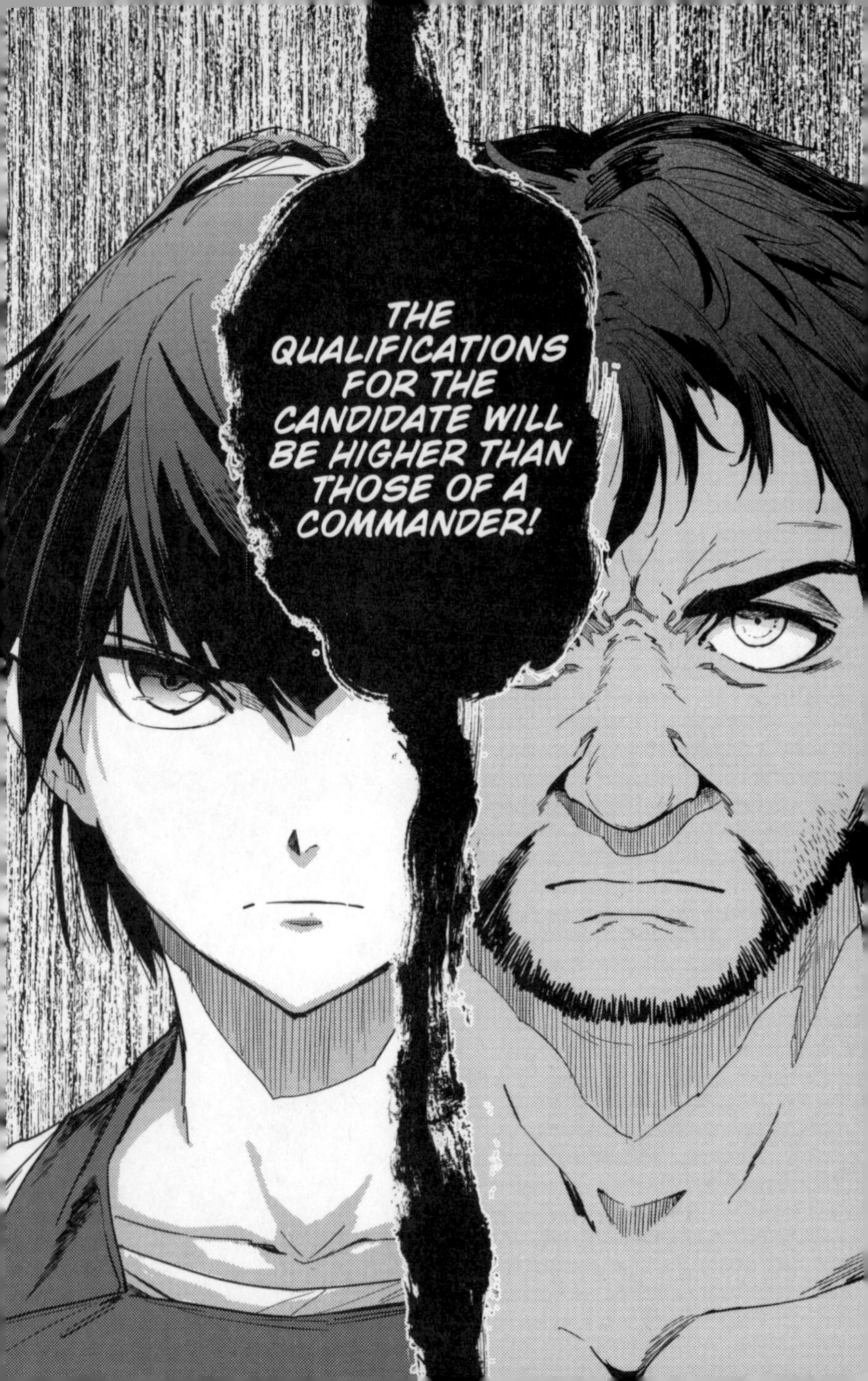
THE QUALIFICATIONS FOR THE CANDIDATE WILL BE HIGHER THAN THOSE OF A COMMANDER!

Hjnowa ga *CRUSH!*

Hijnowa ga CRUSH!

Design Drafts ④

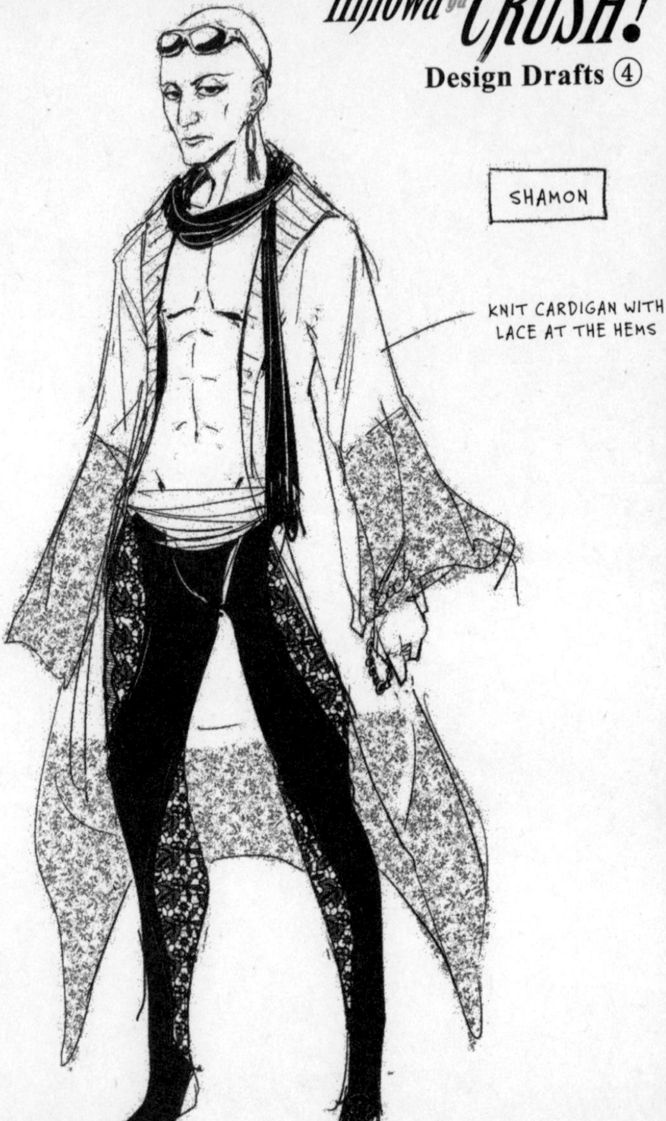
SHAMON
KNIT CARDIGAN WITH LACE AT THE HEMS

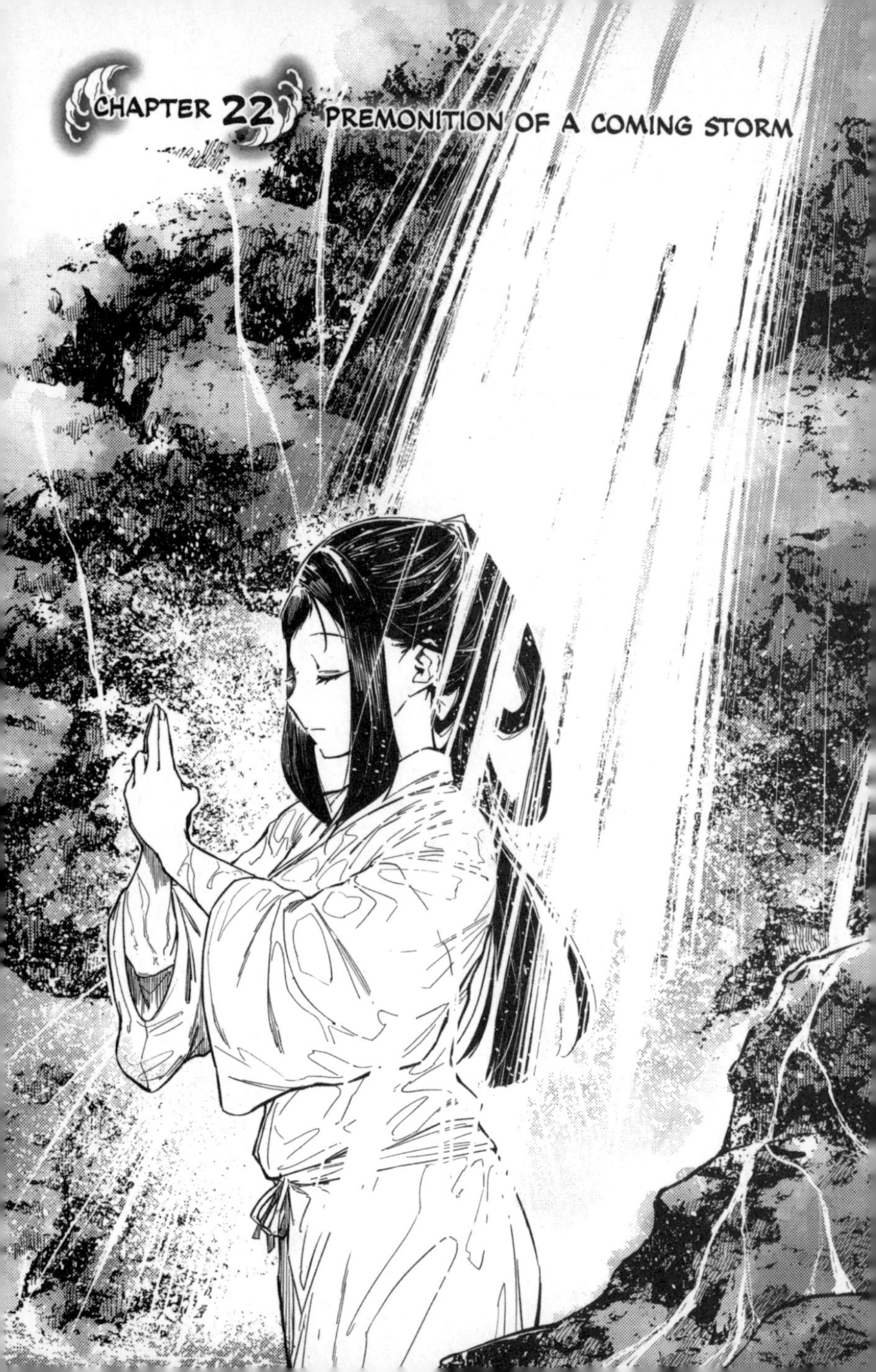
CHAPTER 22
PREMONITION OF A COMING STORM

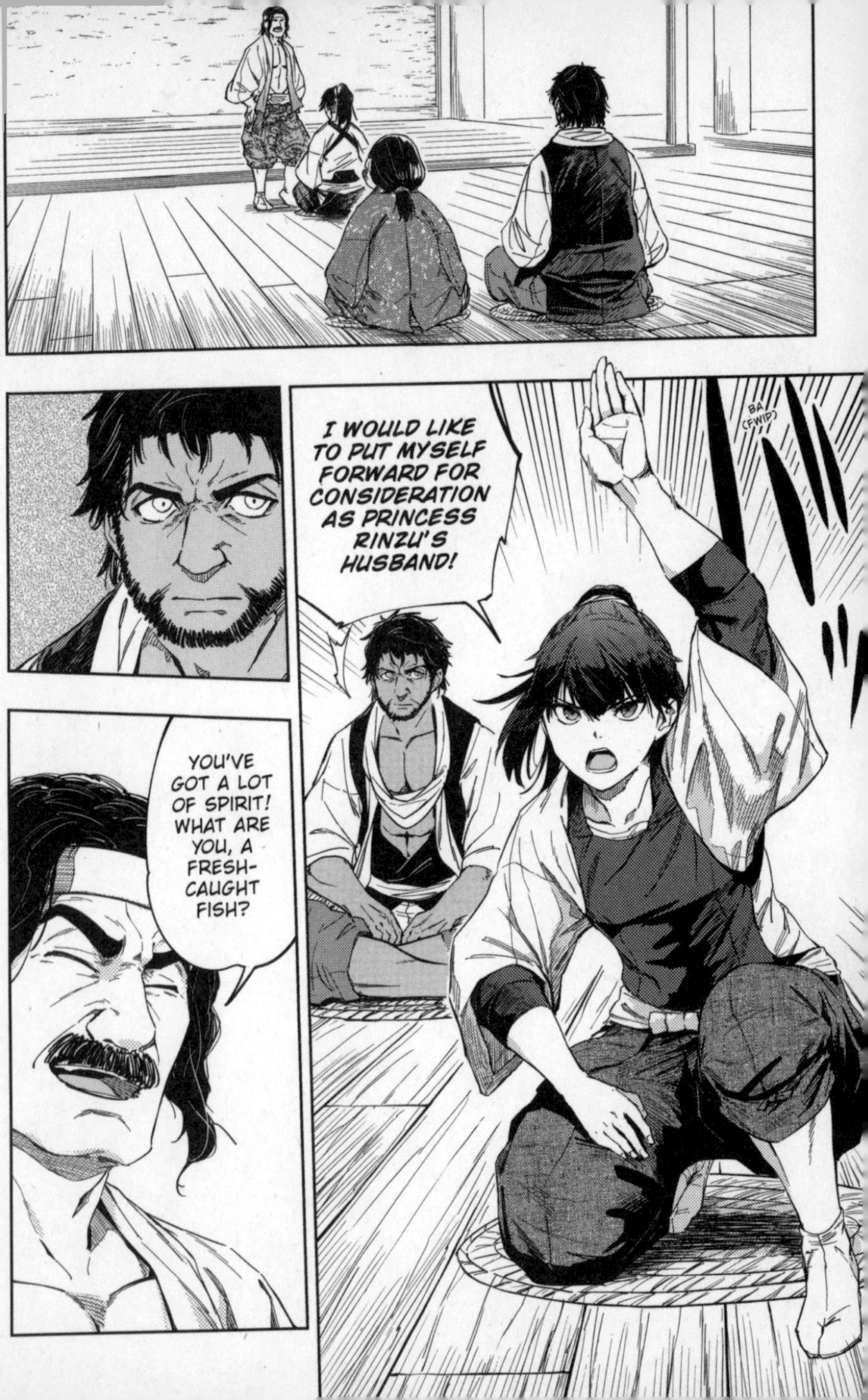
BA (FWIP)
I WOULD LIKE TO PUT MYSELF FORWARD FOR CONSIDERATION AS PRINCESS RINZU'S HUSBAND!
YOU'VE GOT A LOT OF SPIRIT! WHAT ARE YOU, A FRESH-CAUGHT FISH?

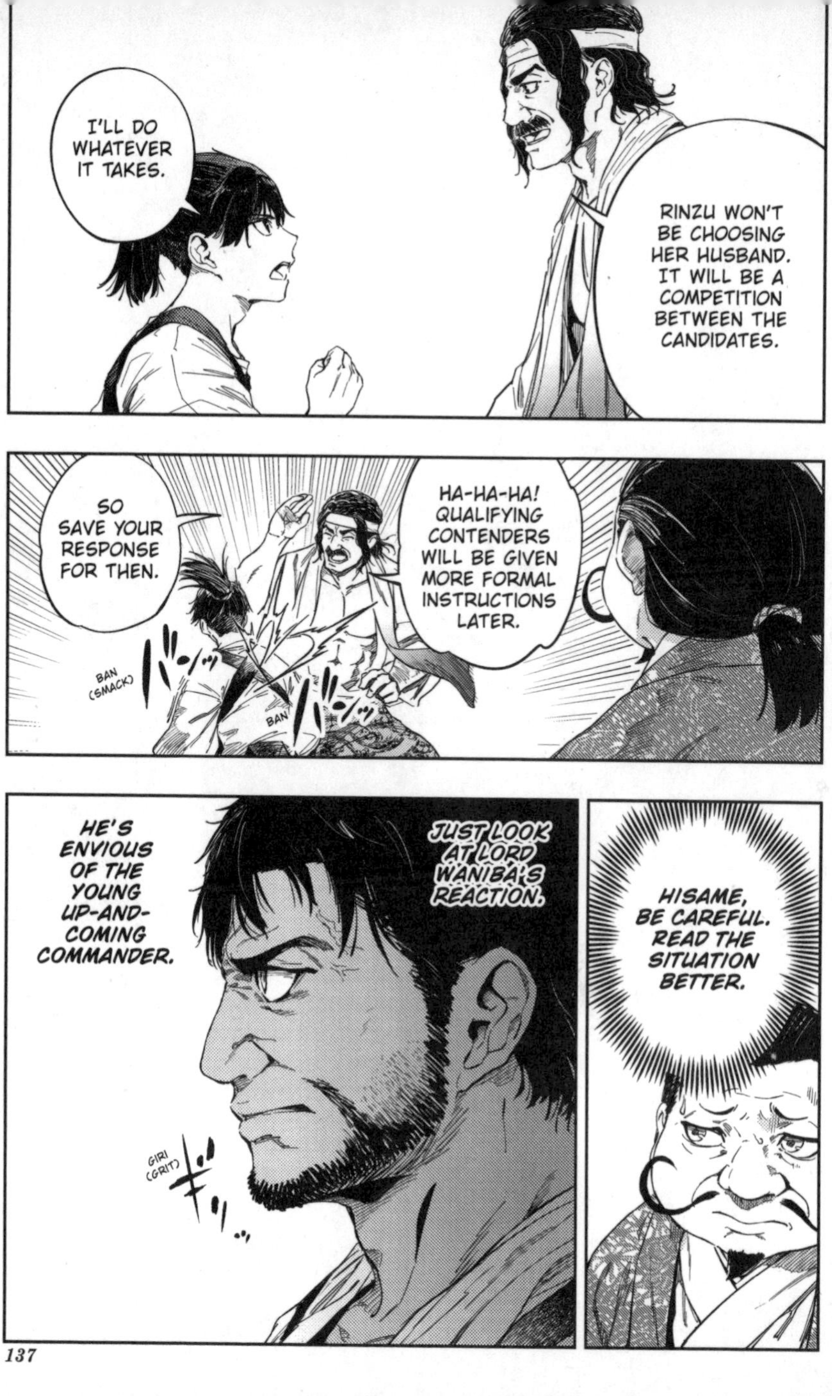
RINZU WON'T BE CHOOSING HER HUSBAND. IT WILL BE A COMPETITION BETWEEN THE CANDIDATES.
I'LL DO WHATEVER IT TAKES.
HA-HA-HA! QUALIFYING CONTENDERS WILL BE GIVEN MORE FORMAL INSTRUCTIONS LATER.
SO SAVE YOUR RESPONSE FOR THEN.
BAN (SMACK)
BAN
HISAME, BE CAREFUL. READ THE SITUATION BETTER.
JUST LOOK AT LORD WANIBA'S REACTION.
HE'S ENVIOUS OF THE YOUNG UP-AND-COMING COMMANDER.
GIRI (GRIT)

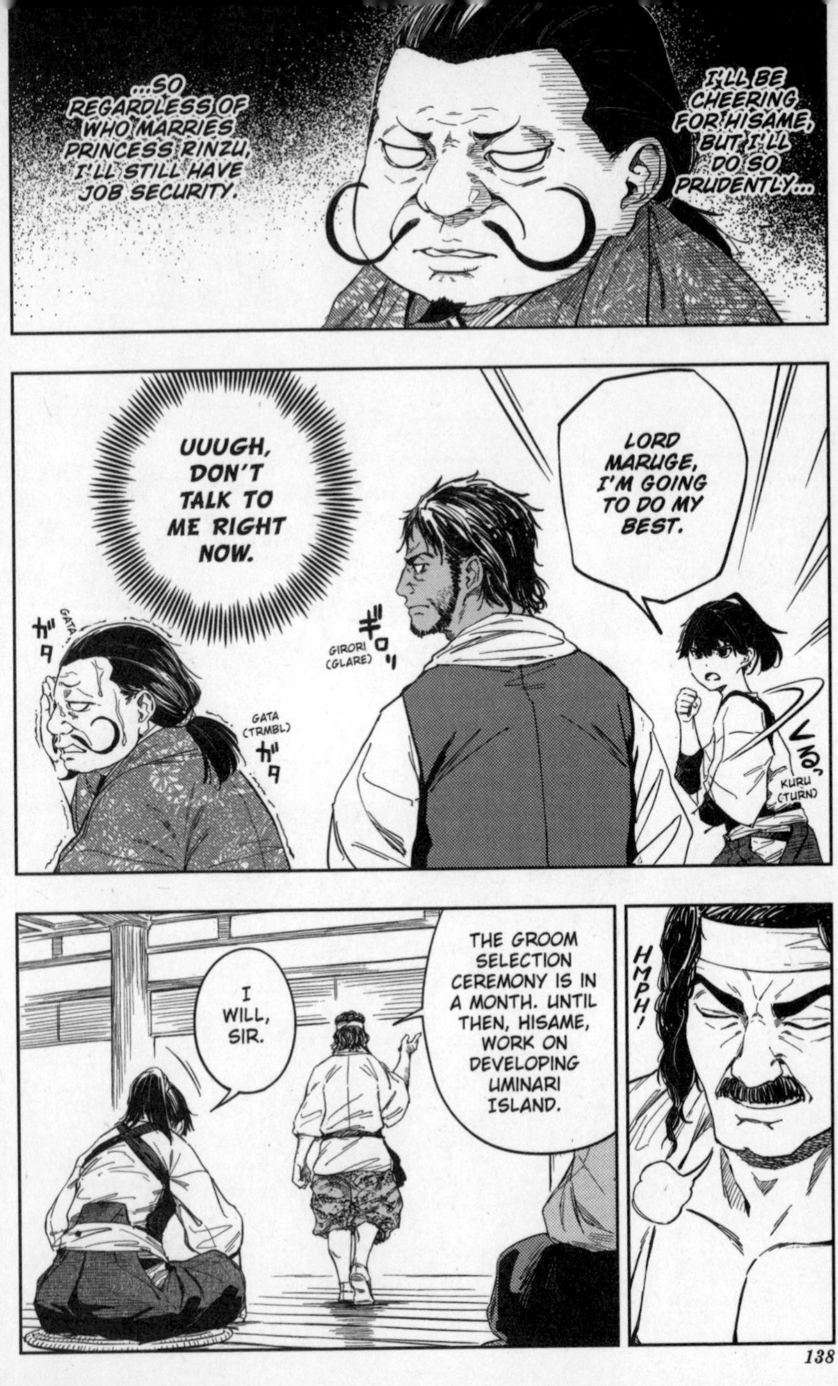
I'LL BE CHEERING FOR HISAME, BUT I'LL DO SO PRUDENTLY...
...SO REGARDLESS OF WHO MARRIES PRINCESS RINZU, I'LL STILL HAVE JOB SECURITY.
LORD MARUGE, I'M GOING TO DO MY BEST.
KURU (TURN)
GIRORI (GLARE)
UUUGH, DON'T TALK TO ME RIGHT NOW.
GATA
GATA (TRMBL)
HMPH!
THE GROOM SELECTION CEREMONY IS IN A MONTH. UNTIL THEN, HISAME, WORK ON DEVELOPING UMINARI ISLAND.
I WILL, SIR.

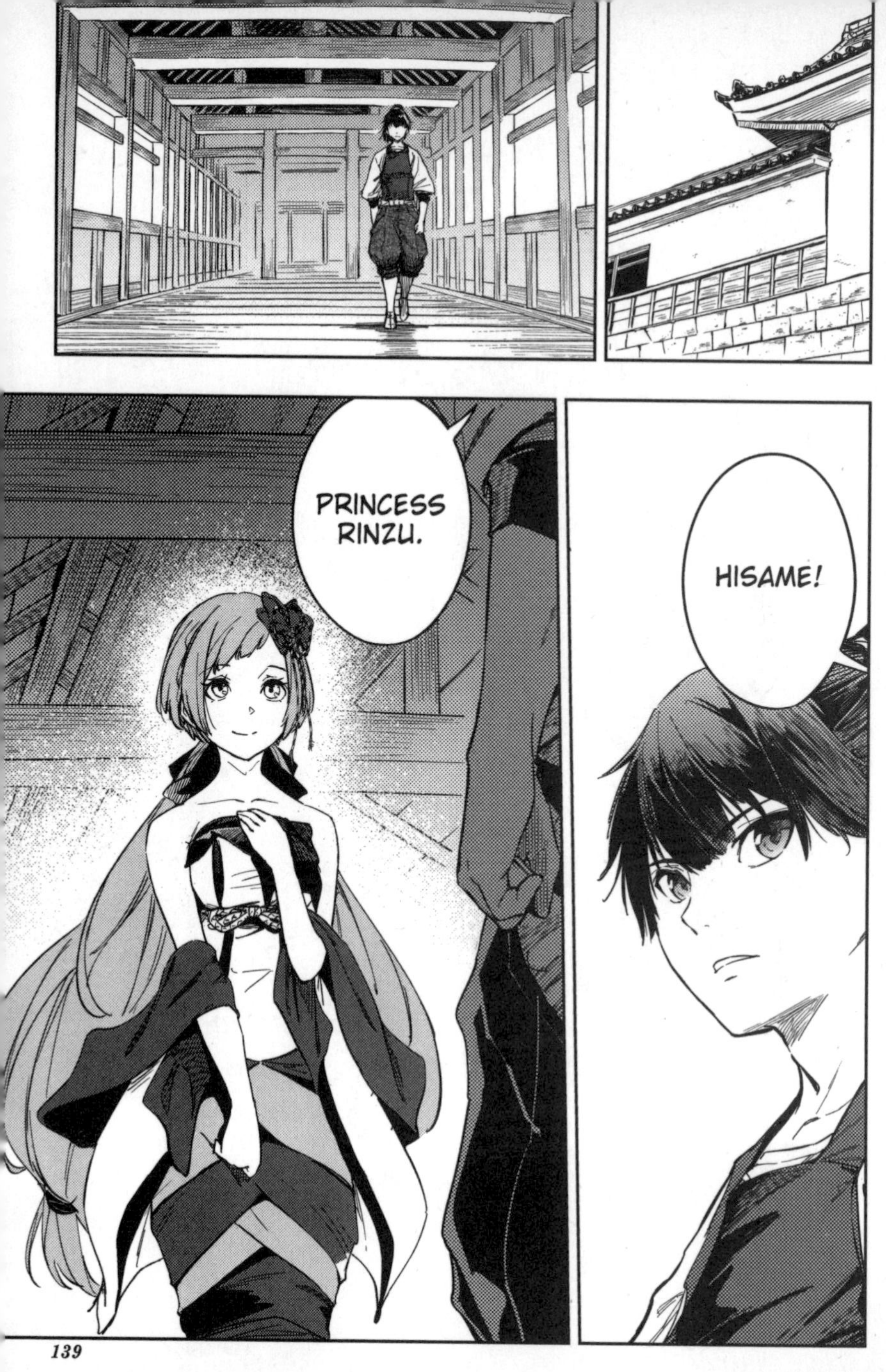
HISAME!
PRINCESS RINZU.

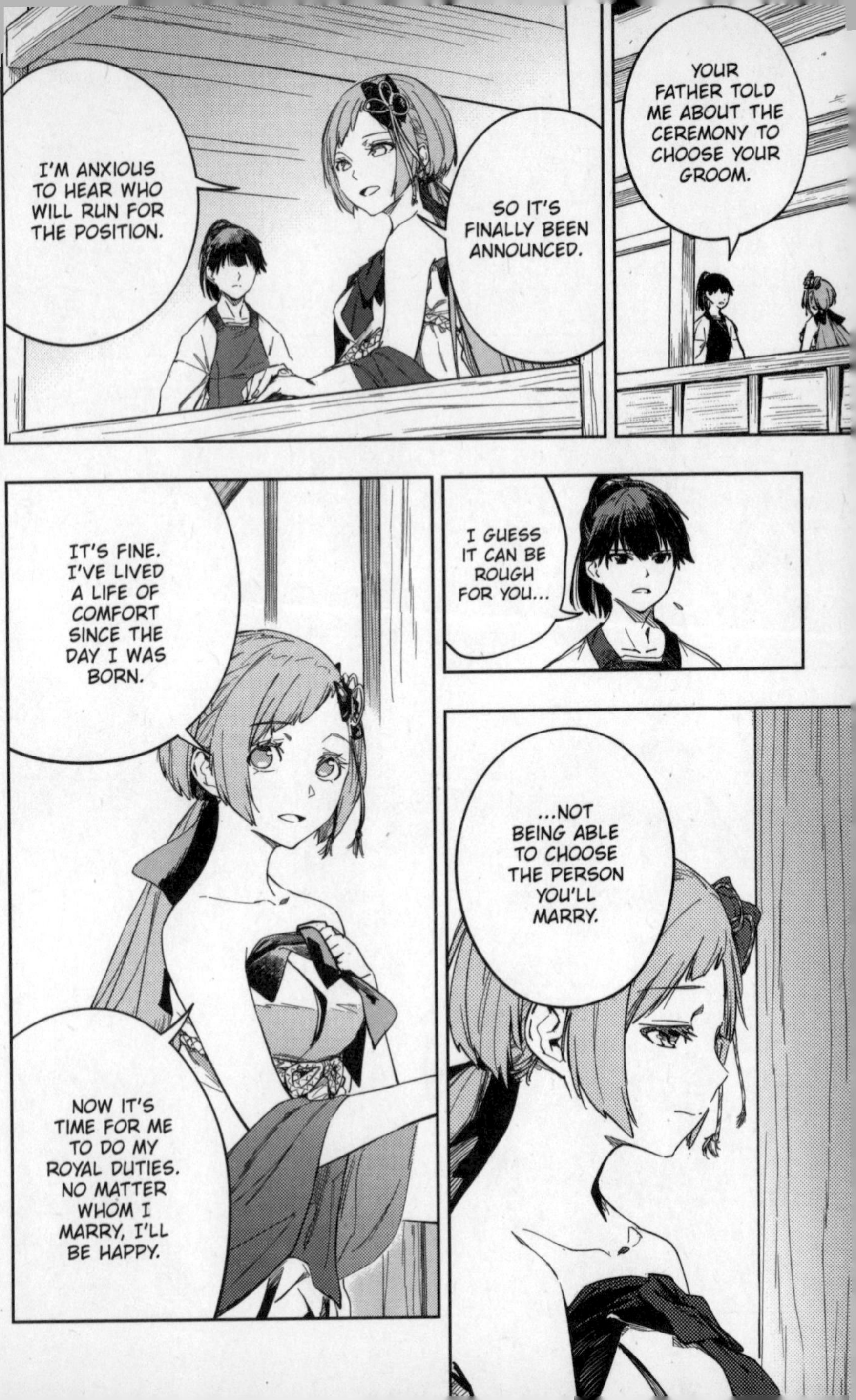
YOUR FATHER TOLD ME ABOUT THE CEREMONY TO CHOOSE YOUR GROOM.
SO IT'S FINALLY BEEN ANNOUNCED.
I'M ANXIOUS TO HEAR WHO WILL RUN FOR THE POSITION.
I GUESS IT CAN BE ROUGH FOR YOU...
...NOT BEING ABLE TO CHOOSE THE PERSON YOU'LL MARRY.
IT'S FINE. I'VE LIVED A LIFE OF COMFORT SINCE THE DAY I WAS BORN.
NOW IT'S TIME FOR ME TO DO MY ROYAL DUTIES. NO MATTER WHOM I MARRY, I'LL BE HAPPY.

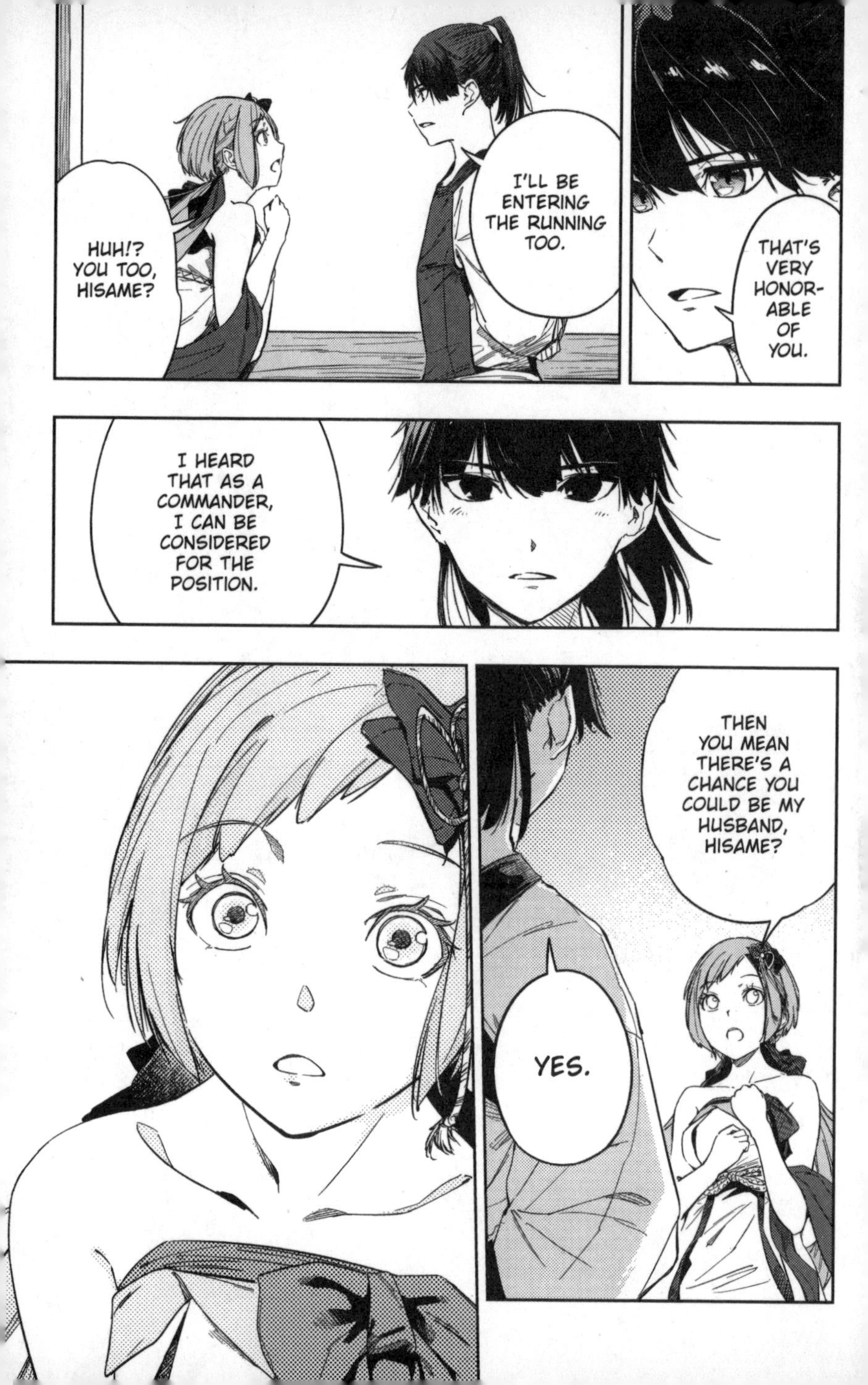
THAT'S VERY HONOR-ABLE OF YOU.
I'LL BE ENTERING THE RUNNING TOO.
HUH!? YOU TOO, HISAME?
I HEARD THAT AS A COMMANDER, I CAN BE CONSIDERED FOR THE POSITION.
THEN YOU MEAN THERE'S A CHANCE YOU COULD BE MY HUSBAND, HISAME?
YES.

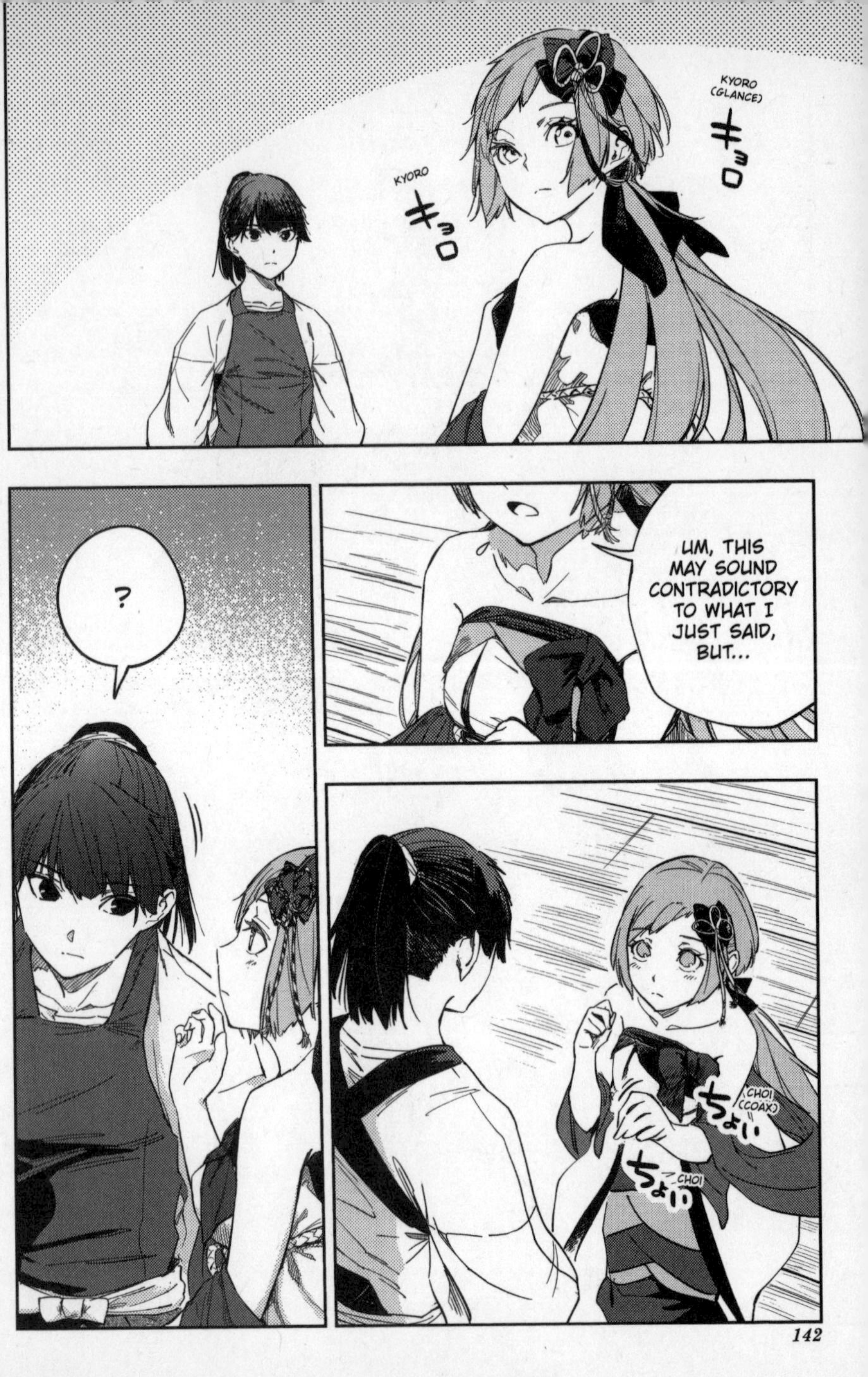
KYORO (GLANCE)
キョロ
KYORO
キョロ
UM, THIS MAY SOUND CONTRADICTORY TO WHAT I JUST SAID, BUT...
ちょい
CHOI (COAX)
ちょい
CHOI
?

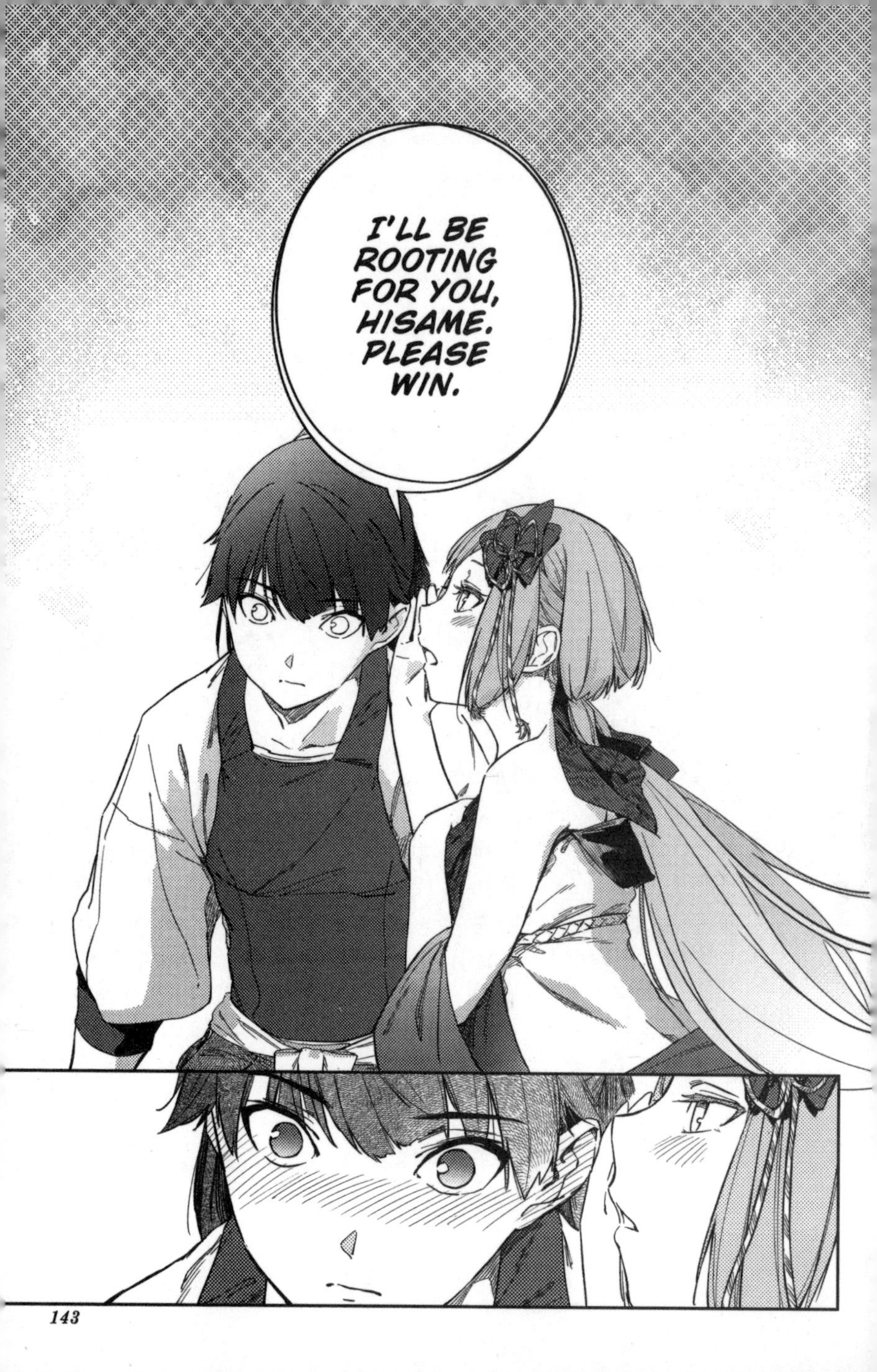
I'LL BE ROOTING FOR YOU, HISAME. PLEASE WIN.

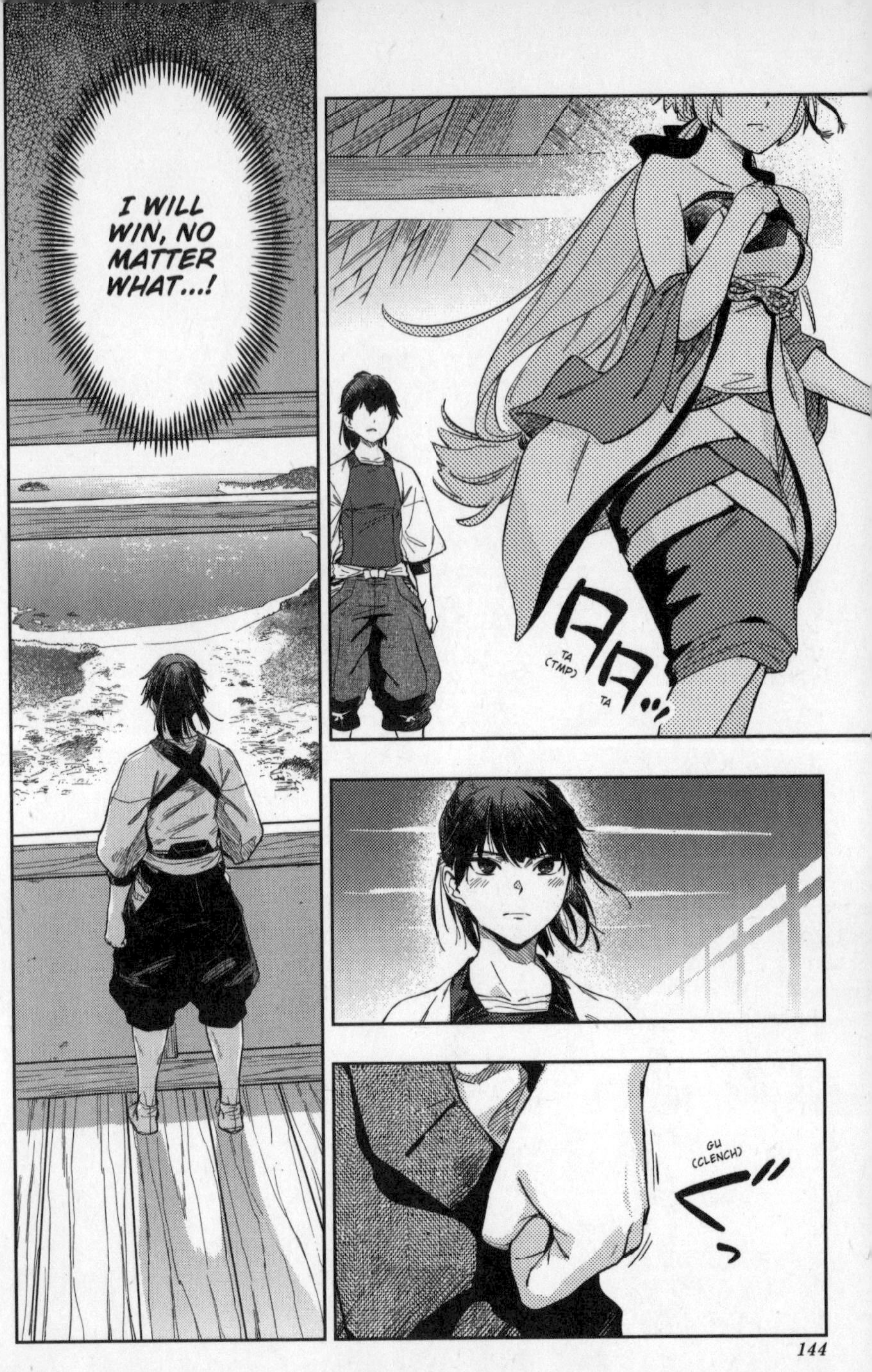
TA (TMP) TA
GU (CLENCH)
I WILL WIN, NO MATTER WHAT...!

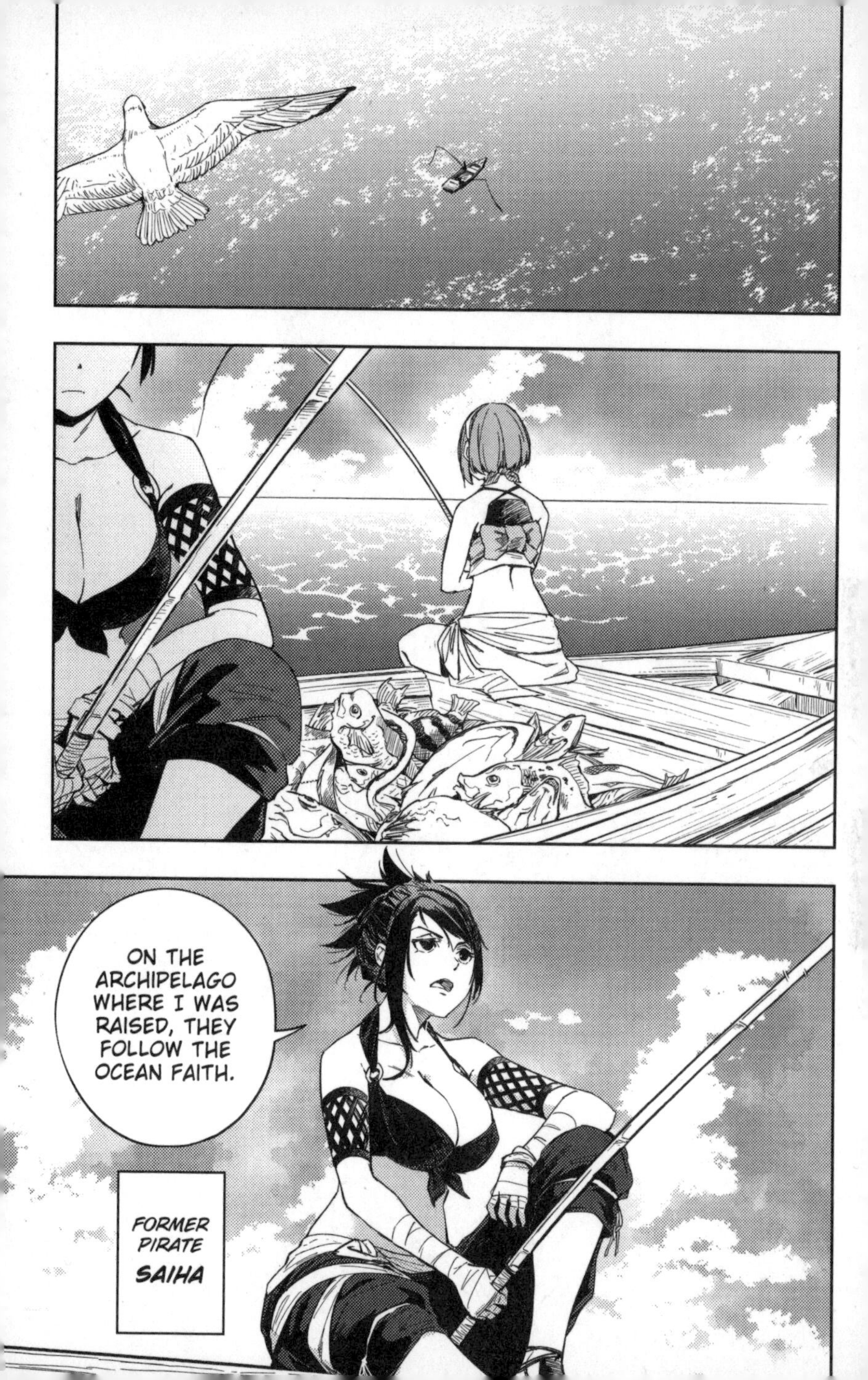
ON THE ARCHIPELAGO WHERE I WAS RAISED, THEY FOLLOW THE OCEAN FAITH.
FORMER PIRATE SAIHA

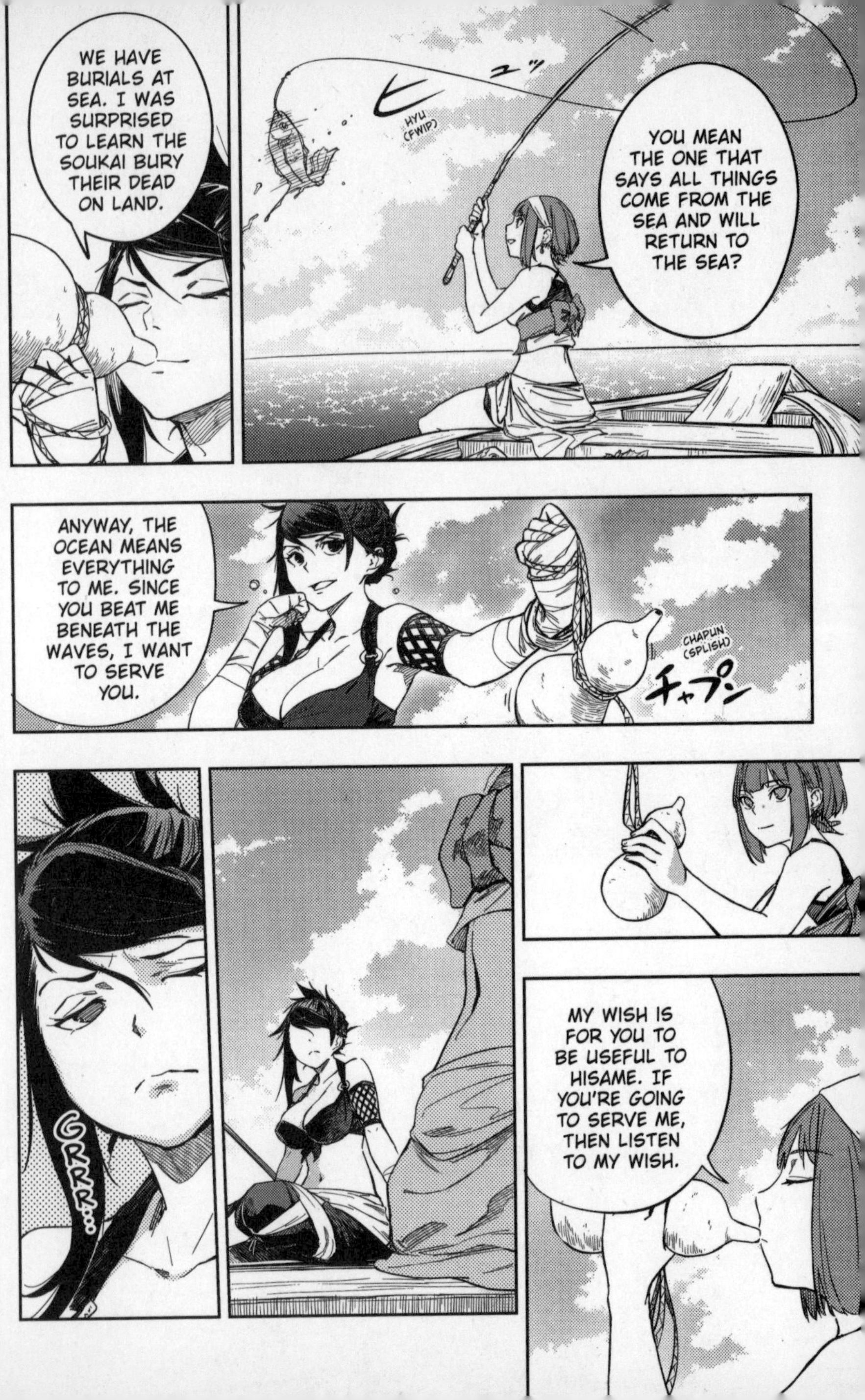

YOU MEAN THE ONE THAT SAYS ALL THINGS COME FROM THE SEA AND WILL RETURN TO THE SEA?
ヒュッ
HYU (FWIP)
WE HAVE BURIALS AT SEA. I WAS SURPRISED TO LEARN THE SOUKAI BURY THEIR DEAD ON LAND.
CHAPUN (SPLISH)
チャプン
ANYWAY, THE OCEAN MEANS EVERYTHING TO ME. SINCE YOU BEAT ME BENEATH THE WAVES, I WANT TO SERVE YOU.
MY WISH IS FOR YOU TO BE USEFUL TO HISAME. IF YOU'RE GOING TO SERVE ME, THEN LISTEN TO MY WISH.
GRRR...

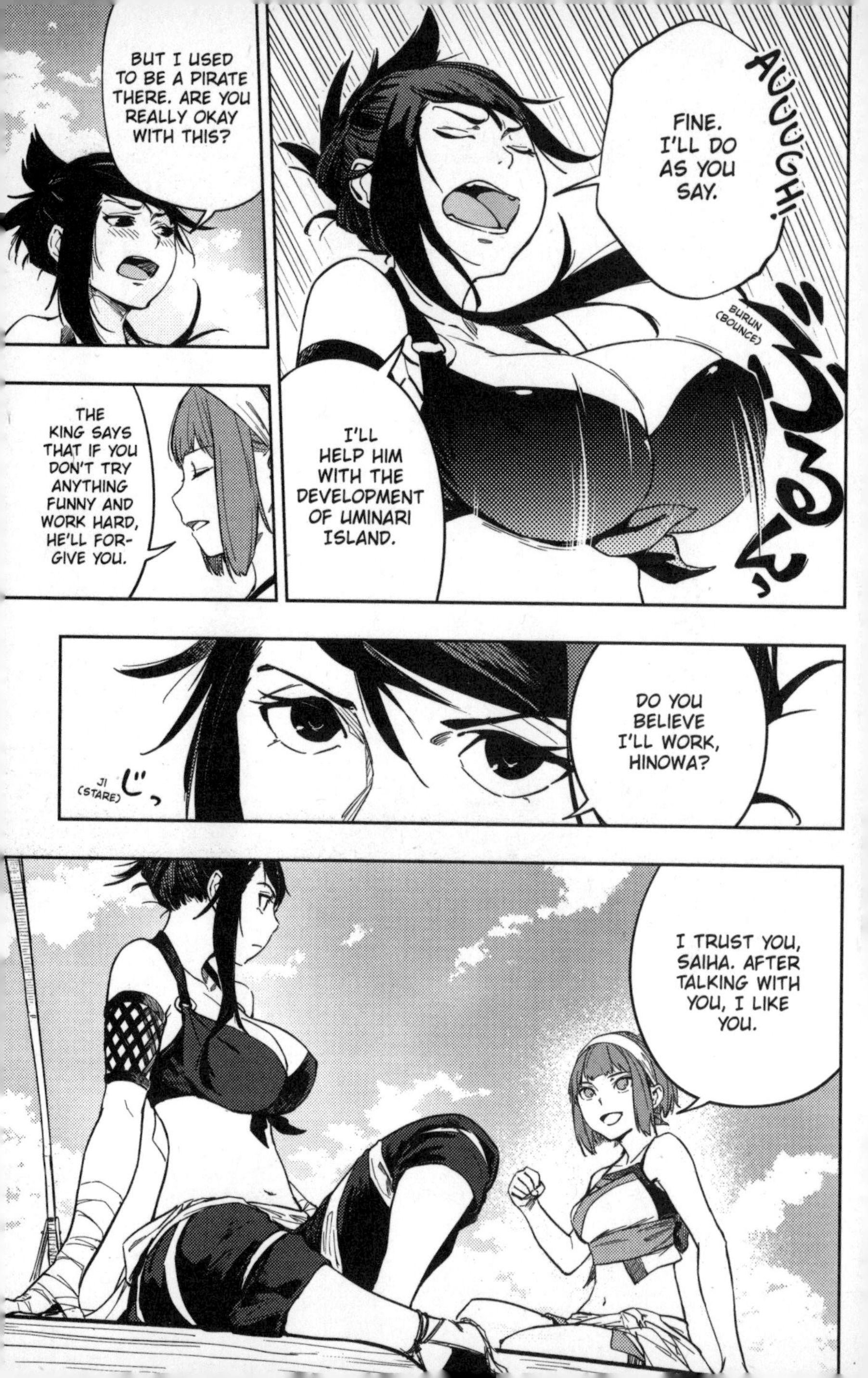
AUUUGH!
FINE. I'LL DO AS YOU SAY.
BURUN (BOUNCE)
I'LL HELP HIM WITH THE DEVELOPMENT OF UMINARI ISLAND.
BUT I USED TO BE A PIRATE THERE. ARE YOU REALLY OKAY WITH THIS?
THE KING SAYS THAT IF YOU DON'T TRY ANYTHING FUNNY AND WORK HARD, HE'LL FOR-GIVE YOU.
DO YOU BELIEVE I'LL WORK, HINOWA?
JI (STARE)
I TRUST YOU, SAIHA. AFTER TALKING WITH YOU, I LIKE YOU.

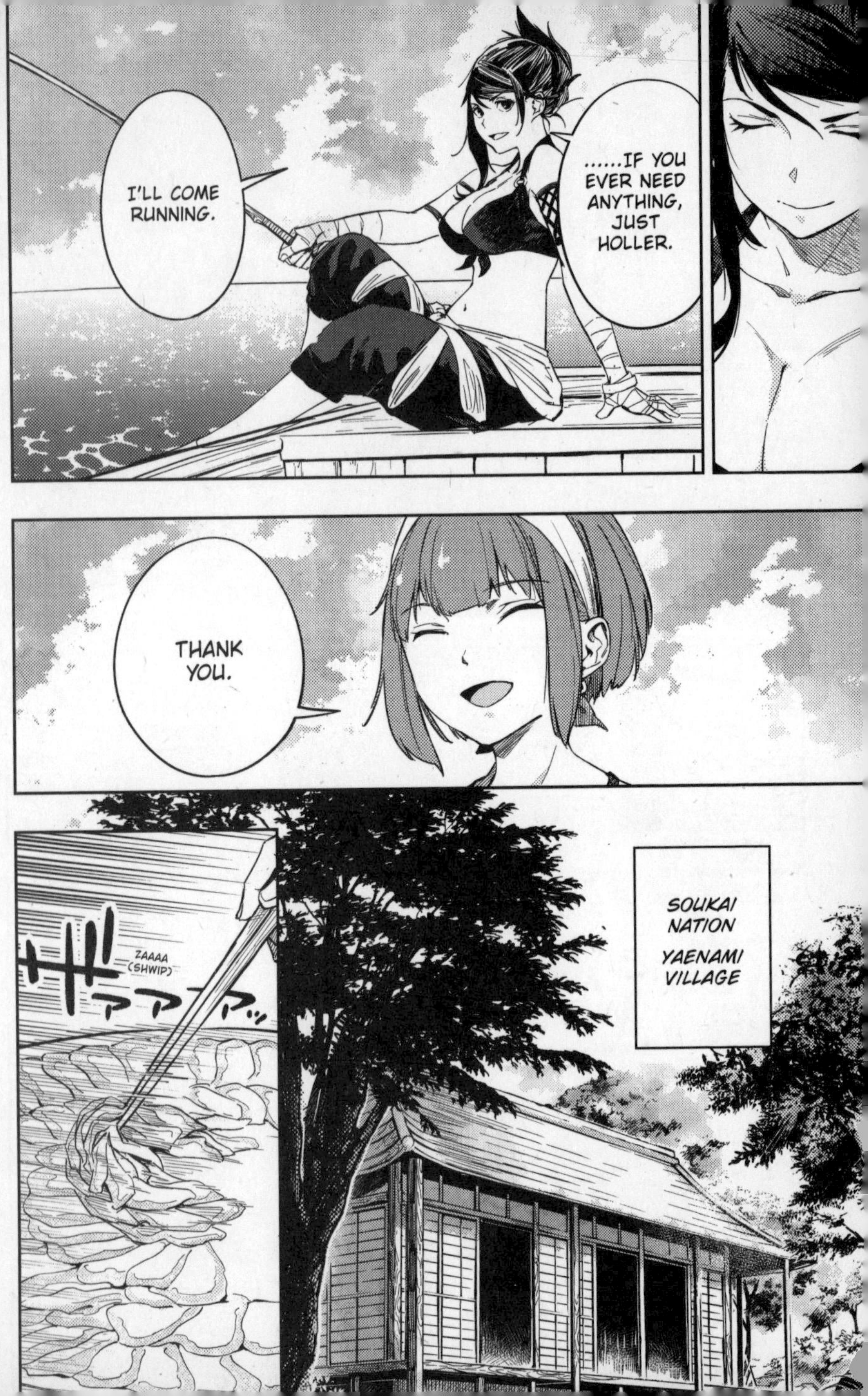
......IF YOU EVER NEED ANYTHING, JUST HOLLER.
I'LL COME RUNNING.
THANK YOU.
SOUKAI NATION
YAENAMI VILLAGE
ザァァァッ
ZAAAA (SHWIP)

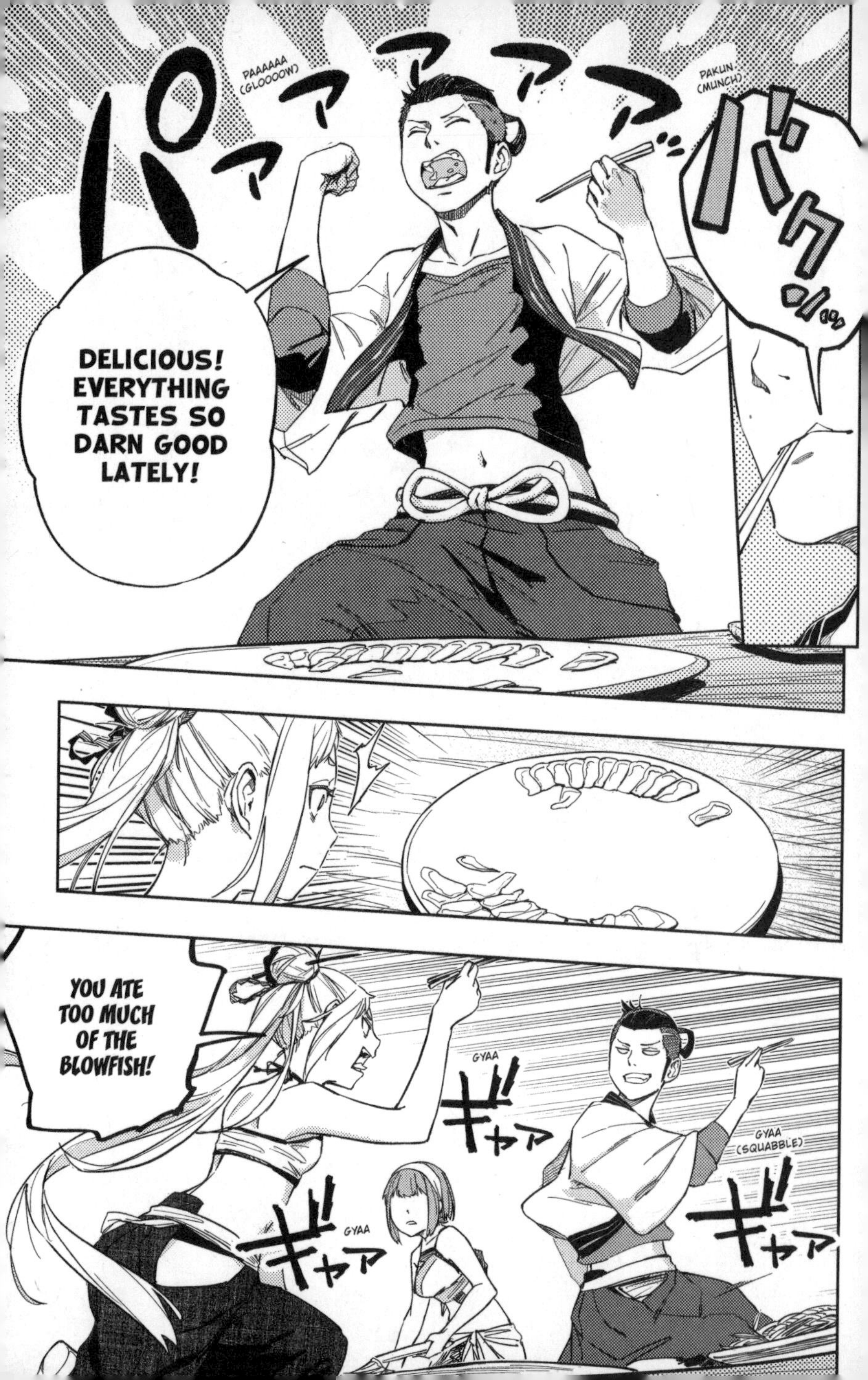
PAKUN (MUNCH)
PAAAAAA (GLOOOOW)
DELICIOUS! EVERYTHING TASTES SO DARN GOOD LATELY!
YOU ATE TOO MUCH OF THE BLOWFISH!
GYAA
GYAA (SQUABBLE)
GYAA

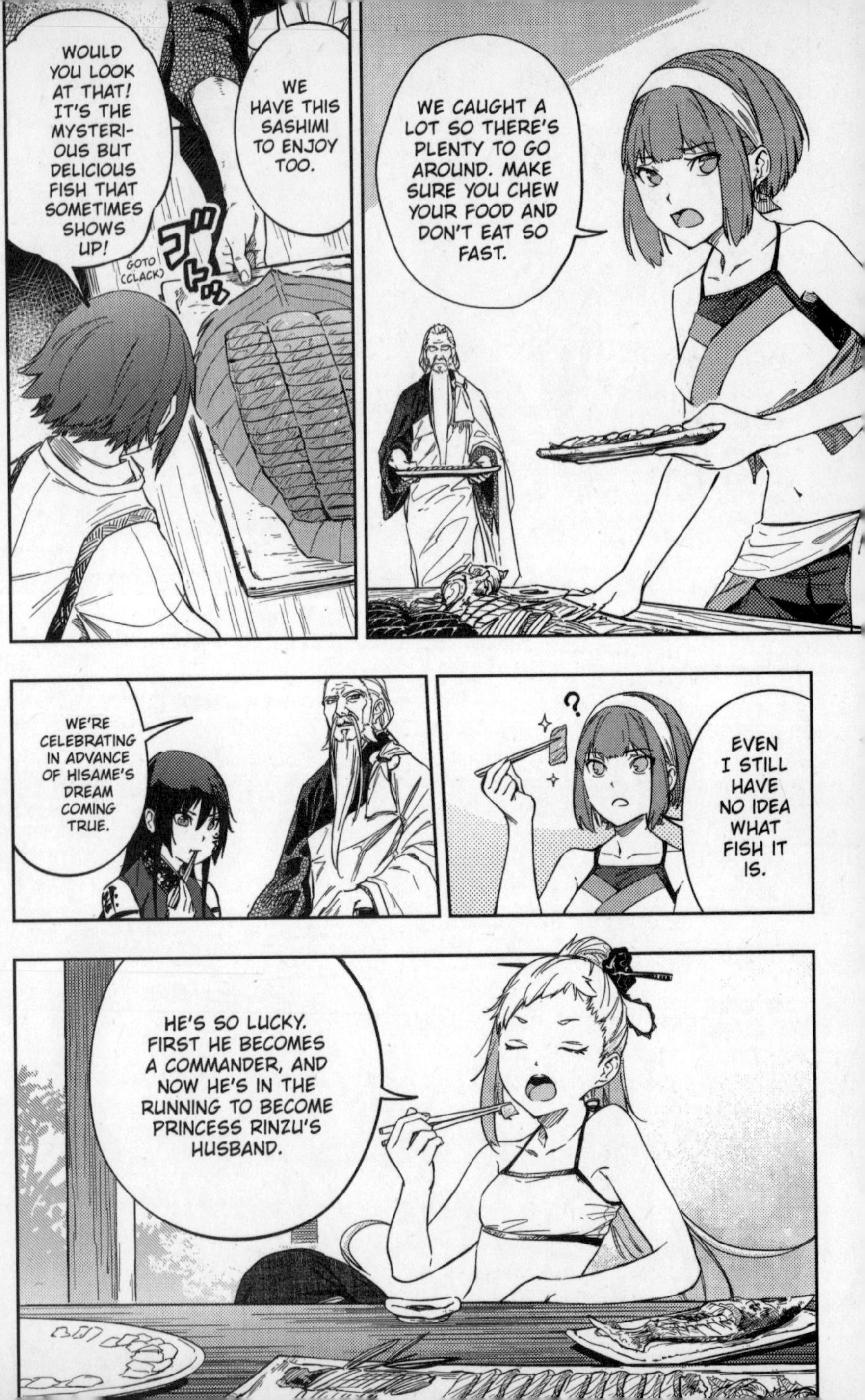
WE CAUGHT A LOT SO THERE'S PLENTY TO GO AROUND. MAKE SURE YOU CHEW YOUR FOOD AND DON'T EAT SO FAST.
WE HAVE THIS SASHIMI TO ENJOY TOO.
WOULD YOU LOOK AT THAT! IT'S THE MYSTERIOUS BUT DELICIOUS FISH THAT SOMETIMES SHOWS UP!
GOTO (CLACK)
EVEN I STILL HAVE NO IDEA WHAT FISH IT IS.
WE'RE CELEBRATING IN ADVANCE OF HISAME'S DREAM COMING TRUE.
HE'S SO LUCKY. FIRST HE BECOMES A COMMANDER, AND NOW HE'S IN THE RUNNING TO BECOME PRINCESS RINZU'S HUSBAND.

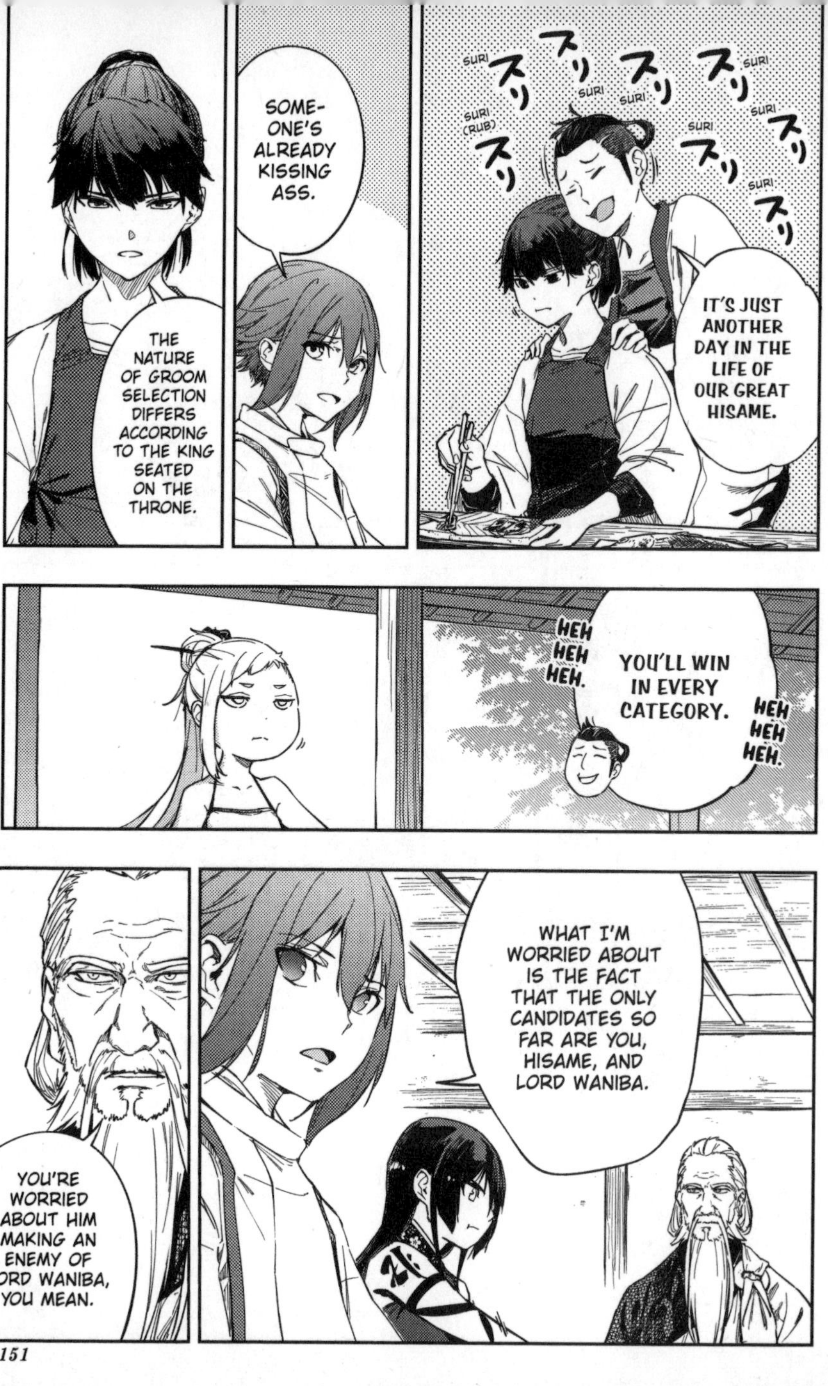
スリ SURI (RUB)
スリ SURI
スリ SURI
スリ SURI
スリ SURI
スリ SURI
スリ SURI
IT'S JUST ANOTHER DAY IN THE LIFE OF OUR GREAT HISAME.
SOME-ONE'S ALREADY KISSING ASS.
THE NATURE OF GROOM SELECTION DIFFERS ACCORDING TO THE KING SEATED ON THE THRONE.
HEH HEH HEH.
YOU'LL WIN IN EVERY CATEGORY.
HEH HEH HEH.
WHAT I'M WORRIED ABOUT IS THE FACT THAT THE ONLY CANDIDATES SO FAR ARE YOU, HISAME, AND LORD WANIBA.
YOU'RE WORRIED ABOUT HIM MAKING AN ENEMY OF LORD WANIBA, YOU MEAN.

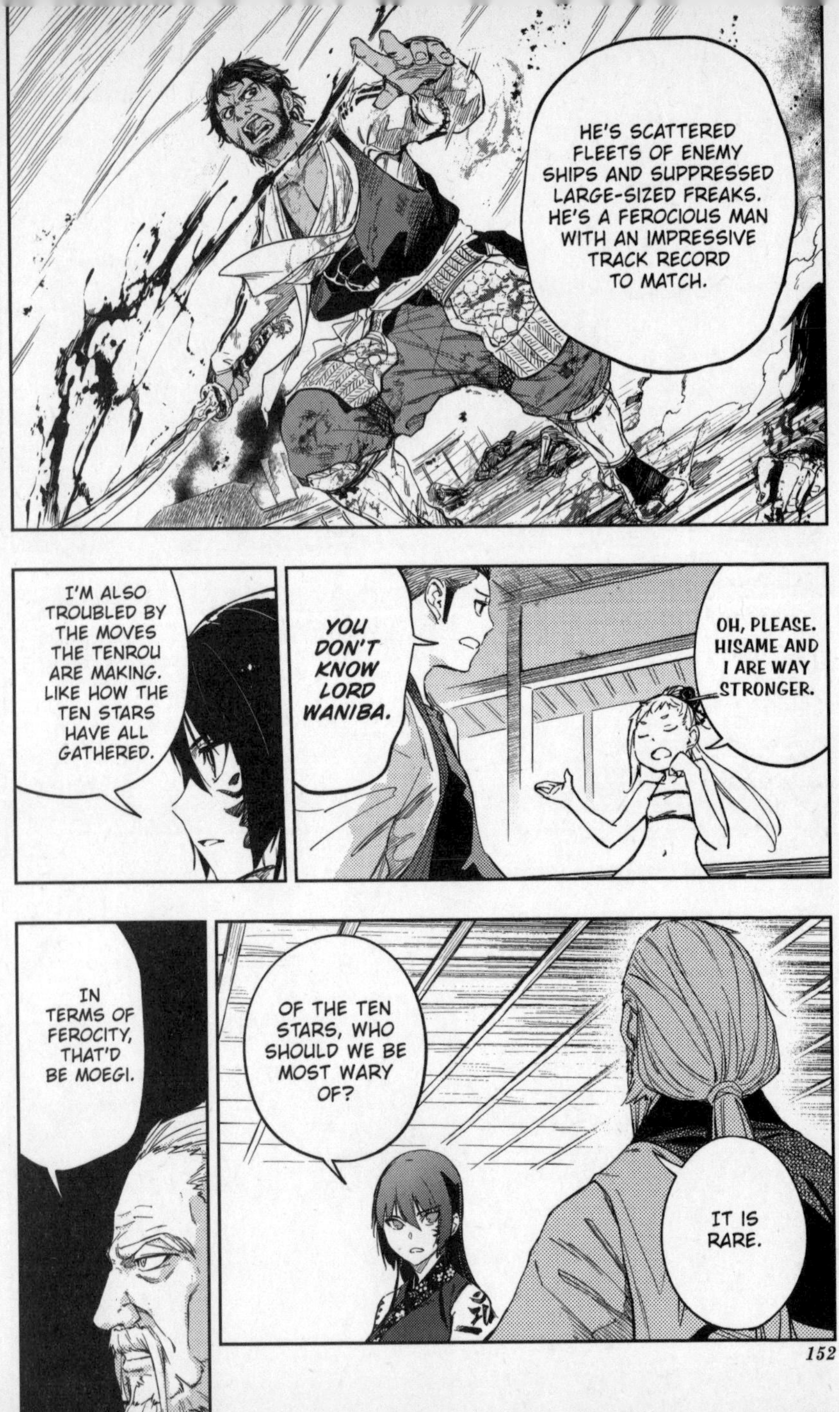
HE'S SCATTERED FLEETS OF ENEMY SHIPS AND SUPPRESSED LARGE-SIZED FREAKS. HE'S A FEROCIOUS MAN WITH AN IMPRESSIVE TRACK RECORD TO MATCH.
OH, PLEASE. HISAME AND I ARE WAY STRONGER.
YOU DON'T KNOW LORD WANIBA.
I'M ALSO TROUBLED BY THE MOVES THE TENROU ARE MAKING. LIKE HOW THE TEN STARS HAVE ALL GATHERED.
IT IS RARE.
OF THE TEN STARS, WHO SHOULD WE BE MOST WARY OF?
IN TERMS OF FEROCITY, THAT'D BE MOEGI.

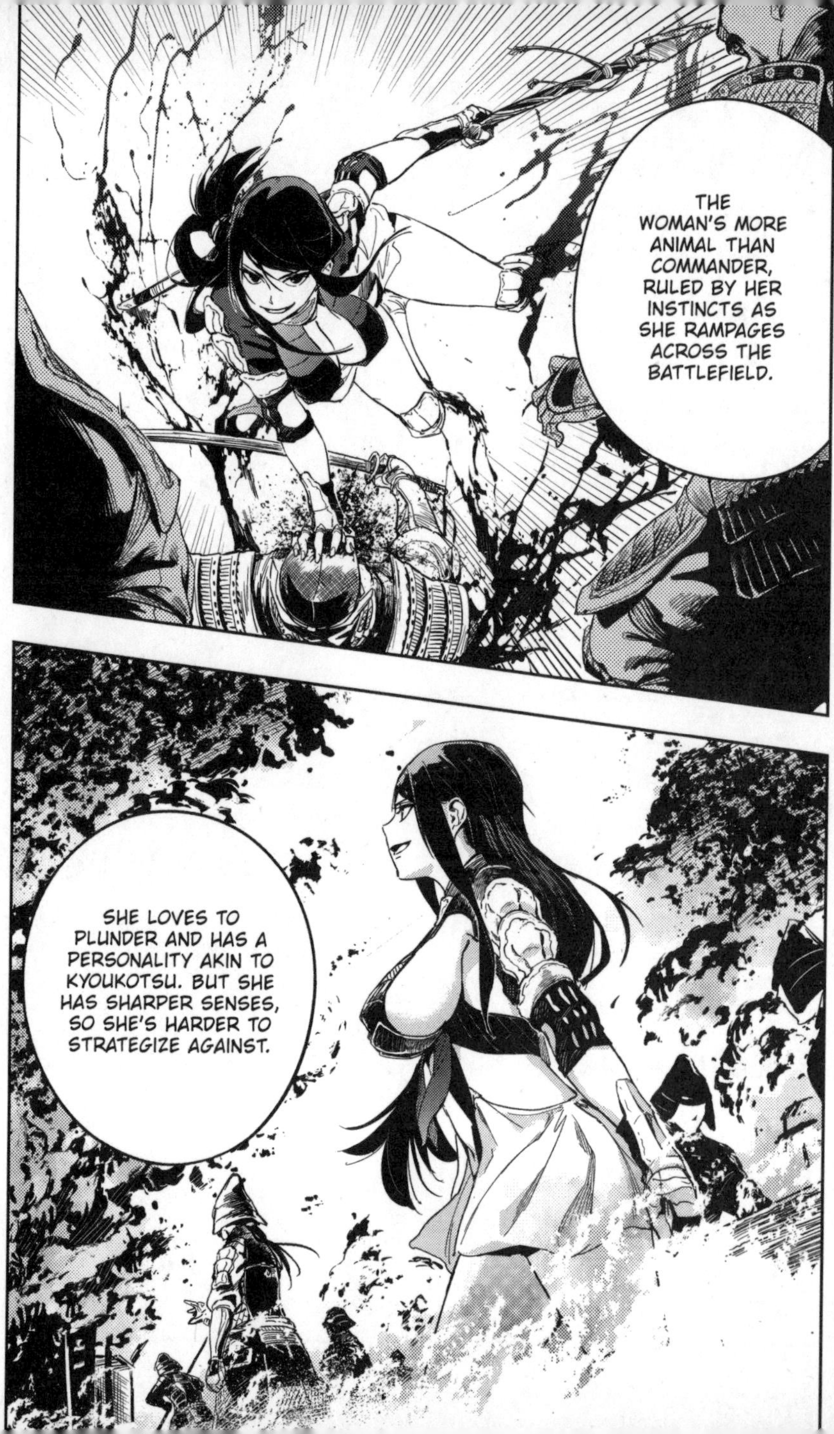
THE WOMAN'S MORE ANIMAL THAN COMMANDER, RULED BY HER INSTINCTS AS SHE RAMPAGES ACROSS THE BATTLEFIELD.
SHE LOVES TO PLUNDER AND HAS A PERSONALITY AKIN TO KYOUKOTSU. BUT SHE HAS SHARPER SENSES, SO SHE'S HARDER TO STRATEGIZE AGAINST.

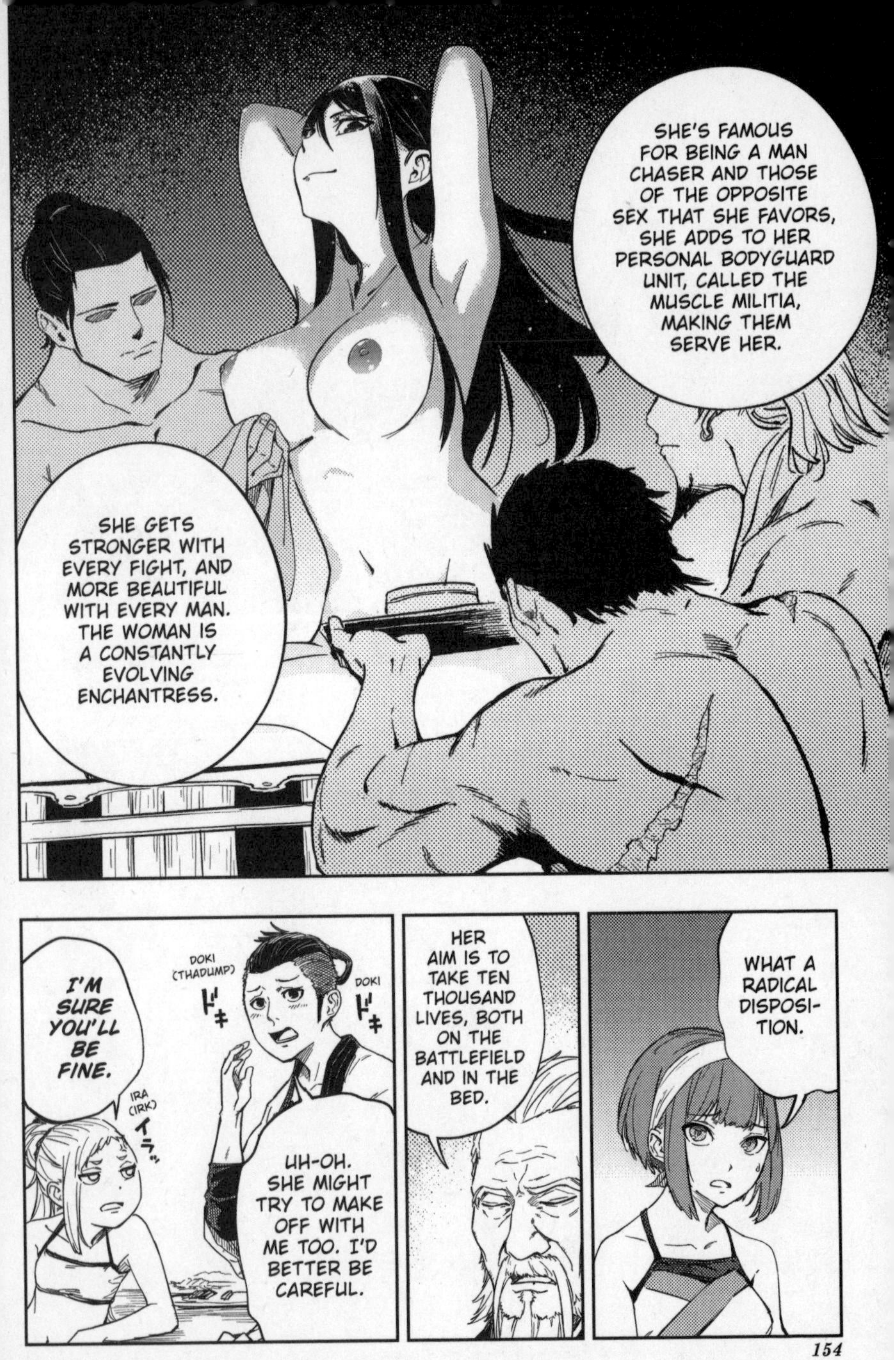
SHE'S FAMOUS FOR BEING A MAN CHASER AND THOSE OF THE OPPOSITE SEX THAT SHE FAVORS, SHE ADDS TO HER PERSONAL BODYGUARD UNIT, CALLED THE MUSCLE MILITIA, MAKING THEM SERVE HER.
SHE GETS STRONGER WITH EVERY FIGHT, AND MORE BEAUTIFUL WITH EVERY MAN. THE WOMAN IS A CONSTANTLY EVOLVING ENCHANTRESS.
WHAT A RADICAL DISPOSITION.
HER AIM IS TO TAKE TEN THOUSAND LIVES, BOTH ON THE BATTLEFIELD AND IN THE BED.
DOKI
ドキ
DOKI (THADUMP)
ドキ
UH-OH. SHE MIGHT TRY TO MAKE OFF WITH ME TOO. I'D BETTER BE CAREFUL.
I'M SURE YOU'LL BE FINE.
IRA (IRK)
イラッ

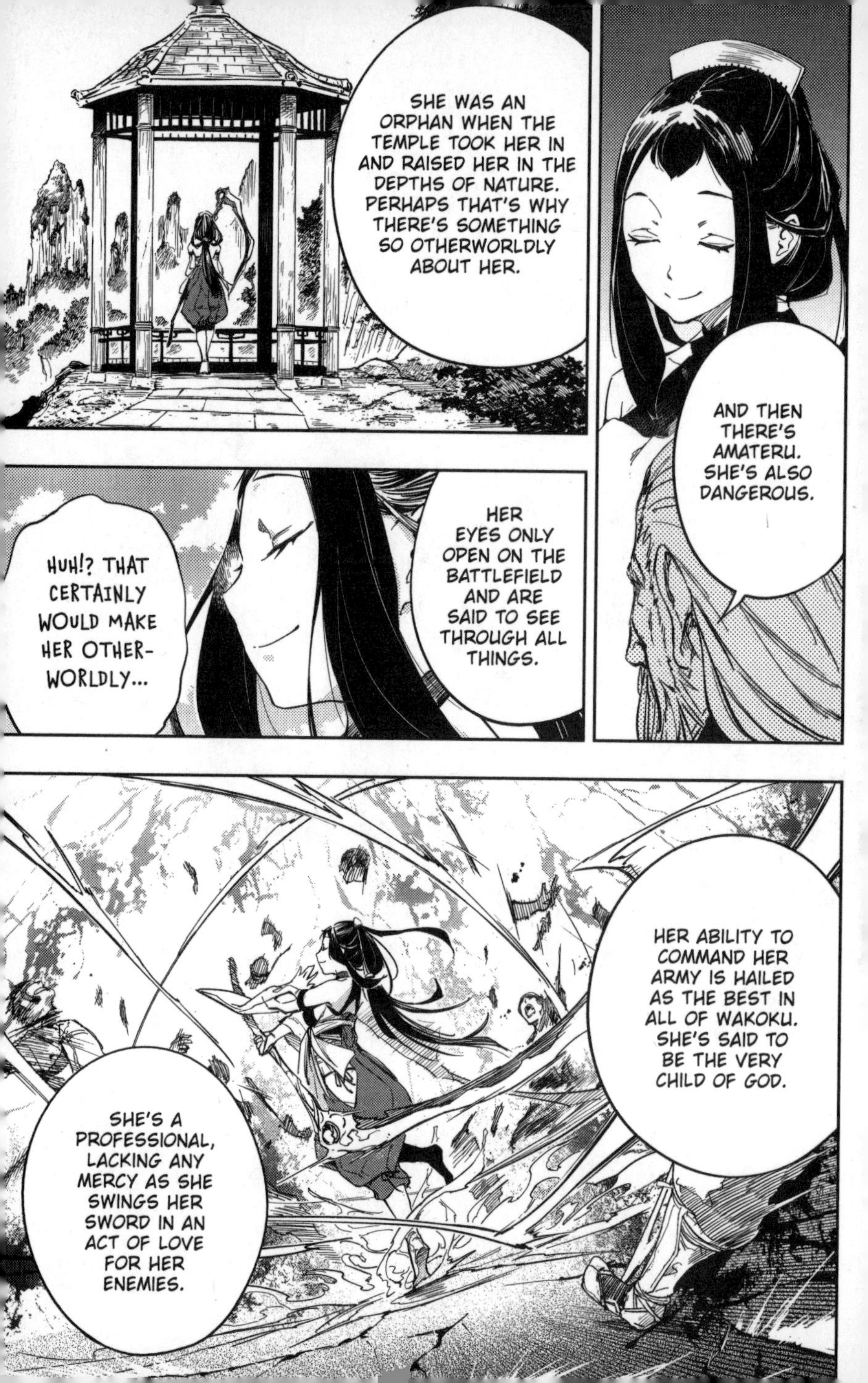
SHE WAS AN ORPHAN WHEN THE TEMPLE TOOK HER IN AND RAISED HER IN THE DEPTHS OF NATURE. PERHAPS THAT'S WHY THERE'S SOMETHING SO OTHERWORLDLY ABOUT HER.
HER EYES ONLY OPEN ON THE BATTLEFIELD AND ARE SAID TO SEE THROUGH ALL THINGS.
HUH!? THAT CERTAINLY WOULD MAKE HER OTHER-WORLDLY...
AND THEN THERE'S AMATERU. SHE'S ALSO DANGEROUS.
HER ABILITY TO COMMAND HER ARMY IS HAILED AS THE BEST IN ALL OF WAKOKU. SHE'S SAID TO BE THE VERY CHILD OF GOD.
SHE'S A PROFESSIONAL, LACKING ANY MERCY AS SHE SWINGS HER SWORD IN AN ACT OF LOVE FOR HER ENEMIES.

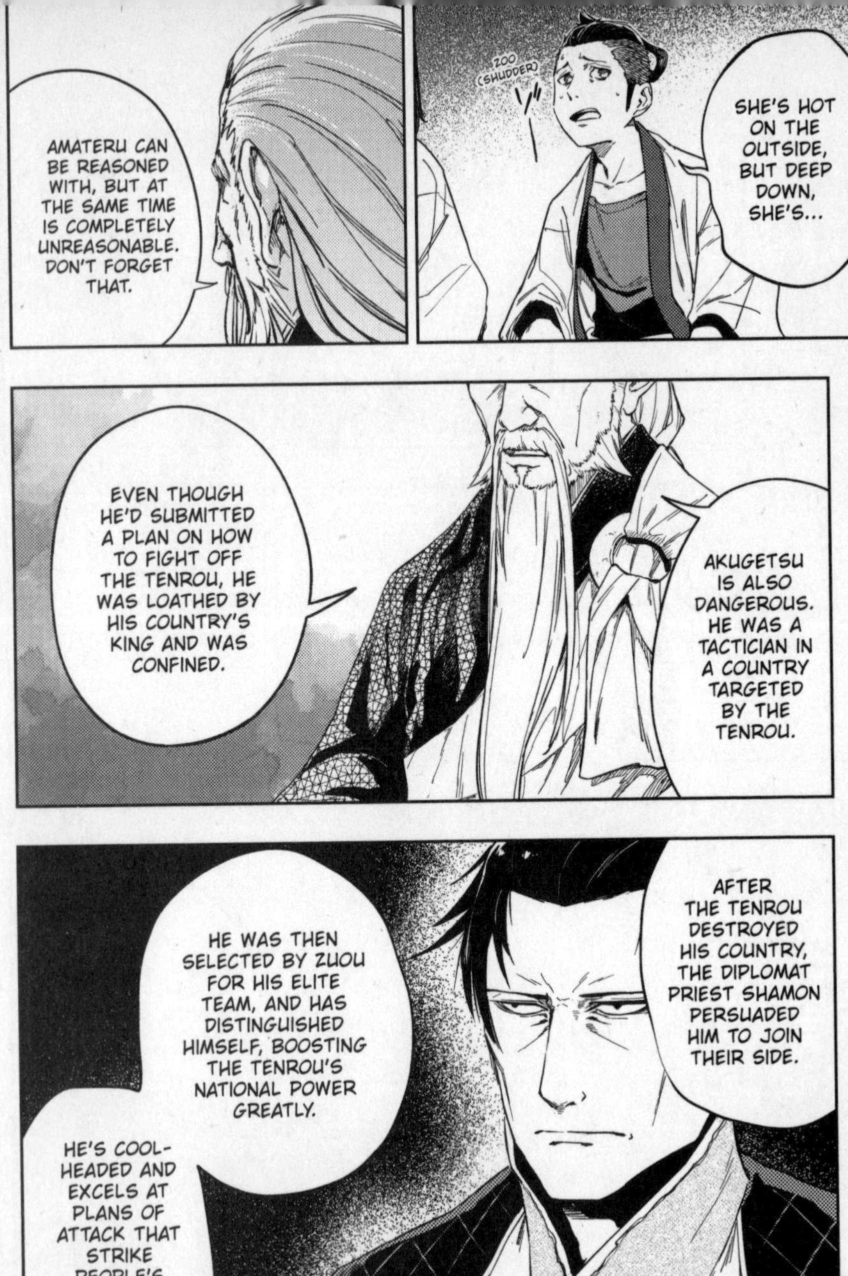
SHE'S HOT ON THE OUTSIDE, BUT DEEP DOWN, SHE'S...
ZOO (SHUDDER)
AMATERU CAN BE REASONED WITH, BUT AT THE SAME TIME IS COMPLETELY UNREASONABLE. DON'T FORGET THAT.
AKUGETSU IS ALSO DANGEROUS. HE WAS A TACTICIAN IN A COUNTRY TARGETED BY THE TENROU.
EVEN THOUGH HE'D SUBMITTED A PLAN ON HOW TO FIGHT OFF THE TENROU, HE WAS LOATHED BY HIS COUNTRY'S KING AND WAS CONFINED.
AFTER THE TENROU DESTROYED HIS COUNTRY, THE DIPLOMAT PRIEST SHAMON PERSUADED HIM TO JOIN THEIR SIDE.
HE WAS THEN SELECTED BY ZUOU FOR HIS ELITE TEAM, AND HAS DISTINGUISHED HIMSELF, BOOSTING THE TENROU'S NATIONAL POWER GREATLY.
HE'S COOL-HEADED AND EXCELS AT PLANS OF ATTACK THAT STRIKE PEOPLE'S HEARTS.

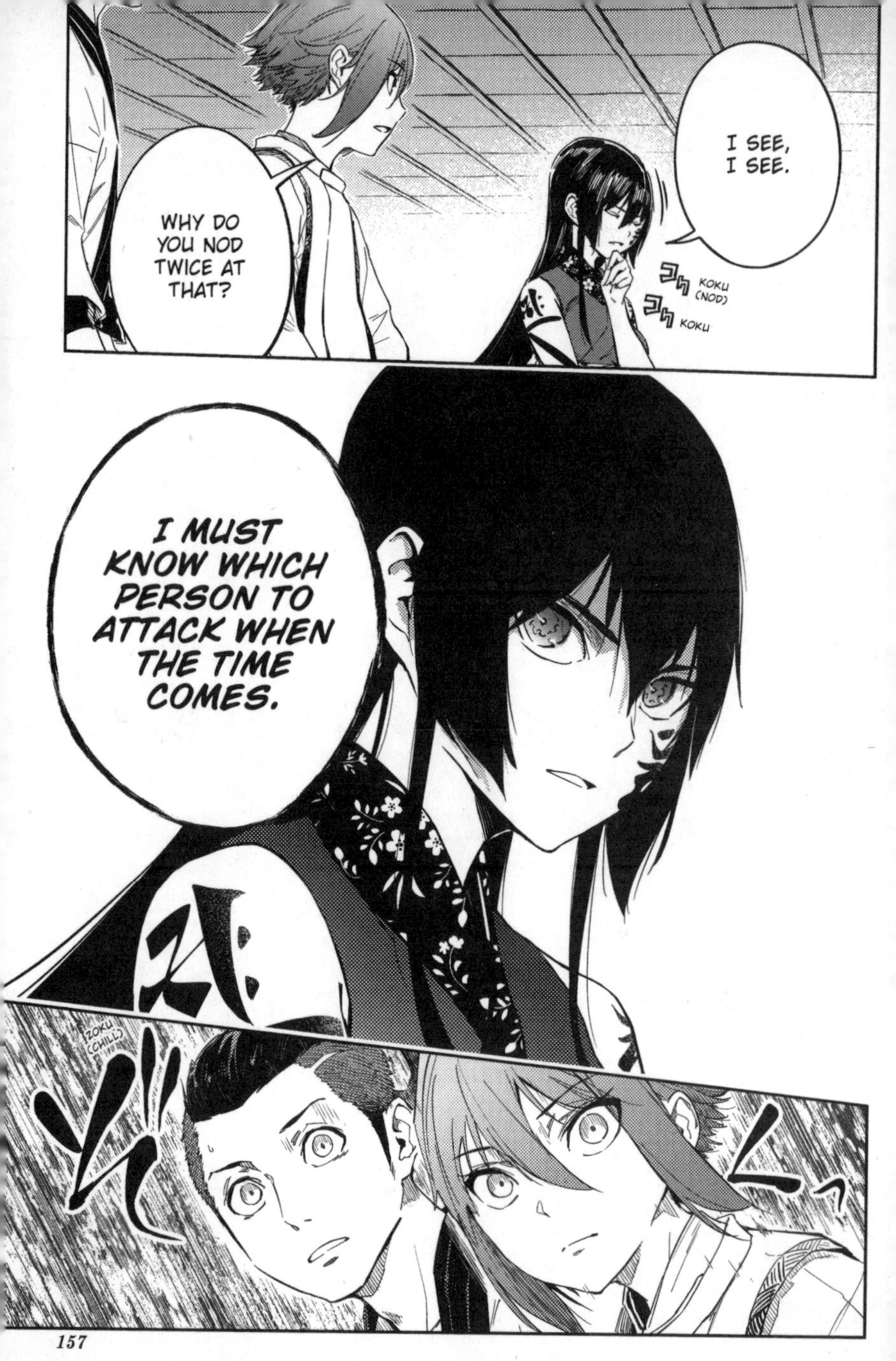
I SEE, I SEE.
コク KOKU (NOD)
コク KOKU
WHY DO YOU NOD TWICE AT THAT?
I MUST KNOW WHICH PERSON TO ATTACK WHEN THE TIME COMES.
ZOKU (CHILL)

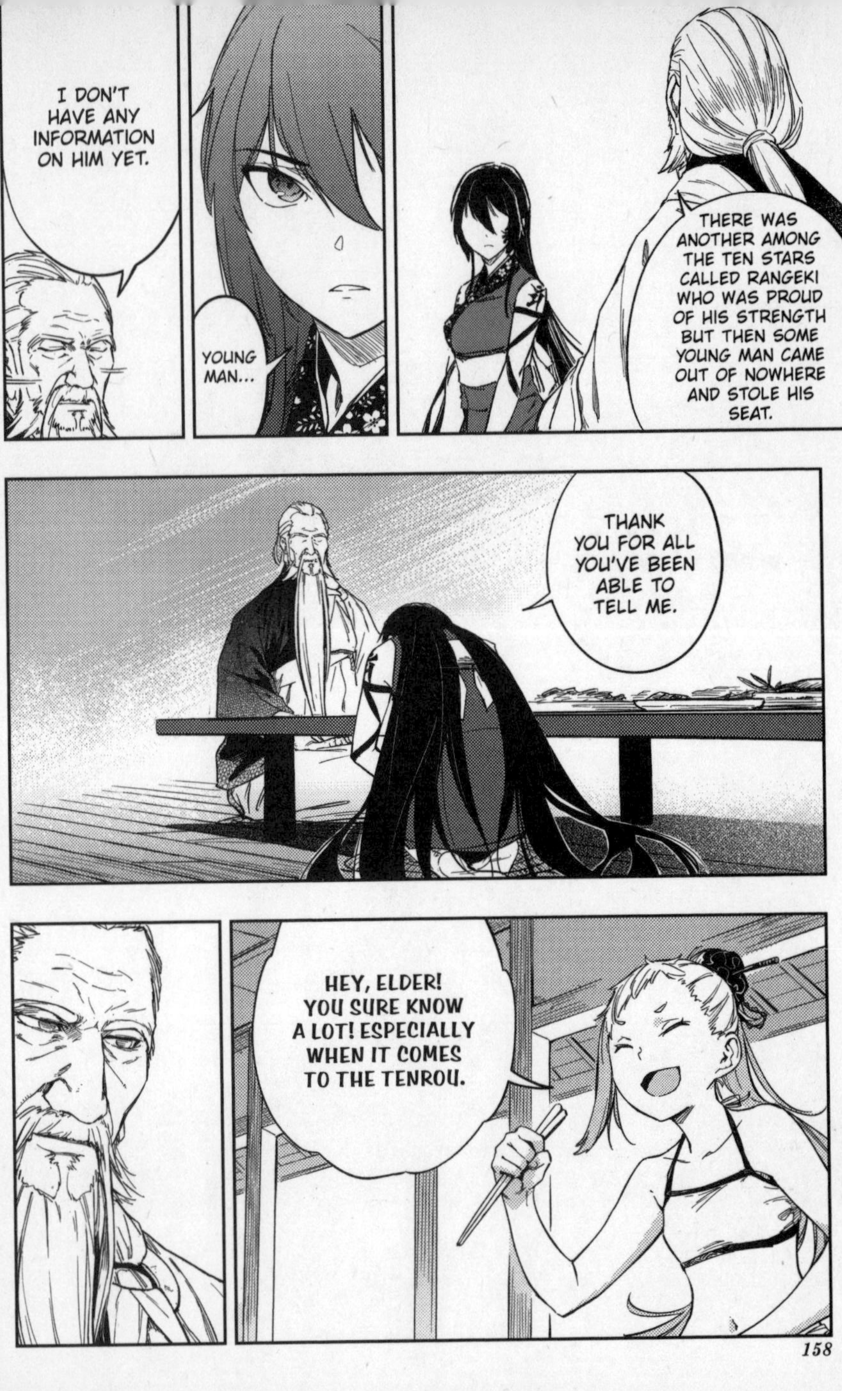
THERE WAS ANOTHER AMONG THE TEN STARS CALLED RANGEKI WHO WAS PROUD OF HIS STRENGTH BUT THEN SOME YOUNG MAN CAME OUT OF NOWHERE AND STOLE HIS SEAT.
YOUNG MAN...
I DON'T HAVE ANY INFORMATION ON HIM YET.
THANK YOU FOR ALL YOU'VE BEEN ABLE TO TELL ME.
HEY, ELDER! YOU SURE KNOW A LOT! ESPECIALLY WHEN IT COMES TO THE TENROU.

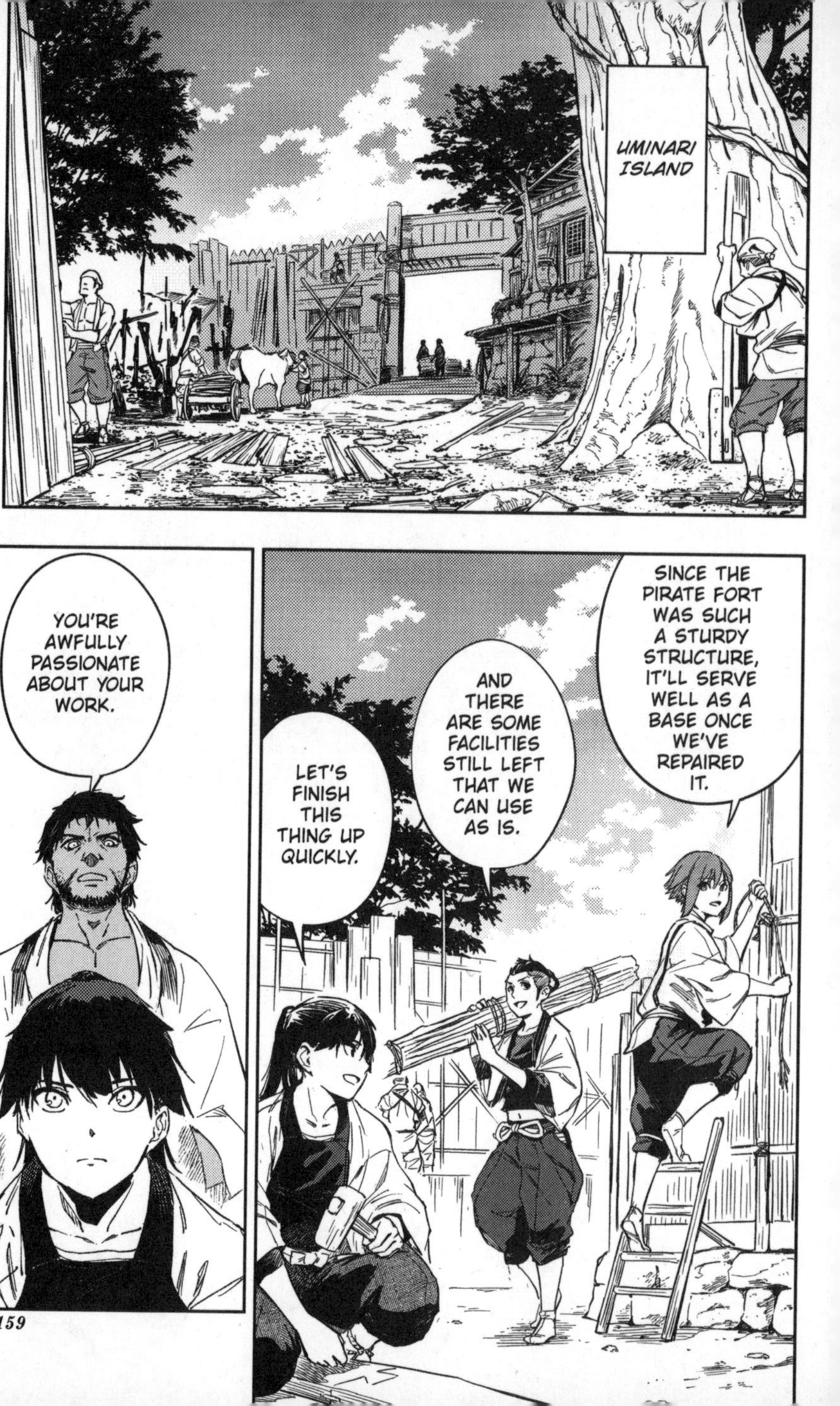
UMINARI ISLAND
SINCE THE PIRATE FORT WAS SUCH A STURDY STRUCTURE, IT'LL SERVE WELL AS A BASE ONCE WE'VE REPAIRED IT.
AND THERE ARE SOME FACILITIES STILL LEFT THAT WE CAN USE AS IS.
LET'S FINISH THIS THING UP QUICKLY.
YOU'RE AWFULLY PASSIONATE ABOUT YOUR WORK.

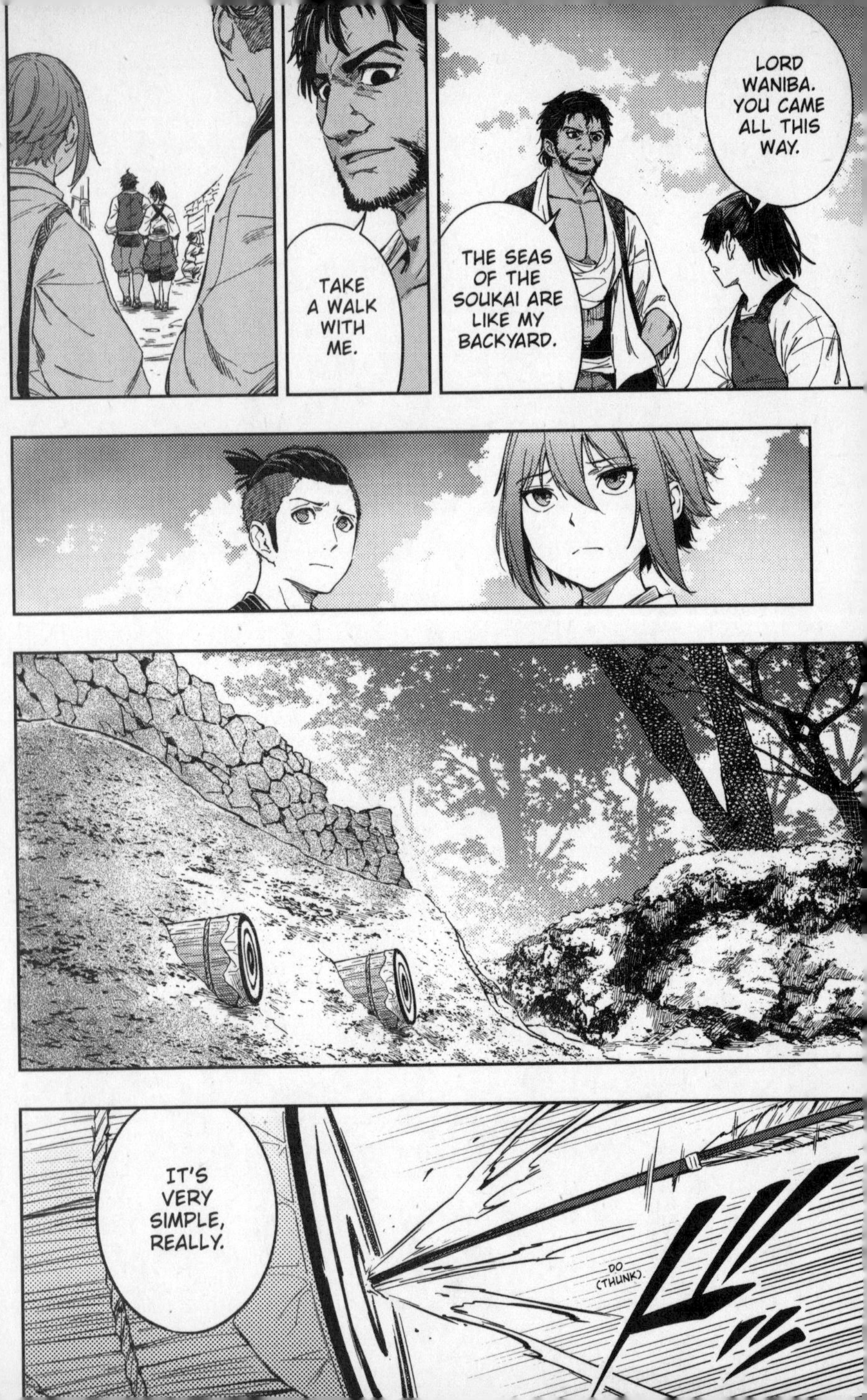
LORD WANIBA. YOU CAME ALL THIS WAY.
THE SEAS OF THE SOUKAI ARE LIKE MY BACKYARD.
TAKE A WALK WITH ME.
IT'S VERY SIMPLE, REALLY.
DO (THUNK)

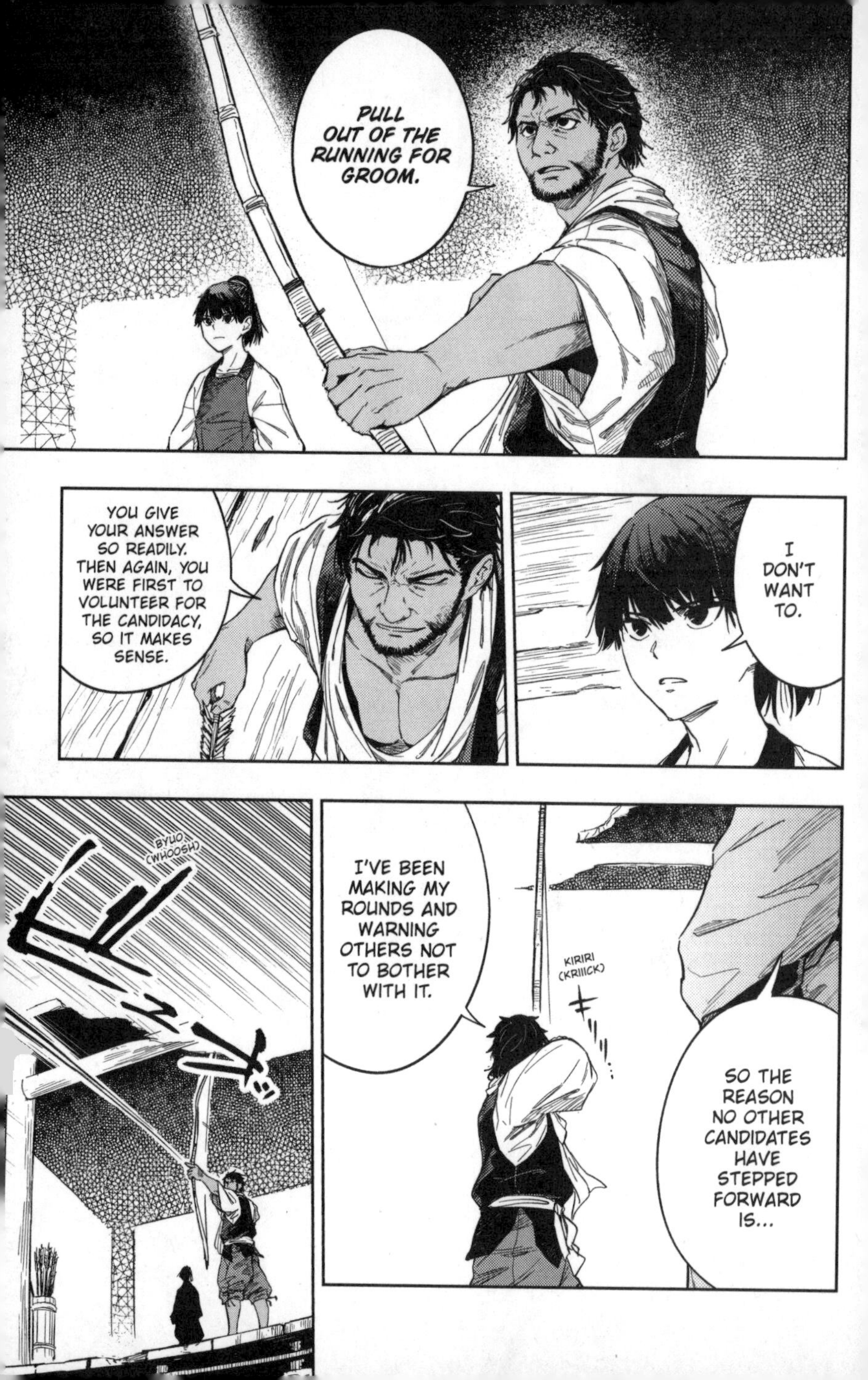
PULL OUT OF THE RUNNING FOR GROOM.
I DON'T WANT TO.
YOU GIVE YOUR ANSWER SO READILY. THEN AGAIN, YOU WERE FIRST TO VOLUNTEER FOR THE CANDIDACY, SO IT MAKES SENSE.
I'VE BEEN MAKING MY ROUNDS AND WARNING OTHERS NOT TO BOTHER WITH IT.
KIRIRI (KRIIICK)
SO THE REASON NO OTHER CANDIDATES HAVE STEPPED FORWARD IS...
BYUO (WHOOSH)

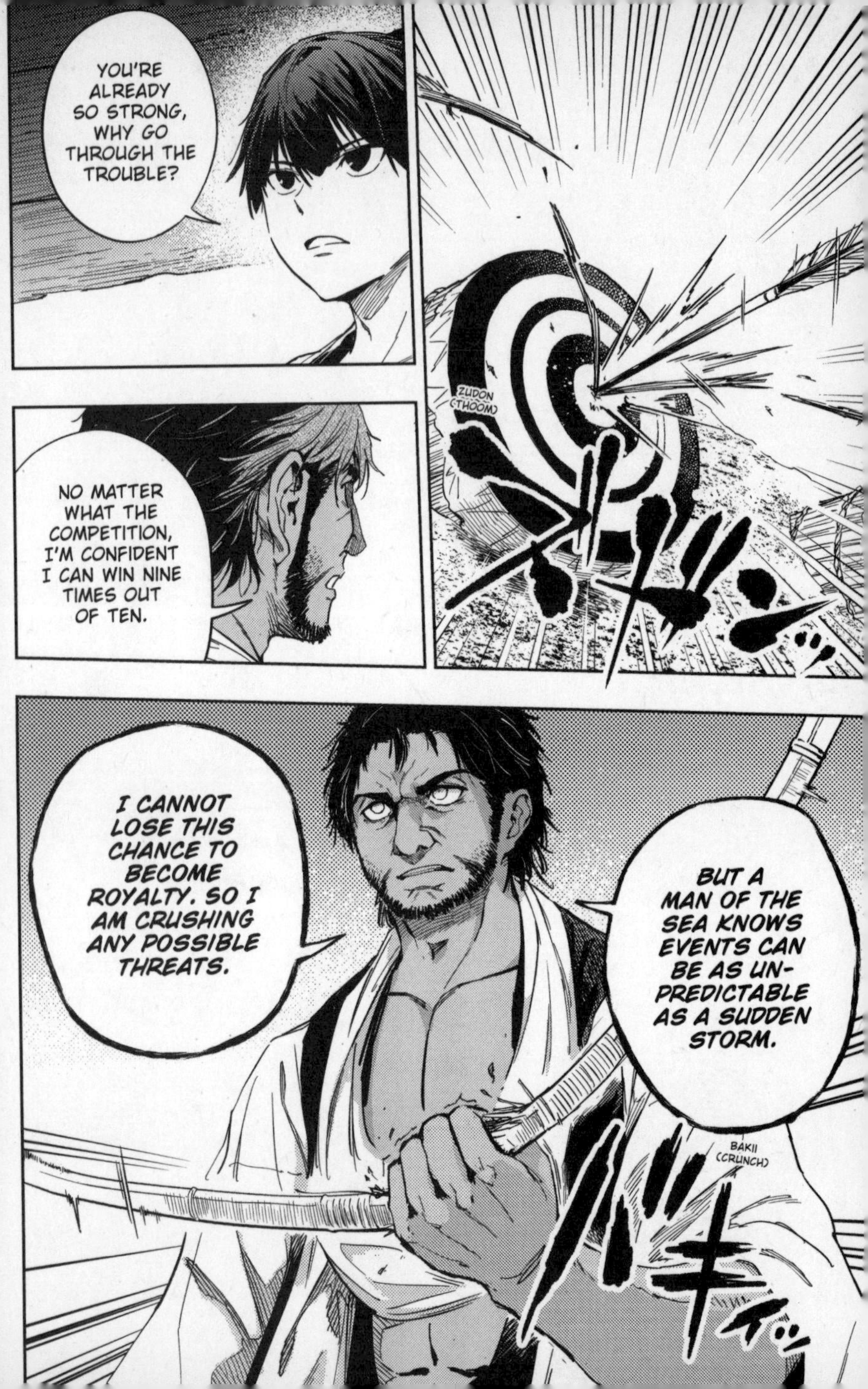
ZUDON (THOOM)
YOU'RE ALREADY SO STRONG, WHY GO THROUGH THE TROUBLE?
NO MATTER WHAT THE COMPETITION, I'M CONFIDENT I CAN WIN NINE TIMES OUT OF TEN.
BUT A MAN OF THE SEA KNOWS EVENTS CAN BE AS UN-PREDICTABLE AS A SUDDEN STORM.
I CANNOT LOSE THIS CHANCE TO BECOME ROYALTY. SO I AM CRUSHING ANY POSSIBLE THREATS.
BAKII (CRUNCH)

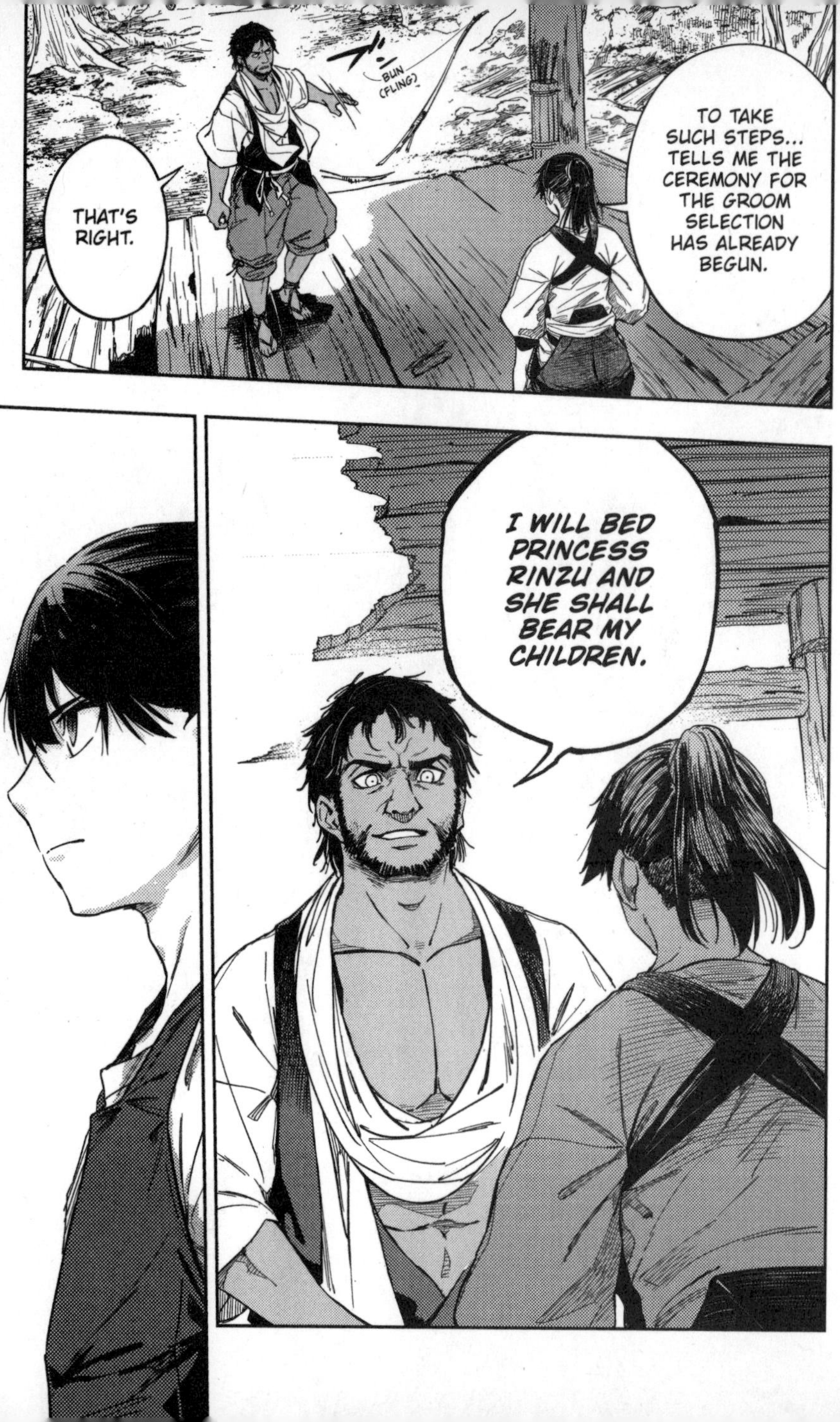
TO TAKE SUCH STEPS... TELLS ME THE CEREMONY FOR THE GROOM SELECTION HAS ALREADY BEGUN.
BUN (FLING)
THAT'S RIGHT.
I WILL BED PRINCESS RINZU AND SHE SHALL BEAR MY CHILDREN.

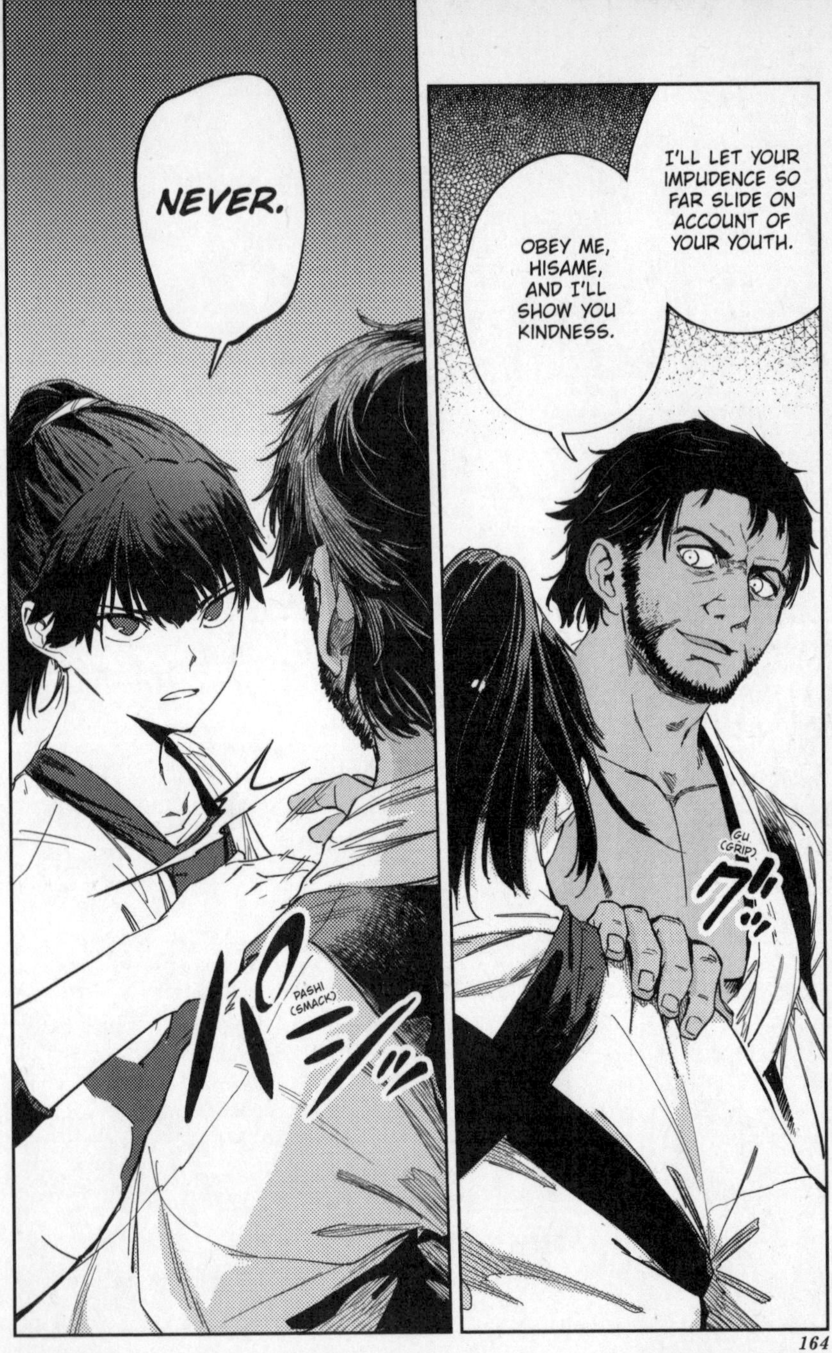
I'LL LET YOUR IMPUDENCE SO FAR SLIDE ON ACCOUNT OF YOUR YOUTH.
OBEY ME, HISAME, AND I'LL SHOW YOU KINDNESS.
GU (GRIP)
NEVER.
PASHI (SMACK)

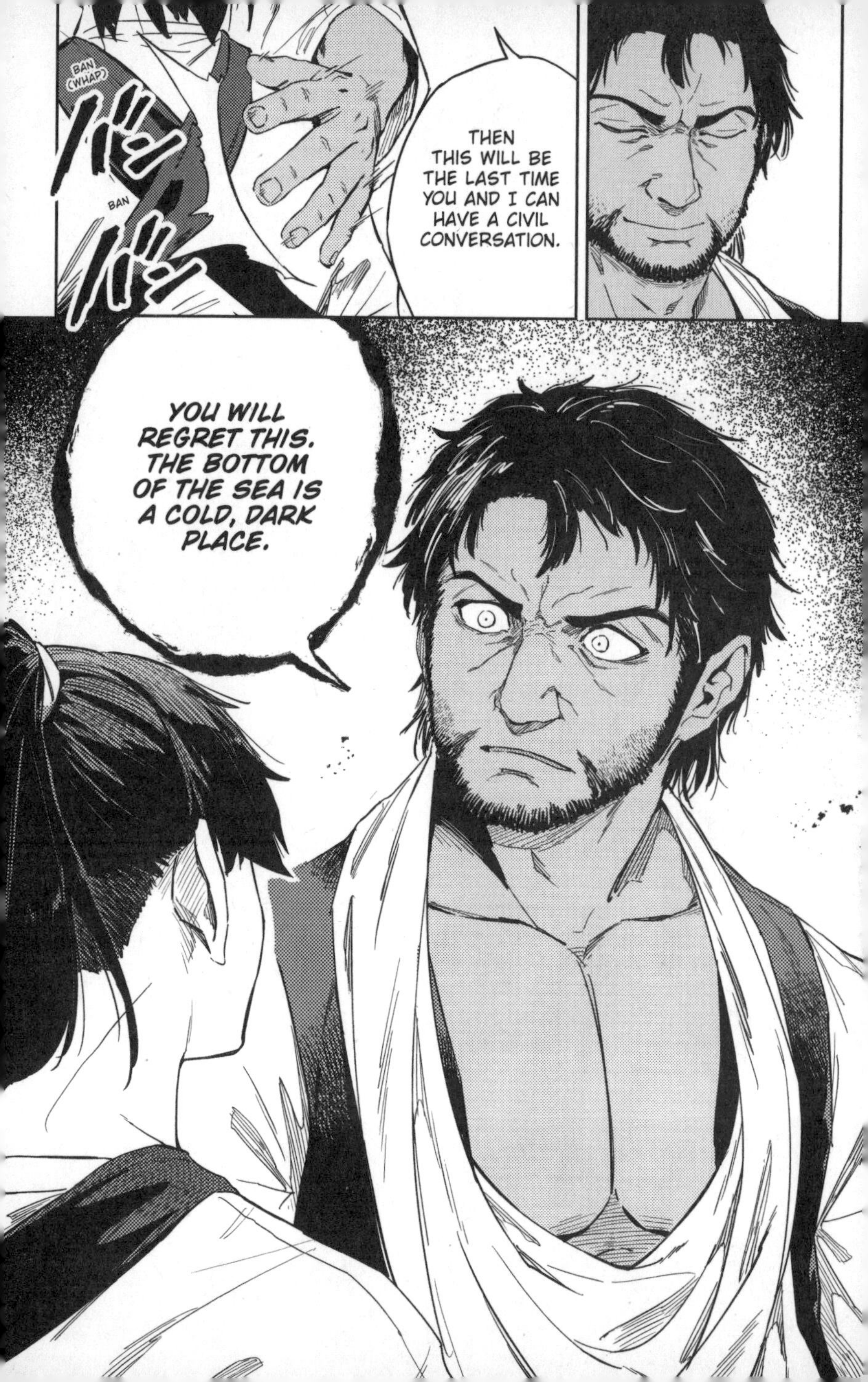
THEN THIS WILL BE THE LAST TIME YOU AND I CAN HAVE A CIVIL CONVERSATION.
BAN (WHAP)
BAN
YOU WILL REGRET THIS. THE BOTTOM OF THE SEA IS A COLD, DARK PLACE.

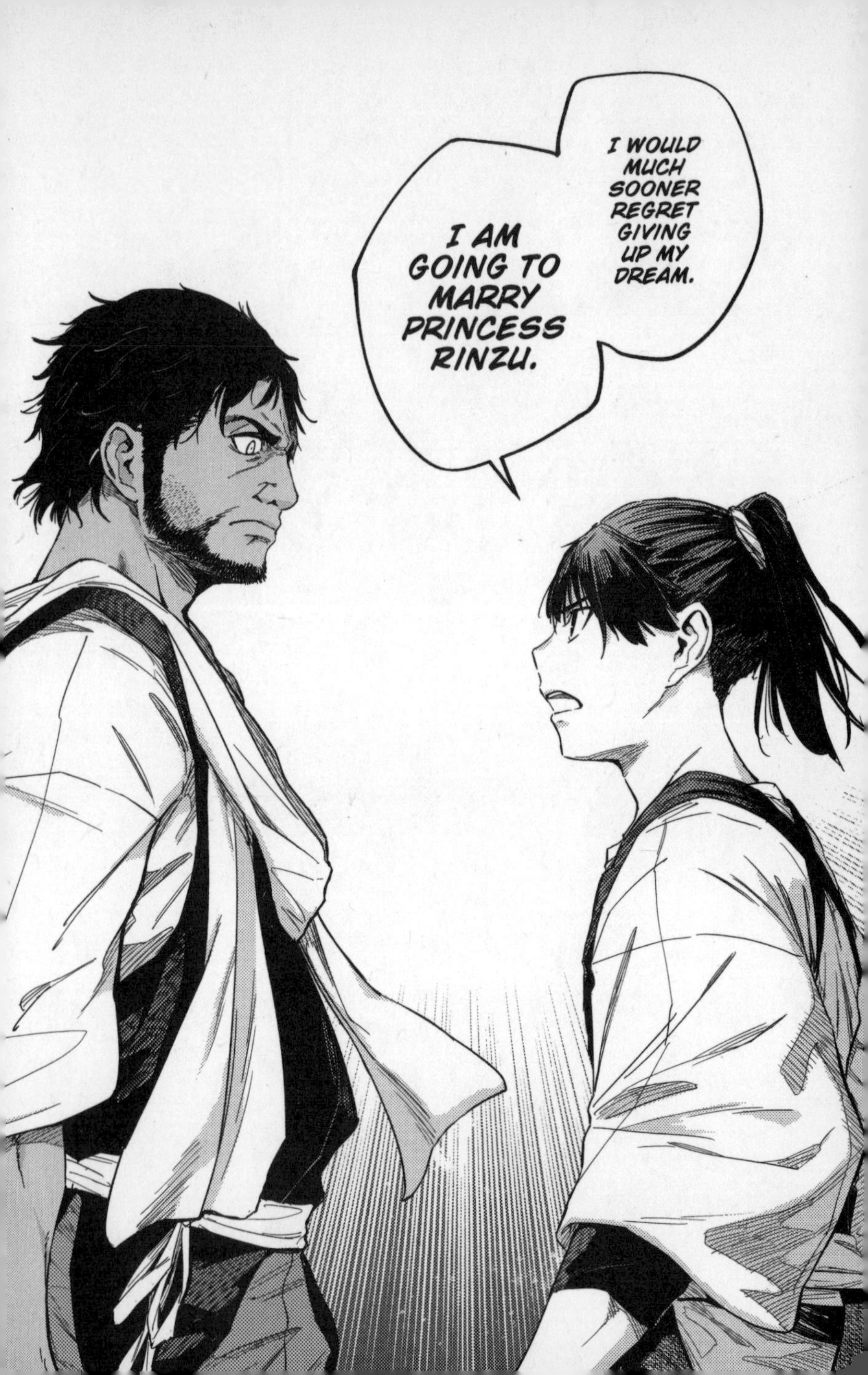
I WOULD MUCH SOONER REGRET GIVING UP MY DREAM.
I AM GOING TO MARRY PRINCESS RINZU.

Hinowa ga CRUSH!

Hinowa ga CRUSH!

Design Drafts ⑤

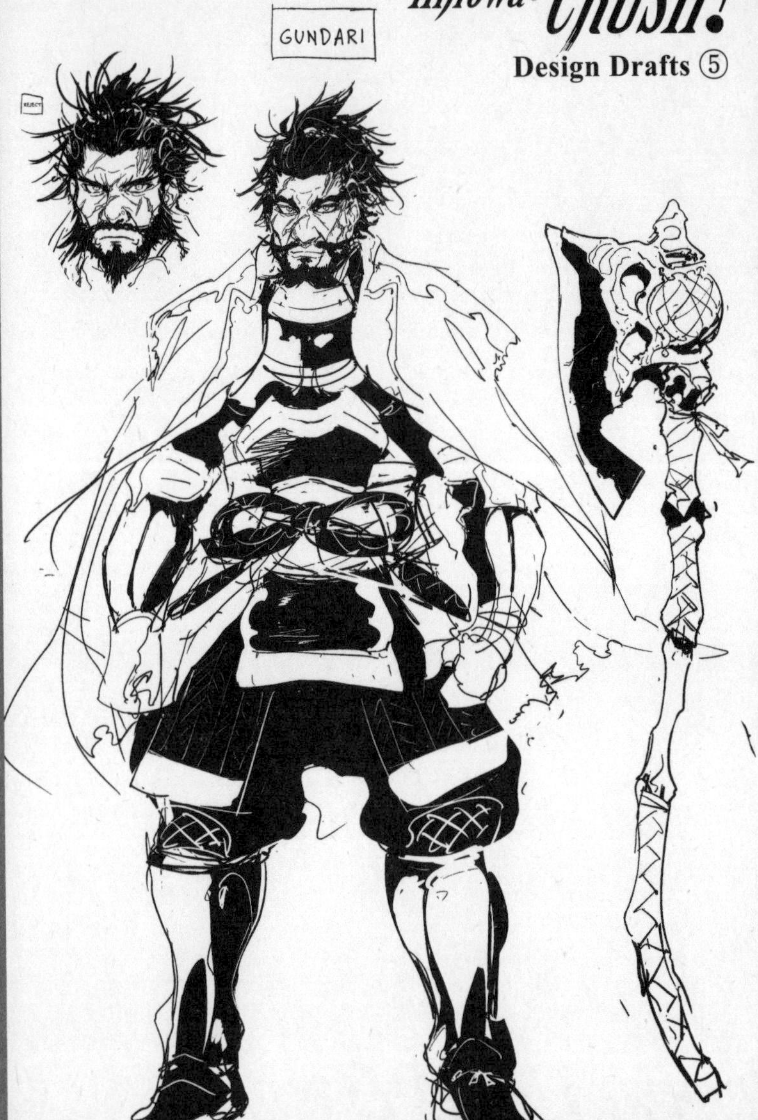
GUNDARI

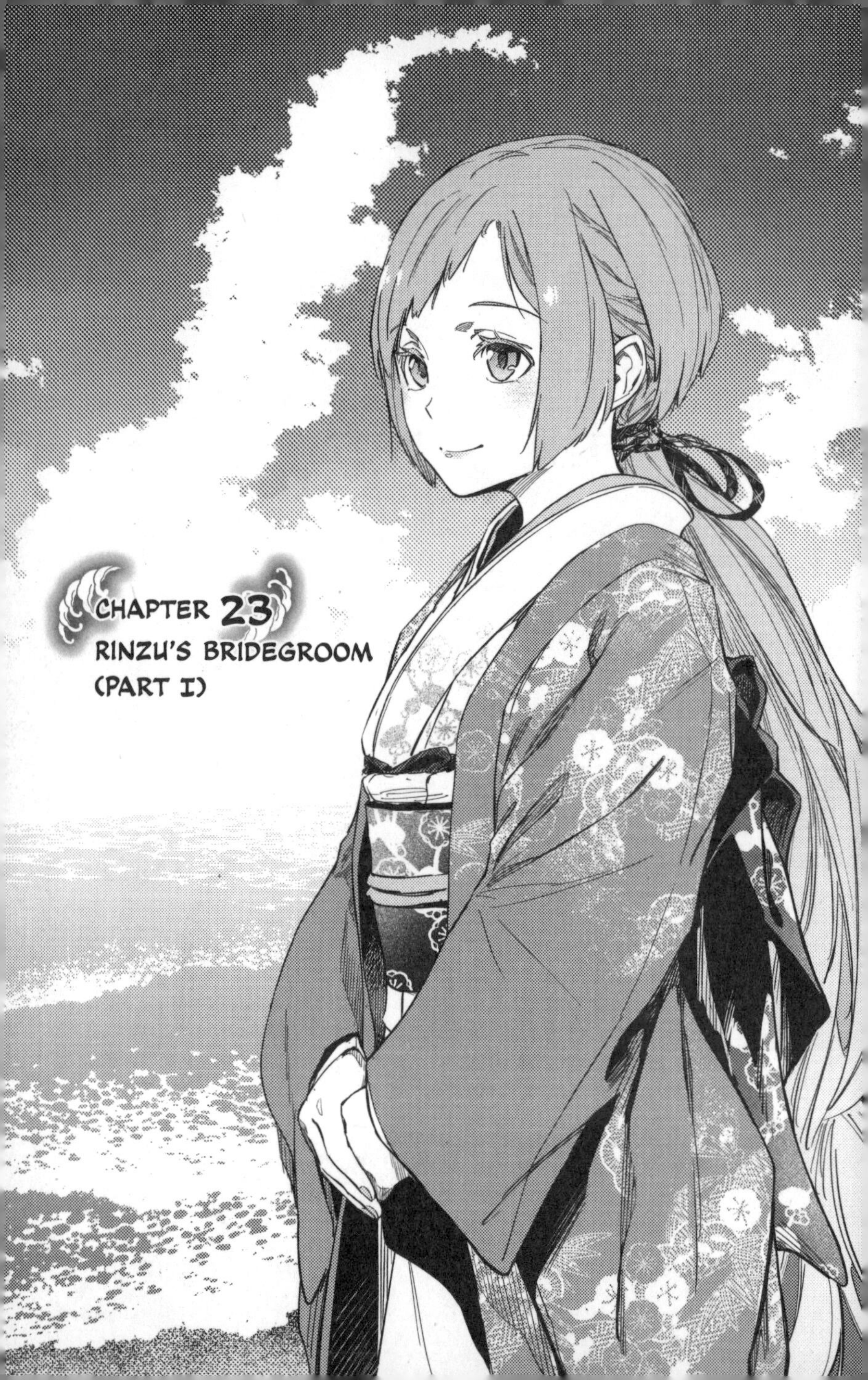
CHAPTER 23
RINZU'S BRIDEGROOM
(PART I)

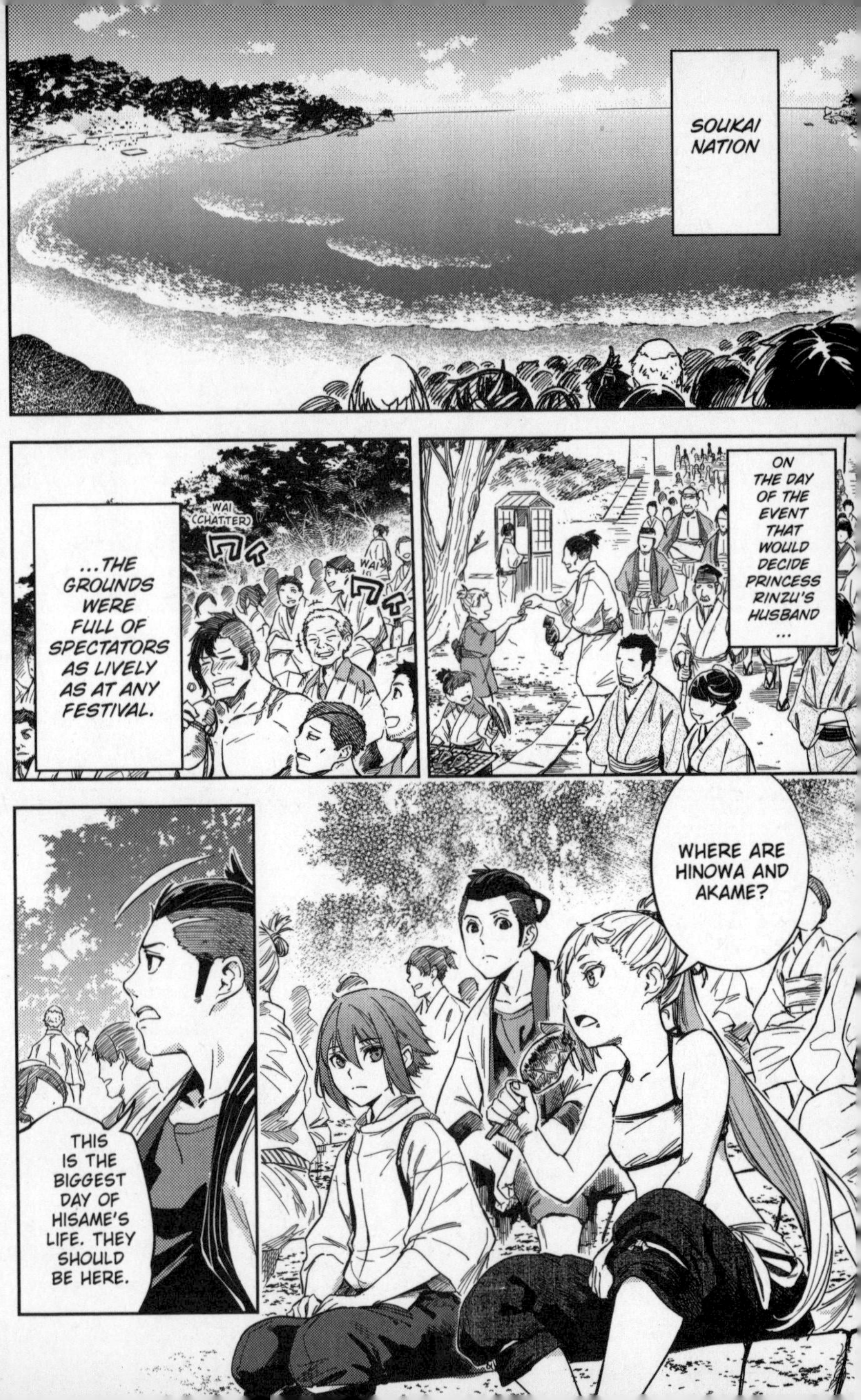
SOUKAI NATION
ON THE DAY OF THE EVENT THAT WOULD DECIDE PRINCESS RINZU'S HUSBAND...
...THE GROUNDS WERE FULL OF SPECTATORS AS LIVELY AS AT ANY FESTIVAL.
WAI (CHATTER)
WAI
WHERE ARE HINOWA AND AKAME?
THIS IS THE BIGGEST DAY OF HISAME'S LIFE. THEY SHOULD BE HERE.

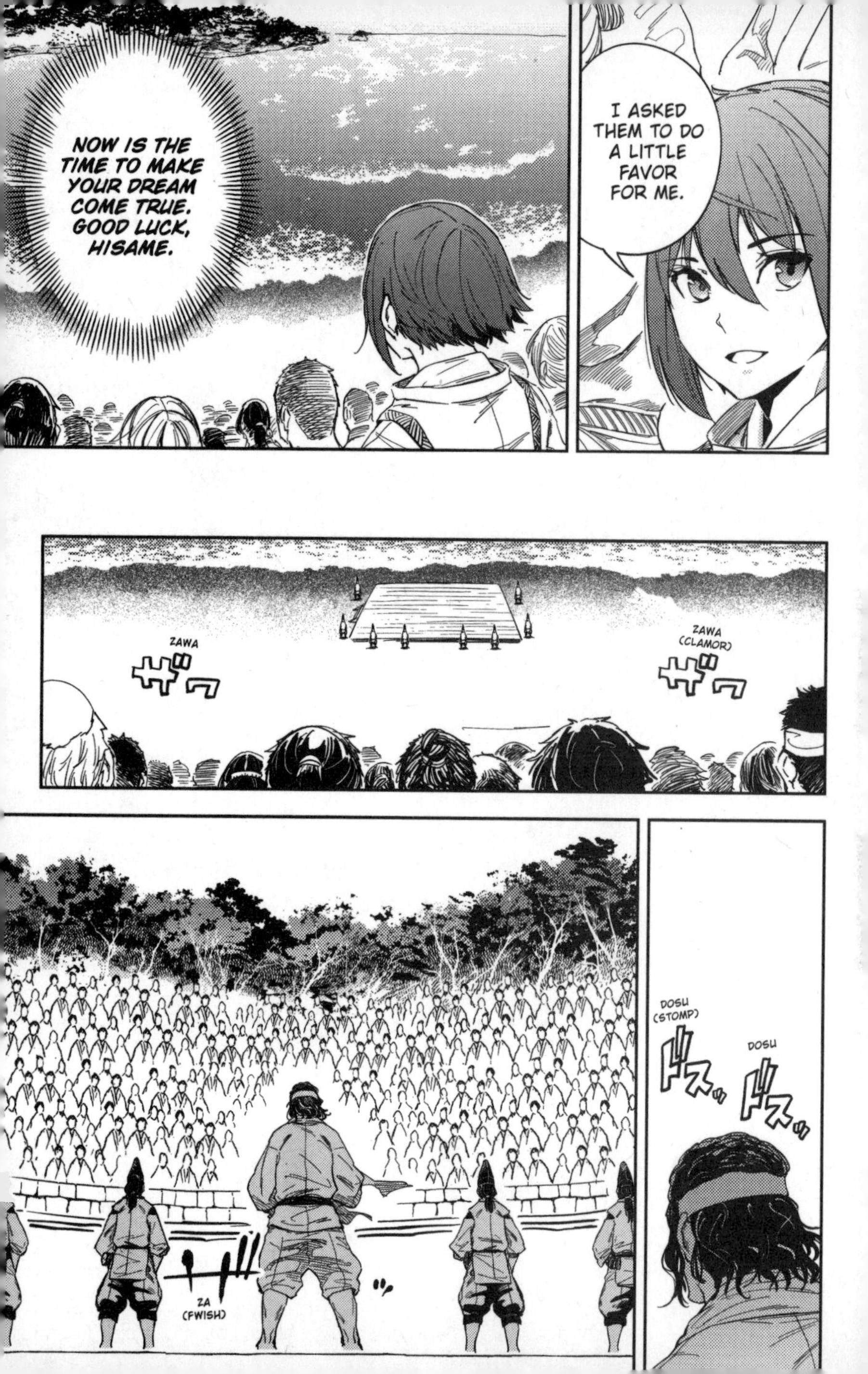
I ASKED THEM TO DO A LITTLE FAVOR FOR ME.
NOW IS THE TIME TO MAKE YOUR DREAM COME TRUE. GOOD LUCK, HISAME.
ZAWA (CLAMOR)
ZAWA
DOSU (STOMP)
DOSU
ZA (FWISH)

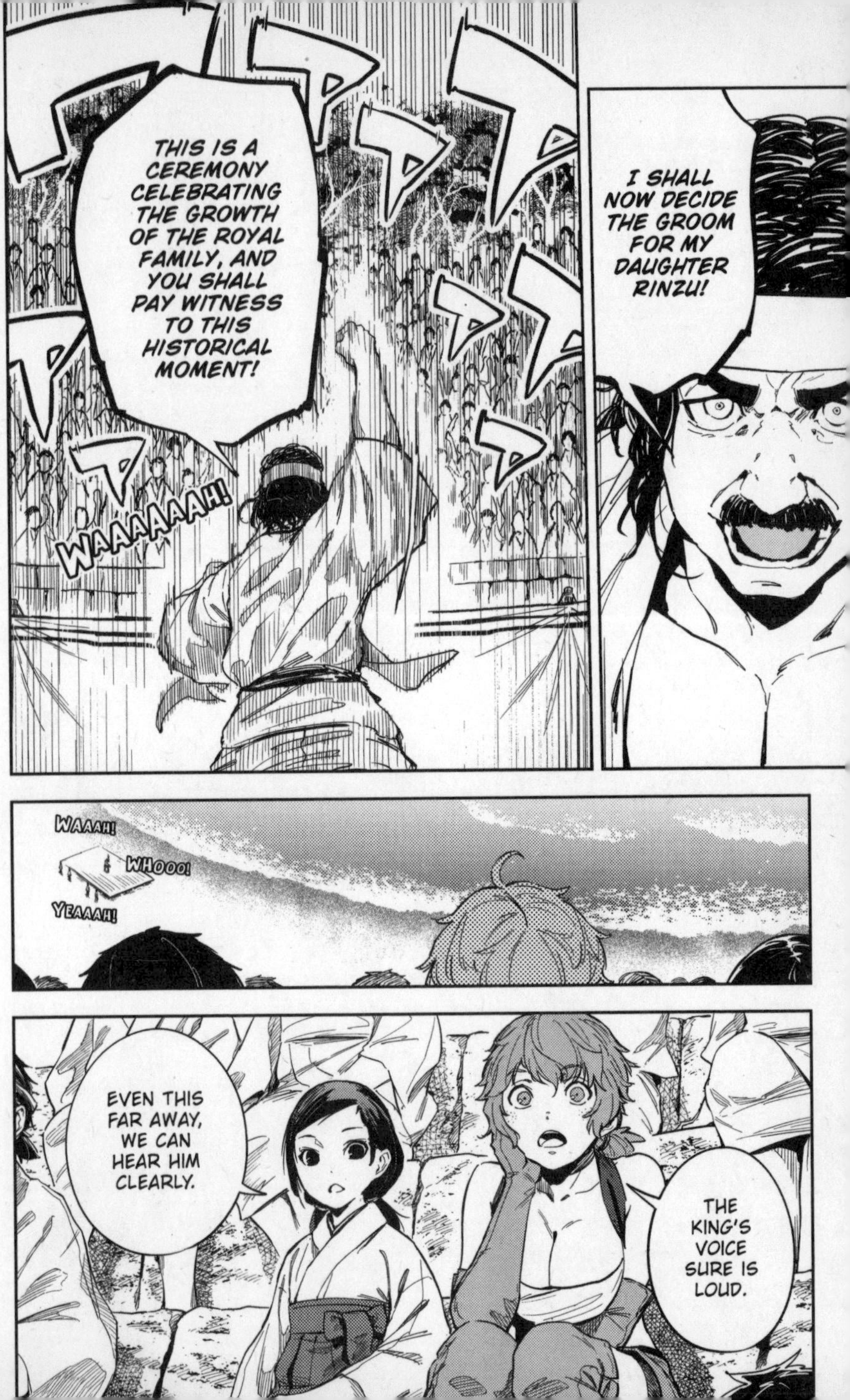
I SHALL NOW DECIDE THE GROOM FOR MY DAUGHTER RINZU!
THIS IS A CEREMONY CELEBRATING THE GROWTH OF THE ROYAL FAMILY, AND YOU SHALL PAY WITNESS TO THIS HISTORICAL MOMENT!
WAAAAAAAH!
WAAAH!
WHOOO!
YEAAAH!
THE KING'S VOICE SURE IS LOUD.
EVEN THIS FAR AWAY, WE CAN HEAR HIM CLEARLY.

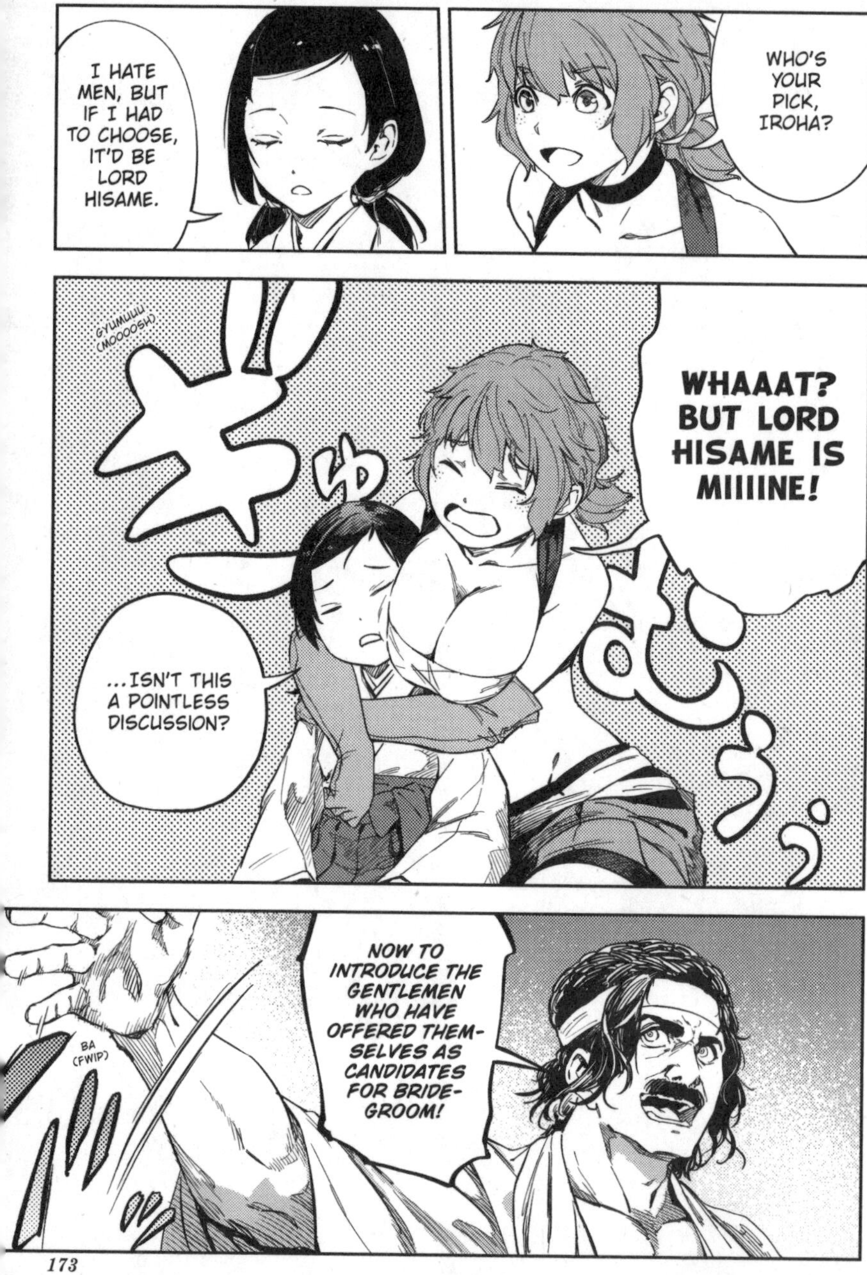
WHO'S YOUR PICK, IROHA?
I HATE MEN, BUT IF I HAD TO CHOOSE, IT'D BE LORD HISAME.
WHAAAT? BUT LORD HISAME IS MIIIINE!
GYUMUUU (MOOOOSH)
...ISN'T THIS A POINTLESS DISCUSSION?
NOW TO INTRODUCE THE GENTLEMEN WHO HAVE OFFERED THEM-SELVES AS CANDIDATES FOR BRIDE-GROOM!
BA (FWIP)

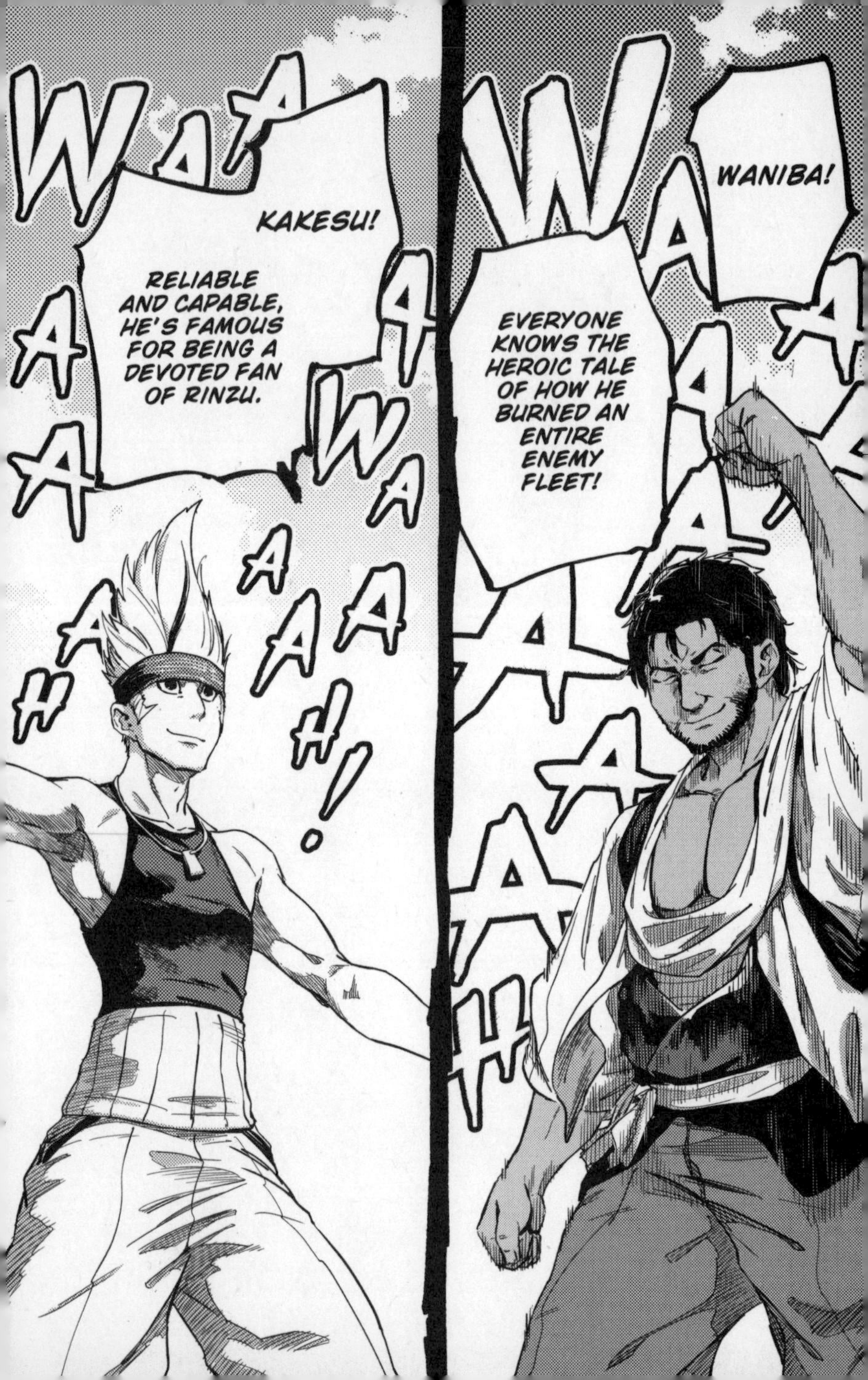
WANIBA!
EVERYONE KNOWS THE HEROIC TALE OF HOW HE BURNED AN ENTIRE ENEMY FLEET!
KAKESU!
RELIABLE AND CAPABLE, HE'S FAMOUS FOR BEING A DEVOTED FAN OF RINZU.

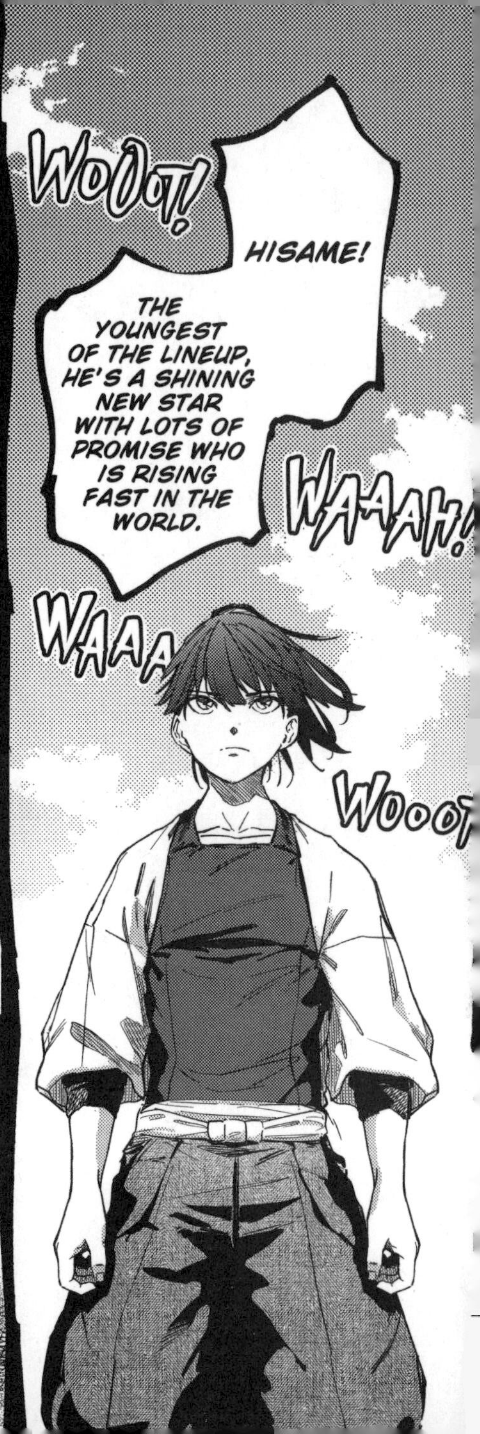
HISAME!
THE YOUNGEST OF THE LINEUP, HE'S A SHINING NEW STAR WITH LOTS OF PROMISE WHO IS RISING FAST IN THE WORLD.
WOOOT!
WAAAH!
WAAA
WOOOT
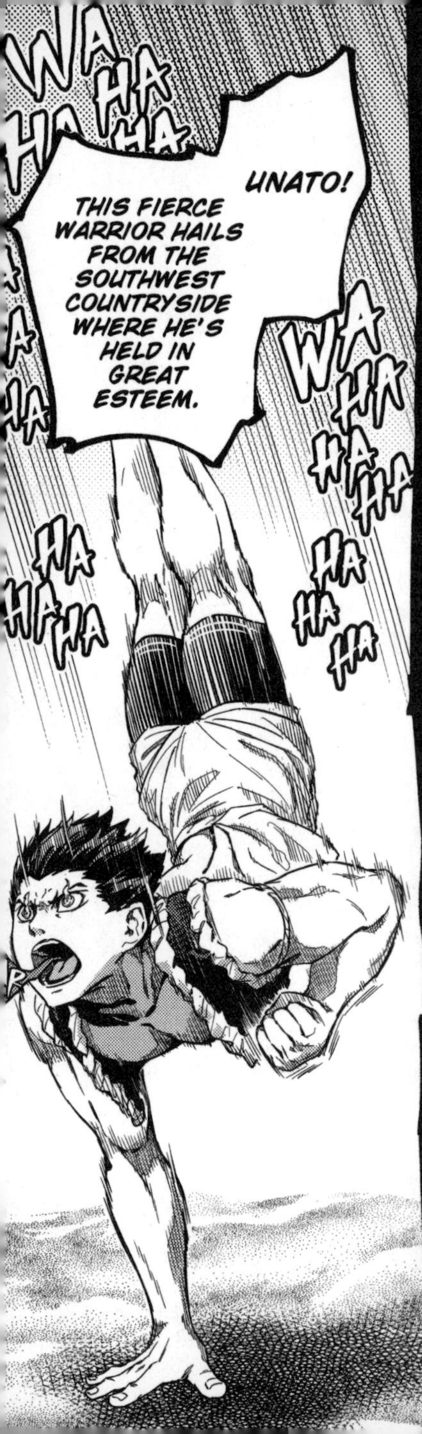
UNATO!
THIS FIERCE WARRIOR HAILS FROM THE SOUTHWEST COUNTRYSIDE WHERE HE'S HELD IN GREAT ESTEEM.
WA HA HA HA
WA HA HA HA
HA HA HA
HA HA HA

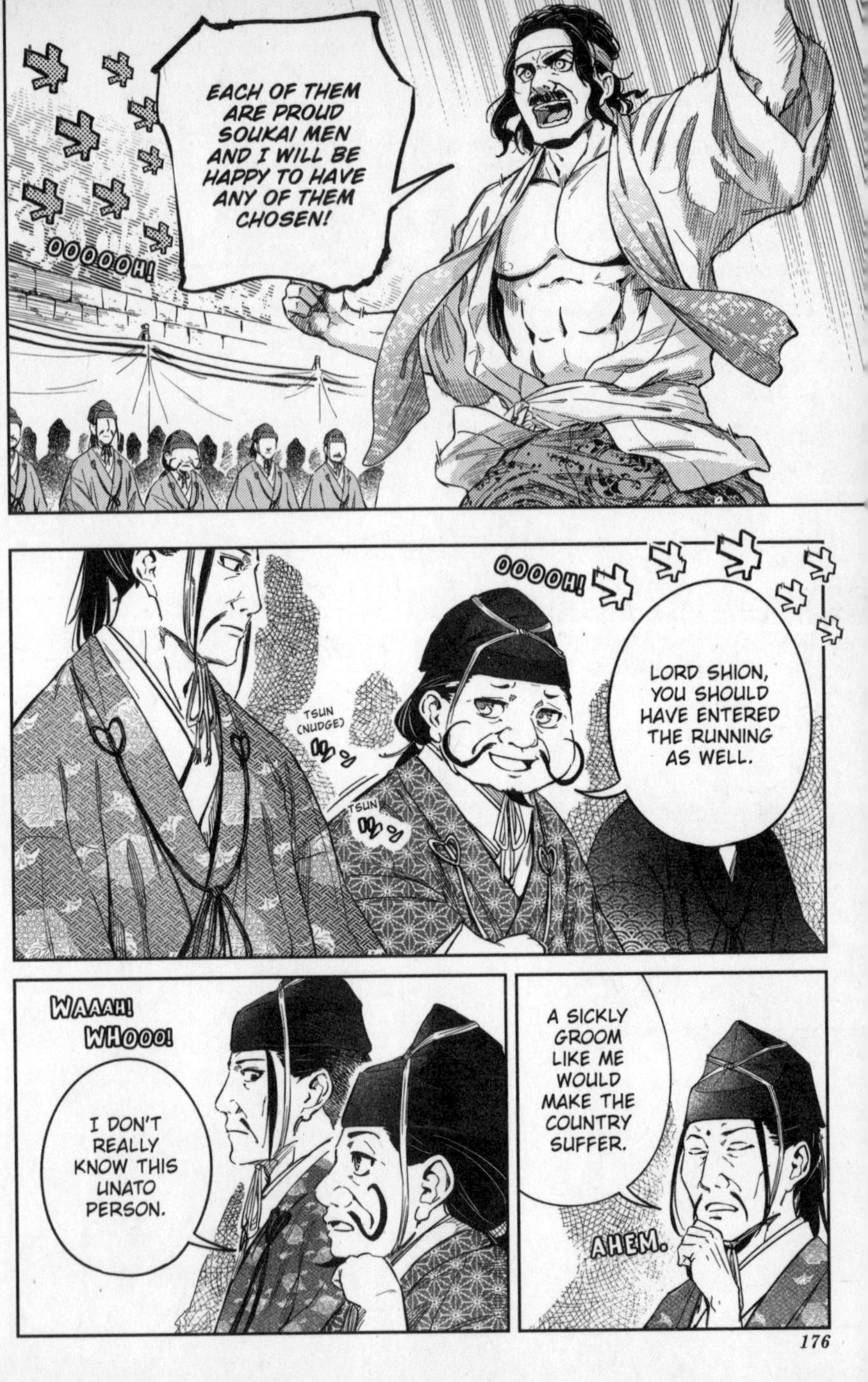
EACH OF THEM ARE PROUD SOUKAI MEN AND I WILL BE HAPPY TO HAVE ANY OF THEM CHOSEN!
OOOOOOH!
OOOOH!
LORD SHION, YOU SHOULD HAVE ENTERED THE RUNNING AS WELL.
TSUN (NUDGE)
TSUN
A SICKLY GROOM LIKE ME WOULD MAKE THE COUNTRY SUFFER.
AHEM.
WAAAH! WHOOO!
I DON'T REALLY KNOW THIS UNATO PERSON.

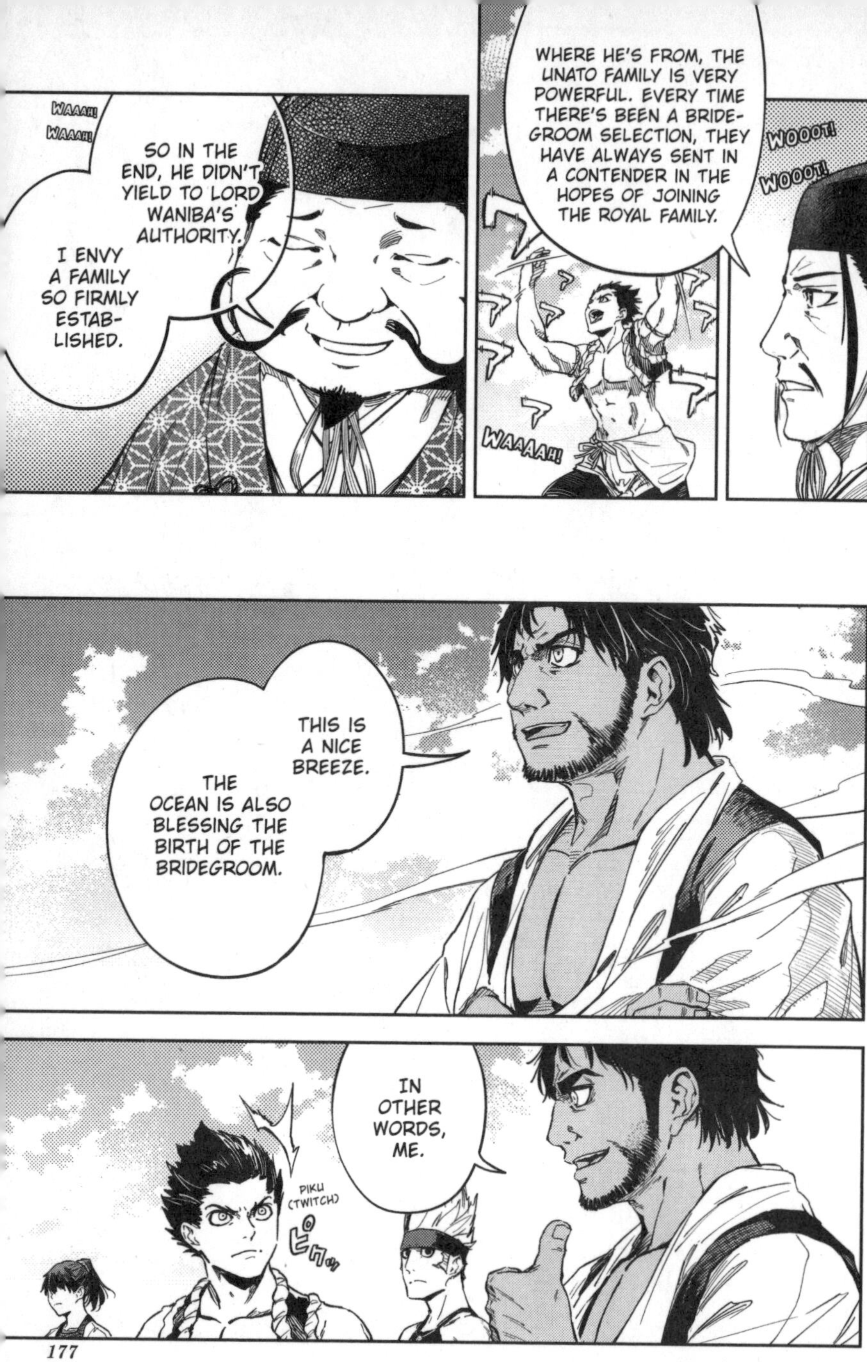

WOOOT!
WOOOT!
WHERE HE'S FROM, THE UNATO FAMILY IS VERY POWERFUL. EVERY TIME THERE'S BEEN A BRIDE-GROOM SELECTION, THEY HAVE ALWAYS SENT IN A CONTENDER IN THE HOPES OF JOINING THE ROYAL FAMILY.
WAAAA!!
WAAAH!
WAAAH!
SO IN THE END, HE DIDN'T YIELD TO LORD WANIBA'S AUTHORITY.
I ENVY A FAMILY SO FIRMLY ESTAB-LISHED.
THIS IS A NICE BREEZE.
THE OCEAN IS ALSO BLESSING THE BIRTH OF THE BRIDEGROOM.
IN OTHER WORDS, ME.
PIKU (TWITCH)

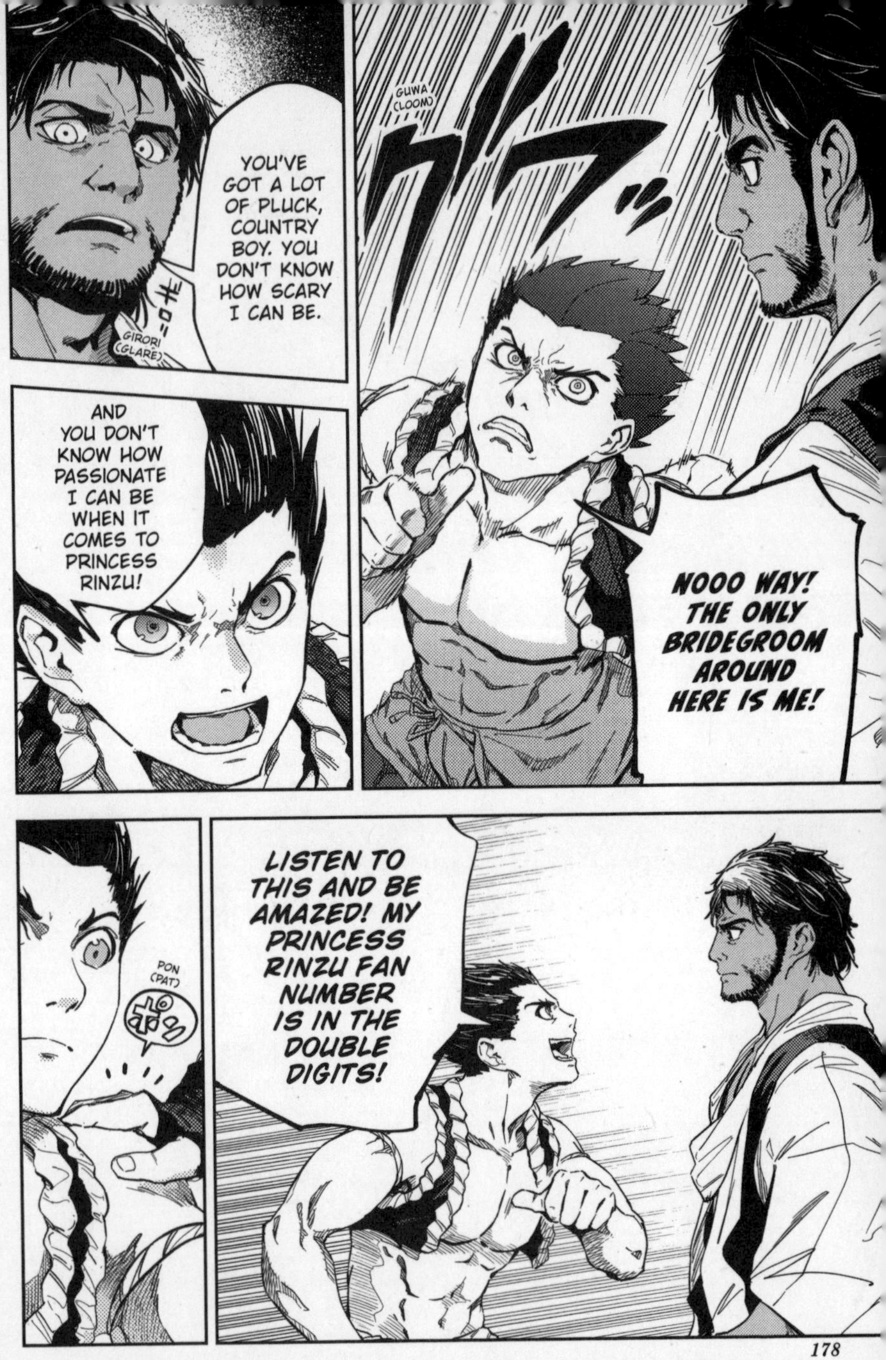
GUWA (LOOM)
NOOO WAY! THE ONLY BRIDEGROOM AROUND HERE IS ME!
YOU'VE GOT A LOT OF PLUCK, COUNTRY BOY. YOU DON'T KNOW HOW SCARY I CAN BE.
GIRORI (GLARE)
AND YOU DON'T KNOW HOW PASSIONATE I CAN BE WHEN IT COMES TO PRINCESS RINZU!
LISTEN TO THIS AND BE AMAZED! MY PRINCESS RINZU FAN NUMBER IS IN THE DOUBLE DIGITS!
PON (PAT)

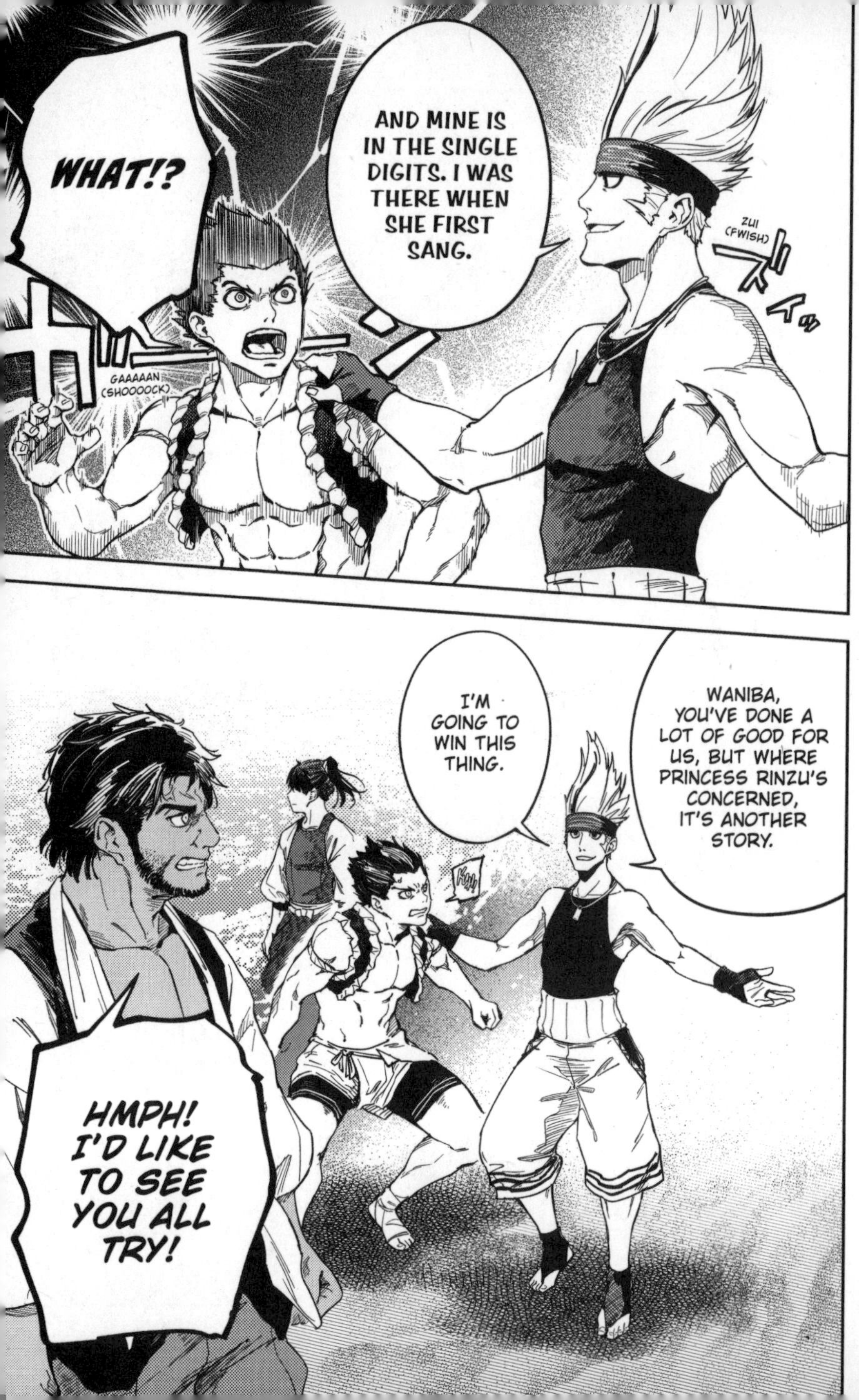
AND MINE IS IN THE SINGLE DIGITS. I WAS THERE WHEN SHE FIRST SANG.
ZUI (FWISH)
WHAT!?
GAAAAAN (SHOOOOCK)
WANIBA, YOU'VE DONE A LOT OF GOOD FOR US, BUT WHERE PRINCESS RINZU'S CONCERNED, IT'S ANOTHER STORY.
I'M GOING TO WIN THIS THING.
HMPH! I'D LIKE TO SEE YOU ALL TRY!

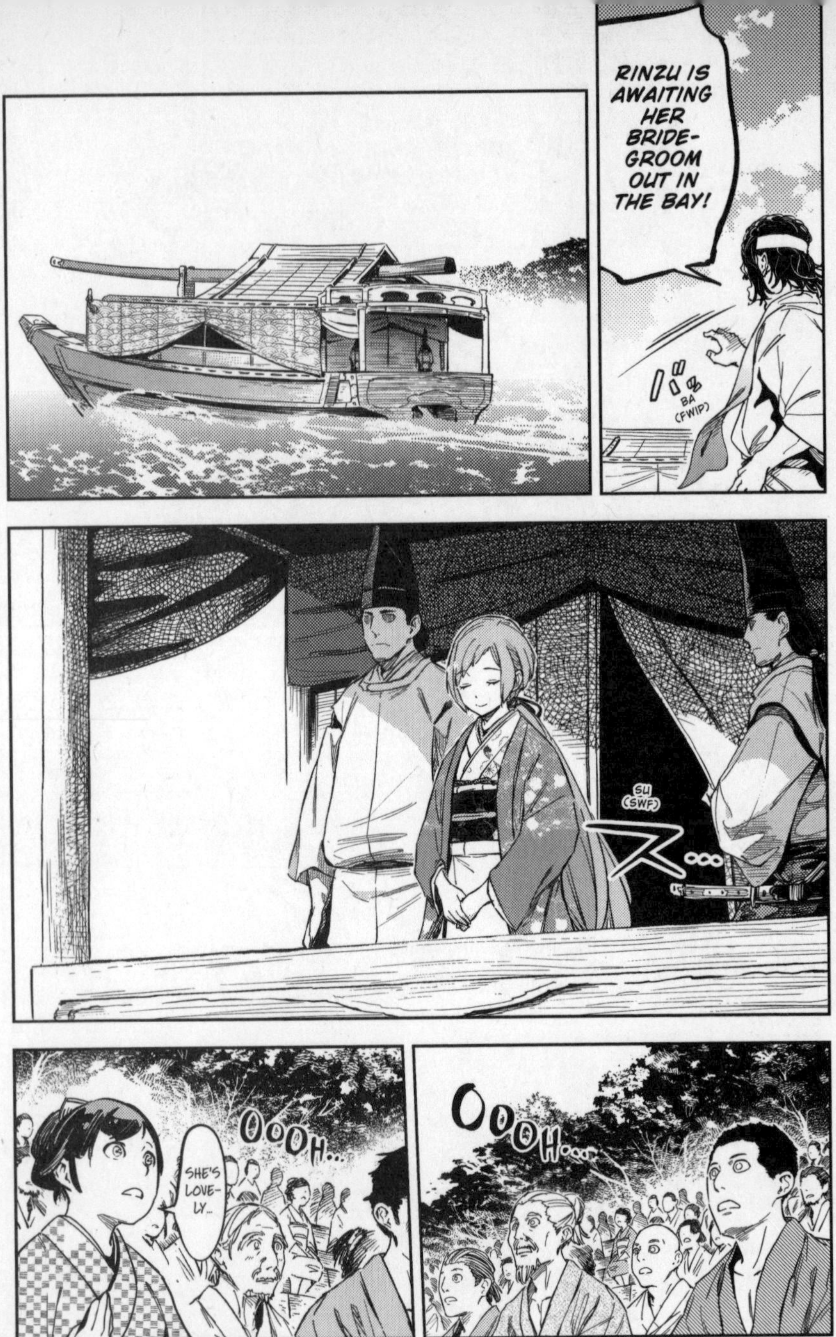
RINZU IS AWAITING HER BRIDE-GROOM OUT IN THE BAY!
BA (FWIP)
SU (SWF)
OOOH...
OOOH...
SHE'S LOVELY...

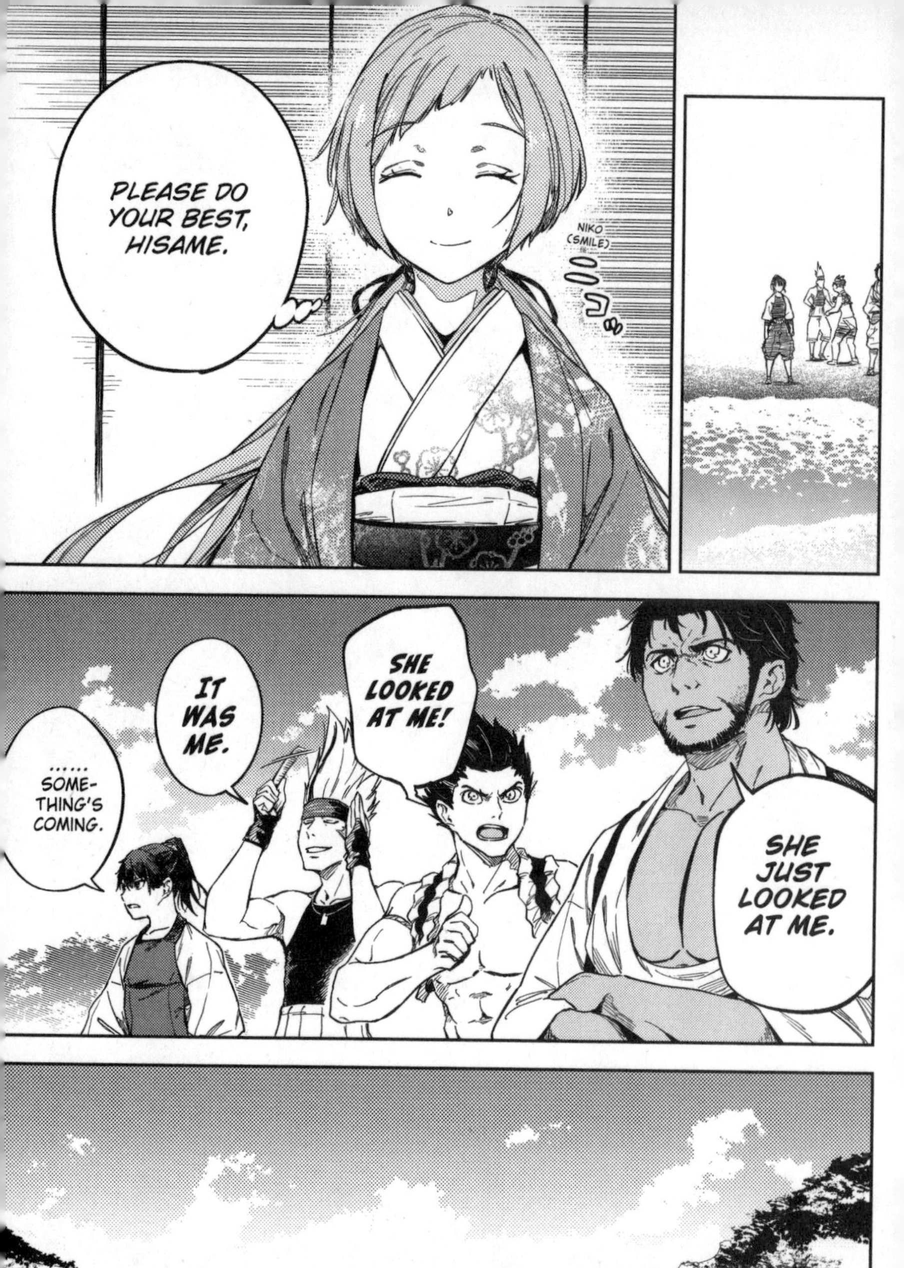
NIKO (SMILE)
PLEASE DO YOUR BEST, HISAME.
SHE JUST LOOKED AT ME.
SHE LOOKED AT ME!
IT WAS ME.
...... SOME-THING'S COMING.

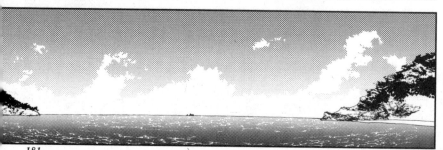

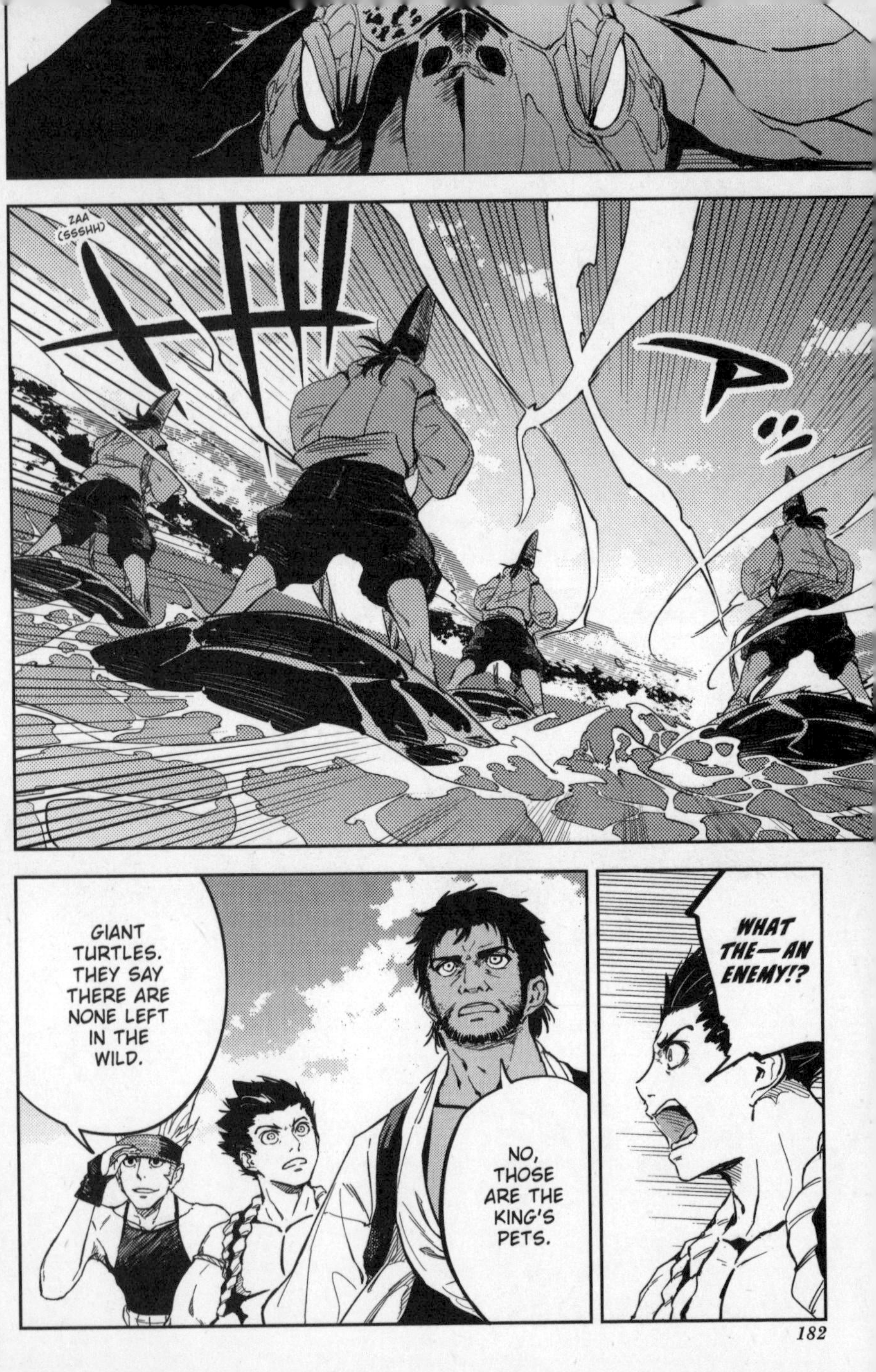
ZAA (SSSHH)
WHAT THE—AN ENEMY!?
GIANT TURTLES. THEY SAY THERE ARE NONE LEFT IN THE WILD.
NO, THOSE ARE THE KING'S PETS.

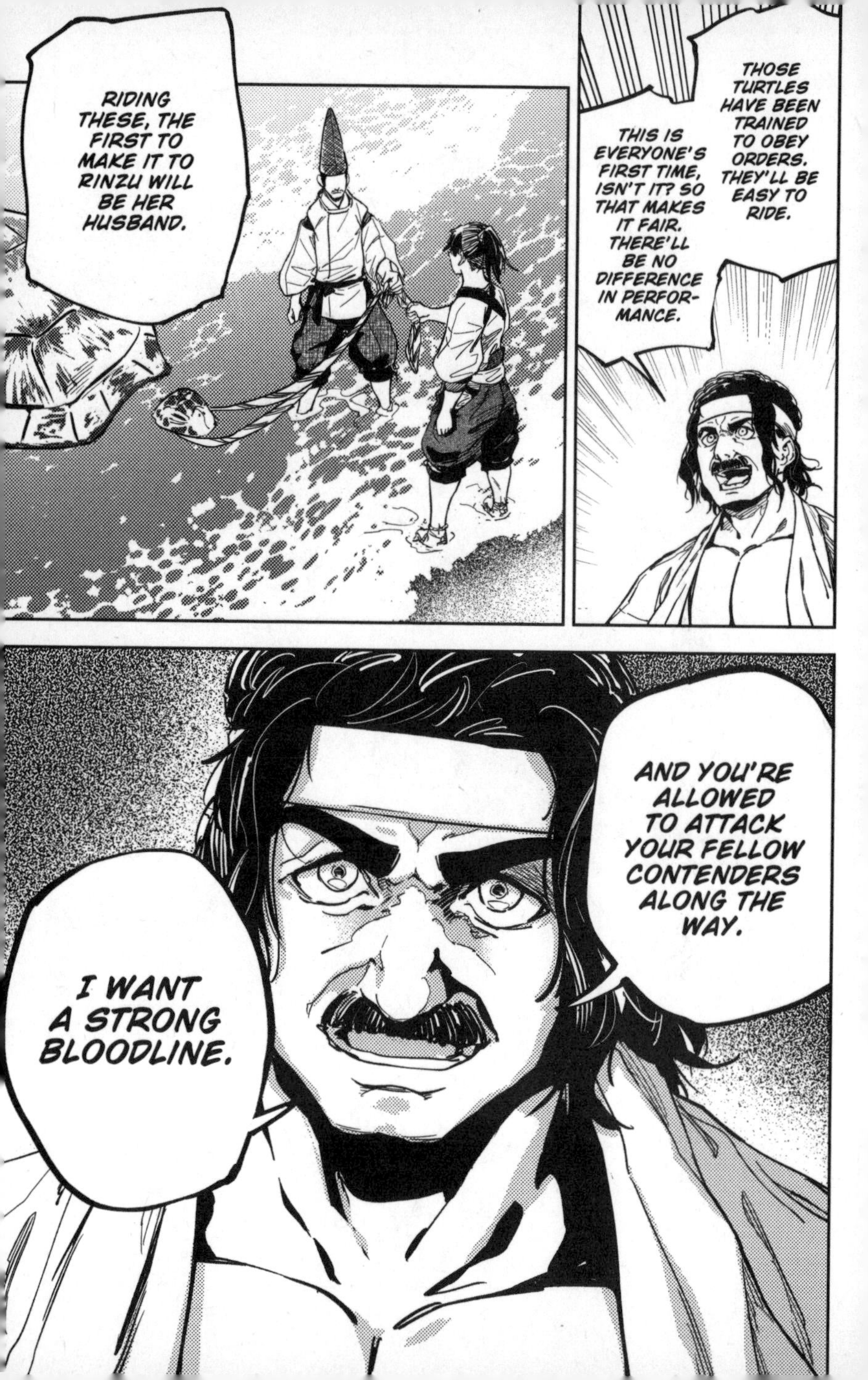
THOSE TURTLES HAVE BEEN TRAINED TO OBEY ORDERS. THEY'LL BE EASY TO RIDE.
THIS IS EVERYONE'S FIRST TIME, ISN'T IT? SO THAT MAKES IT FAIR. THERE'LL BE NO DIFFERENCE IN PERFOR-MANCE.
RIDING THESE, THE FIRST TO MAKE IT TO RINZU WILL BE HER HUSBAND.
AND YOU'RE ALLOWED TO ATTACK YOUR FELLOW CONTENDERS ALONG THE WAY.
I WANT A STRONG BLOODLINE.

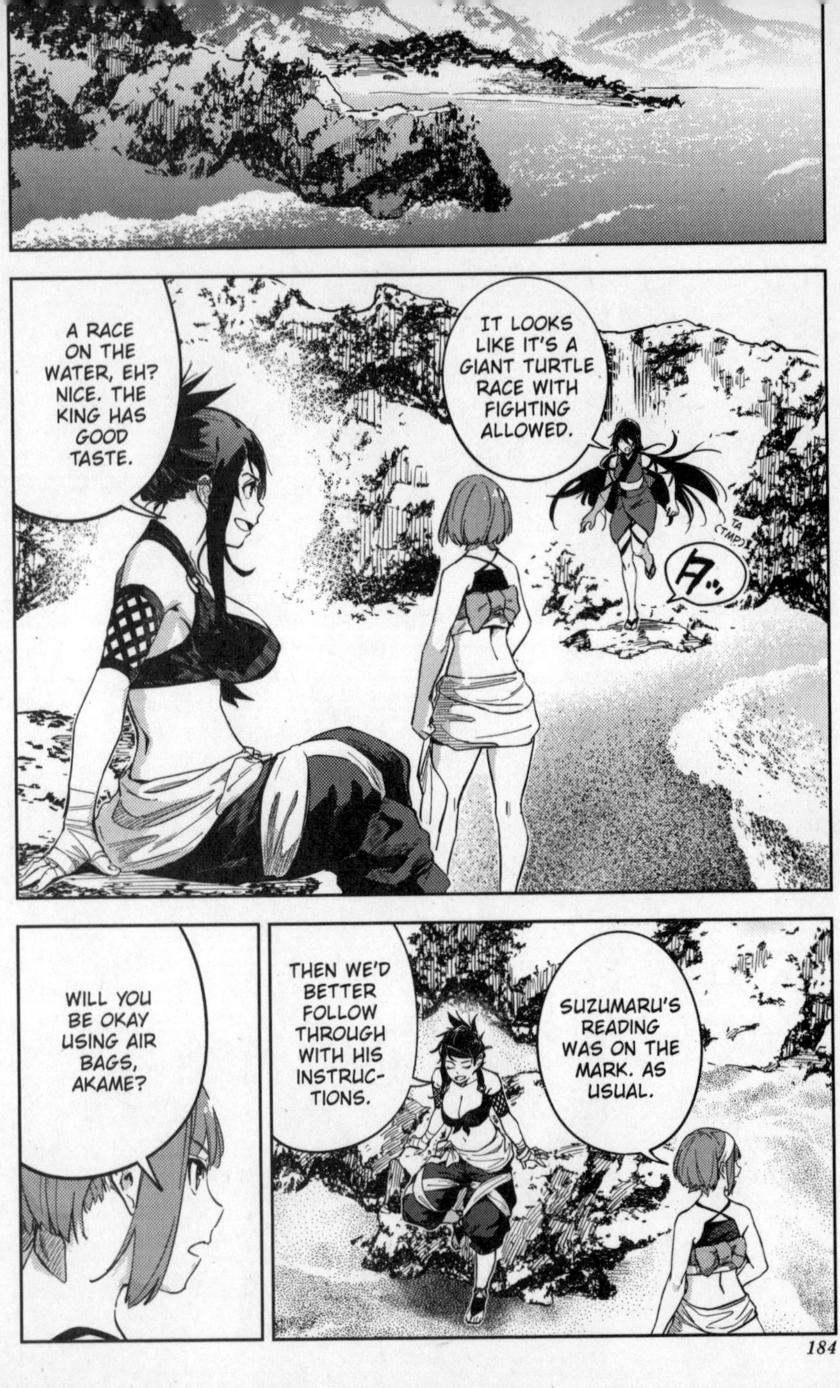
IT LOOKS LIKE IT'S A GIANT TURTLE RACE WITH FIGHTING ALLOWED.
タッ
TA (TMP)
A RACE ON THE WATER, EH? NICE. THE KING HAS GOOD TASTE.
SUZUMARU'S READING WAS ON THE MARK. AS USUAL.
THEN WE'D BETTER FOLLOW THROUGH WITH HIS INSTRUC-TIONS.
WILL YOU BE OKAY USING AIR BAGS, AKAME?

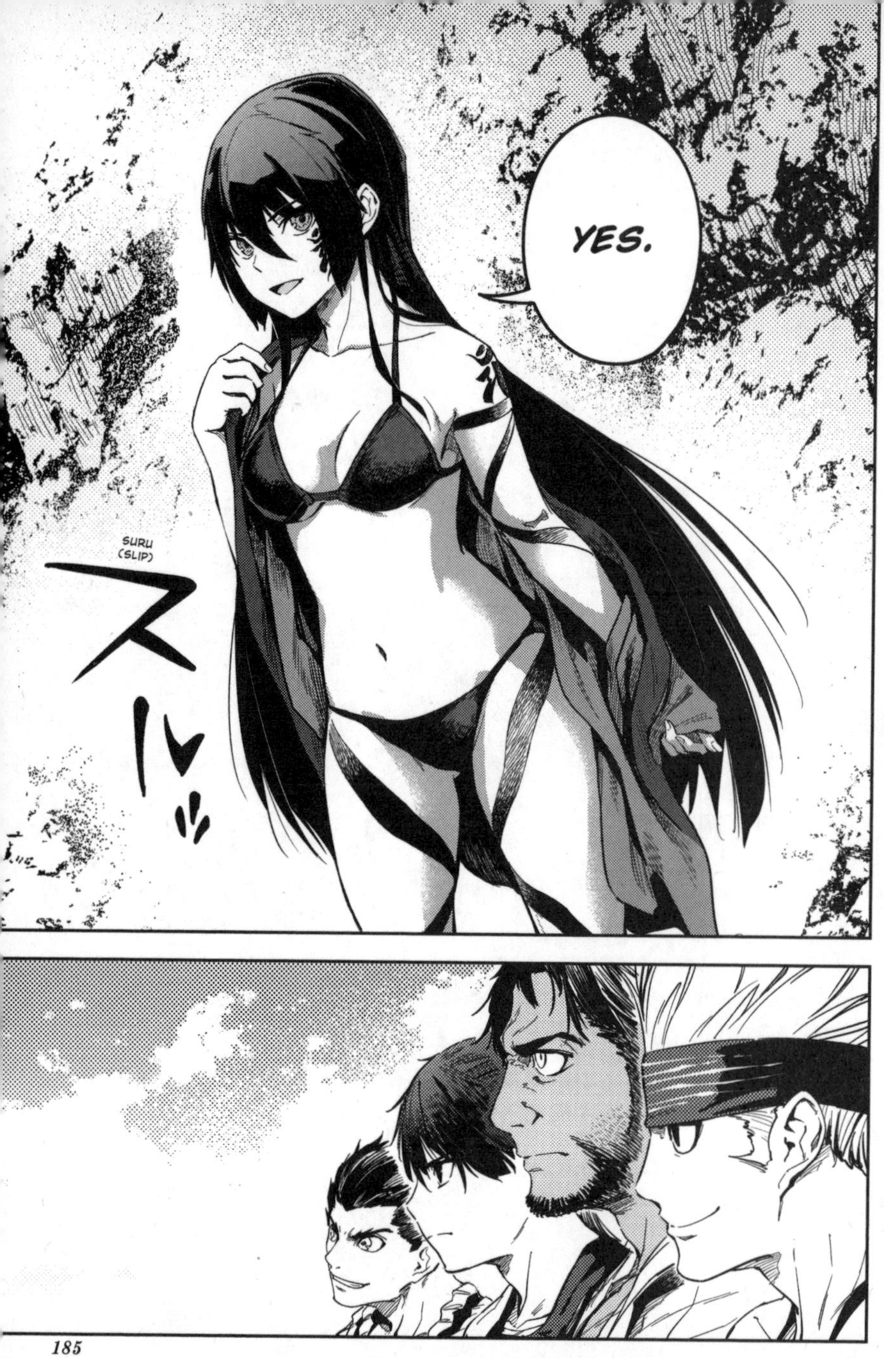
YES.
SURU
(SLIP)
スル

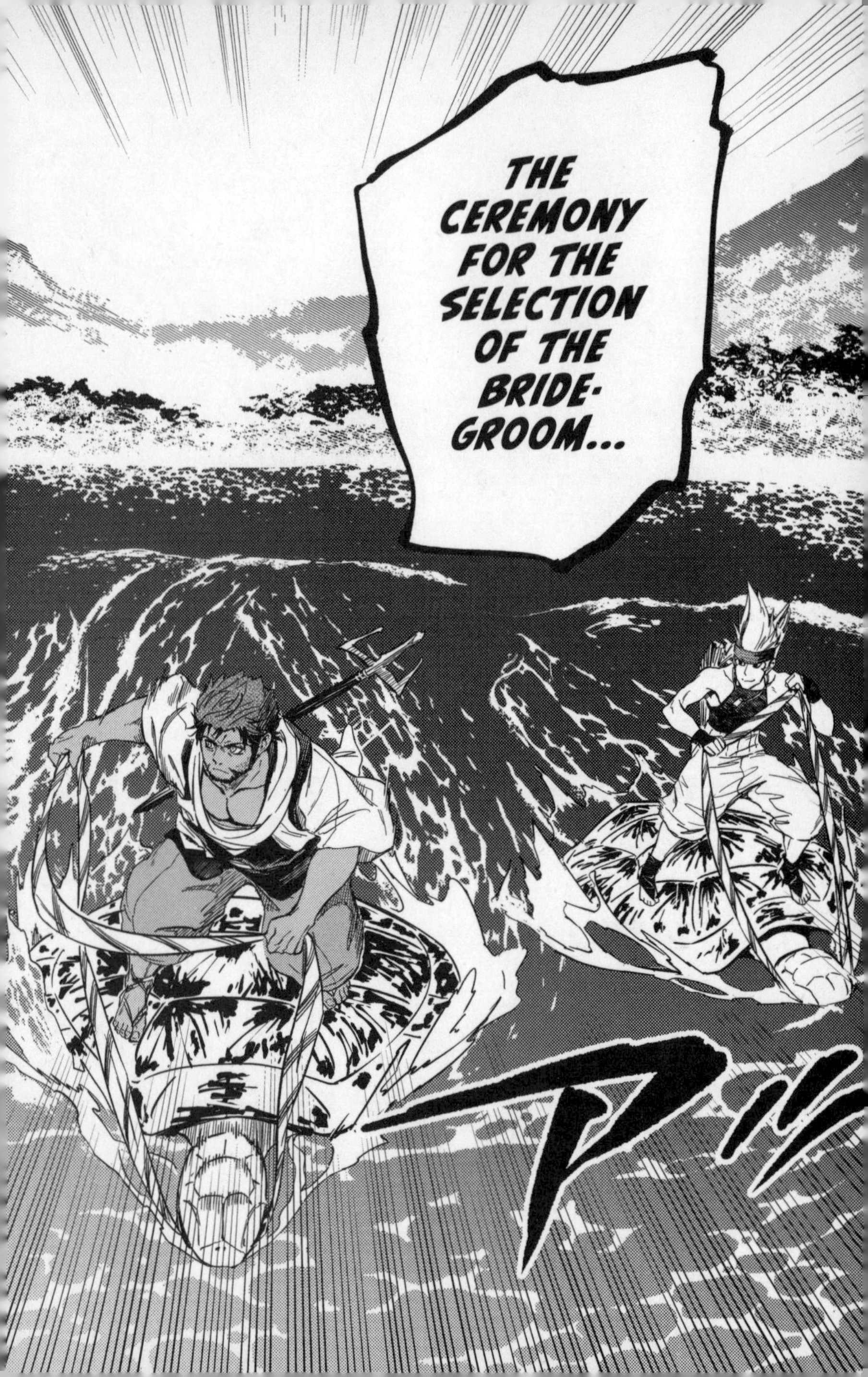
THE CEREMONY FOR THE SELECTION OF THE BRIDE-GROOM...

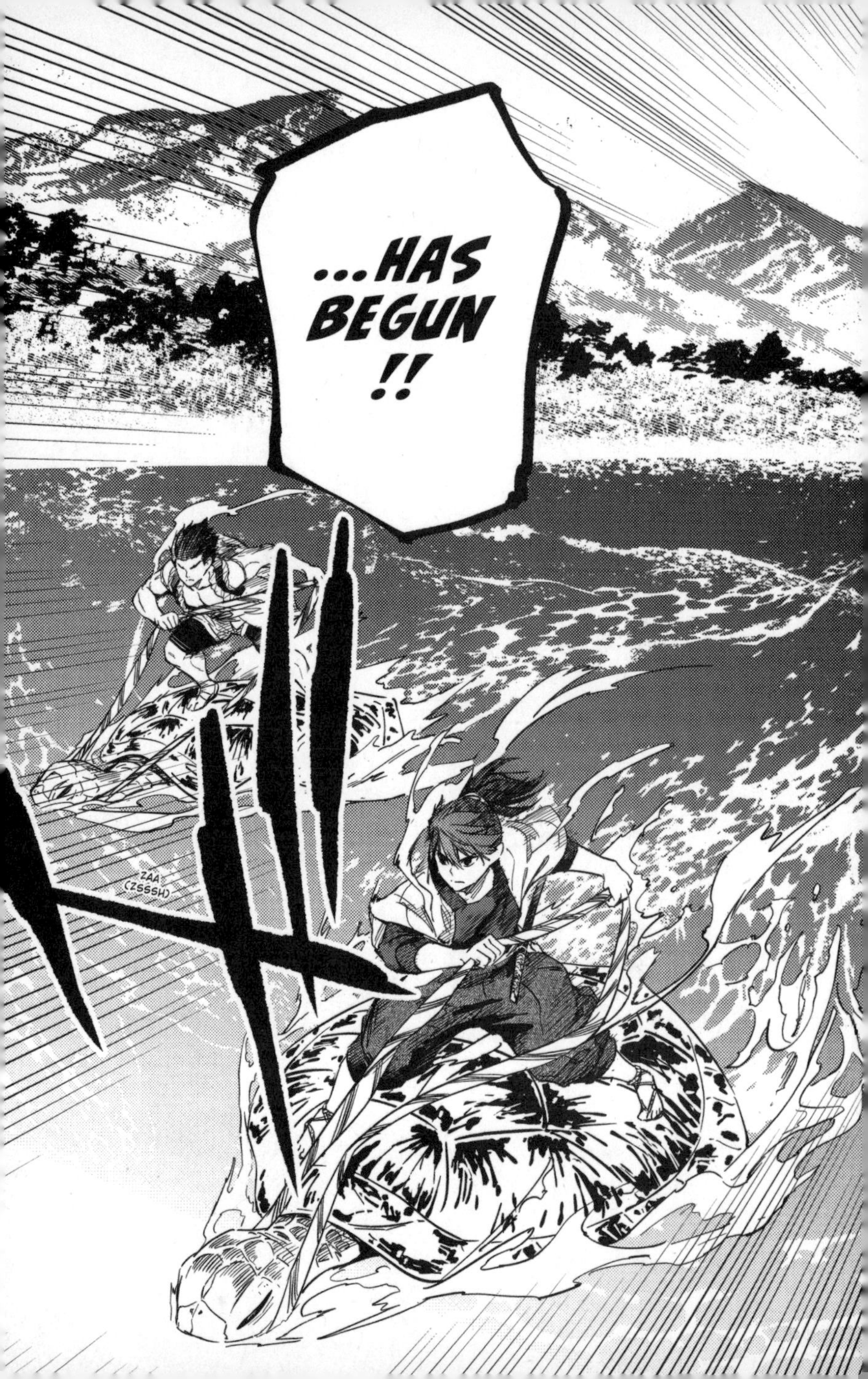
...HAS BEGUN!!
ZAA (ZSSSH)

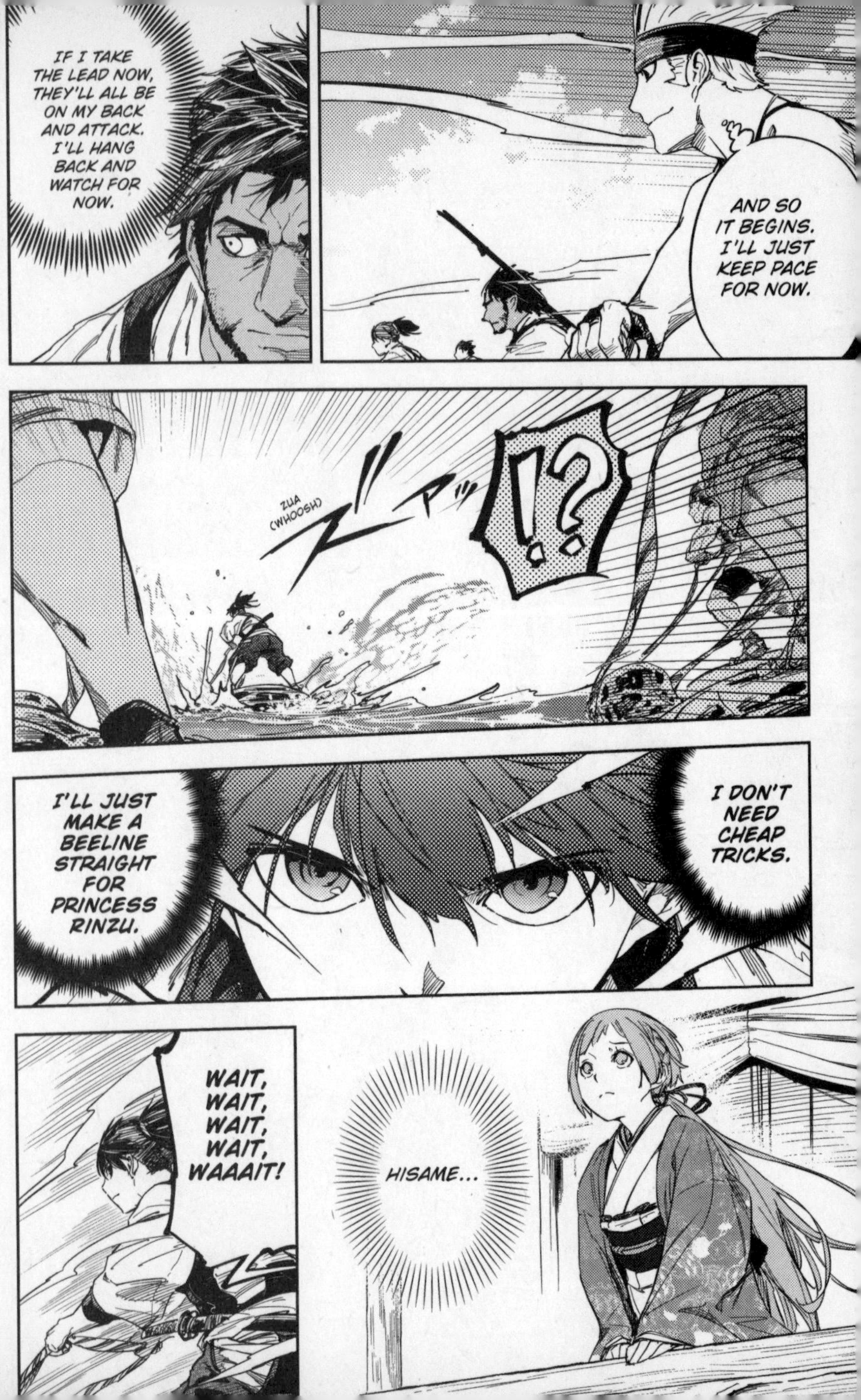
AND SO IT BEGINS. I'LL JUST KEEP PACE FOR NOW.
IF I TAKE THE LEAD NOW, THEY'LL ALL BE ON MY BACK AND ATTACK. I'LL HANG BACK AND WATCH FOR NOW.
!?
ZUA (WHOOSH)
I DON'T NEED CHEAP TRICKS.
I'LL JUST MAKE A BEELINE STRAIGHT FOR PRINCESS RINZU.
HISAME...
WAIT, WAIT, WAIT, WAIT, WAAAIT!

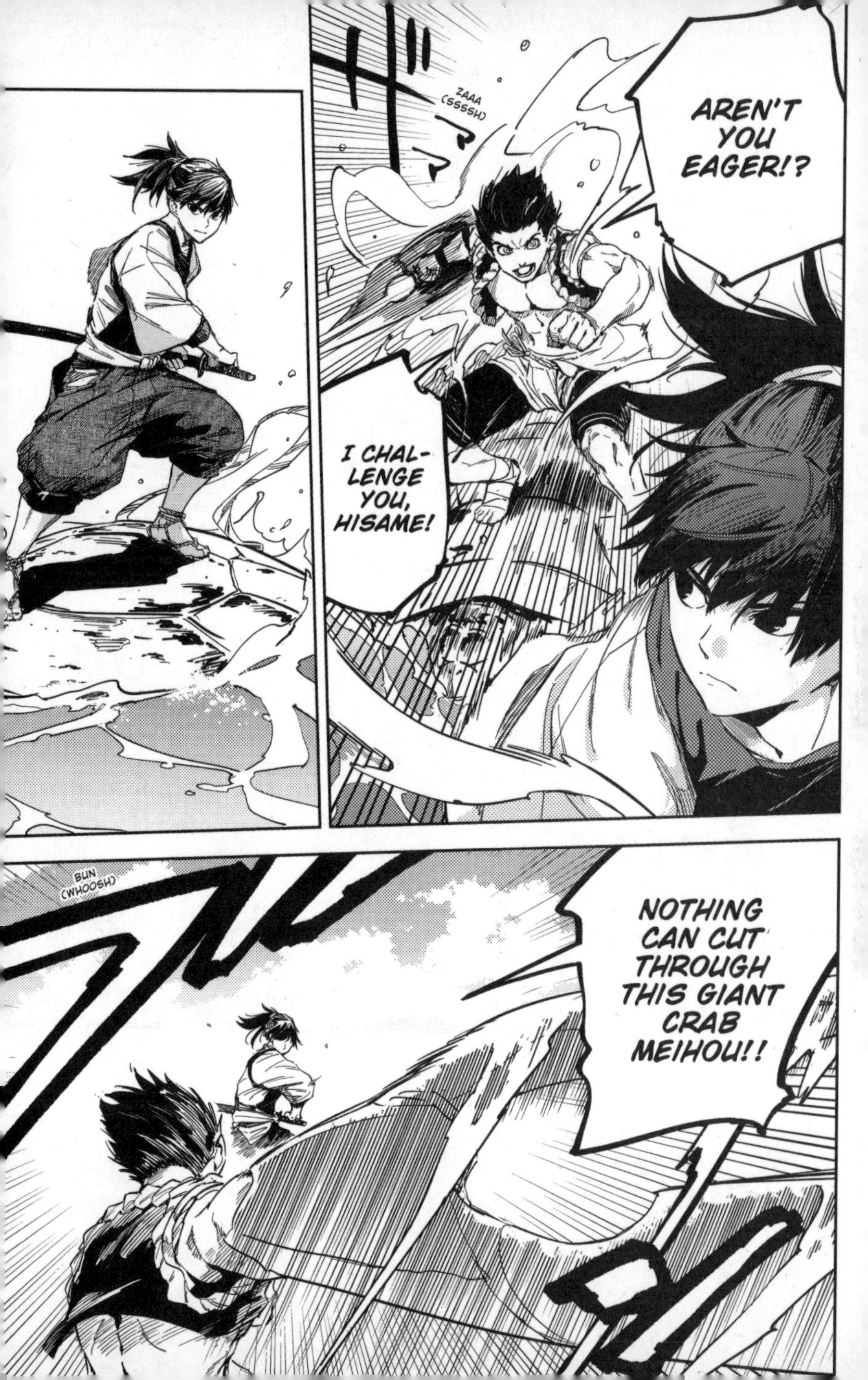
AREN'T YOU EAGER!?
ZAAA (SSSSH)
I CHAL-LENGE YOU, HISAME!
NOTHING CAN CUT THROUGH THIS GIANT CRAB MEIHOU!!
BUN (WHOOSH)

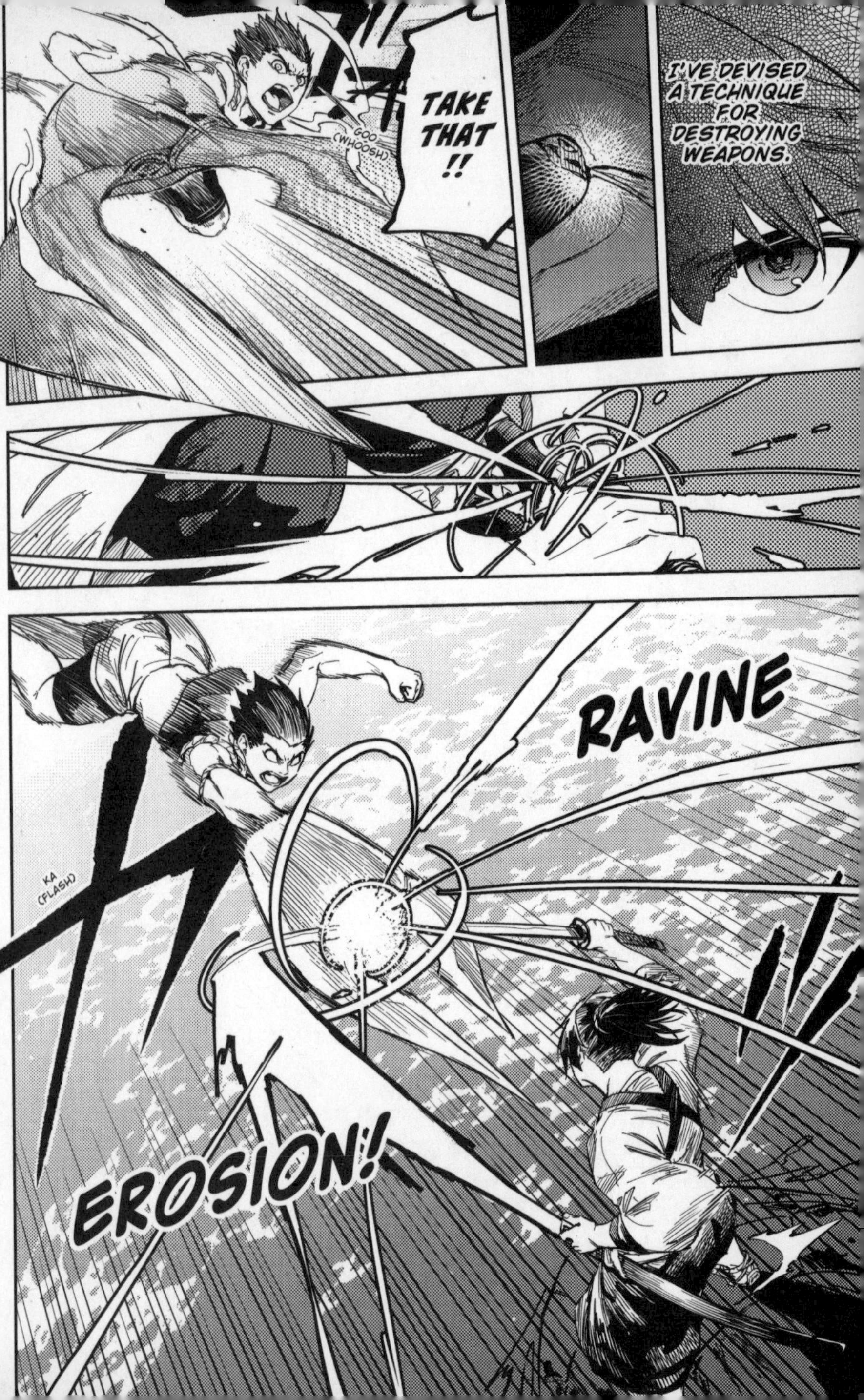
I'VE DEVISED A TECHNIQUE FOR DESTROYING WEAPONS.
TAKE THAT!!
GOO (WHOOSH)
KA (FLASH)
RAVINE
EROSION!

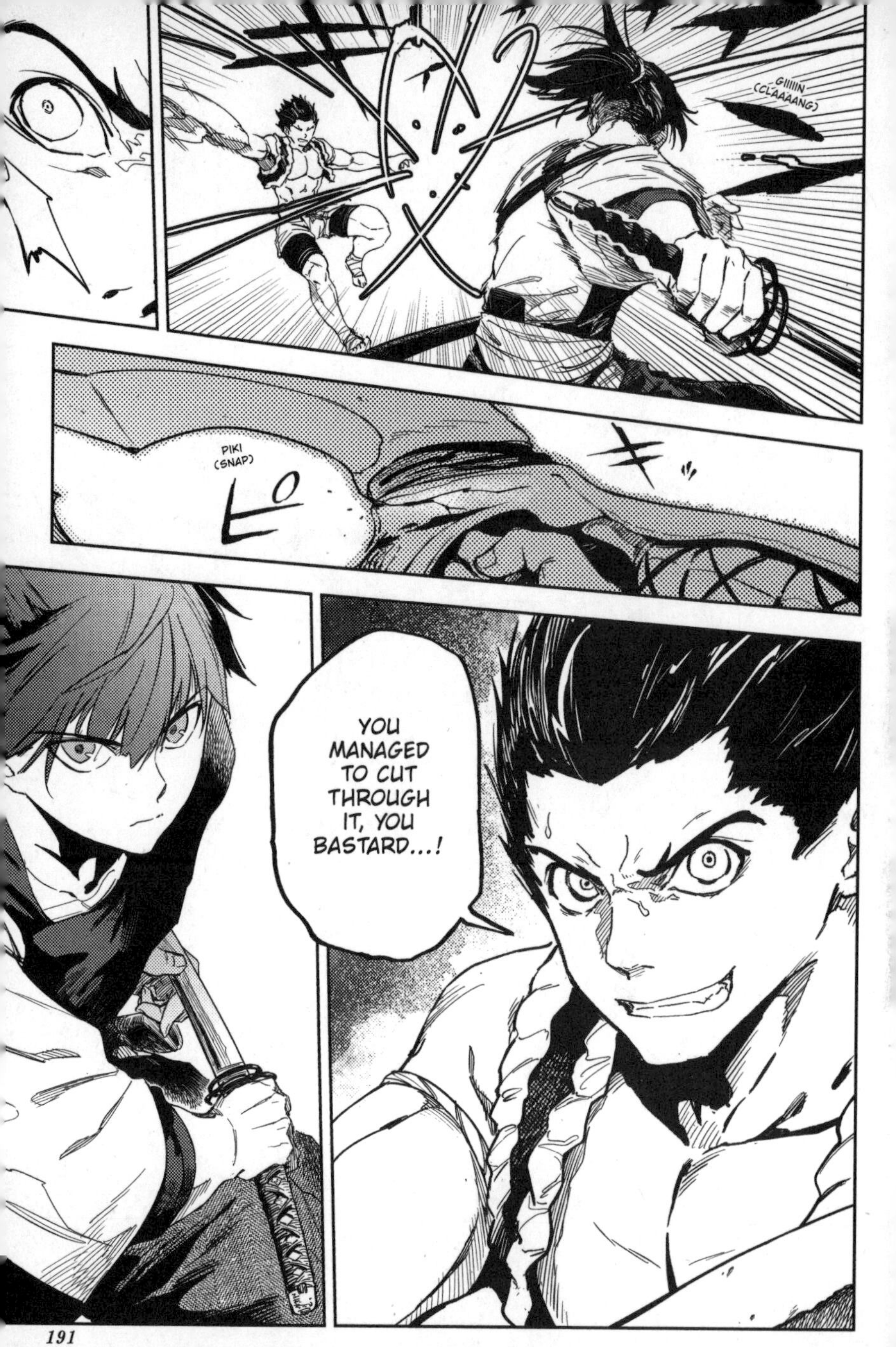
GIIIIN
(CLAAAANG)
PIKI
(SNAP)
YOU MANAGED TO CUT THROUGH IT, YOU BASTARD...!

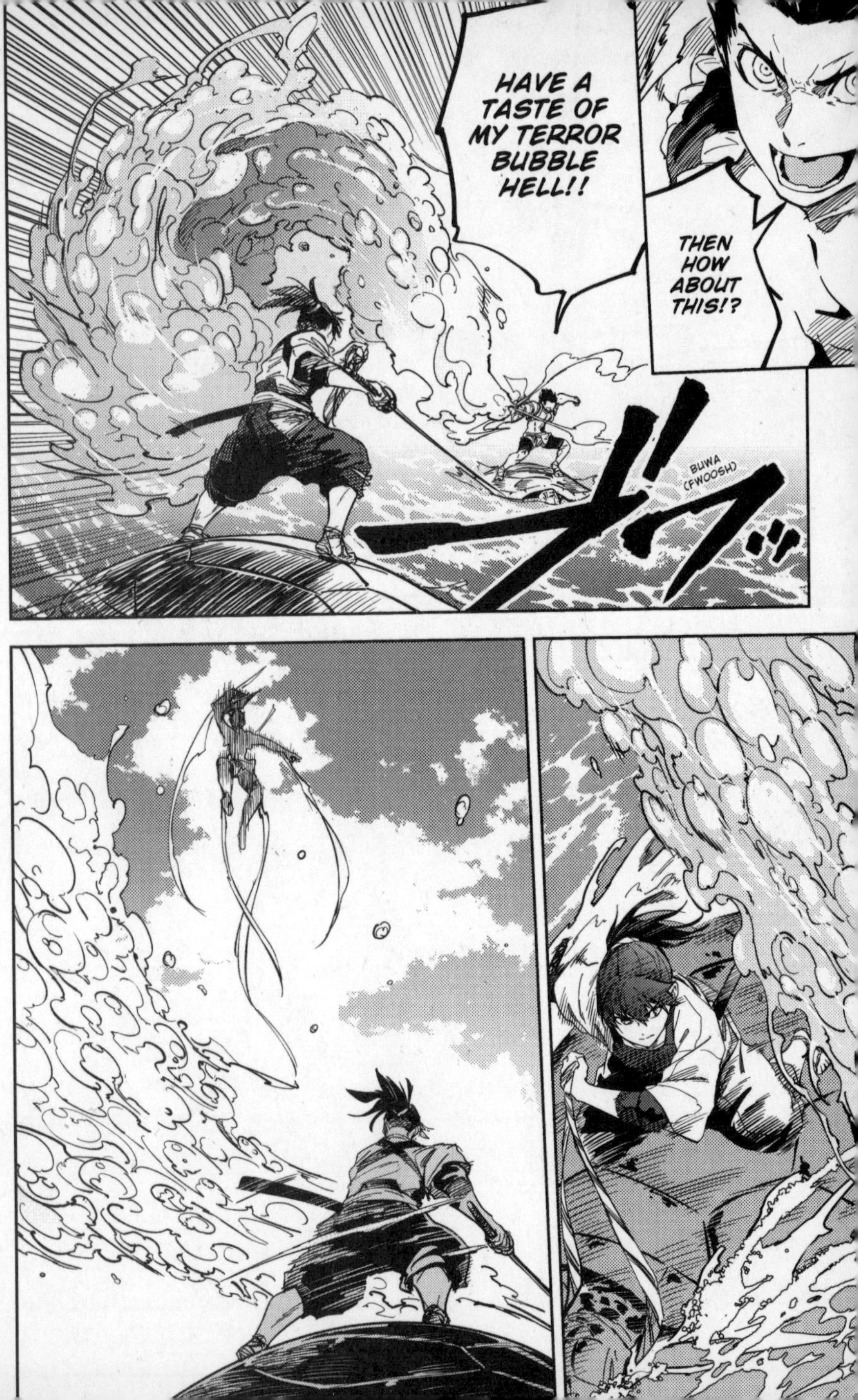
THEN HOW ABOUT THIS!?
HAVE A TASTE OF MY TERROR BUBBLE HELL!!
BUWA (FWOOSH)

I'M IMPRESSED YOU COULD FIGURE OUT THE BUBBLES CONSIDERING IT'S YOUR FIRST ENCOUNTER!

ANNOUNCING THE NAME OF YOUR ATTACK GAVE ME A HINT.

GOGIN (CLANG)

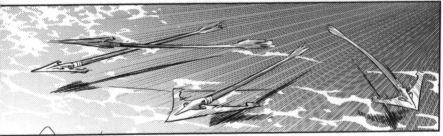

193

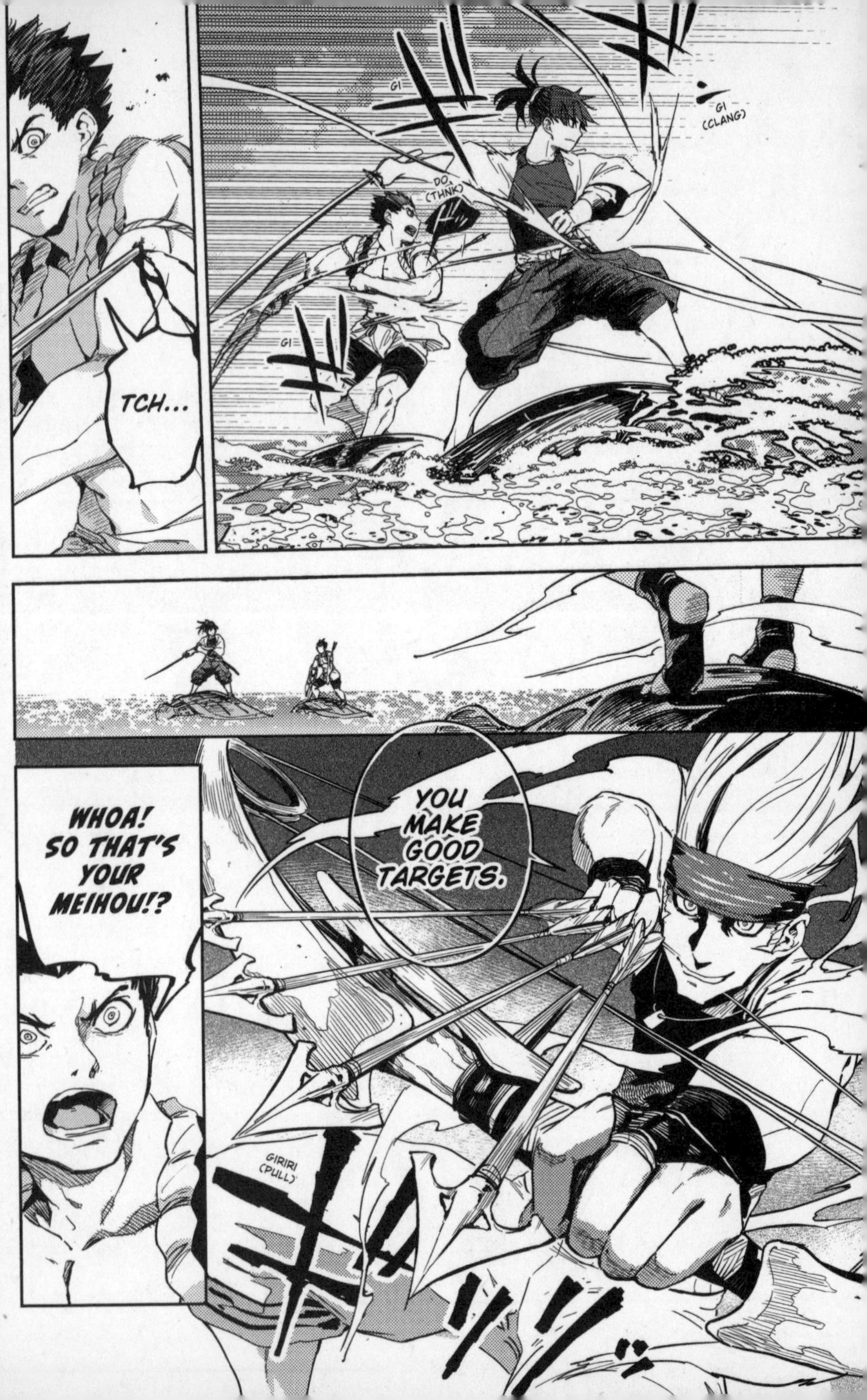
GI (CLANG)
GI
DO (THNK)
GI
TCH...
YOU MAKE GOOD TARGETS.
GIRIRI (PULL)
WHOA! SO THAT'S YOUR MEIHOU!?

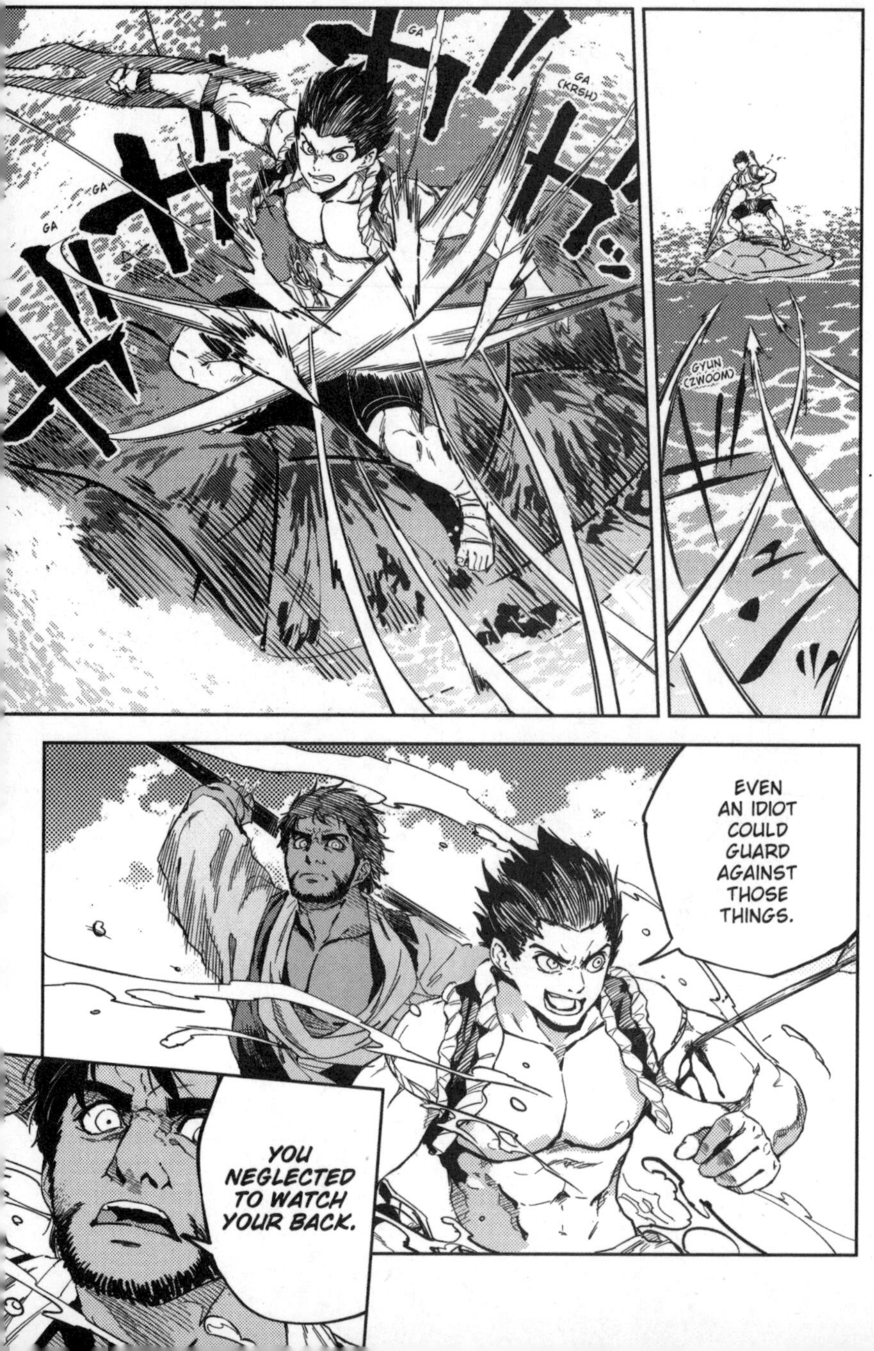
GYUN (ZWOOM)
GA (KRSH)
GA
GA
GA
EVEN AN IDIOT COULD GUARD AGAINST THOSE THINGS.
YOU NEGLECTED TO WATCH YOUR BACK.

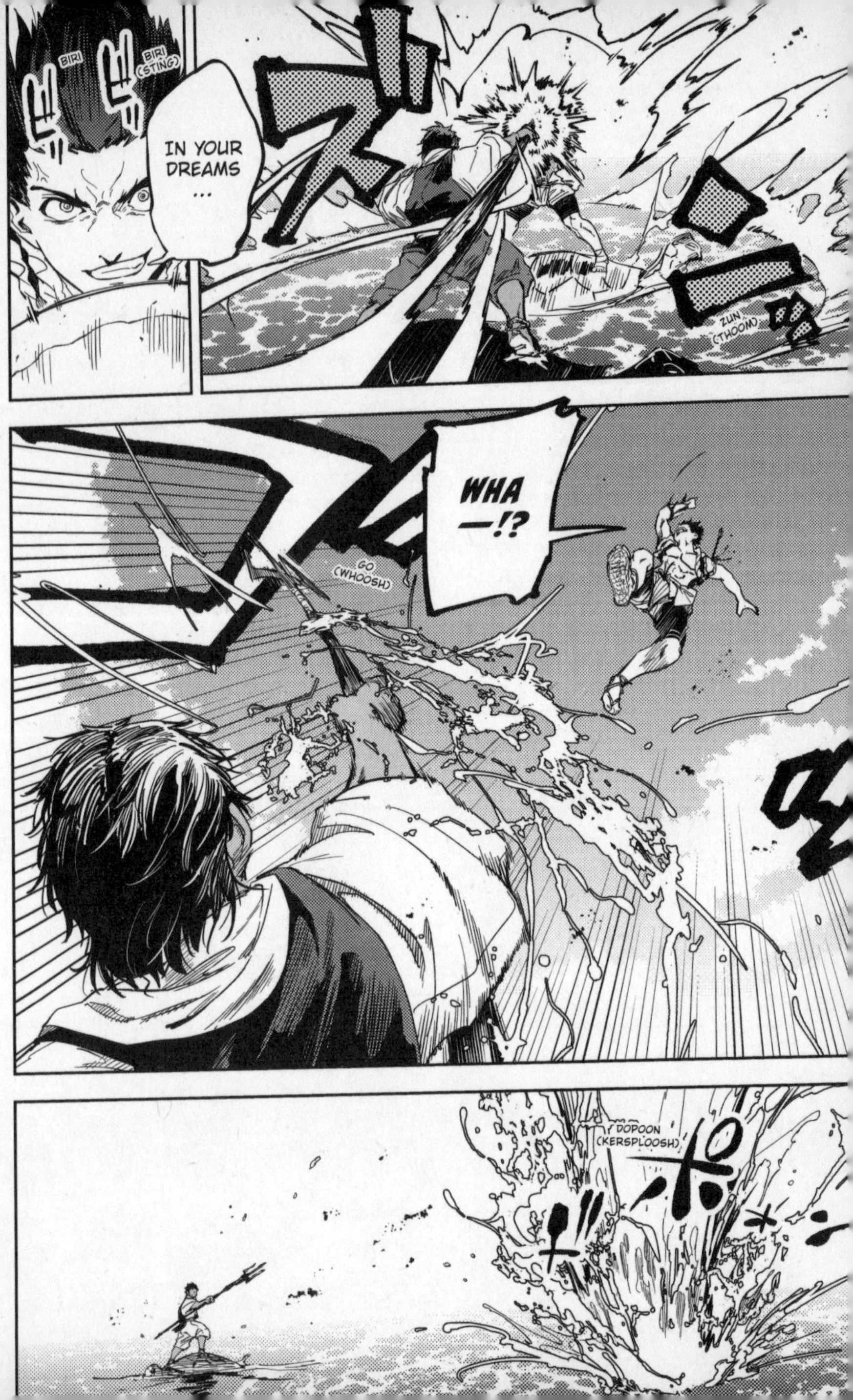
ZUN (THOOM)
BIRI BIRI (STING)
IN YOUR DREAMS ...
WHA —!?
GO (WHOOSH)
DOPOON (KERSPLOOSH)

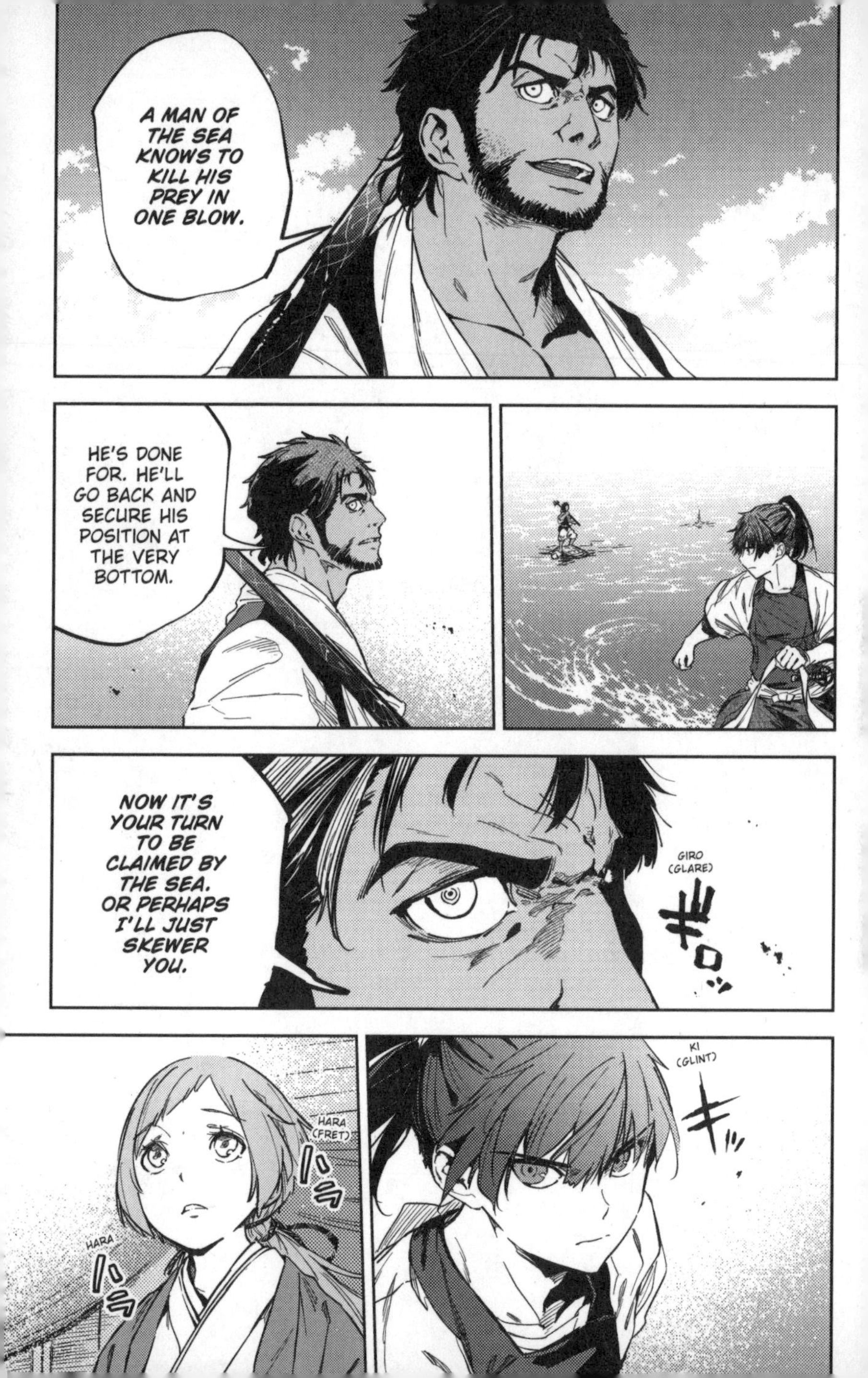
A MAN OF THE SEA KNOWS TO KILL HIS PREY IN ONE BLOW.
HE'S DONE FOR. HE'LL GO BACK AND SECURE HIS POSITION AT THE VERY BOTTOM.
NOW IT'S YOUR TURN TO BE CLAIMED BY THE SEA. OR PERHAPS I'LL JUST SKEWER YOU.
GIRO (GLARE)
KI (GLINT)
HARA (FRET)
HARA

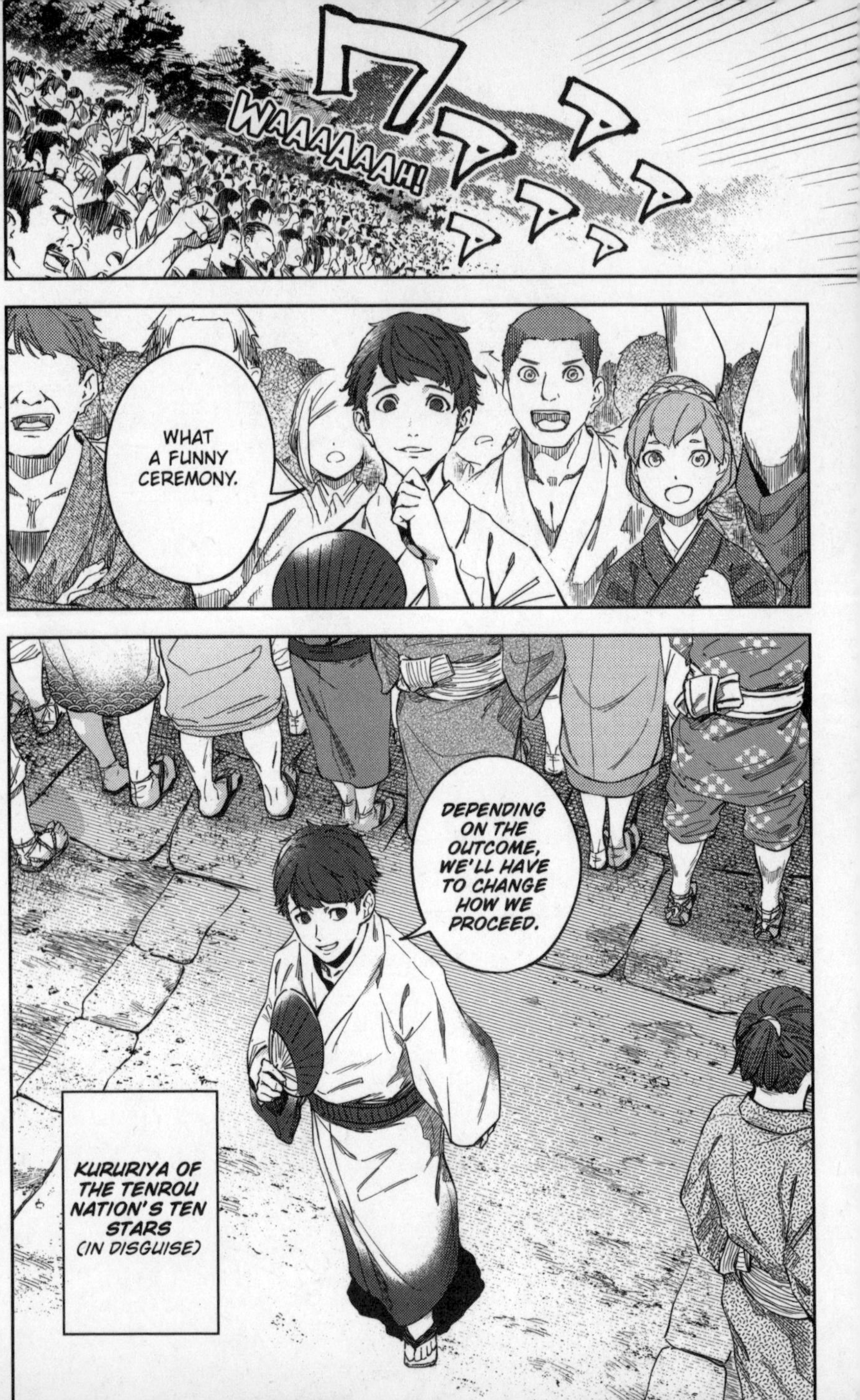
WAAAAAAAH!
WHAT A FUNNY CEREMONY.
DEPENDING ON THE OUTCOME, WE'LL HAVE TO CHANGE HOW WE PROCEED.
KURURIYA OF THE TENROU NATION'S TEN STARS (IN DISGUISE)

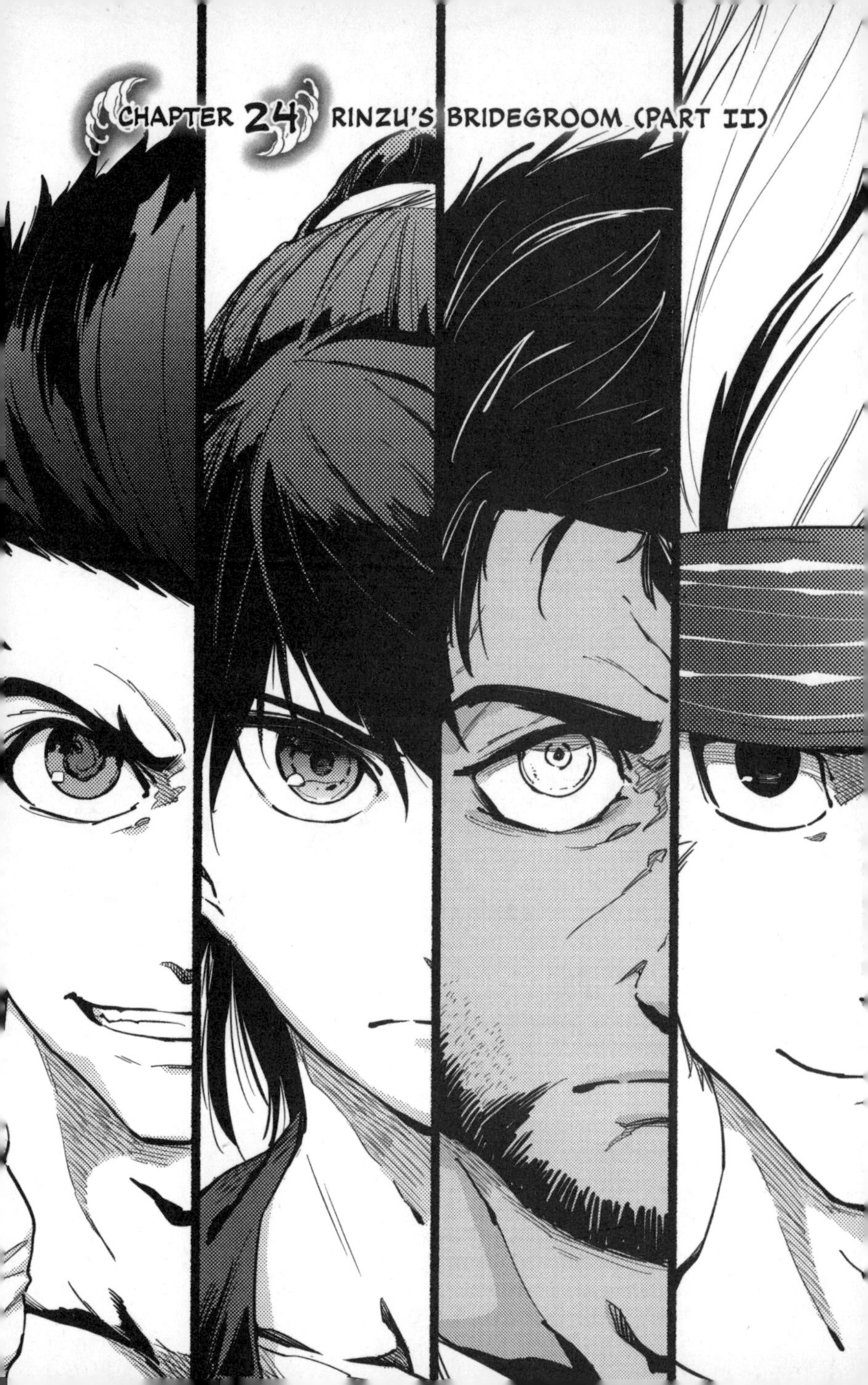
CHAPTER 24 RINZU'S BRIDEGROOM (PART II)

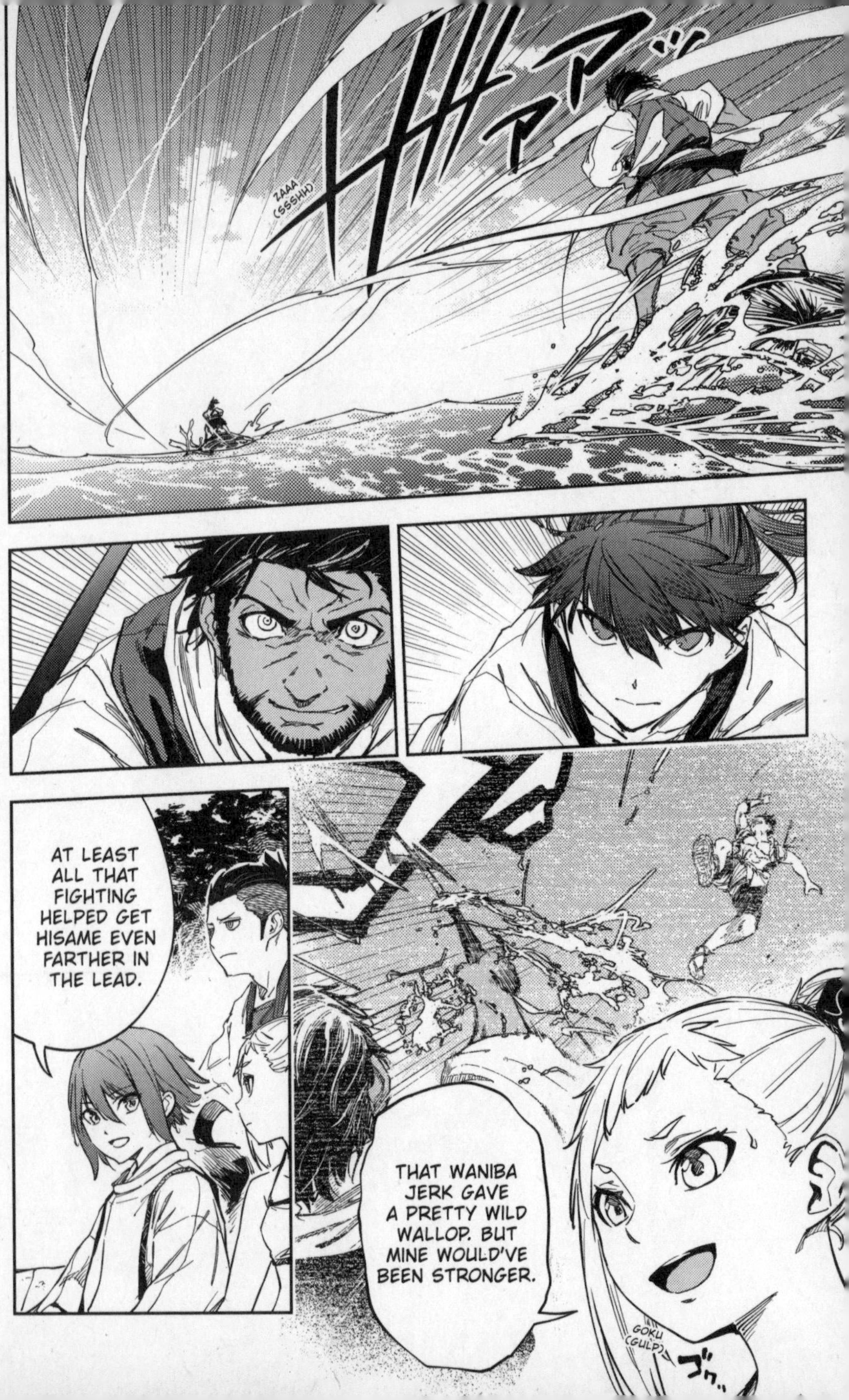
ZAAA (SSSHH)
AT LEAST ALL THAT FIGHTING HELPED GET HISAME EVEN FARTHER IN THE LEAD.
THAT WANIBA JERK GAVE A PRETTY WILD WALLOP. BUT MINE WOULD'VE BEEN STRONGER.
GOKU (GULP)

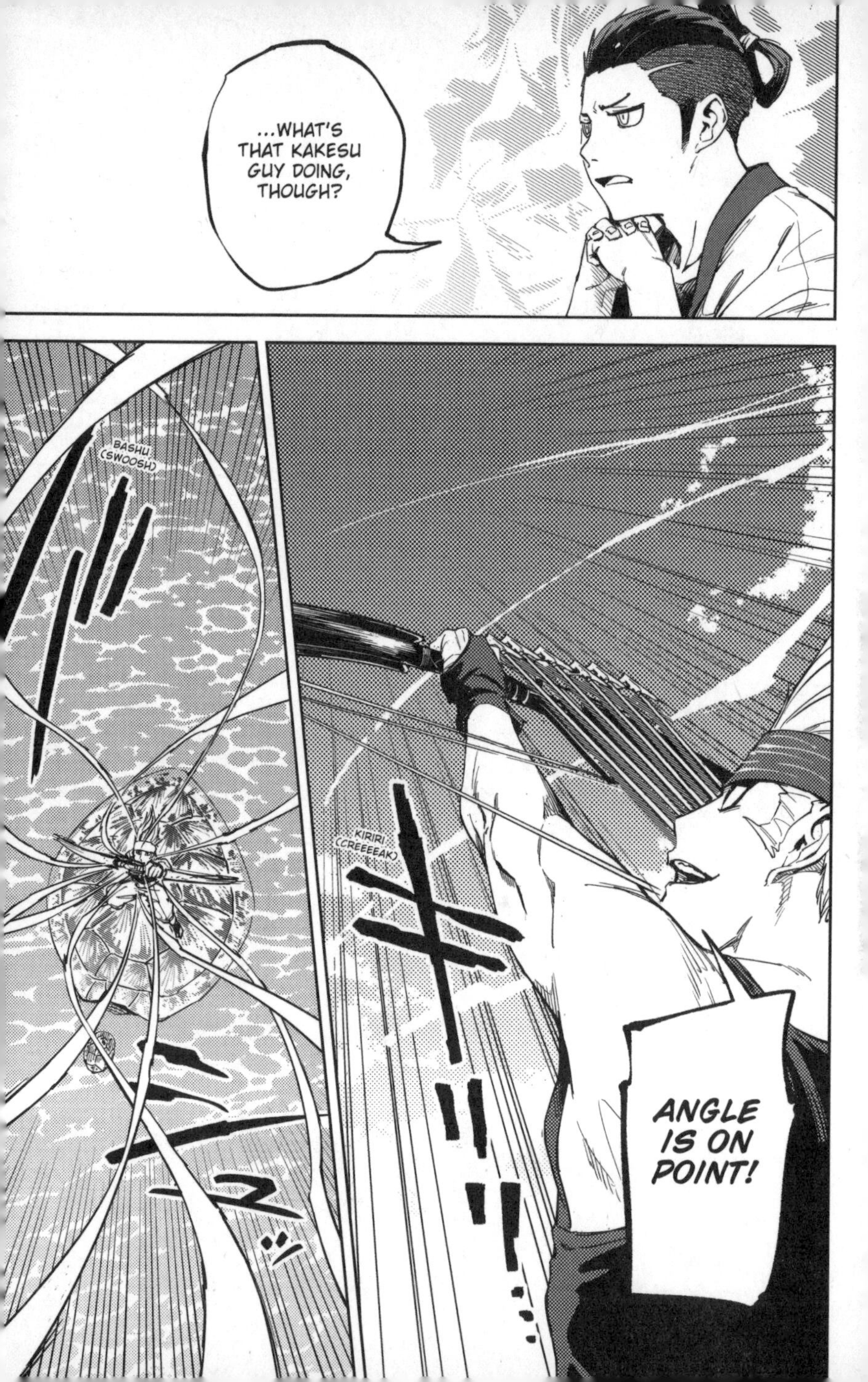
...WHAT'S THAT KAKESU GUY DOING, THOUGH?
KIRIRI (CREEEEAK)
ANGLE IS ON POINT!
BASHU (SWOOSH)

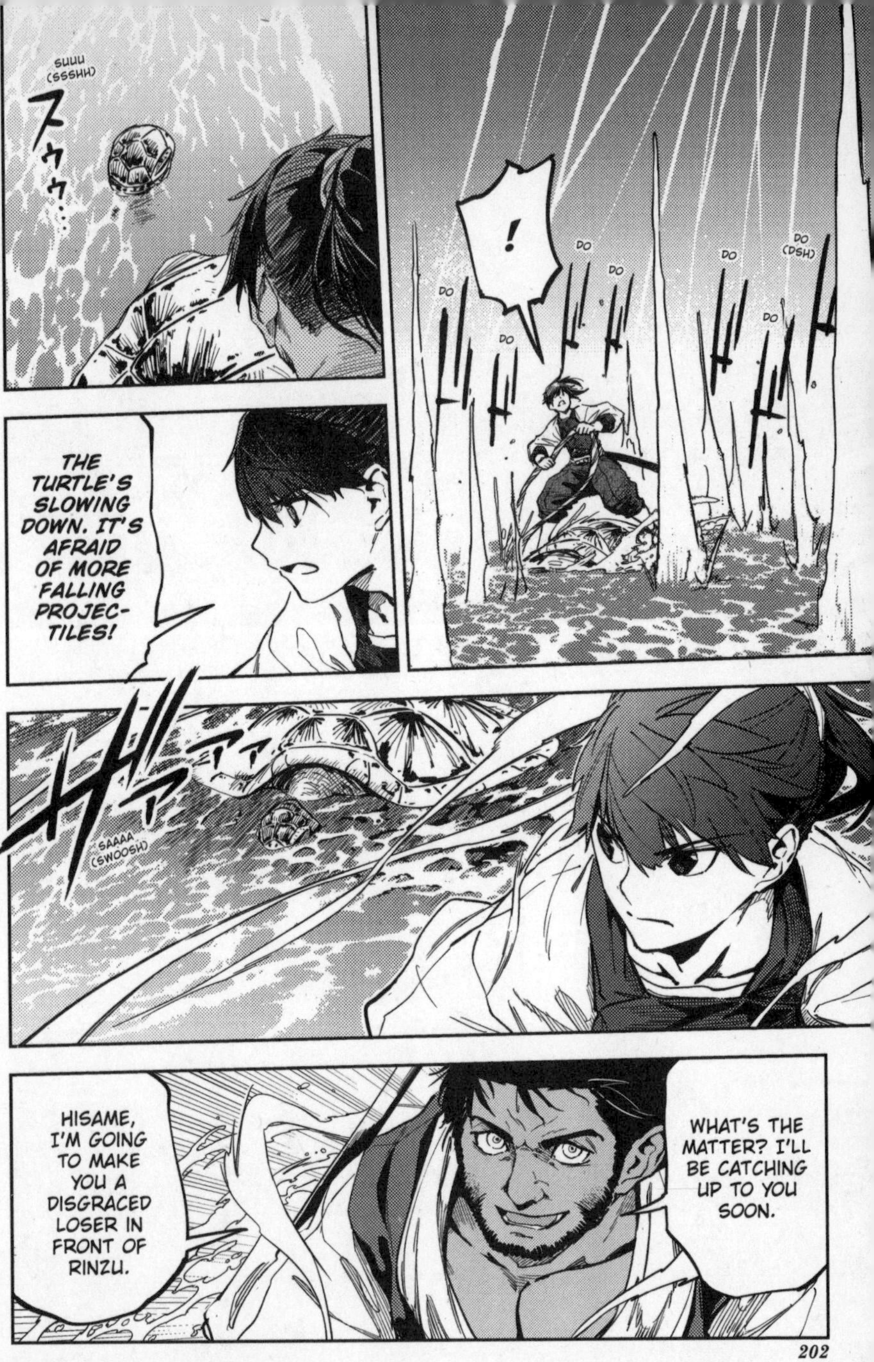
!
DO
DO
DO
DO
DO
DO
DO (DSH)
SUUU (SSSHH)
THE TURTLE'S SLOWING DOWN. IT'S AFRAID OF MORE FALLING PROJEC- TILES!
SAAAA (SWOOSH)
WHAT'S THE MATTER? I'LL BE CATCHING UP TO YOU SOON.
HISAME, I'M GOING TO MAKE YOU A DISGRACED LOSER IN FRONT OF RINZU.

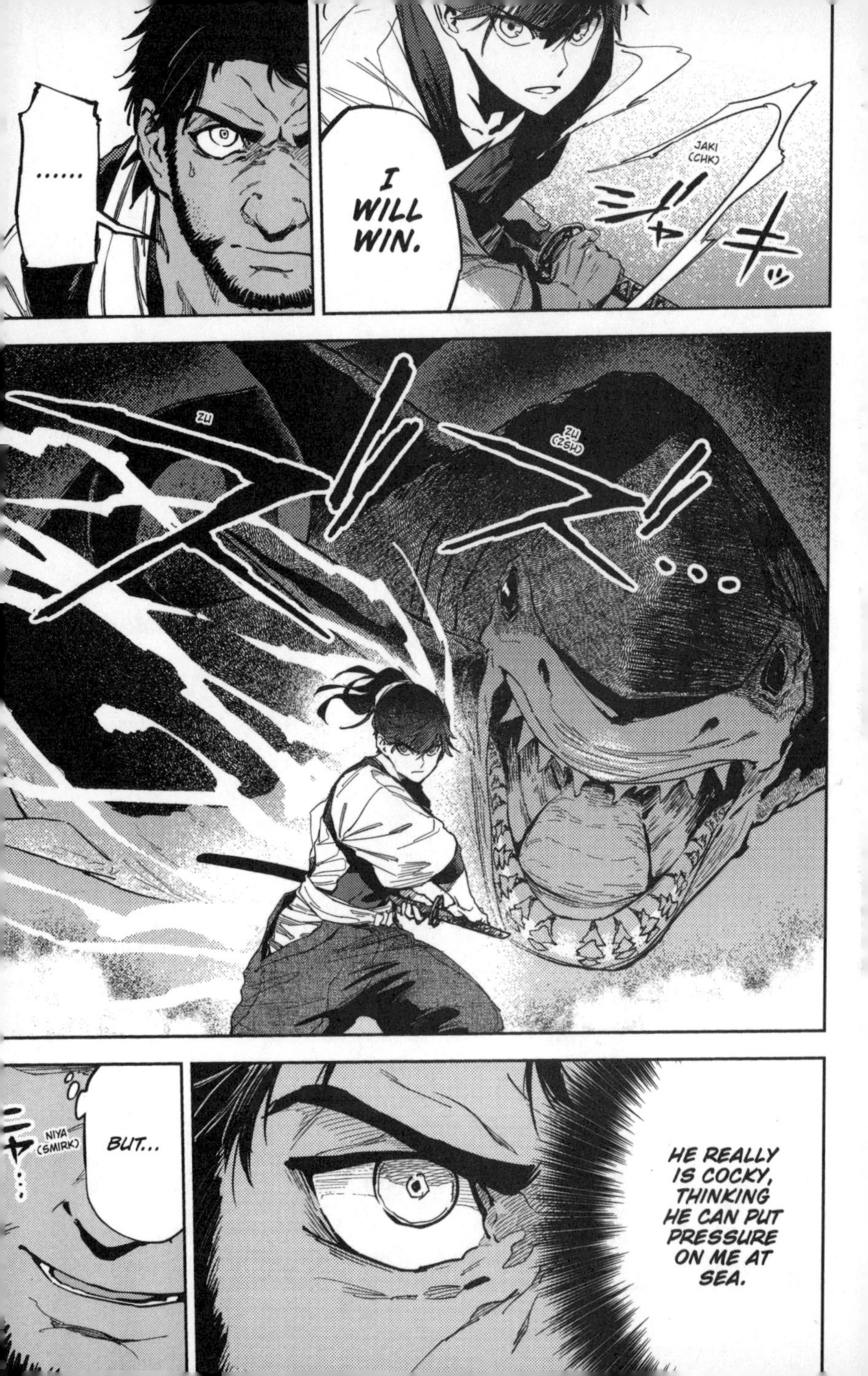
I WILL WIN.
JAKI (CHK)
......
ZU (ZSH)
ZU
HE REALLY IS COCKY, THINKING HE CAN PUT PRESSURE ON ME AT SEA.
BUT...
NIYA (SMIRK)

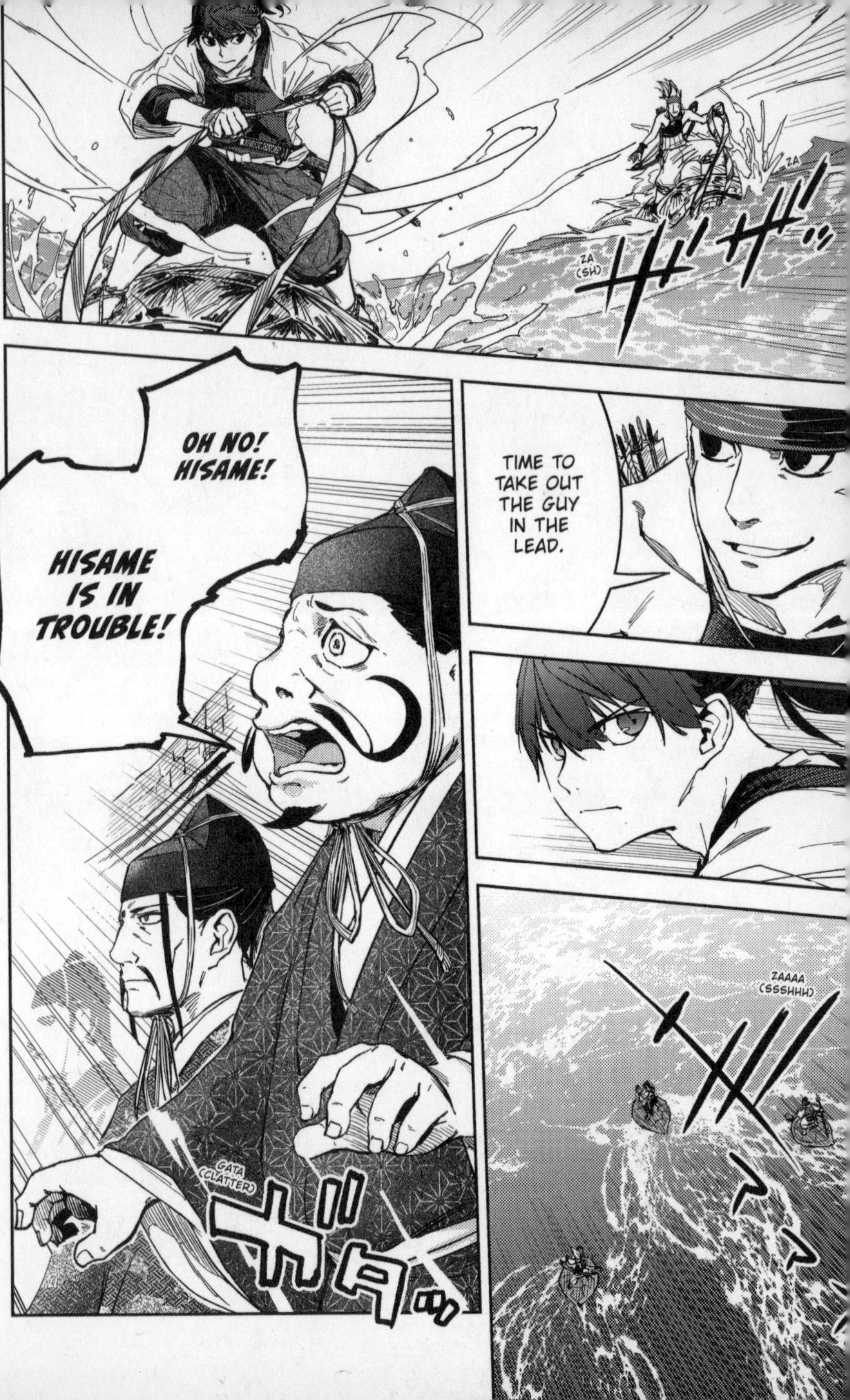
ZA
ZA (SH)
TIME TO TAKE OUT THE GUY IN THE LEAD.
ZAAAA (SSSHHH)
OH NO! HISAME!
HISAME IS IN TROUBLE!
GATA (CLATTER)

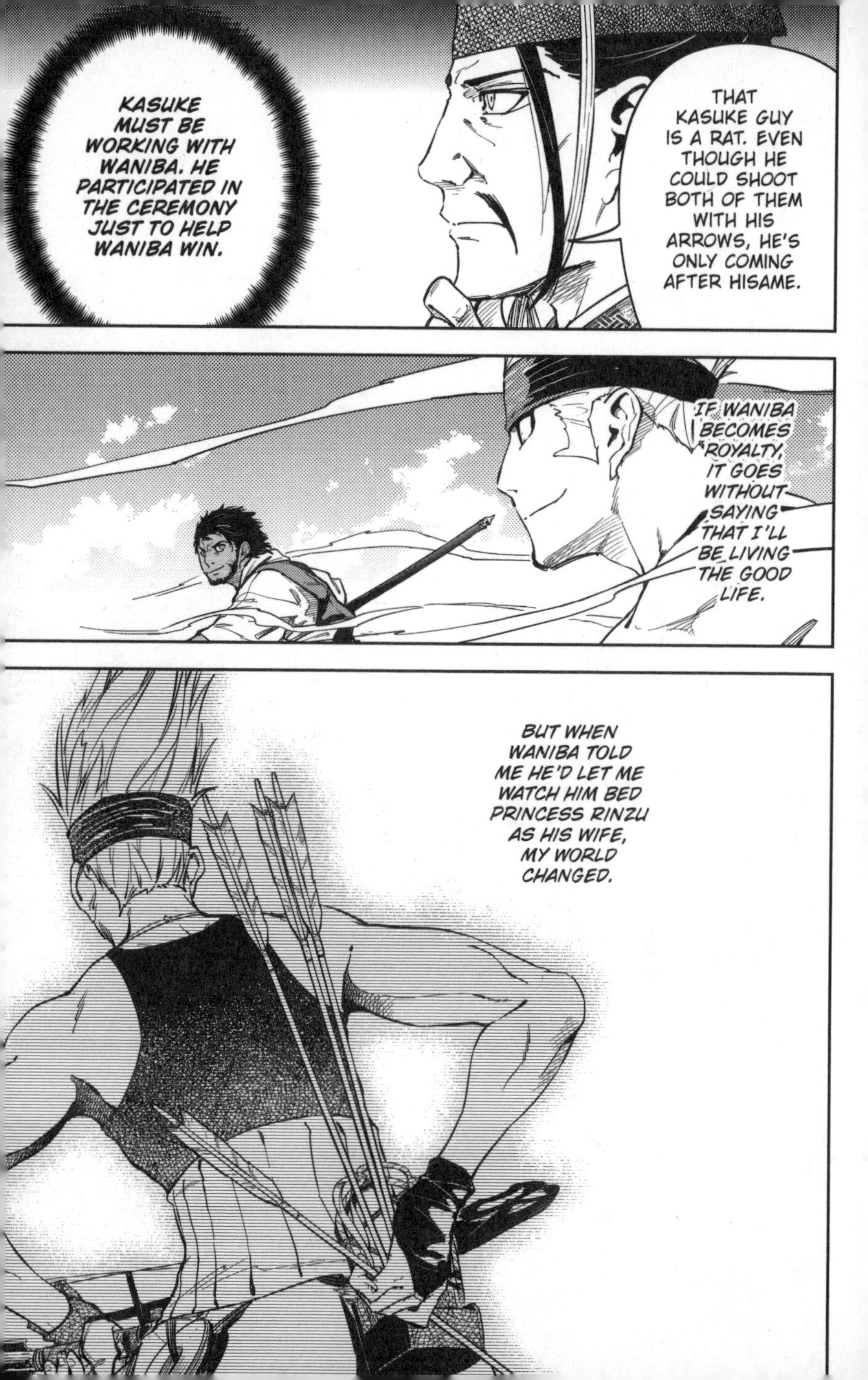
THAT KASUKE GUY IS A RAT. EVEN THOUGH HE COULD SHOOT BOTH OF THEM WITH HIS ARROWS, HE'S ONLY COMING AFTER HISAME.
KASUKE MUST BE WORKING WITH WANIBA. HE PARTICIPATED IN THE CEREMONY JUST TO HELP WANIBA WIN.
IF WANIBA BECOMES ROYALTY, IT GOES WITHOUT SAYING THAT I'LL BE LIVING THE GOOD LIFE.
BUT WHEN WANIBA TOLD ME HE'D LET ME WATCH HIM BED PRINCESS RINZU AS HIS WIFE, MY WORLD CHANGED.

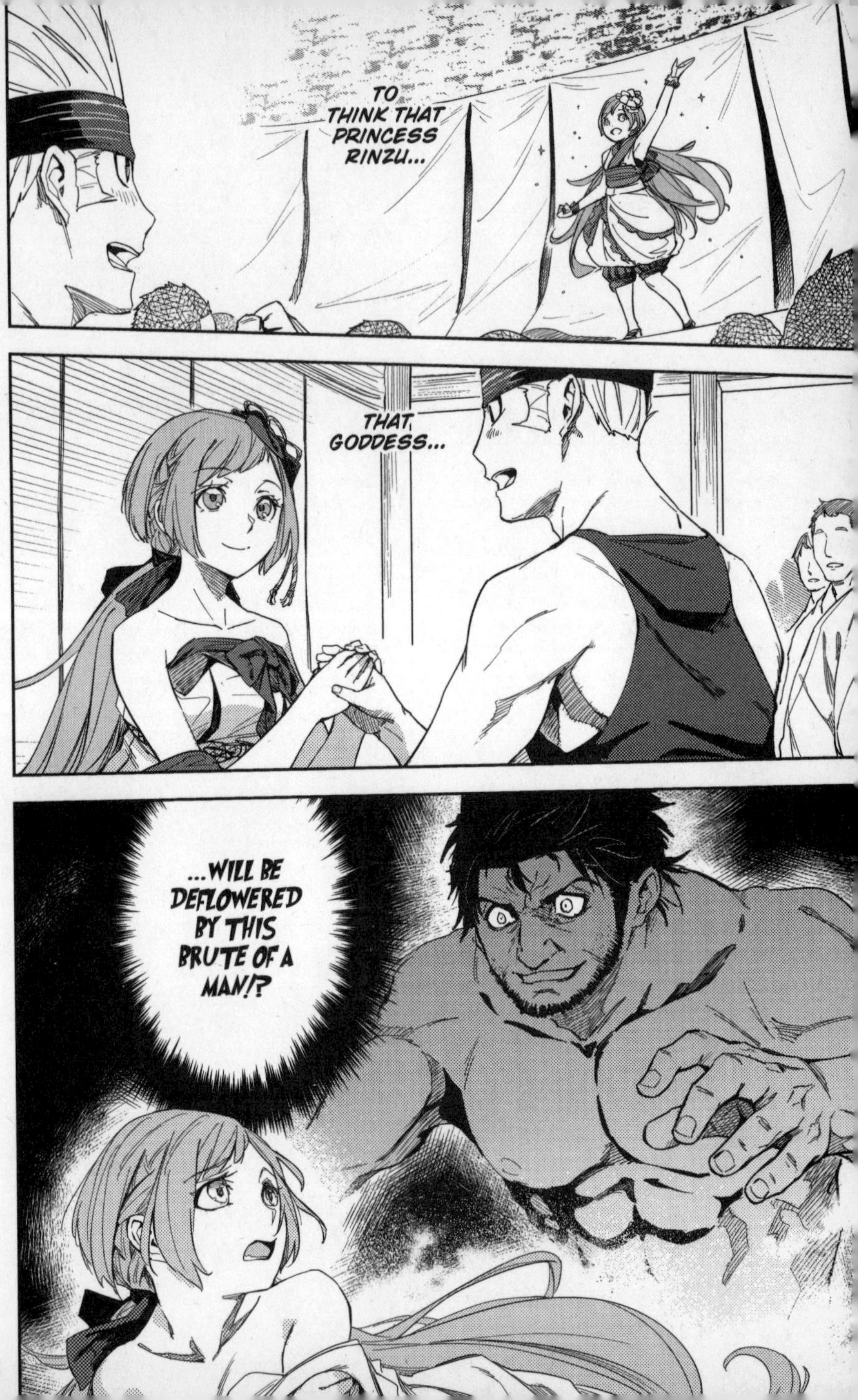
TO THINK THAT PRINCESS RINZU...
THAT GODDESS...
...WILL BE DEFLOWERED BY THIS BRUTE OF A MAN!?

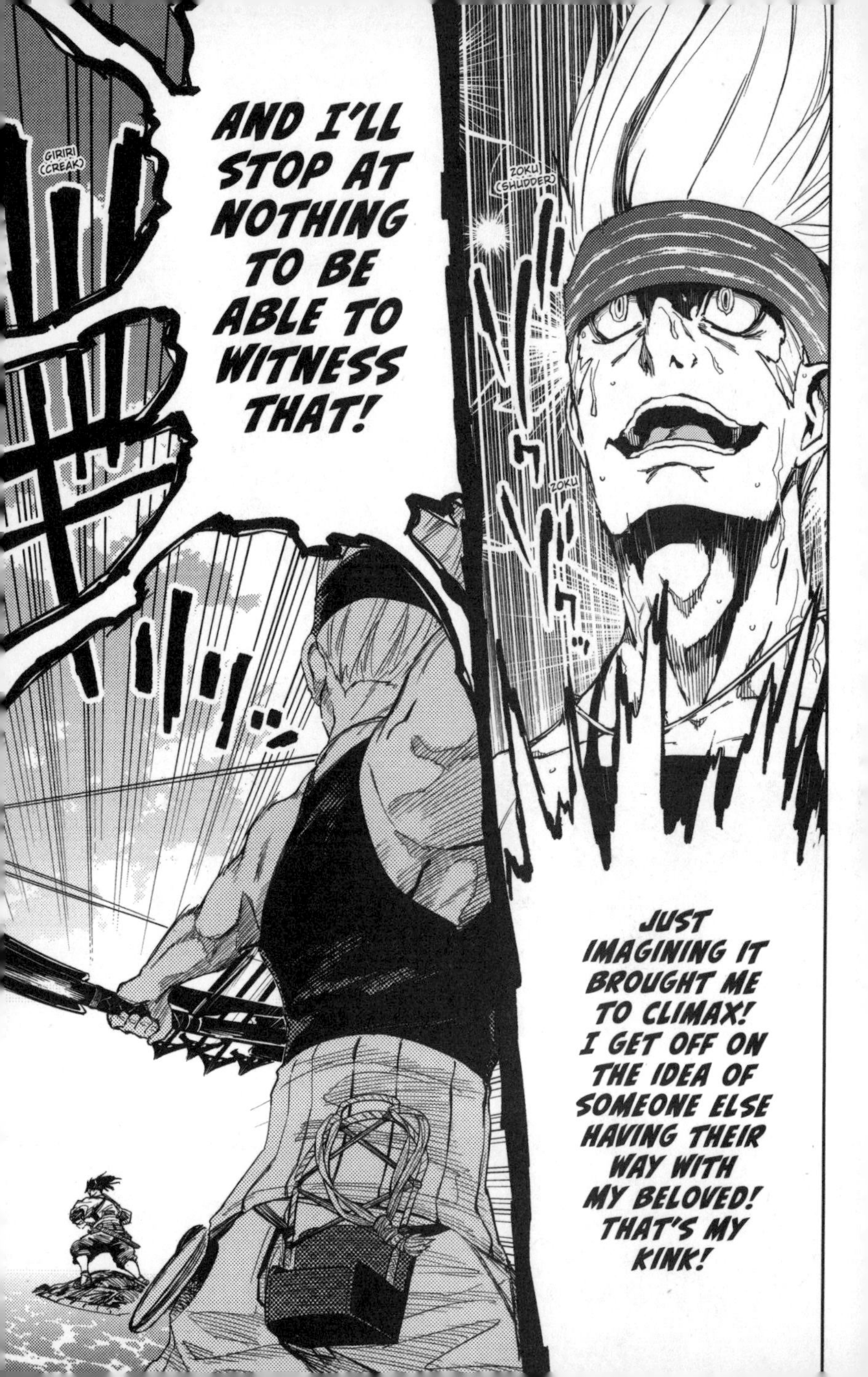
ZOKU (SHUDDER)
ZOKU
JUST IMAGINING IT BROUGHT ME TO CLIMAX! I GET OFF ON THE IDEA OF SOMEONE ELSE HAVING THEIR WAY WITH MY BELOVED! THAT'S MY KINK!
AND I'LL STOP AT NOTHING TO BE ABLE TO WITNESS THAT!
GIRIRI (CREAK)

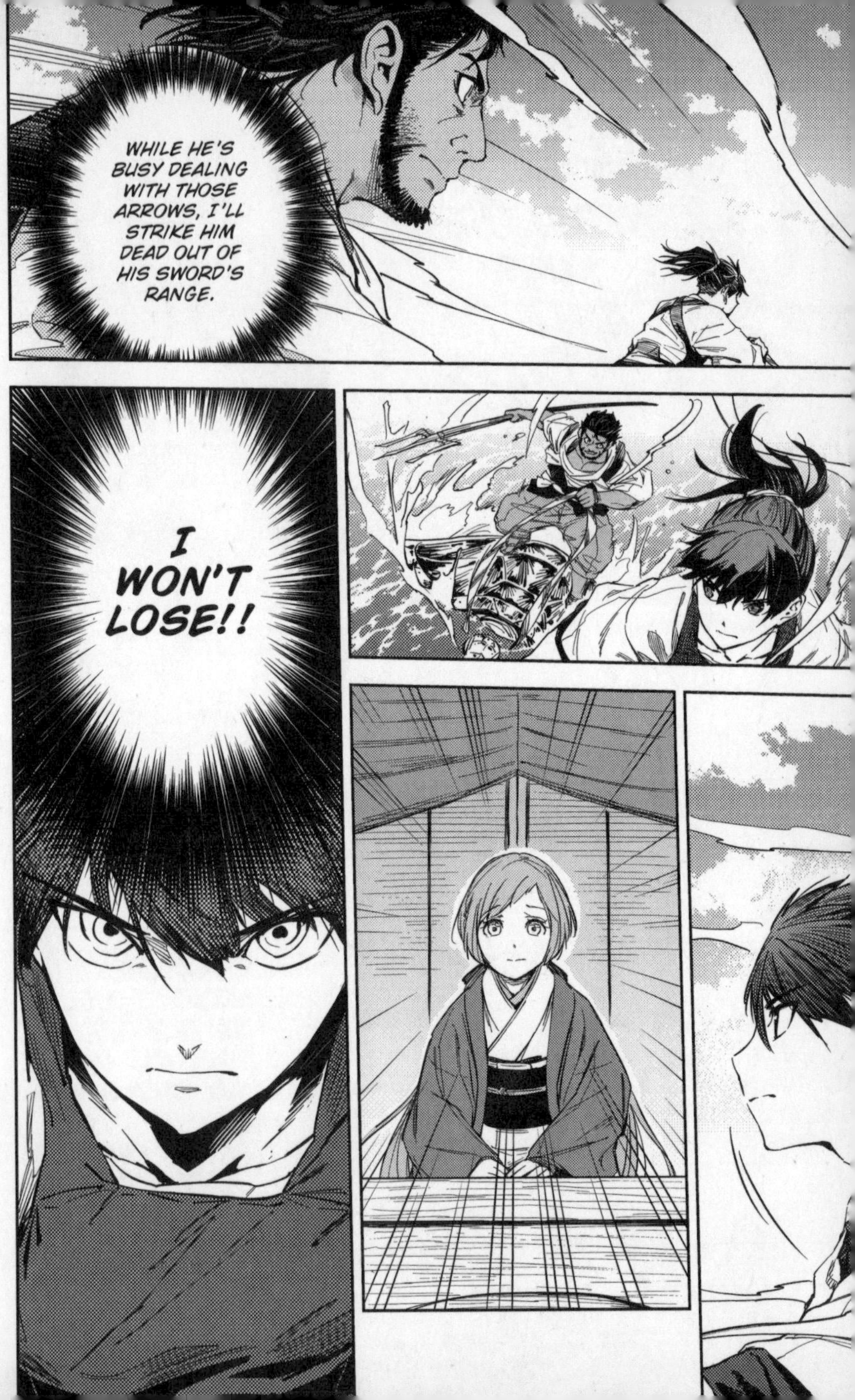
WHILE HE'S BUSY DEALING WITH THOSE ARROWS, I'LL STRIKE HIM DEAD OUT OF HIS SWORD'S RANGE.
I WON'T LOSE!!

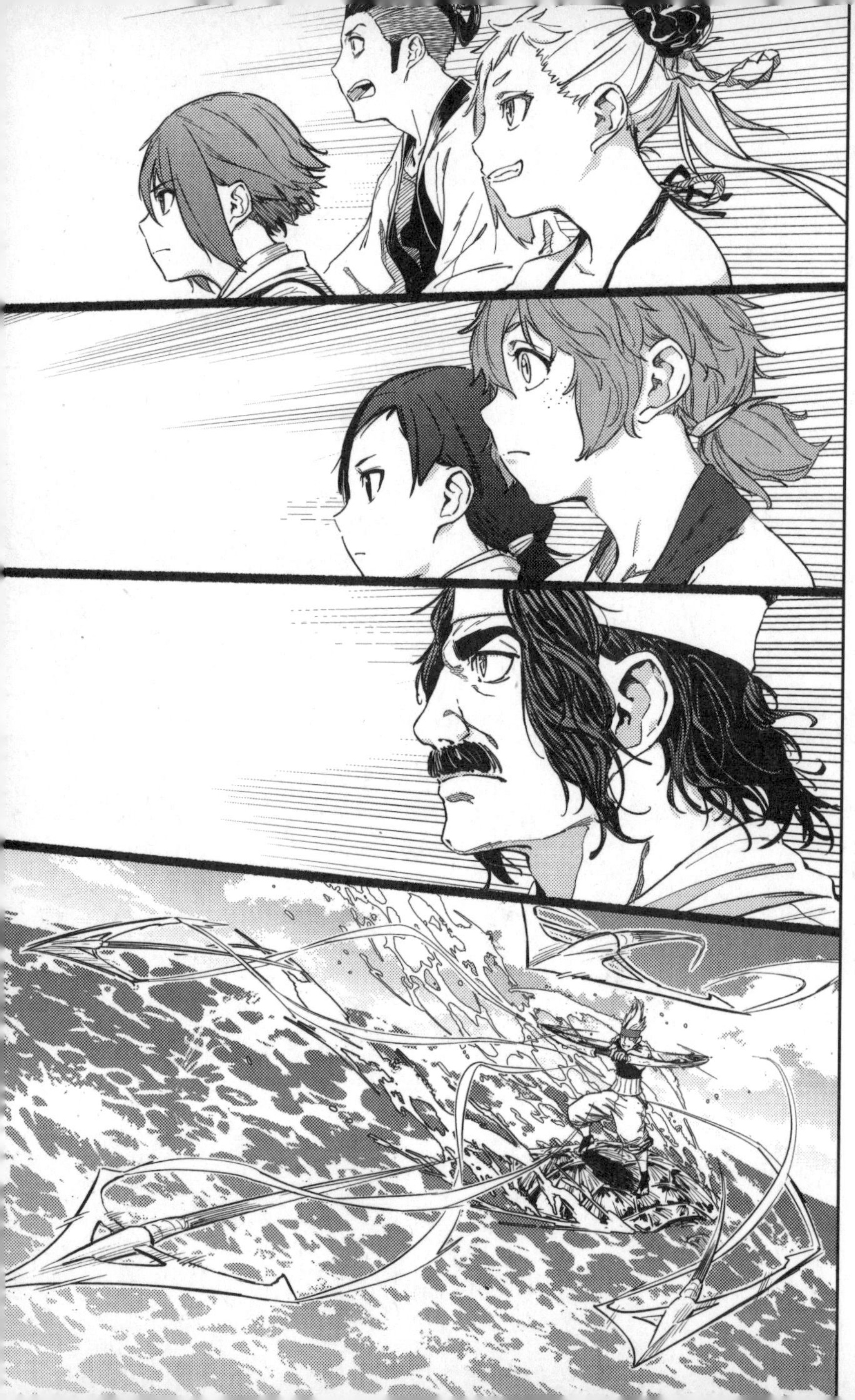

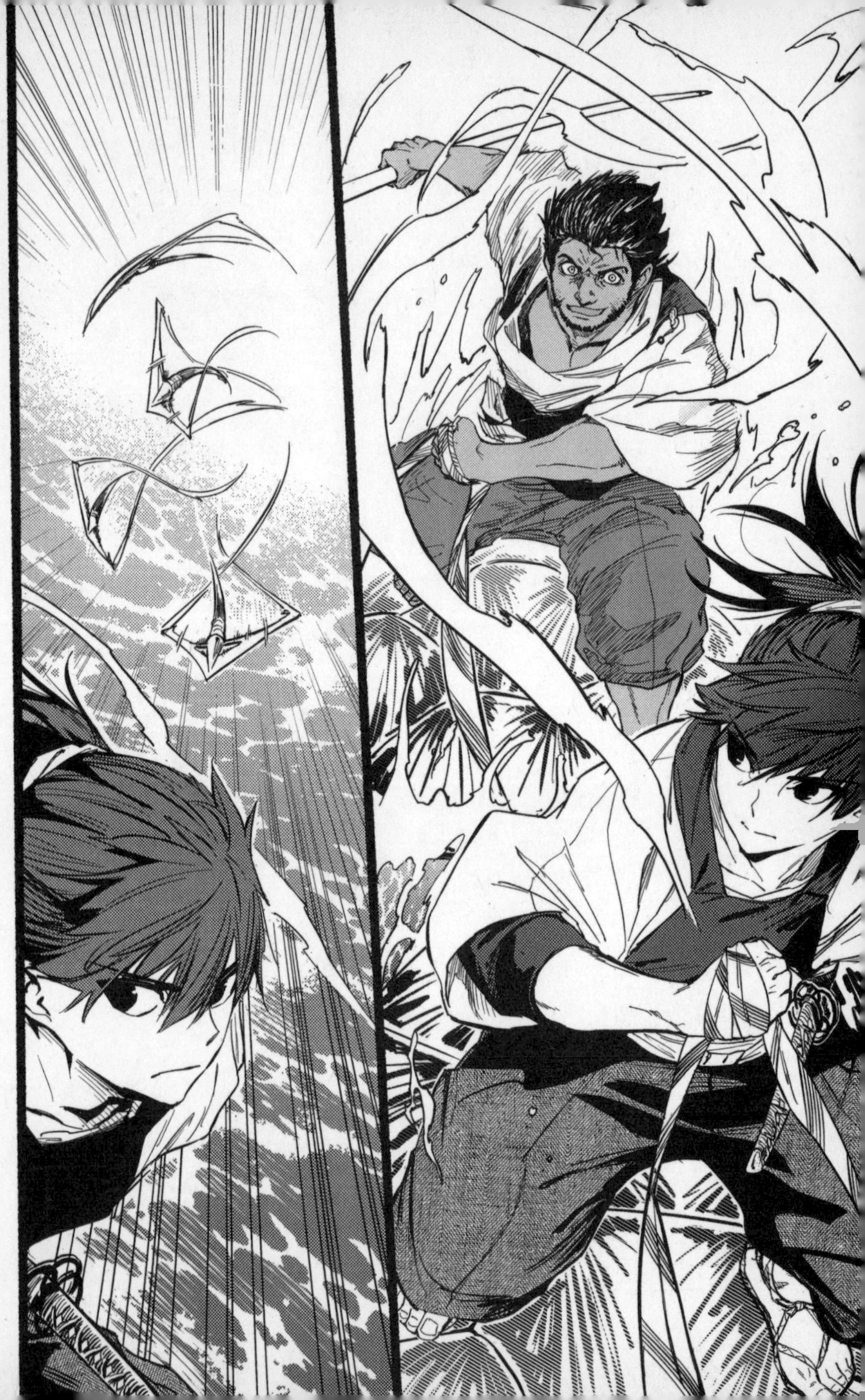

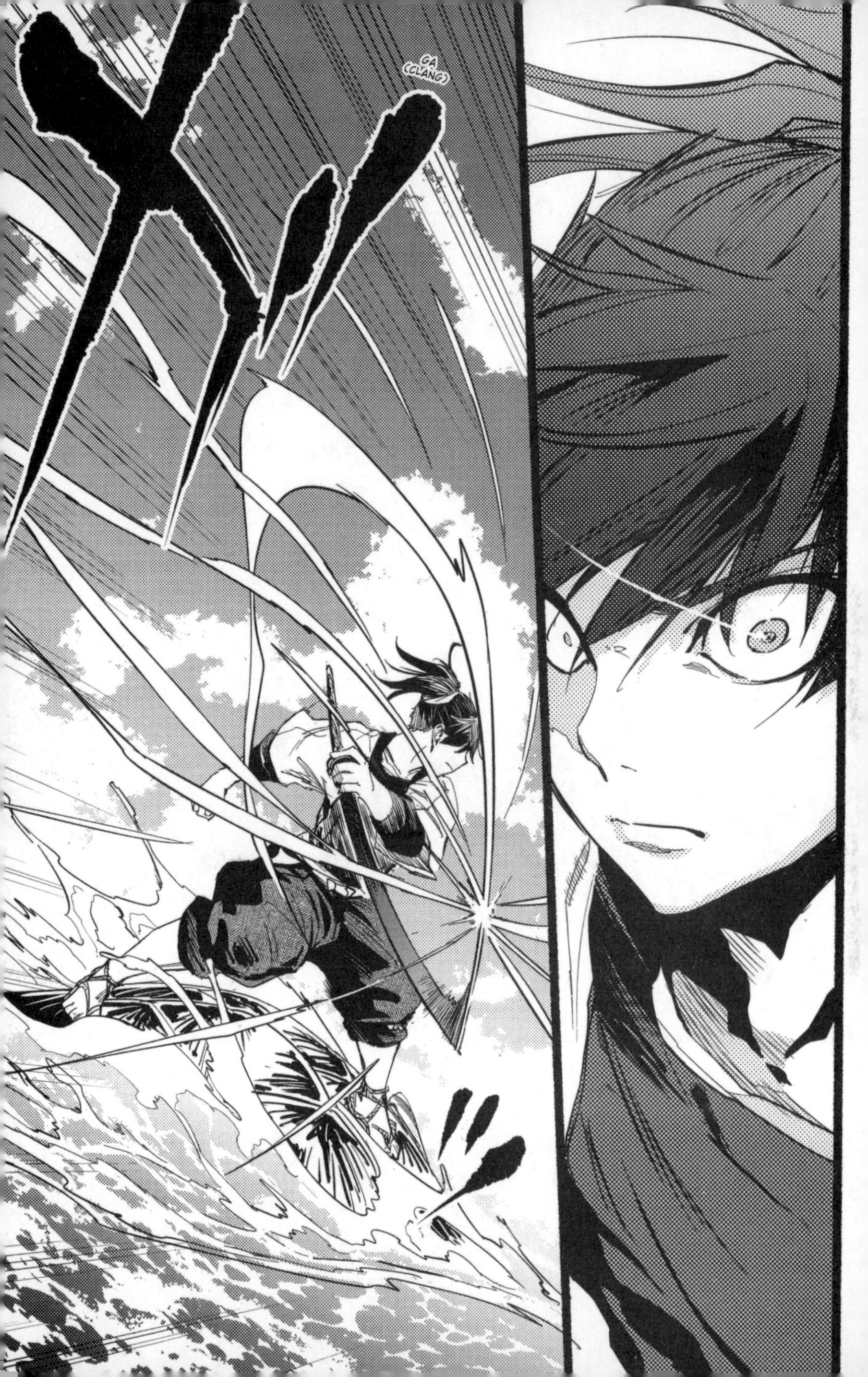
GA
(CLANG)

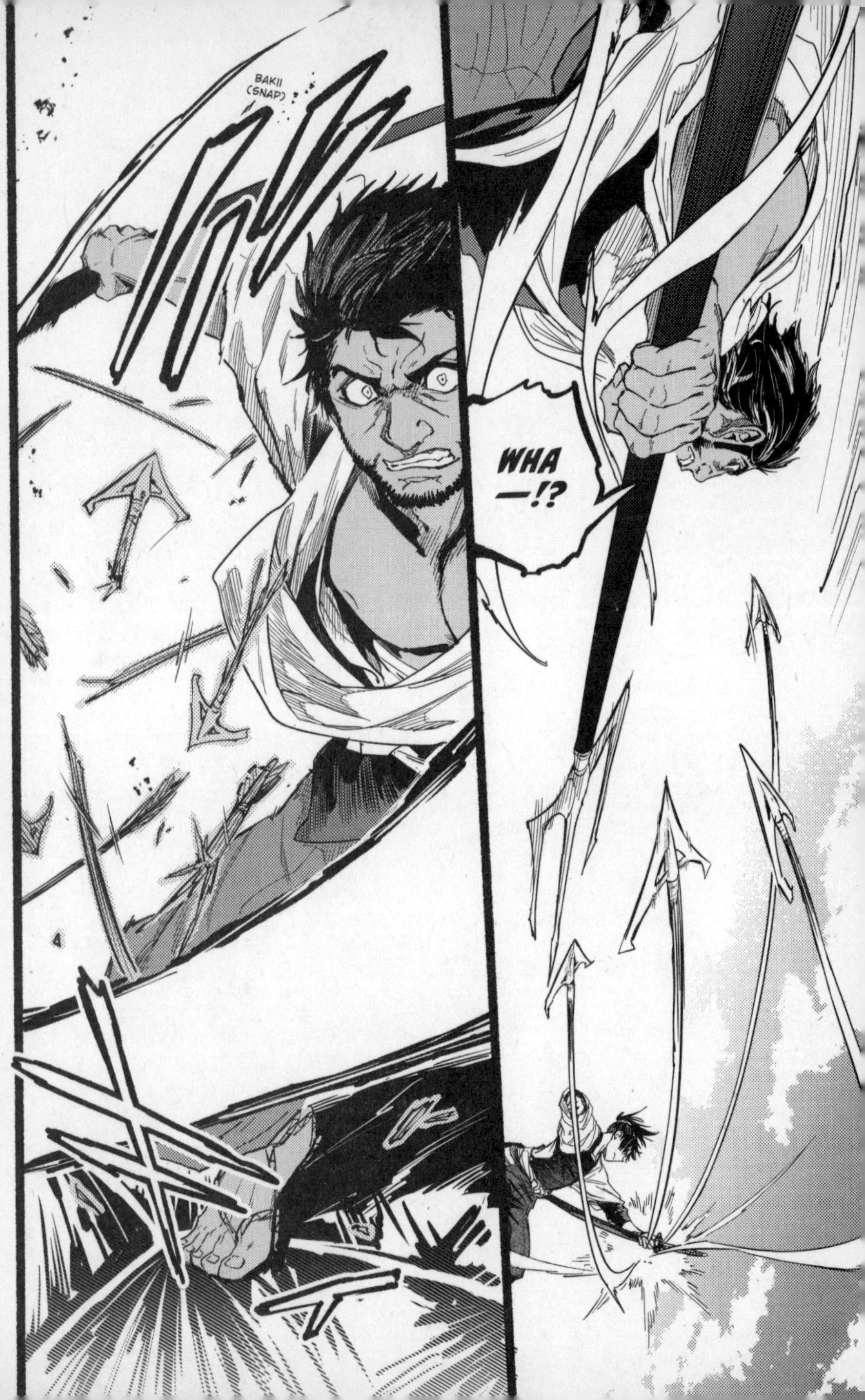
WHA—!?
BAKII (SNAP)

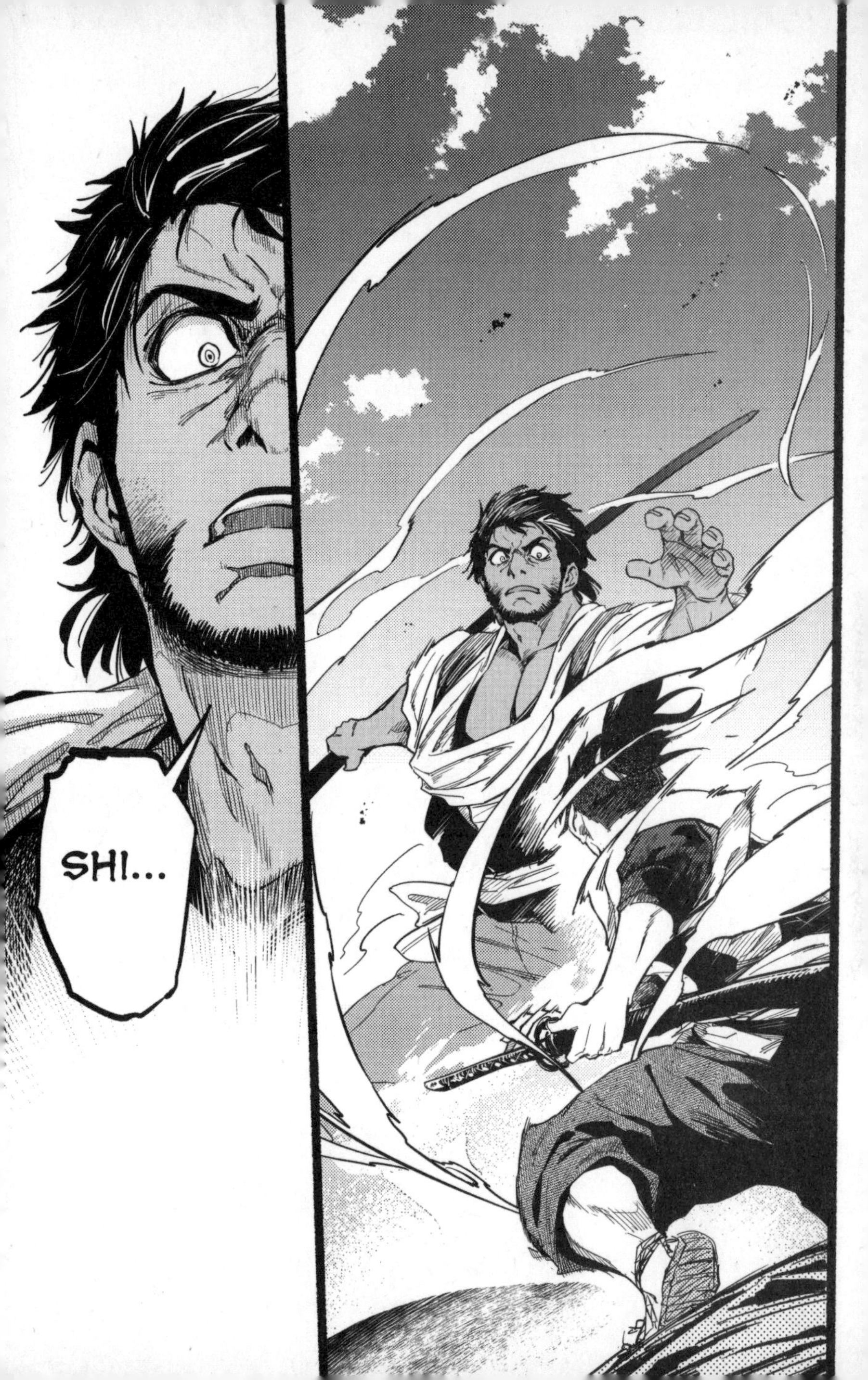
SHI...

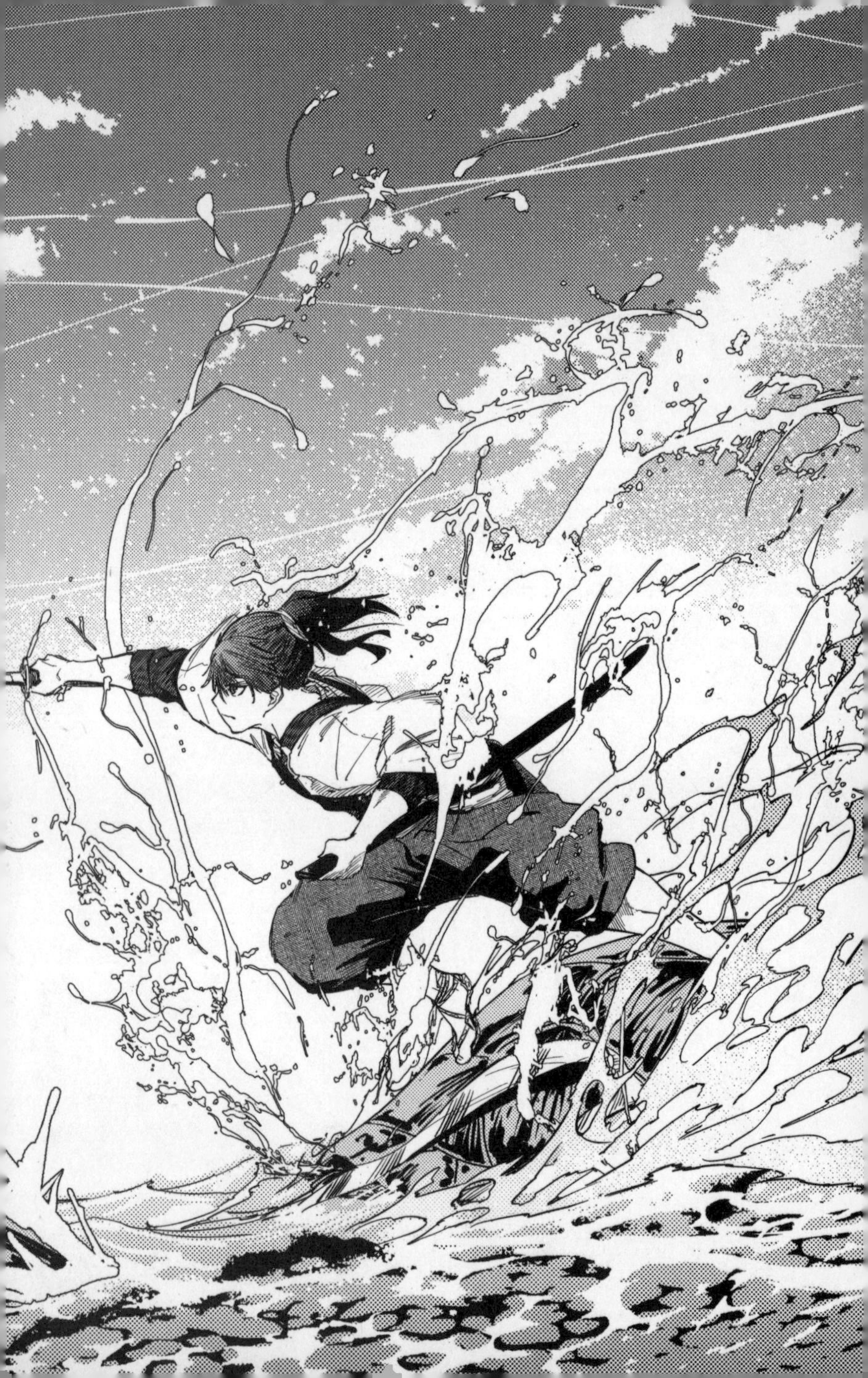

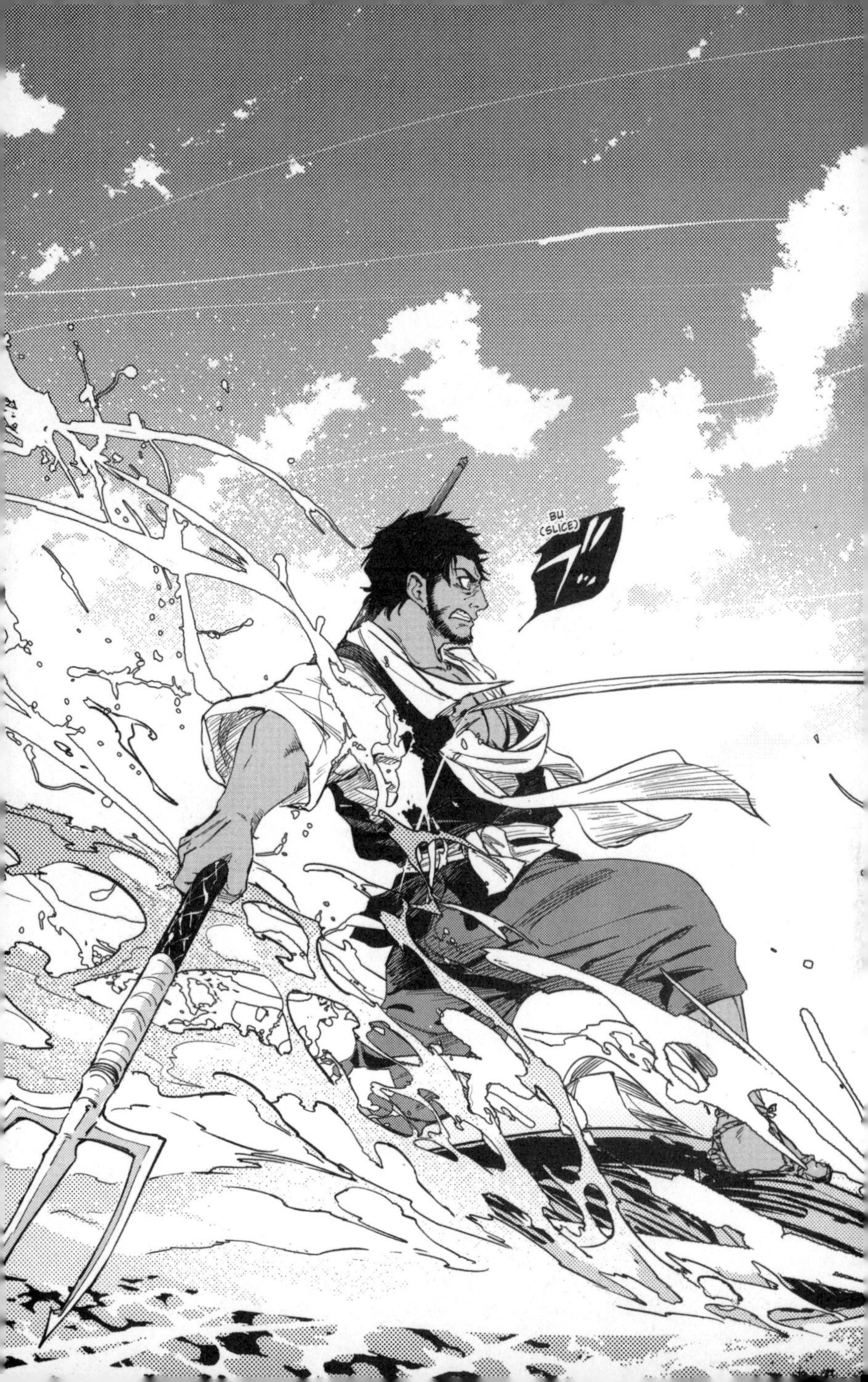
BU
(SLICE)

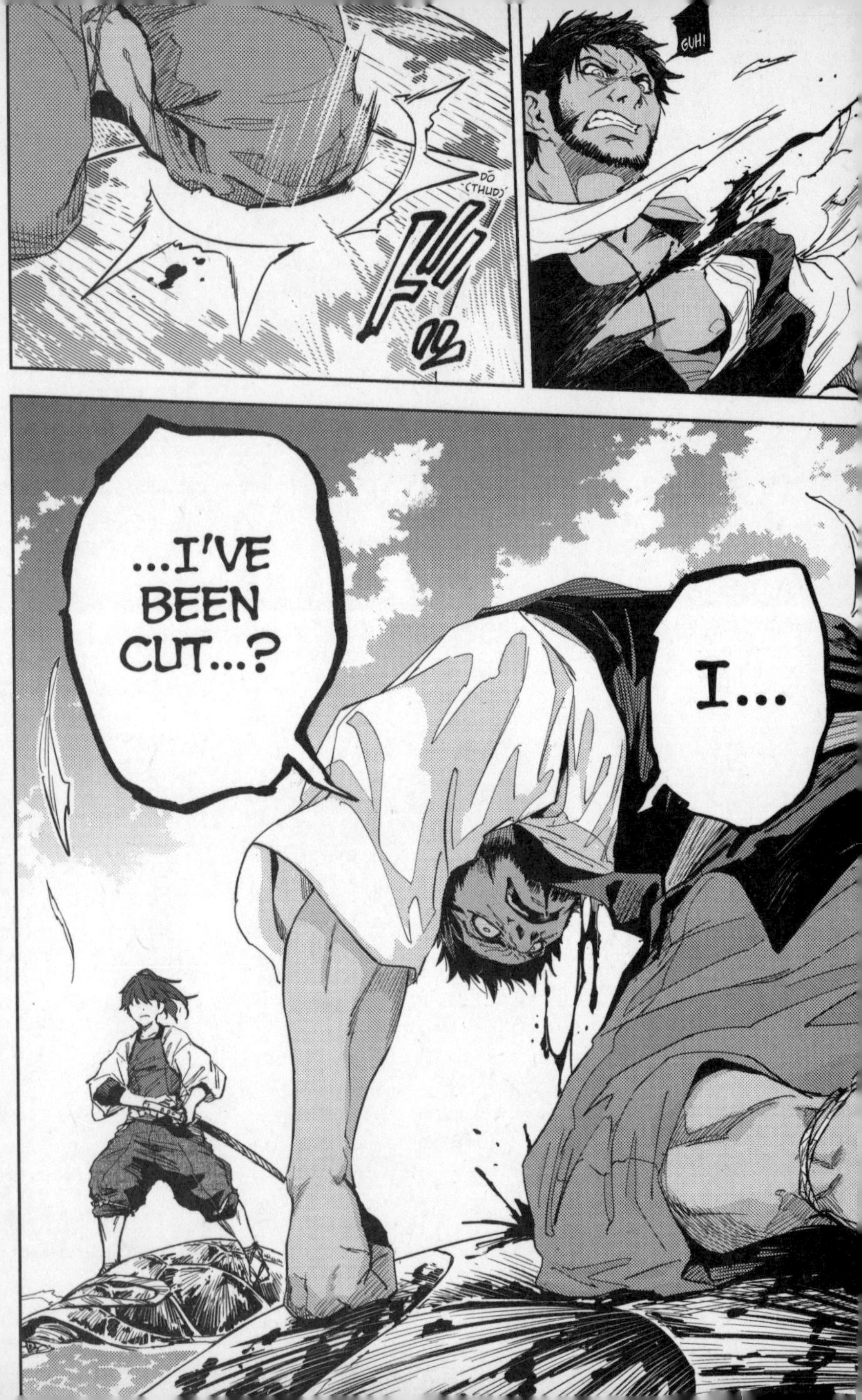
GUH!
DO
-(THUD)-
I...
...I'VE BEEN CUT...?

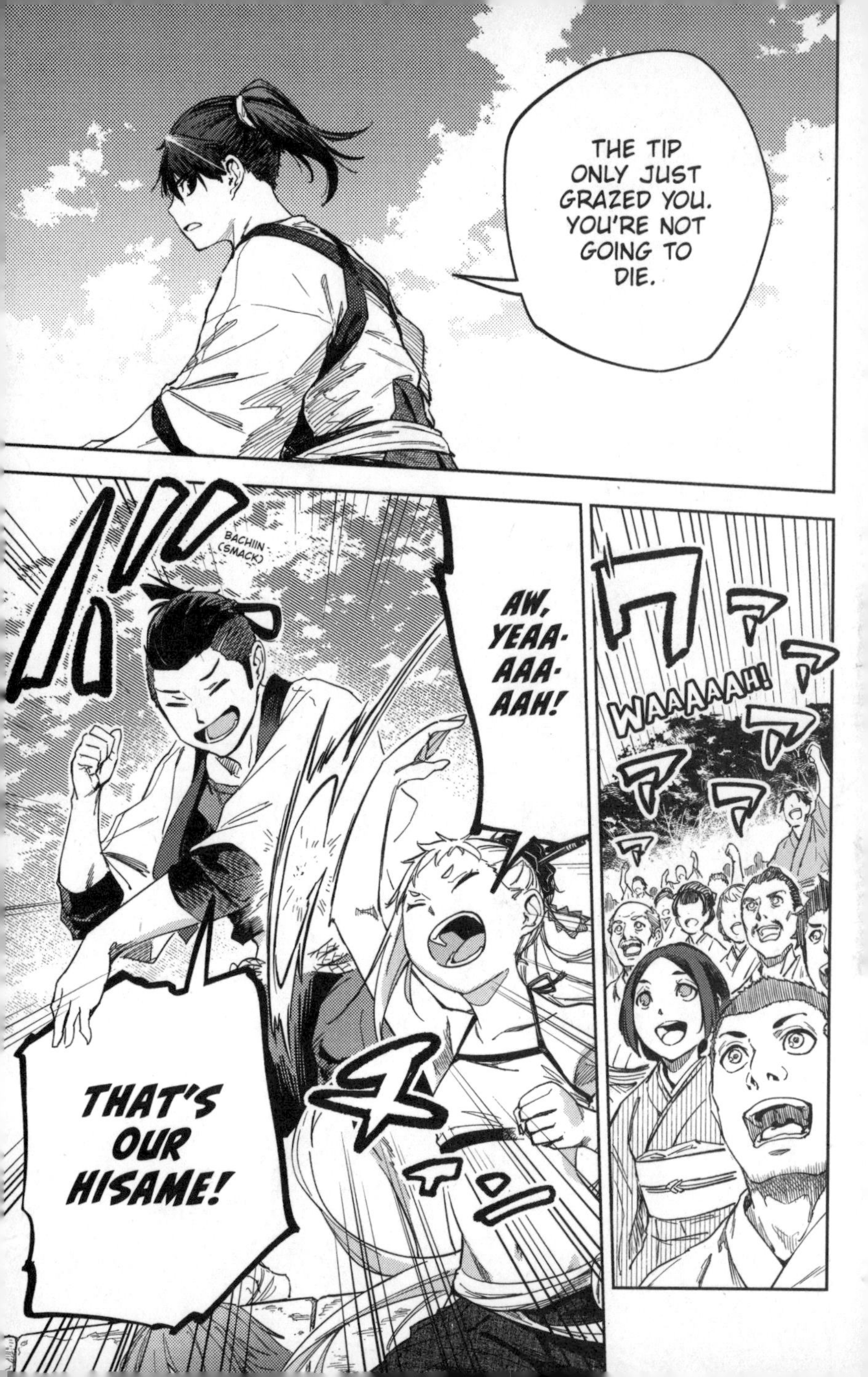
THE TIP ONLY JUST GRAZED YOU. YOU'RE NOT GOING TO DIE.
WAAAAAH!
AW, YEAA-AAA-AAH!
BACHIIN (SMACK)
THAT'S OUR HISAME!

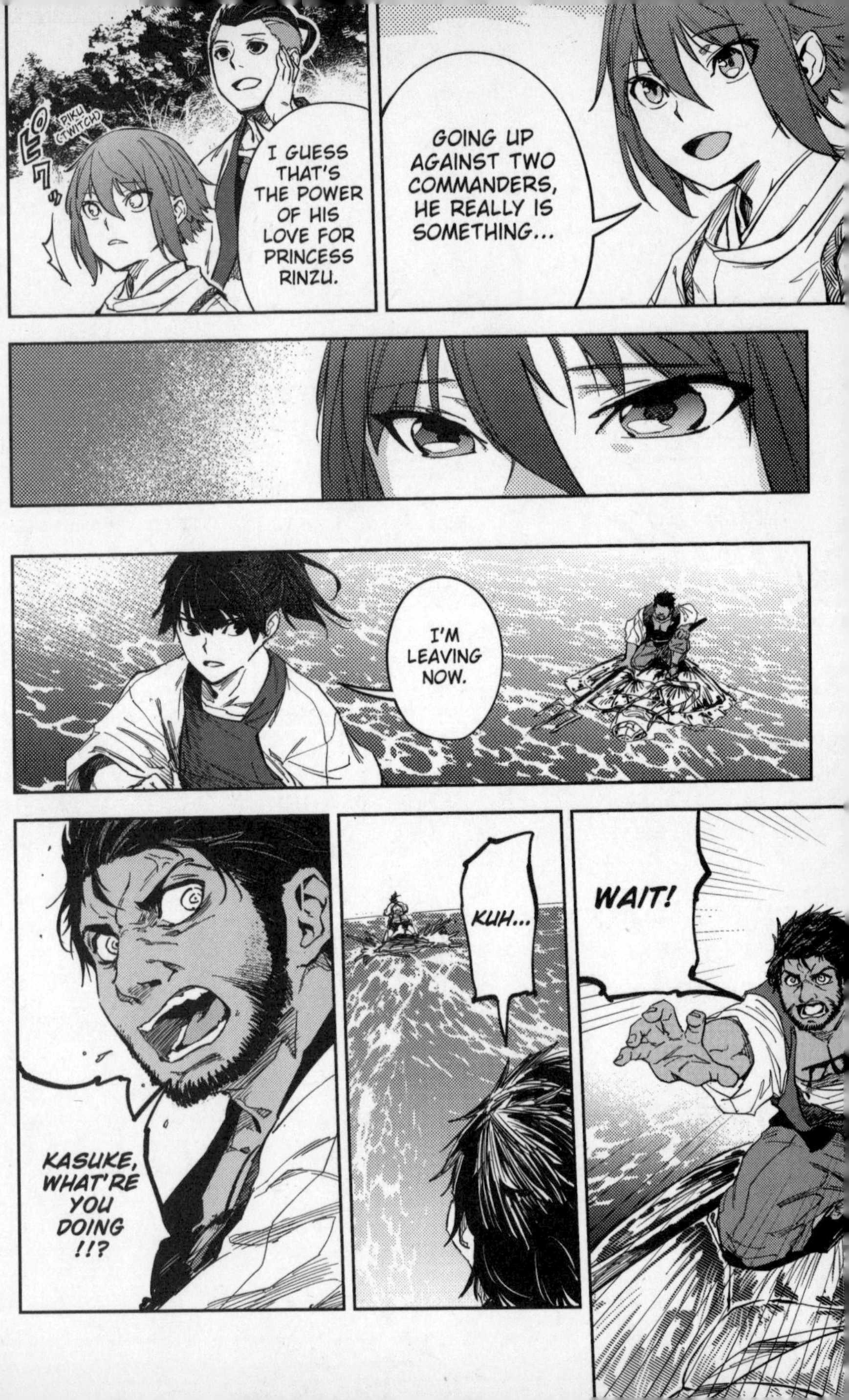
GOING UP AGAINST TWO COMMANDERS, HE REALLY IS SOMETHING...
I GUESS THAT'S THE POWER OF HIS LOVE FOR PRINCESS RINZU.
ピクッ
PIKU (TWITCH)
I'M LEAVING NOW.
WAIT!
KUH...
KASUKE, WHAT'RE YOU DOING!!?

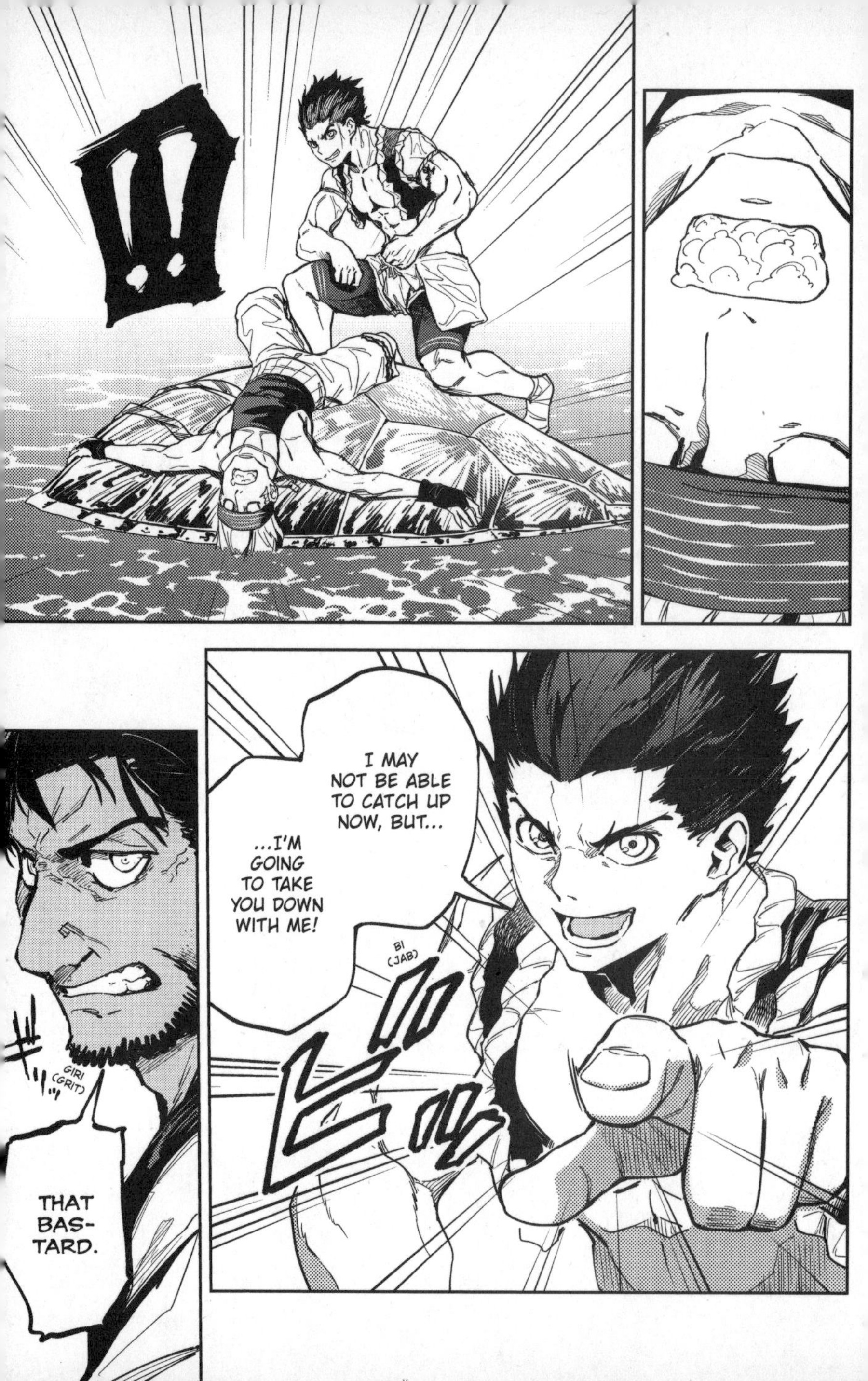
!!
I MAY NOT BE ABLE TO CATCH UP NOW, BUT...
...I'M GOING TO TAKE YOU DOWN WITH ME!
BI (JAB)
GIRI (GRIT)
THAT BAS-TARD.

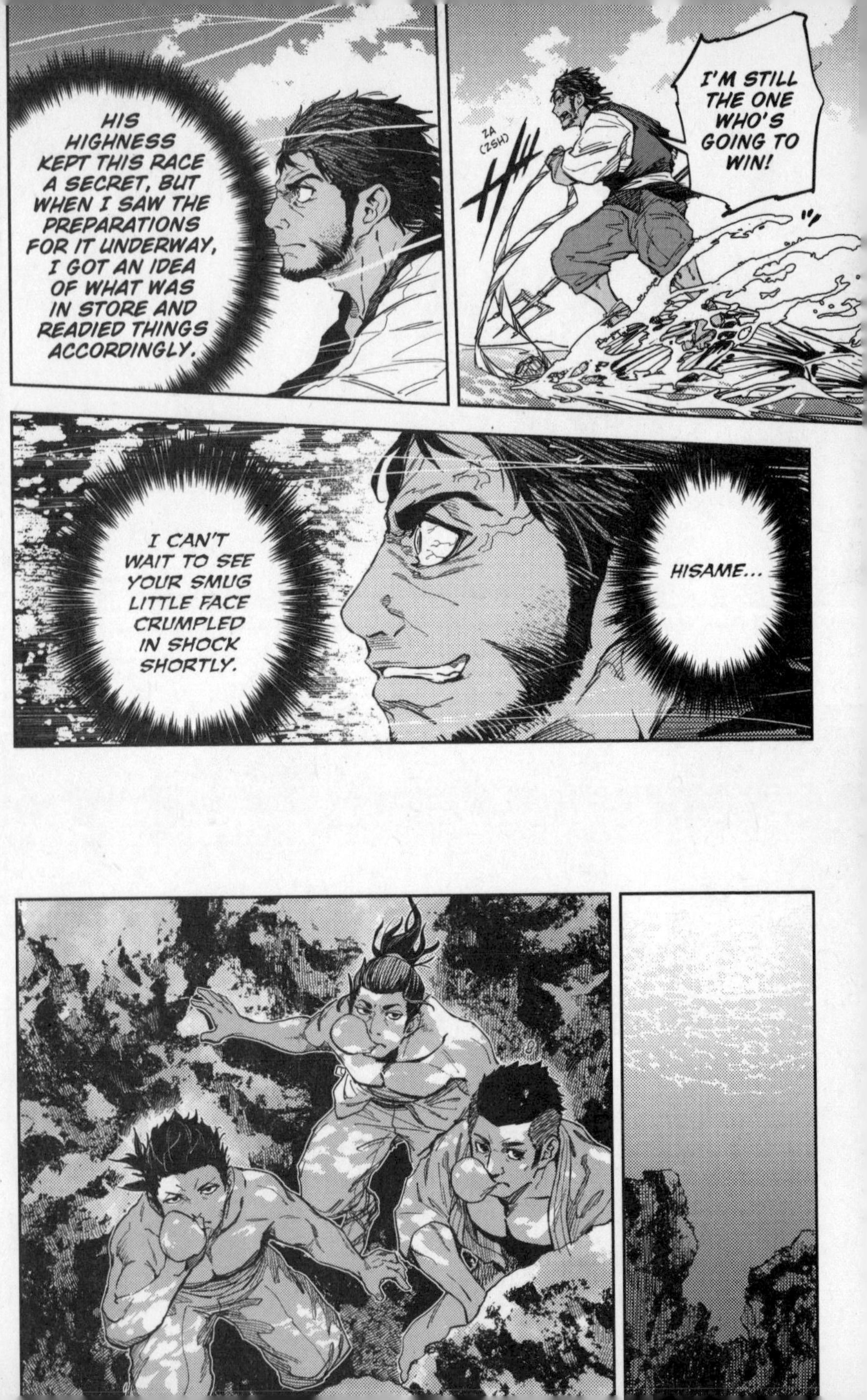
I'M STILL THE ONE WHO'S GOING TO WIN!
ZA (ZSH)
HIS HIGHNESS KEPT THIS RACE A SECRET, BUT WHEN I SAW THE PREPARATIONS FOR IT UNDERWAY, I GOT AN IDEA OF WHAT WAS IN STORE AND READIED THINGS ACCORDINGLY.
HISAME...
I CAN'T WAIT TO SEE YOUR SMUG LITTLE FACE CRUMPLED IN SHOCK SHORTLY.

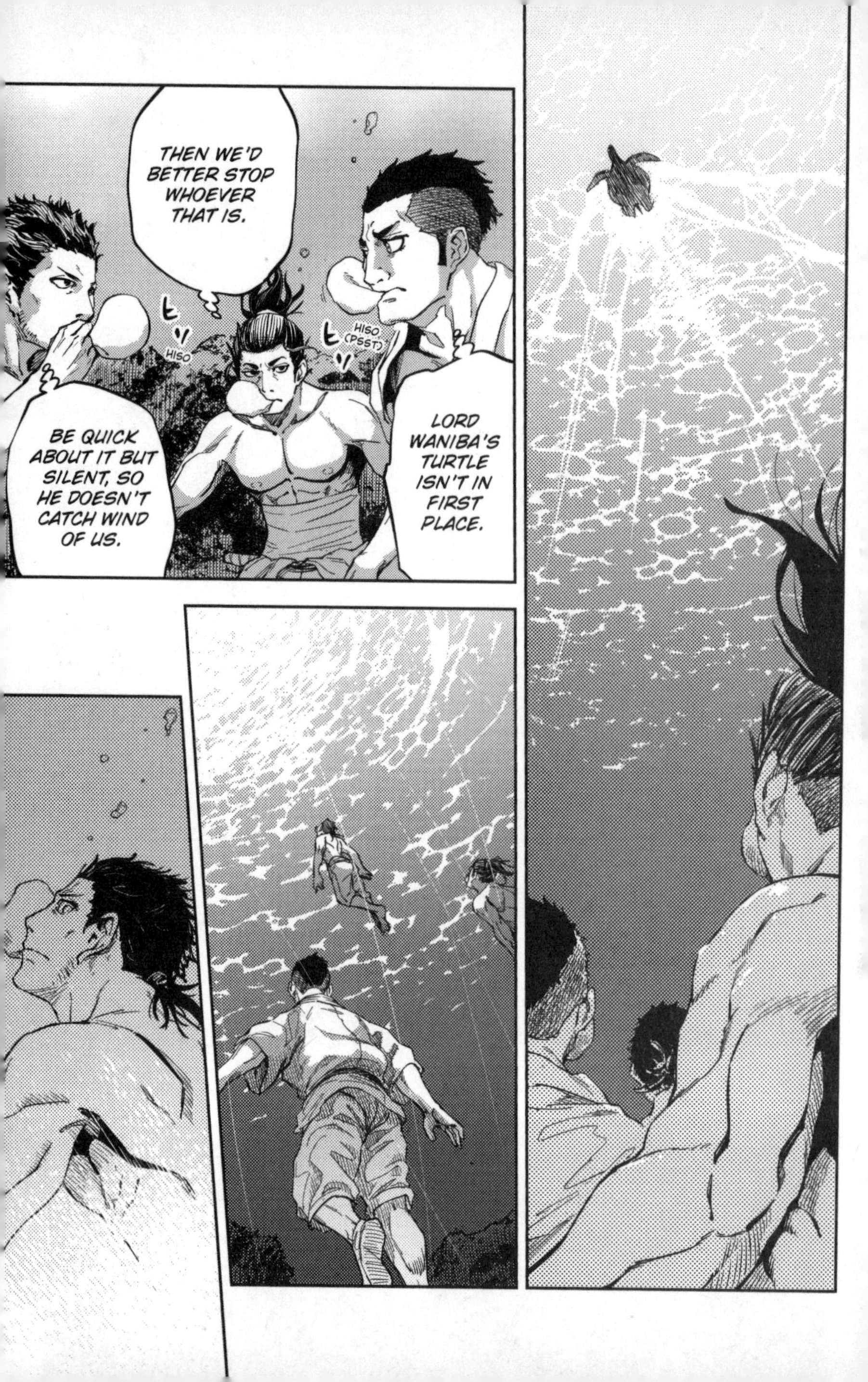
HISO (PSST)
LORD WANIBA'S TURTLE ISN'T IN FIRST PLACE.
THEN WE'D BETTER STOP WHOEVER THAT IS.
HISO
BE QUICK ABOUT IT BUT SILENT, SO HE DOESN'T CATCH WIND OF US.

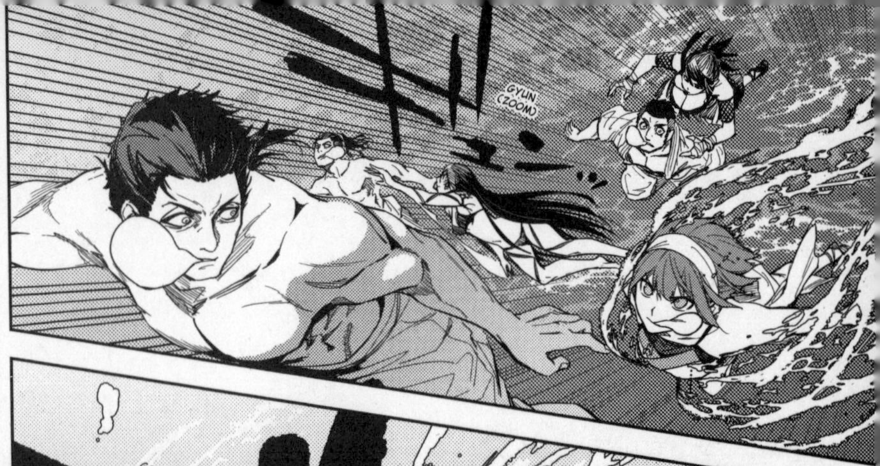
GYUN
(ZOOM)
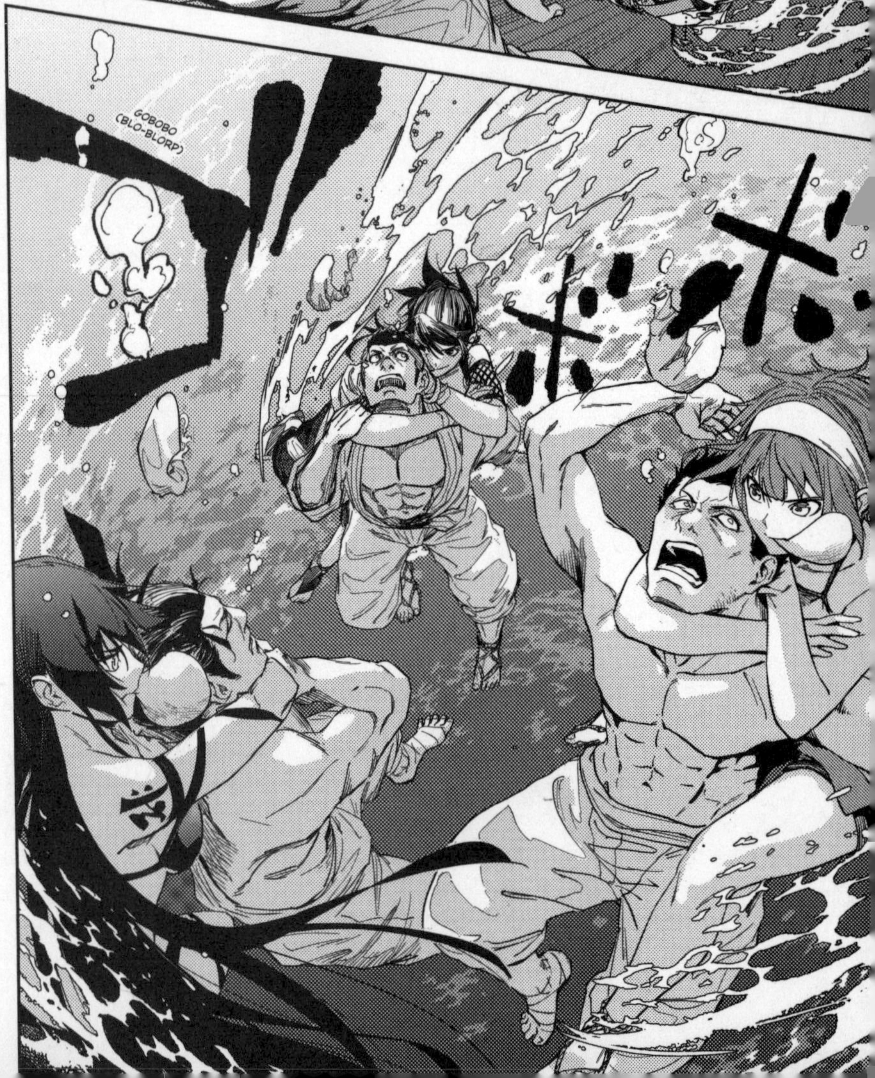
GOBOBO
(BLO-BLORP)

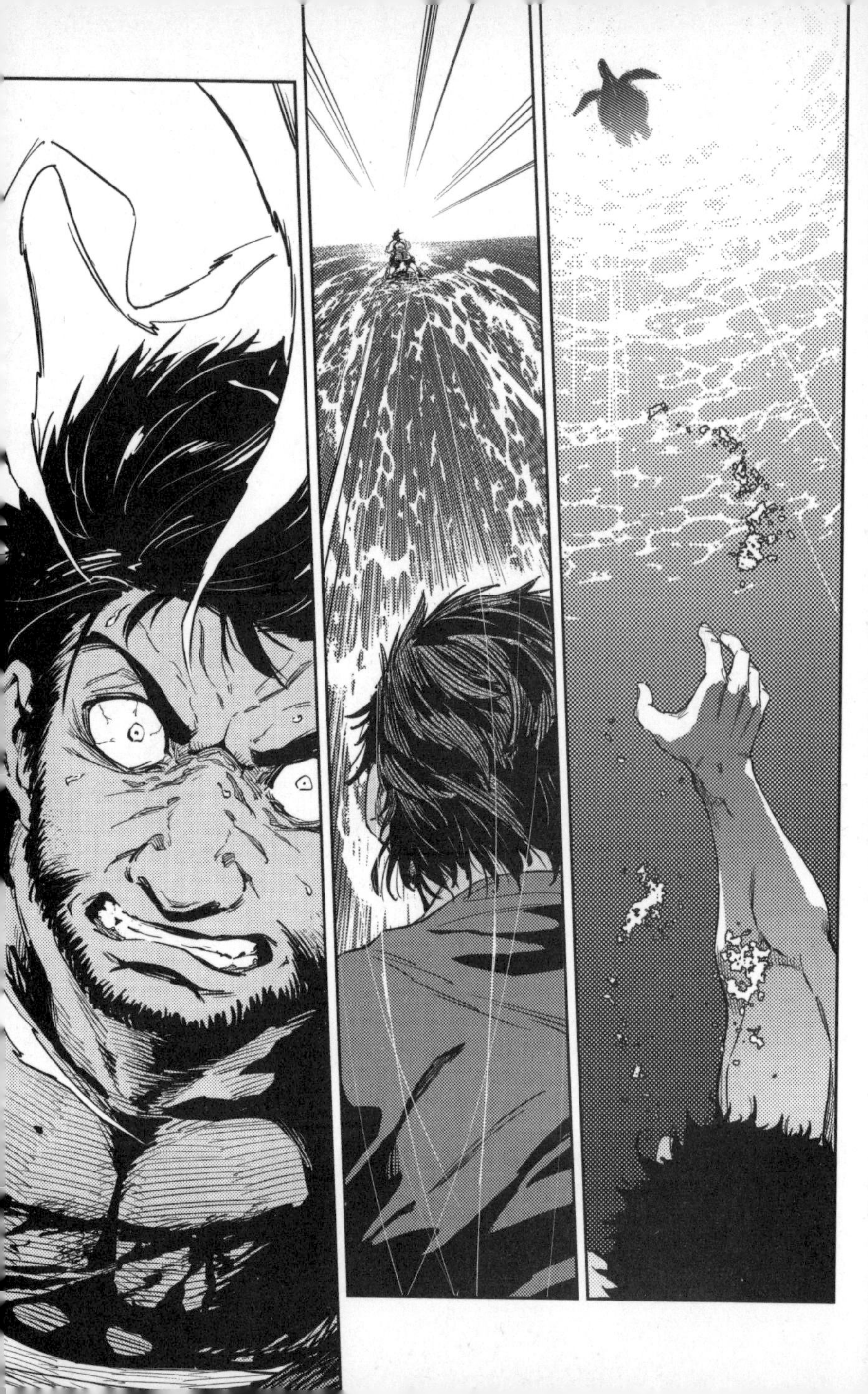

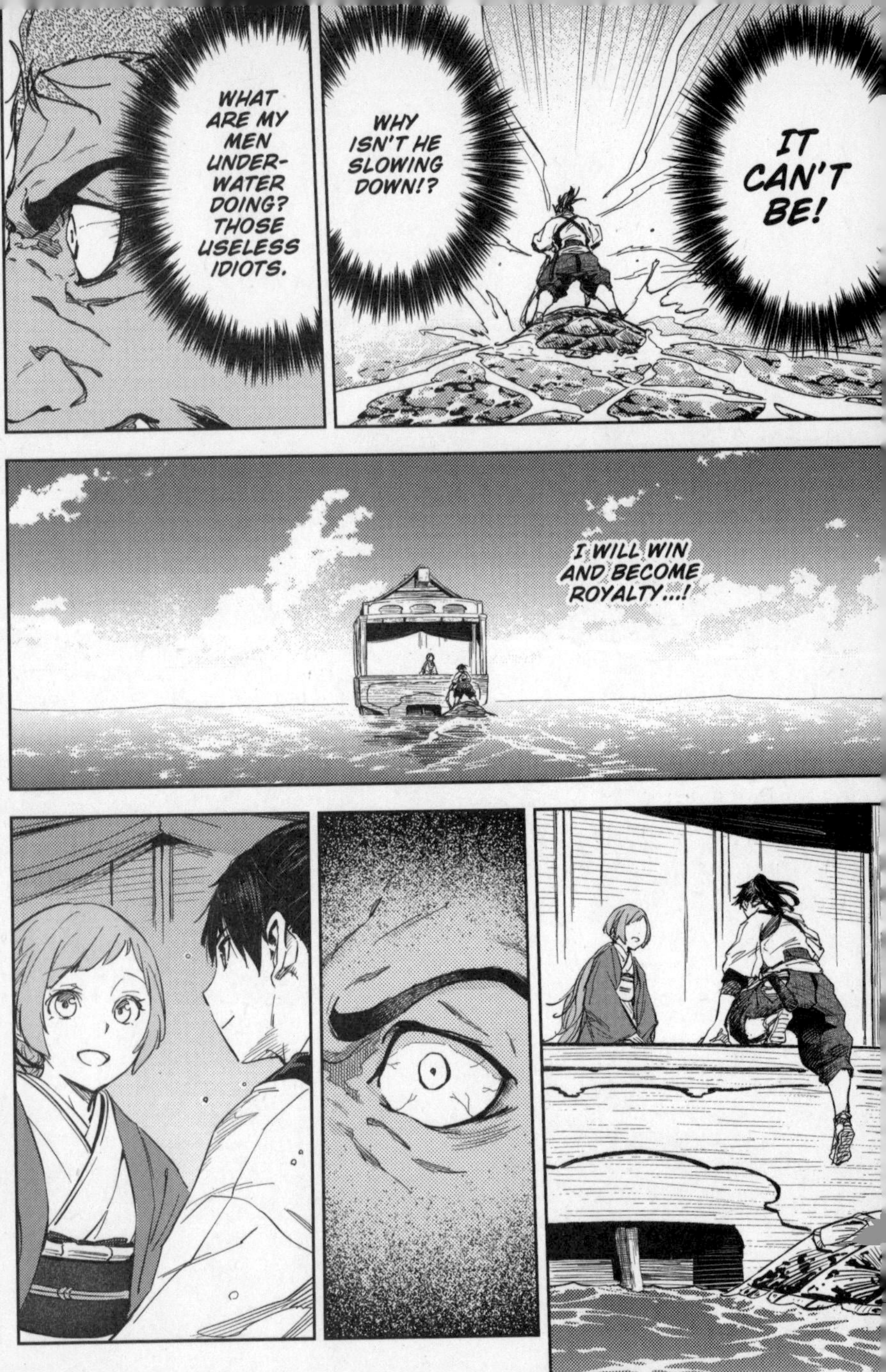
IT CAN'T BE!
WHY ISN'T HE SLOWING DOWN!?
WHAT ARE MY MEN UNDER-WATER DOING? THOSE USELESS IDIOTS.
I WILL WIN AND BECOME ROYALTY...!

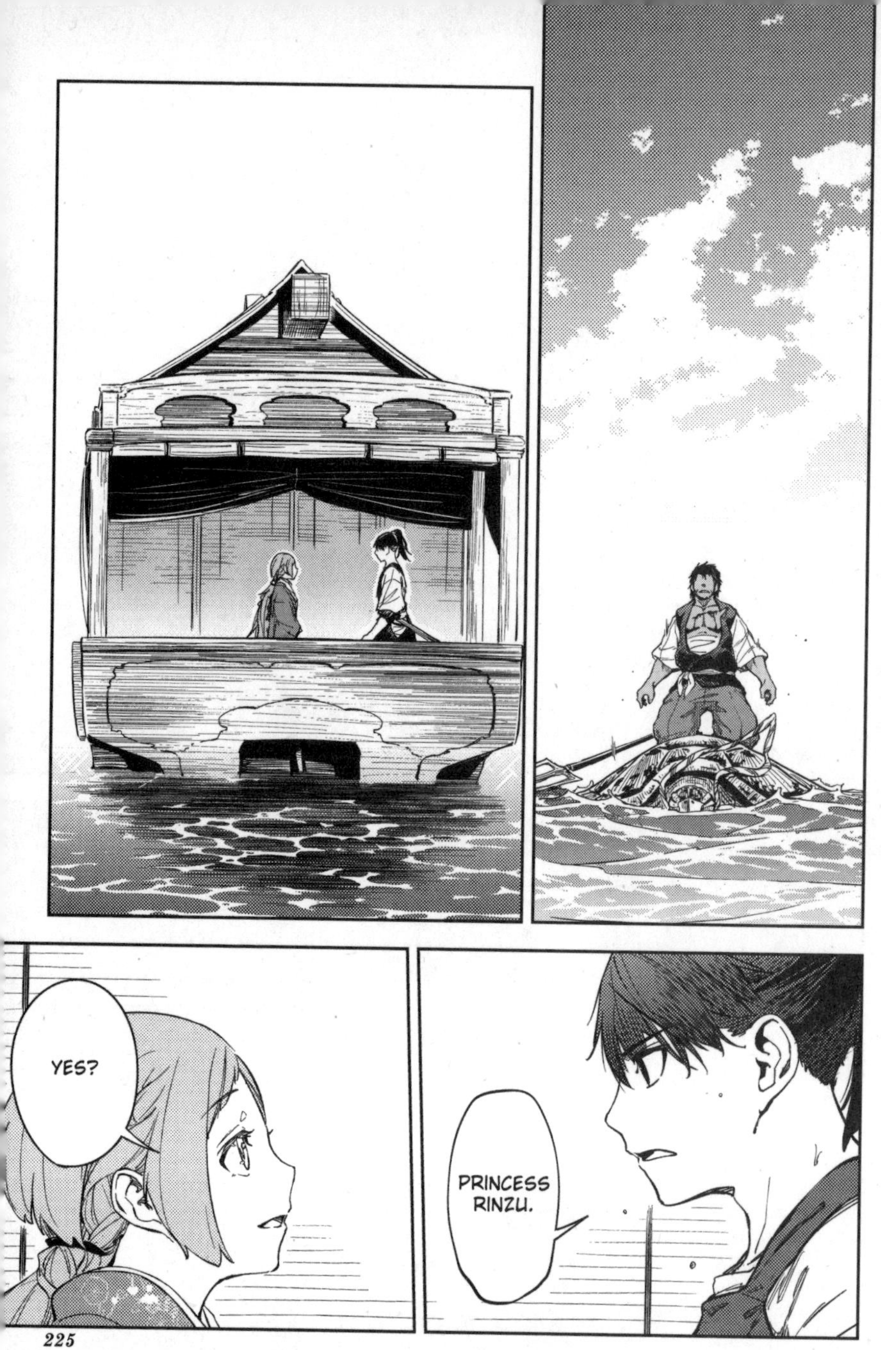
PRINCESS RINZU.
YES?

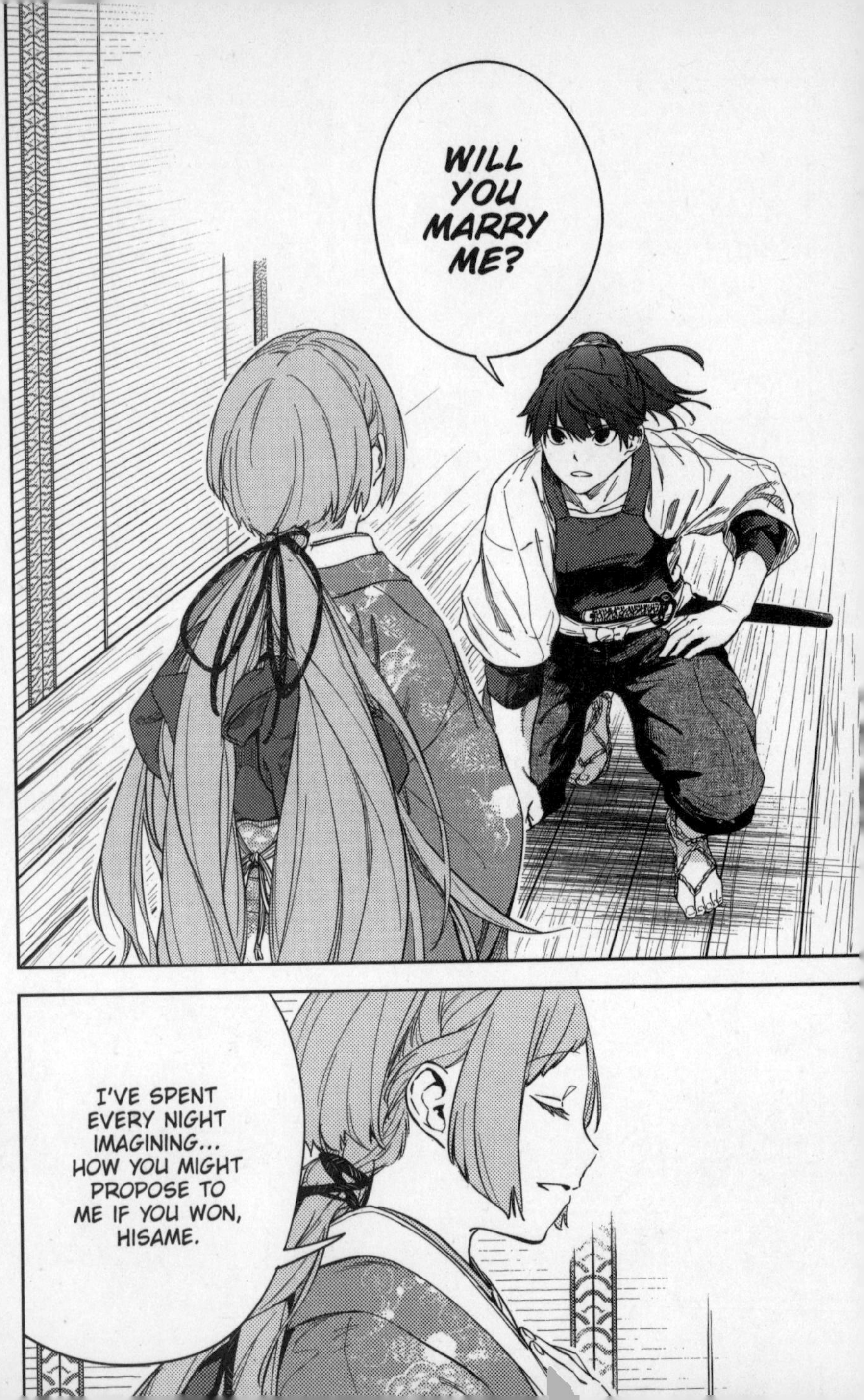
WILL YOU MARRY ME?
I'VE SPENT EVERY NIGHT IMAGINING... HOW YOU MIGHT PROPOSE TO ME IF YOU WON, HISAME.

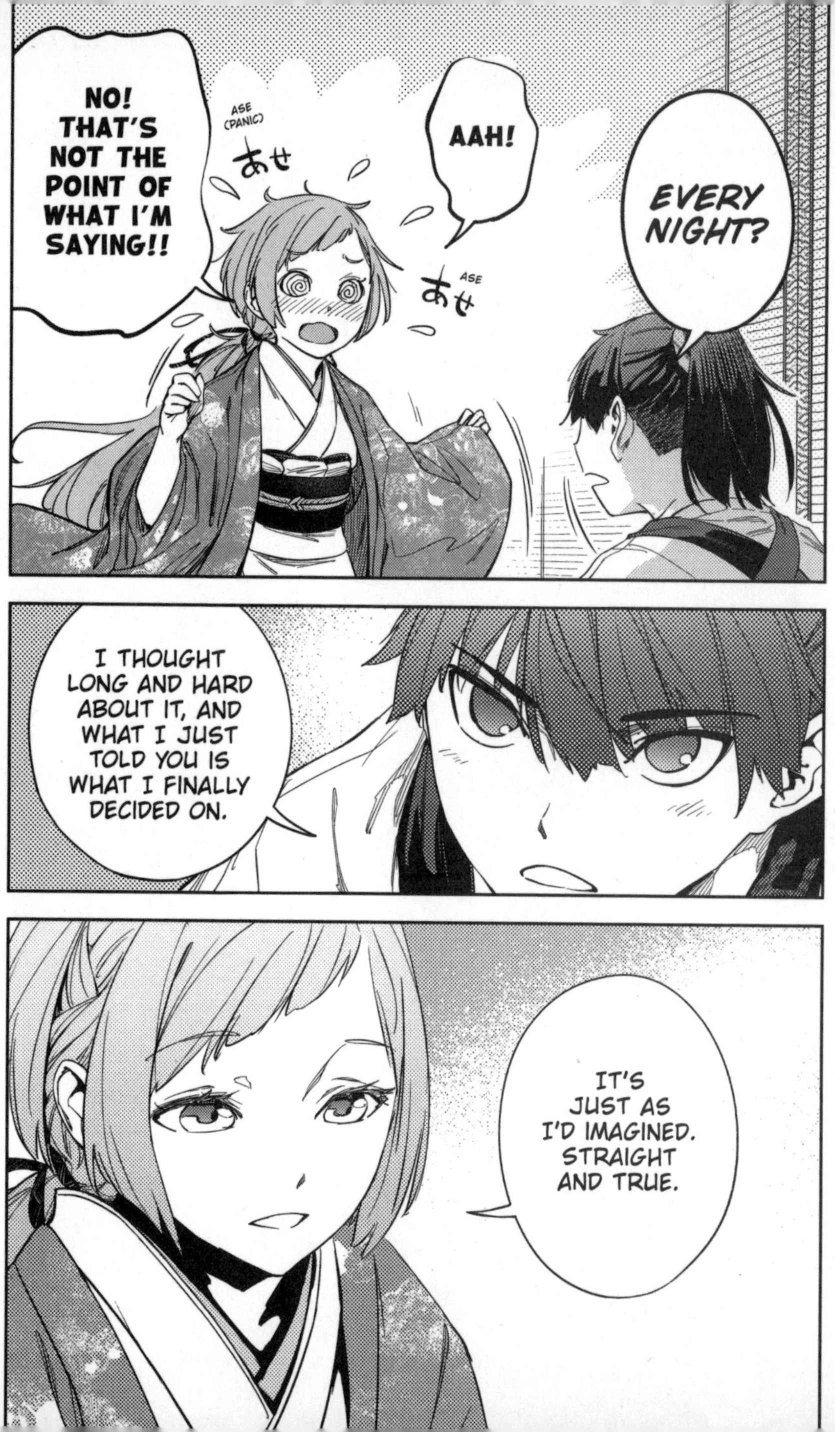
EVERY NIGHT?
AAH!
ASE
あせ
ASE (PANIC)
あせ
NO! THAT'S NOT THE POINT OF WHAT I'M SAYING!!
I THOUGHT LONG AND HARD ABOUT IT, AND WHAT I JUST TOLD YOU IS WHAT I FINALLY DECIDED ON.
IT'S JUST AS I'D IMAGINED. STRAIGHT AND TRUE.

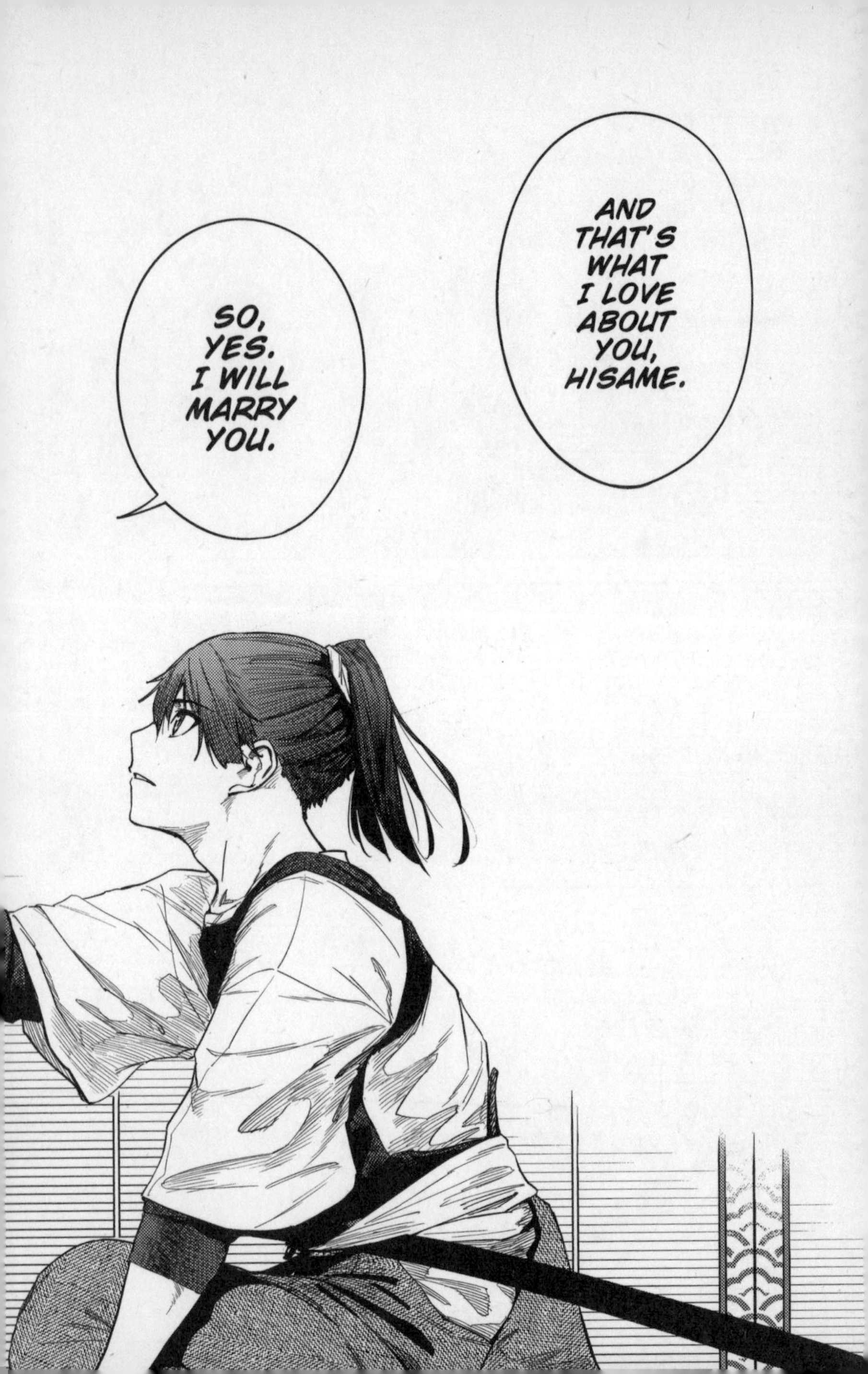
AND THAT'S WHAT I LOVE ABOUT YOU, HISAME.
SO, YES. I WILL MARRY YOU.

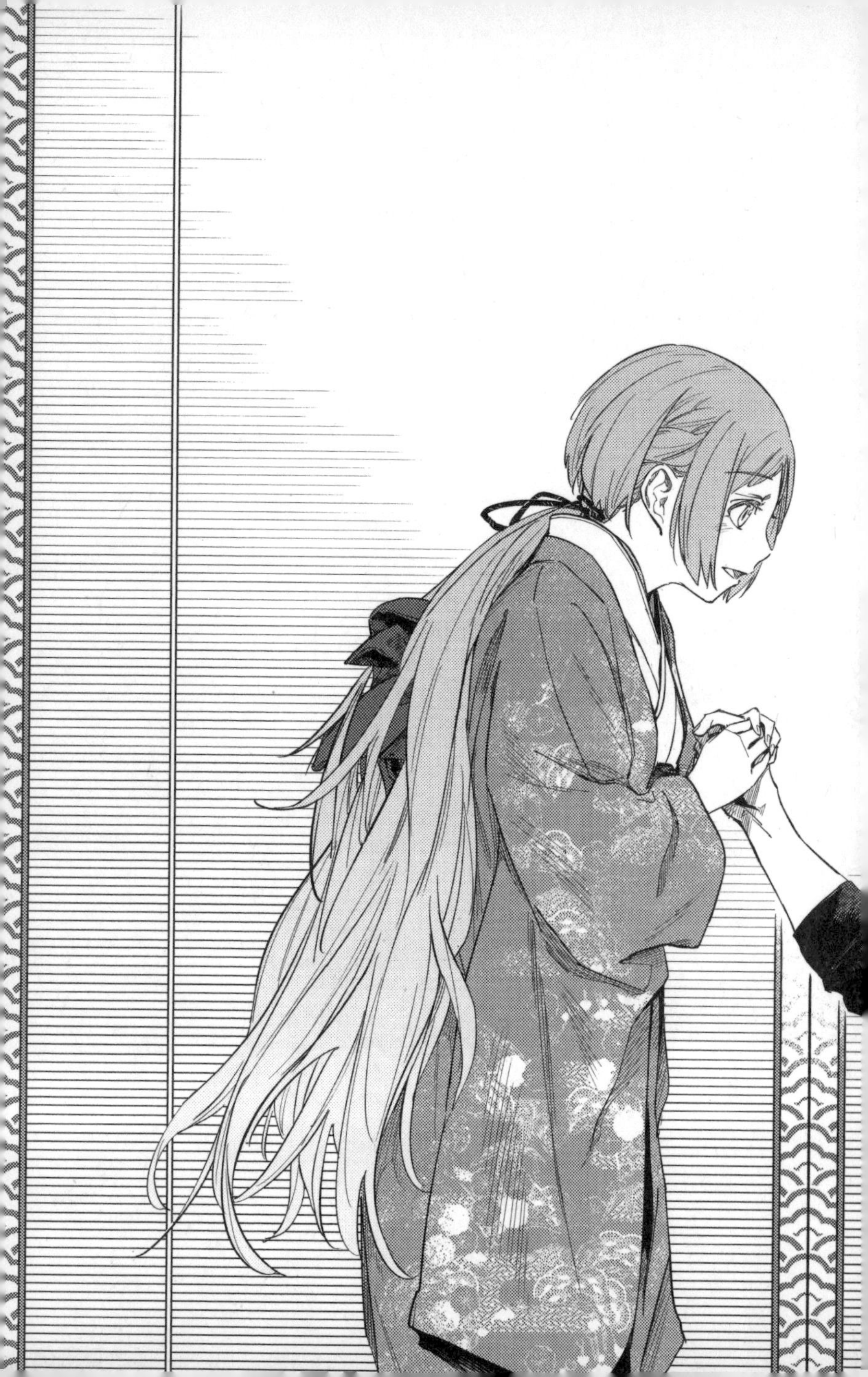

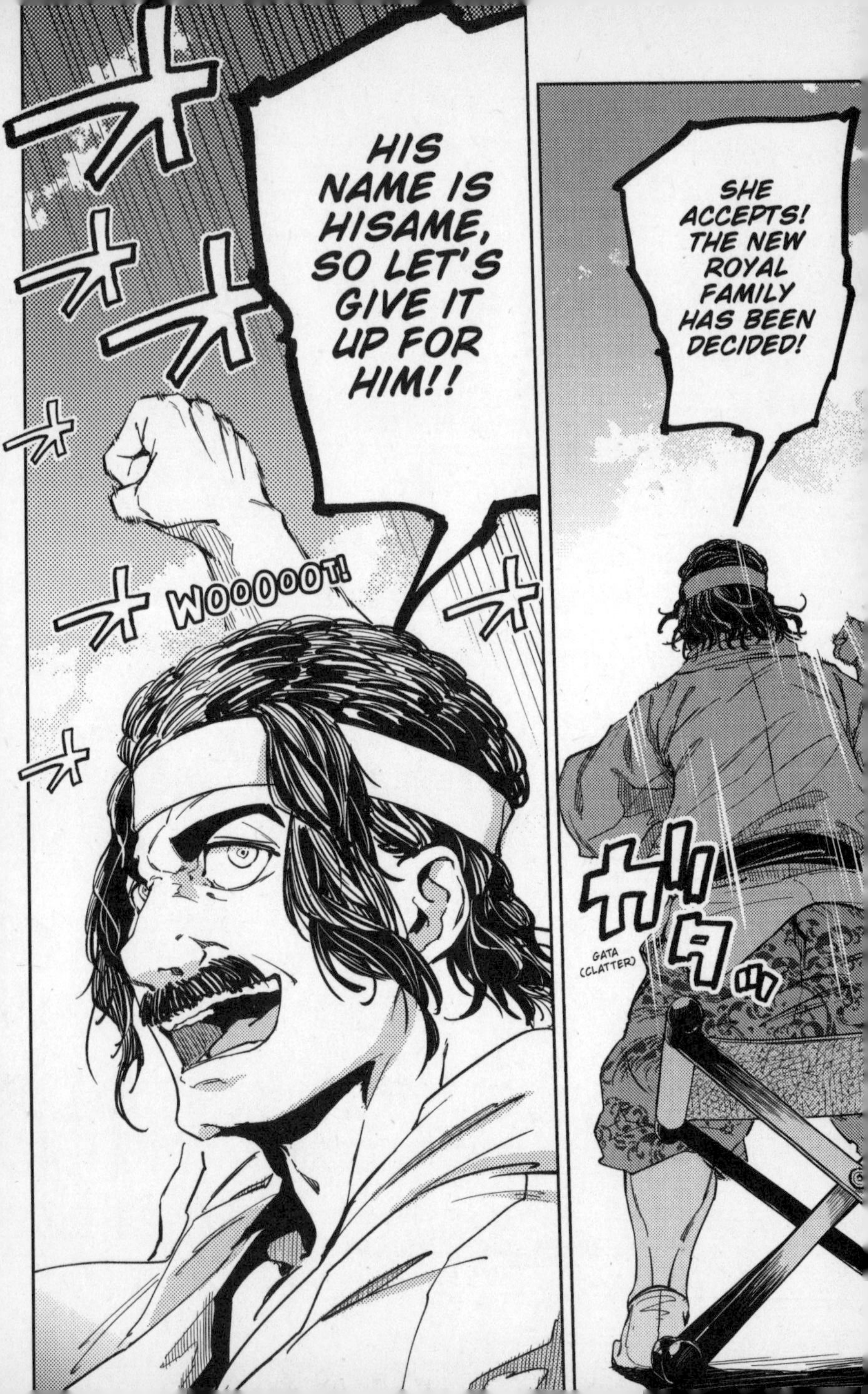
SHE ACCEPTS! THE NEW ROYAL FAMILY HAS BEEN DECIDED!
ガタッ
GATA (CLATTER)
HIS NAME IS HISAME, SO LET'S GIVE IT UP FOR HIM!!
WOOOOOT!

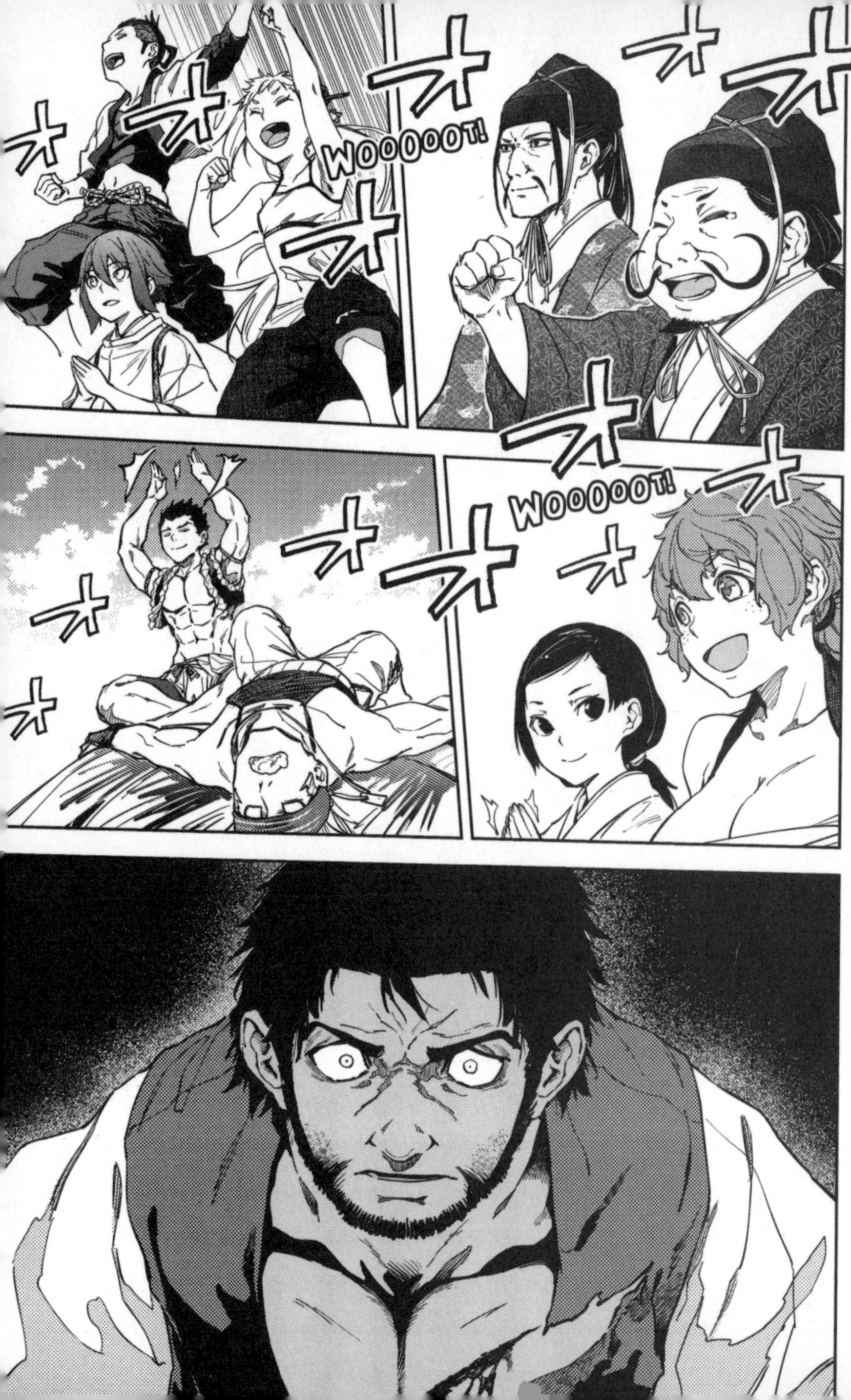
WOOOOOT!
WOOOOOT!

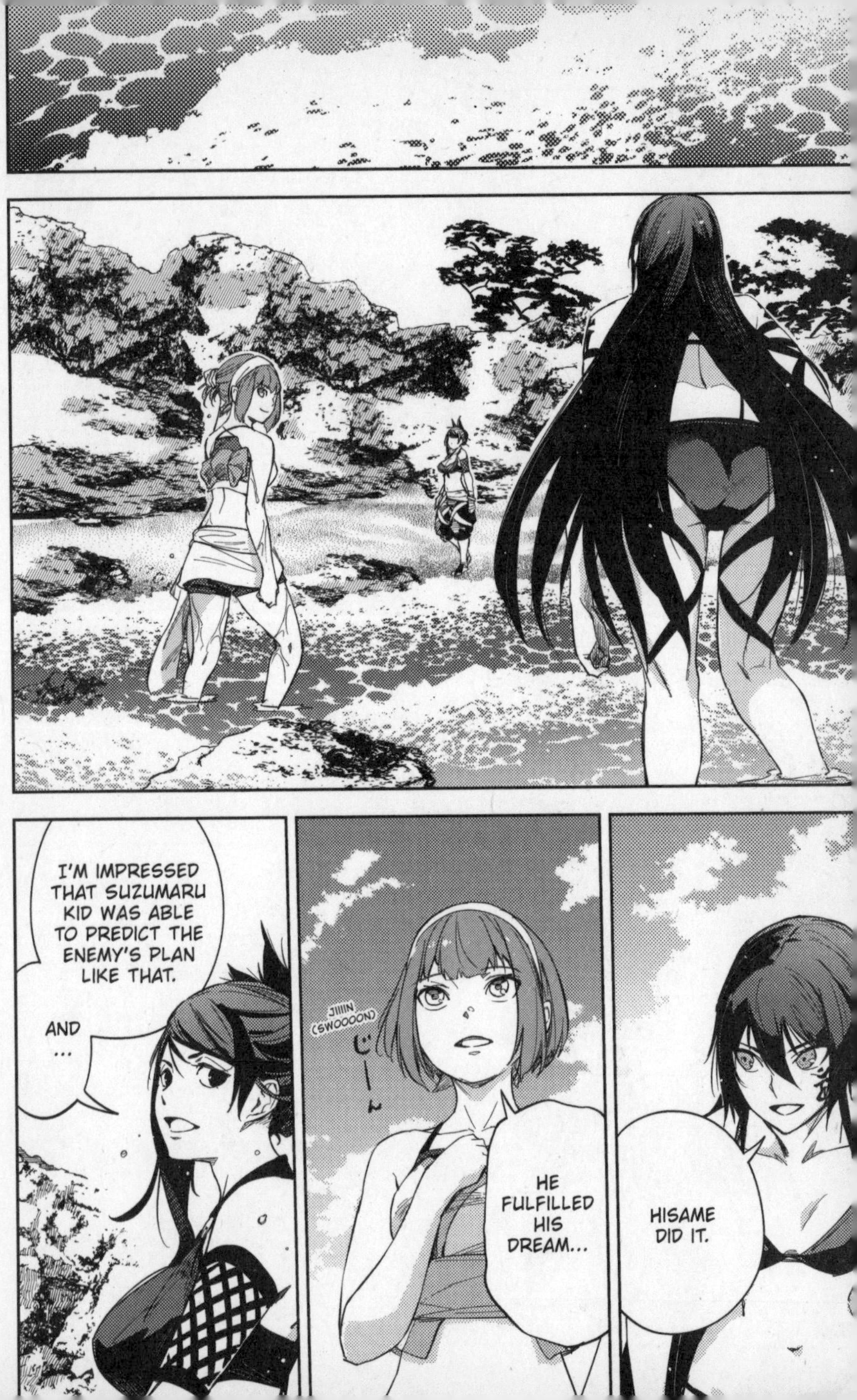
HISAME DID IT.
JIIIIN (SWOOOON)
HE FULFILLED HIS DREAM...
I'M IMPRESSED THAT SUZUMARU KID WAS ABLE TO PREDICT THE ENEMY'S PLAN LIKE THAT.
AND ...

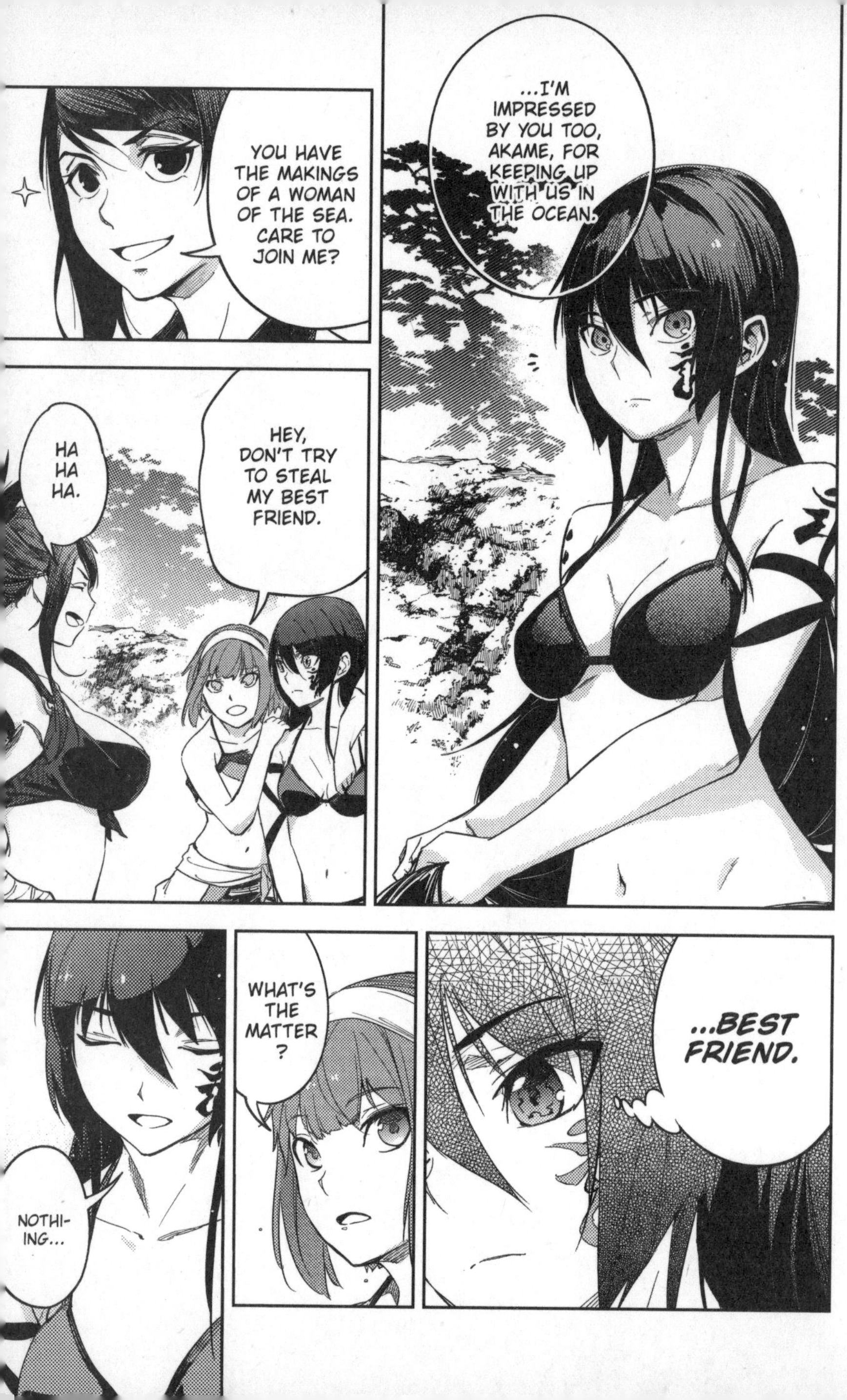
...I'M IMPRESSED BY YOU TOO, AKAME, FOR KEEPING UP WITH US IN THE OCEAN.
YOU HAVE THE MAKINGS OF A WOMAN OF THE SEA. CARE TO JOIN ME?
HEY, DON'T TRY TO STEAL MY BEST FRIEND.
HA HA HA.
...BEST FRIEND.
WHAT'S THE MATTER?
NOTHI-ING...

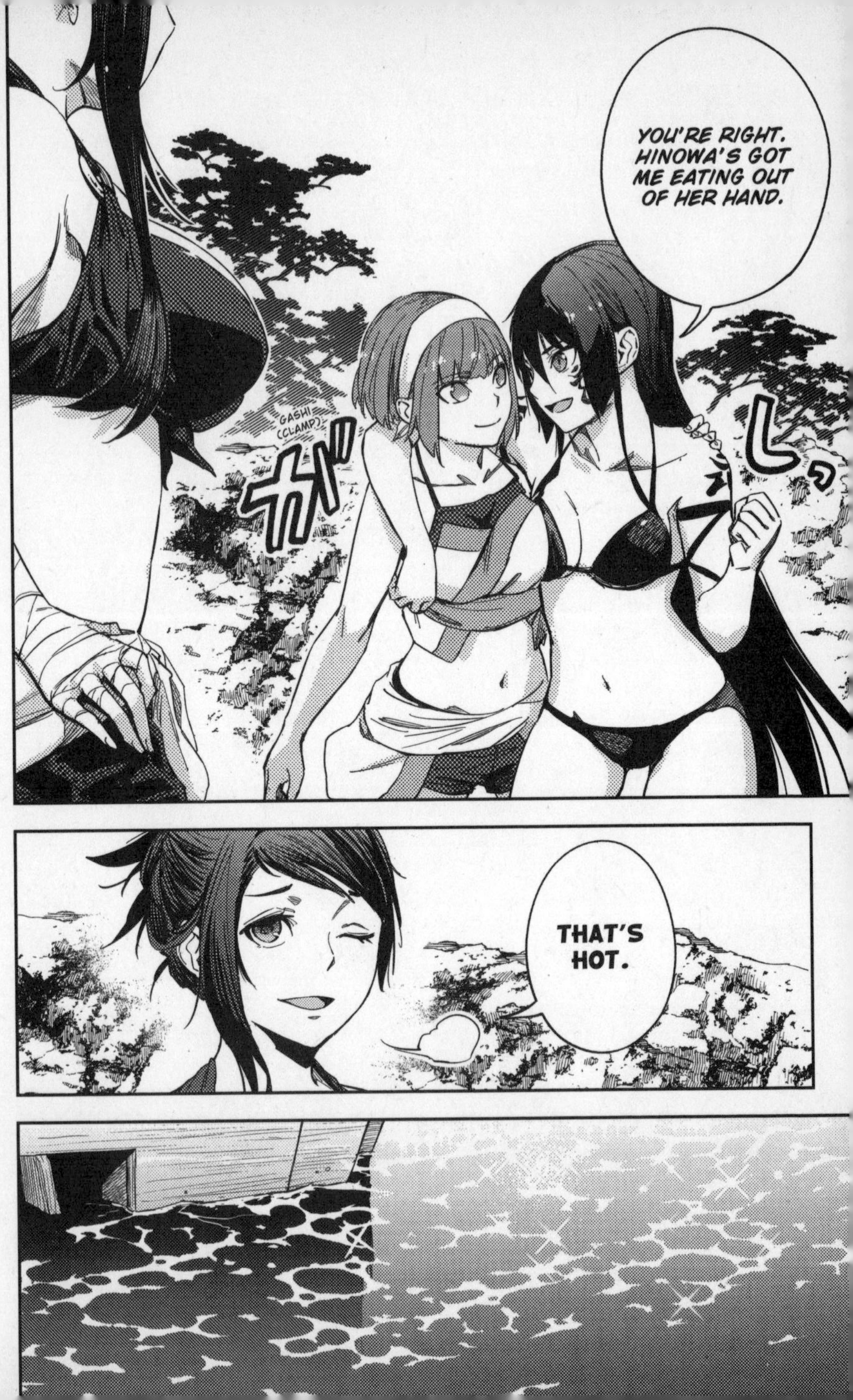
YOU'RE RIGHT. HINOWA'S GOT ME EATING OUT OF HER HAND.
しっ
GASHI (CLAMP)
ガ
THAT'S HOT.

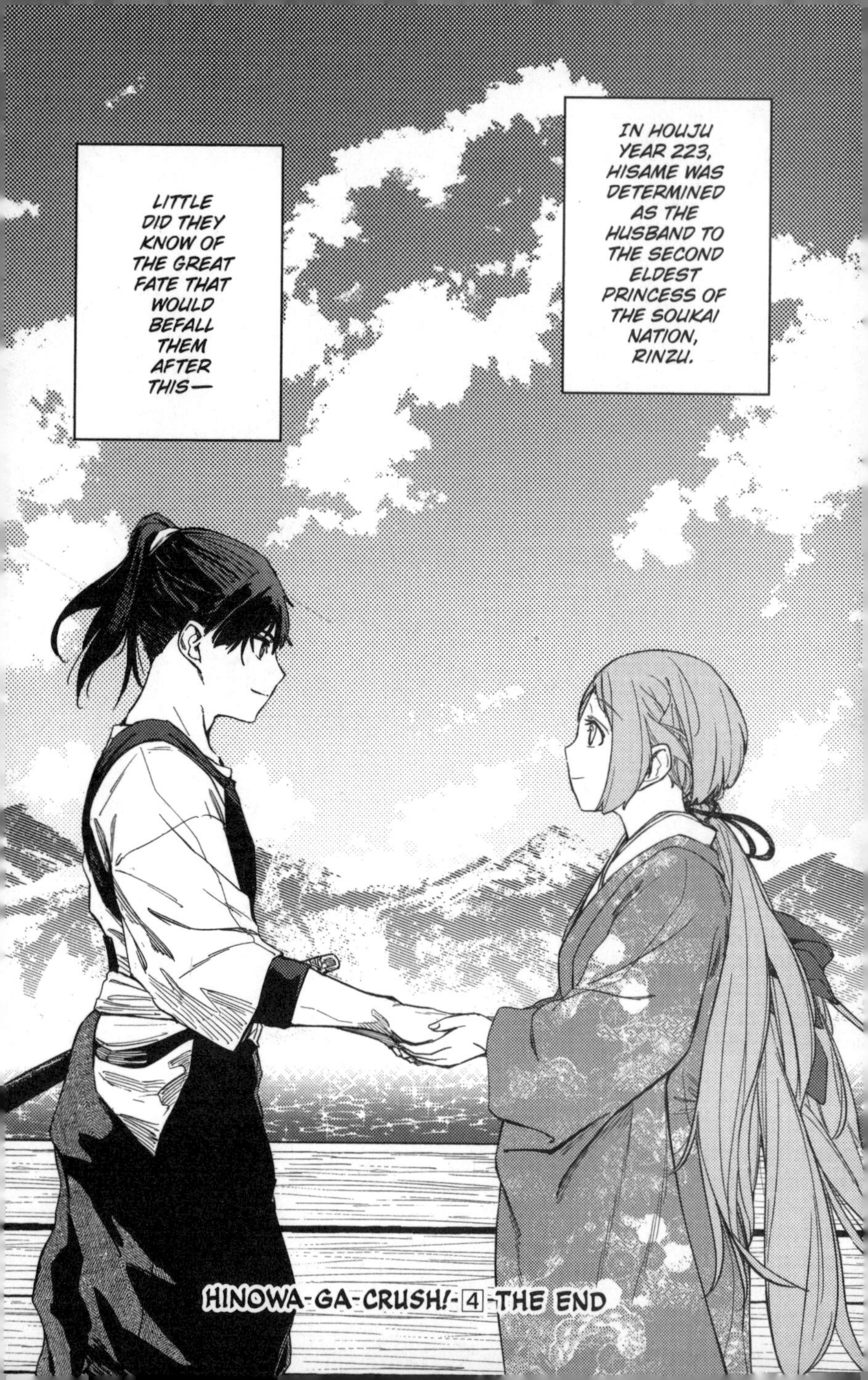
IN HOUJU YEAR 223, HISAME WAS DETERMINED AS THE HUSBAND TO THE SECOND ELDEST PRINCESS OF THE SOUKAI NATION, RINZU.
LITTLE DID THEY KNOW OF THE GREAT FATE THAT WOULD BEFALL THEM AFTER THIS—
HINOWA-GA-CRUSH!-4-THE END

Takahiro's PostScript

HELLO, EVERYONE. THIS IS THE WRITER OF THIS STORY, TAKAHIRO. I'D LIKE TO TAKE THIS OPPORTUNITY TO SHARE SOME ADDITIONAL INFORMATION AND SPOILERS REGARDING EACH CHAPTER FROM THIS FOURTH VOLUME.

★*CHAPTER 18*
IN THIS CHAPTER, THE KING OF THE TENROU NATION, ZUOU, AS WELL AS THE TEN STARS ASSEMBLE. A LOT OF NEW CHARACTERS ARE BEING INTRODUCED, SO I MADE SURE TO MAKE THEM ALL DISCERNIBLE AND UNIQUE. THOUGH I SAY THEY HAVE ASSEMBLED, I ASSURE YOU ONE OF THEM IS MISSING FROM THE LINEUP.

★*CHAPTER 19*
THIS IS THE FIRST TIME WANIBA MAKES AN APPEARANCE. SINCE INTRODUCING TOO MANY NEW CHARACTERS IN ONE GO MAKES IT RISKY THAT READERS WON'T BE ABLE TO REMEMBER WHO'S WHO, I PUT IT OFF AS LONG AS I COULD. BUT THE TENROU SIDE GOT SO MANY NEW ADDITIONS THAT THE SOUKAI SIDE WILL ALSO BE GETTING MORE COMMANDERS. SO FAR, HINOWA AND THE GANG HAVE ONLY BEEN ON THE DEFENSE, SO I WROTE THEM ENGAGING IN AN OFFENSIVE FIGHT.

★*CHAPTER 20*
THIS IS THE CHAPTER WHERE HINOWA AND HER UNIT WORK REALLY HARD. UNDERWATER FIGHTS ARE COOL AND SOMETHING YOU DON'T SEE EVERY DAY. WHILE THE MAIN STORYLINE IS MOVING ALONG, THE TEN STARS ARE ALSO ESTABLISHING THEIR OWN CHARACTERS. IT FEELS LIKE EVERYONE'S SO HARD ON YOMIHIME. SHE PUTS UP WITH A LOT.

★*CHAPTER 21*
EVEN THOUGH THERE WAS A LINE-UP OF STRONG FIGHTERS, WE FINALLY HAD OUR FIRST DEATH. I NEEDED HINOWA TO HAVE TO FACE DEATH HEAD ON AT LEAST ONCE. NAHASHU OF THE TEN STARS SEEMS TO HAVE REMEMBERED THINGS BUT ONLY VAGUELY.

★*CHAPTER 22*
I WROTE ABOUT THE PROGRESSION OF HISAME AND WANIBA'S CONTENTIOUS RELATIONSHIP WHILE MAKING NODS TO EVENTS TO COME. ONCE YOU READ UP TO VOLUME 6 OR SO, YOU MIGHT WANT TO TAKE A LOOK AT THESE CHAPTERS AGAIN. MAGURE IS SO HIM, TRYING TO COME OFF AS NEUTRAL WHILE SECRETLY CHEERING FOR HISAME. THE ILLUSTRATION ON THE CHAPTER'S FRONTISPIECE IS OF AMATERU-SAN MEDITATING UNDER A WATERFALL.

★*CHAPTER 23 & 24*
THE CHOOSING OF RINZU'S HUSBAND. I MADE IT THE KIND OF COMPETITION YOU'D SEE FROM AN OCEAN NATION. UNATO AND KAKESU WILL BE MAKING APPEARANCES AGAIN, SO PLEASE BE SURE TO REMEMBER THEM. AND THE SOUKAI NATION SURE HAS A LOT OF KINKY GUYS.

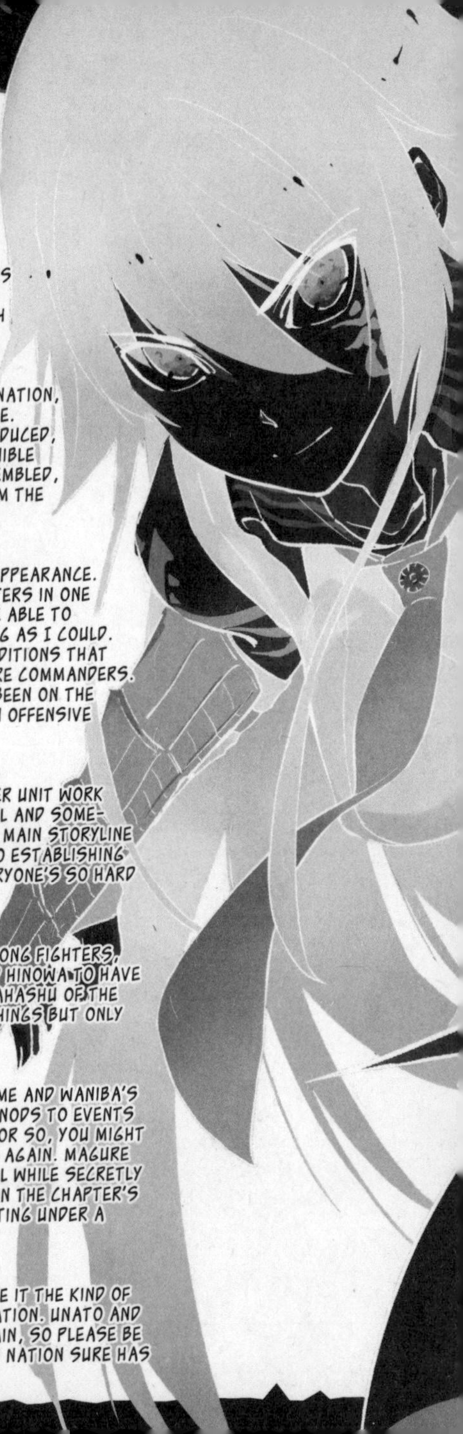

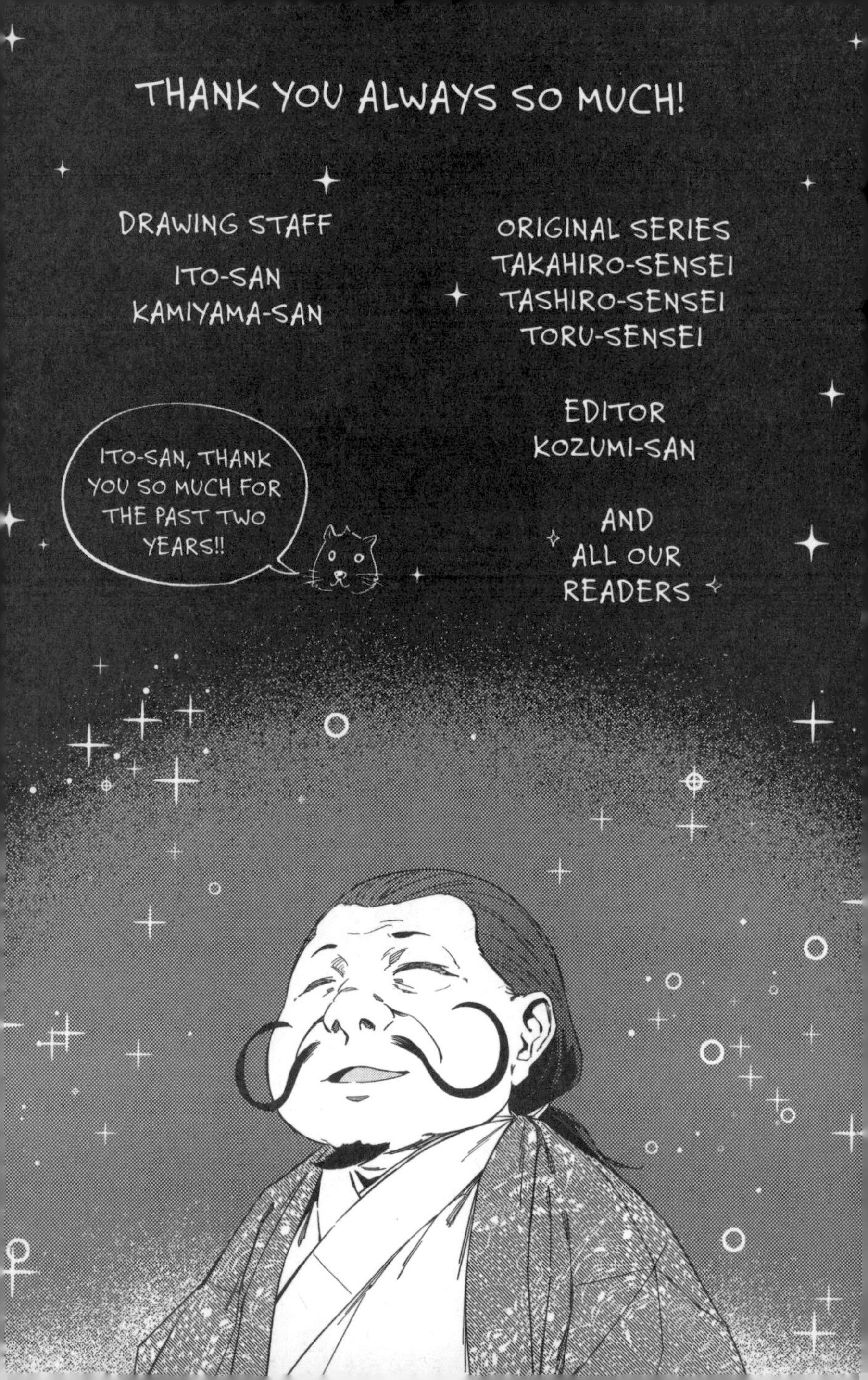
THANK YOU ALWAYS SO MUCH!
DRAWING STAFF
ITO-SAN
KAMIYAMA-SAN
ORIGINAL SERIES
TAKAHIRO-SENSEI
TASHIRO-SENSEI
TORU-SENSEI
EDITOR
KOZUMI-SAN
AND
ALL OUR
READERS
ITO-SAN, THANK YOU SO MUCH FOR THE PAST TWO YEARS!!

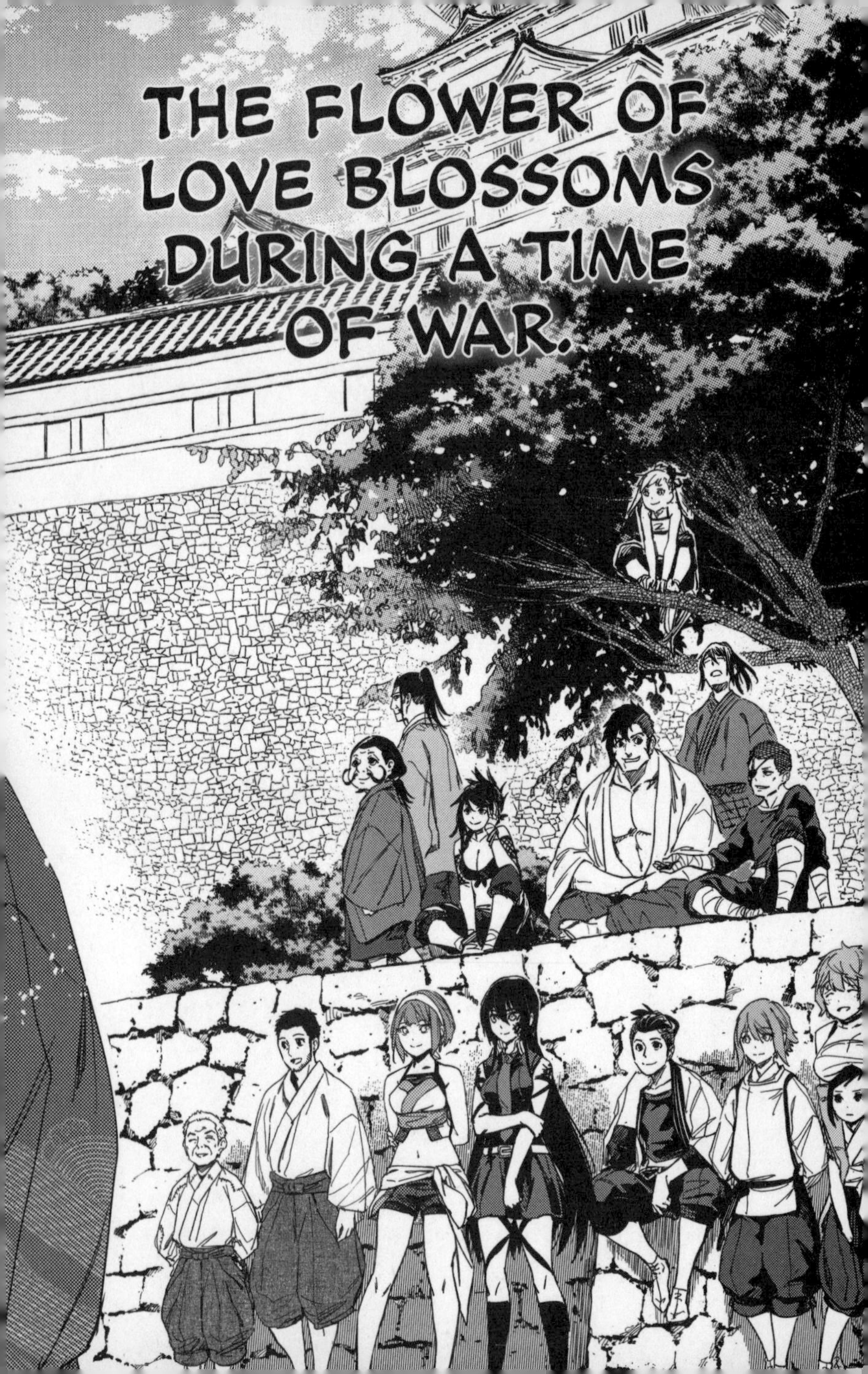
THE FLOWER OF LOVE BLOSSOMS DURING A TIME OF WAR.

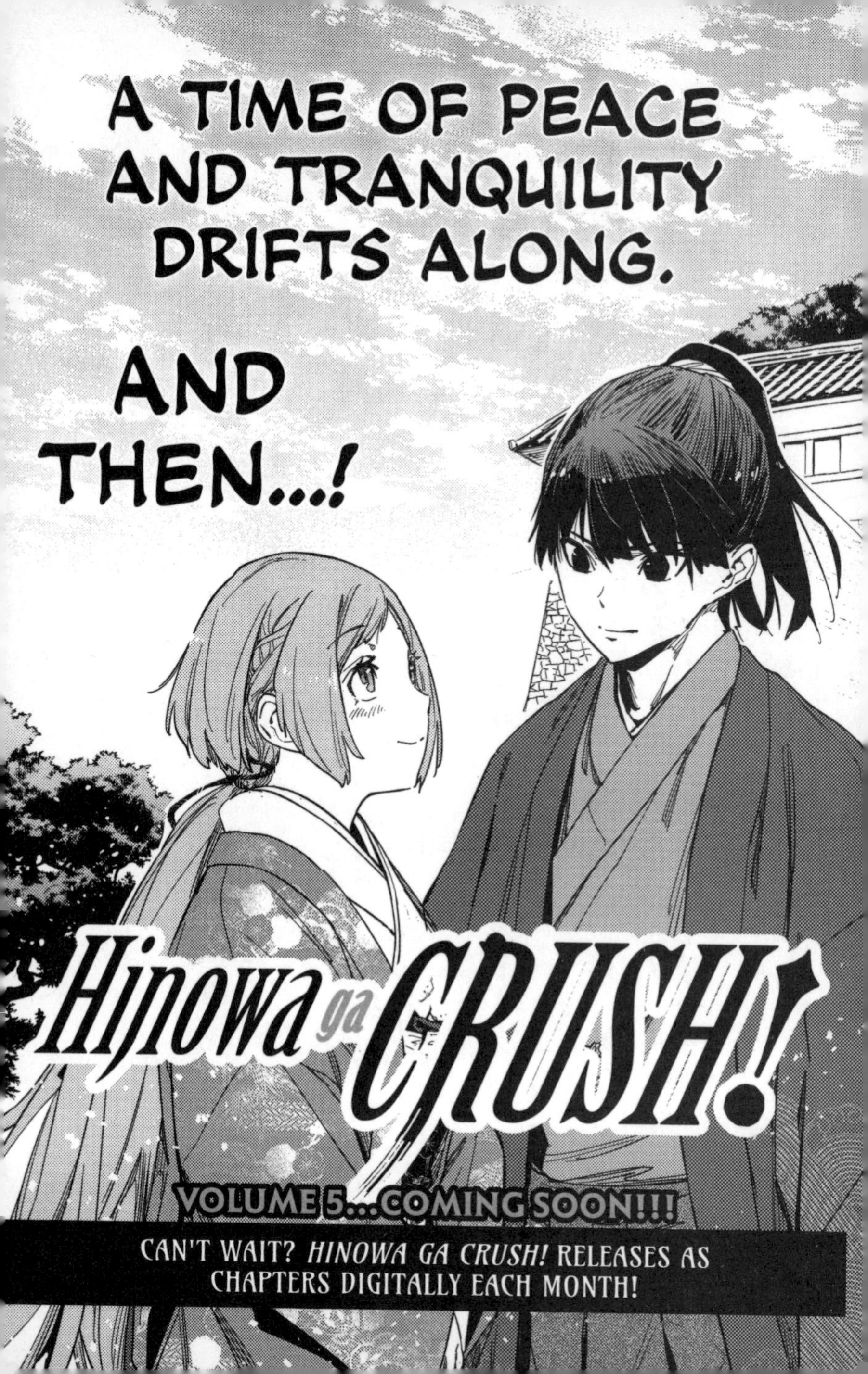
A TIME OF PEACE AND TRANQUILITY DRIFTS ALONG.
AND THEN...!
Hinowa ga CRUSH!
VOLUME 5... COMING SOON!!!
CAN'T WAIT? *HINOWA GA CRUSH!* RELEASES AS CHAPTERS DIGITALLY EACH MONTH!

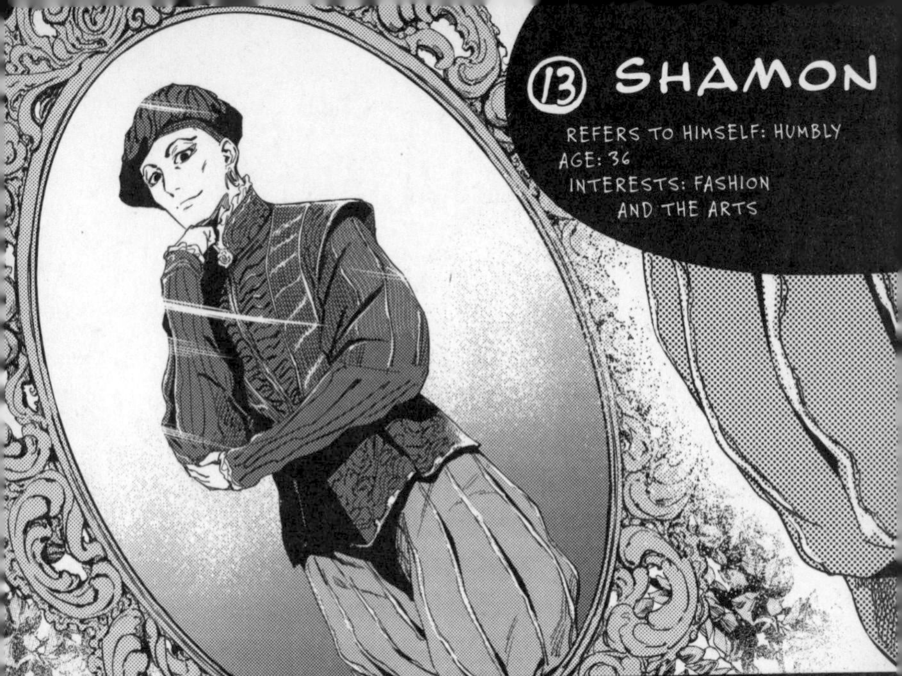
⑬ SHAMON
REFERS TO HIMSELF: HUMBLY
AGE: 36
INTERESTS: FASHION AND THE ARTS

HINOWA GA CRUSH!

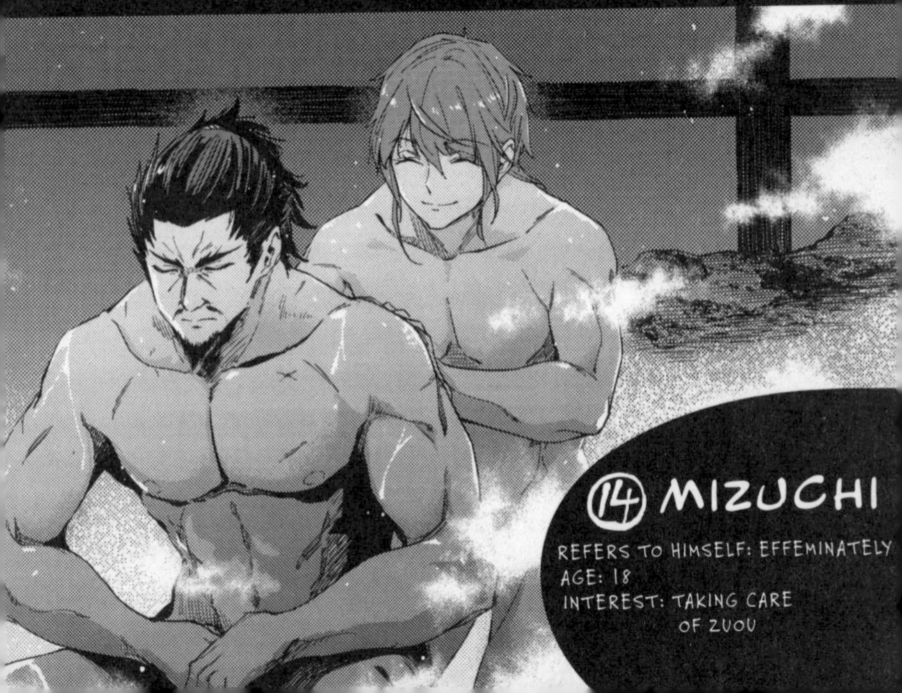
⑭ MIZUCHI
REFERS TO HIMSELF: EFFEMINATELY
AGE: 18
INTEREST: TAKING CARE OF ZUOU

HinoWa ga CRUSH! ④

STORY: TAKAHIRO **ART: strelka**

Translation: Christine Dashiell

Lettering: Rochelle Gancio & Phil Christie

HINOWA GA YUKU! Volume 4 © 2019 Takahiro, strelka / SQUARE ENIX CO., LTD.
First published in Japan in 2019 by SQUARE ENIX CO., LTD. English translation rights arranged with SQUARE ENIX CO., LTD. and Yen Press, LLC through Tuttle-Mori Agency, Inc., Tokyo.

English translation © 2020 by SQUARE ENIX CO., LTD.

Yen Press
150 West 30th Street, 19th Floor
New York, NY 10001

Visit us at yenpress.com
facebook.com/yenpress
twitter.com/yenpress
yenpress.tumblr.com
instagram.com/yenpress

First Yen Press Edition: August 2020
The chapters in this volume were originally published as ebooks by Yen Press.

Yen Press is an imprint of Yen Press, LLC.
The Yen Press name and logo are trademarks of Yen Press, LLC.

The publisher is not responsible for websites (or their content) that are not owned by the publisher.

Library of Congress Control Number: 2018946467

ISBNs: 978-1-9753-1516-0 (paperback)
978-1-9753-1515-3 (ebook)

10 9 8 7 6 5 4 3 2 1

WOR

Printed in the United States of America

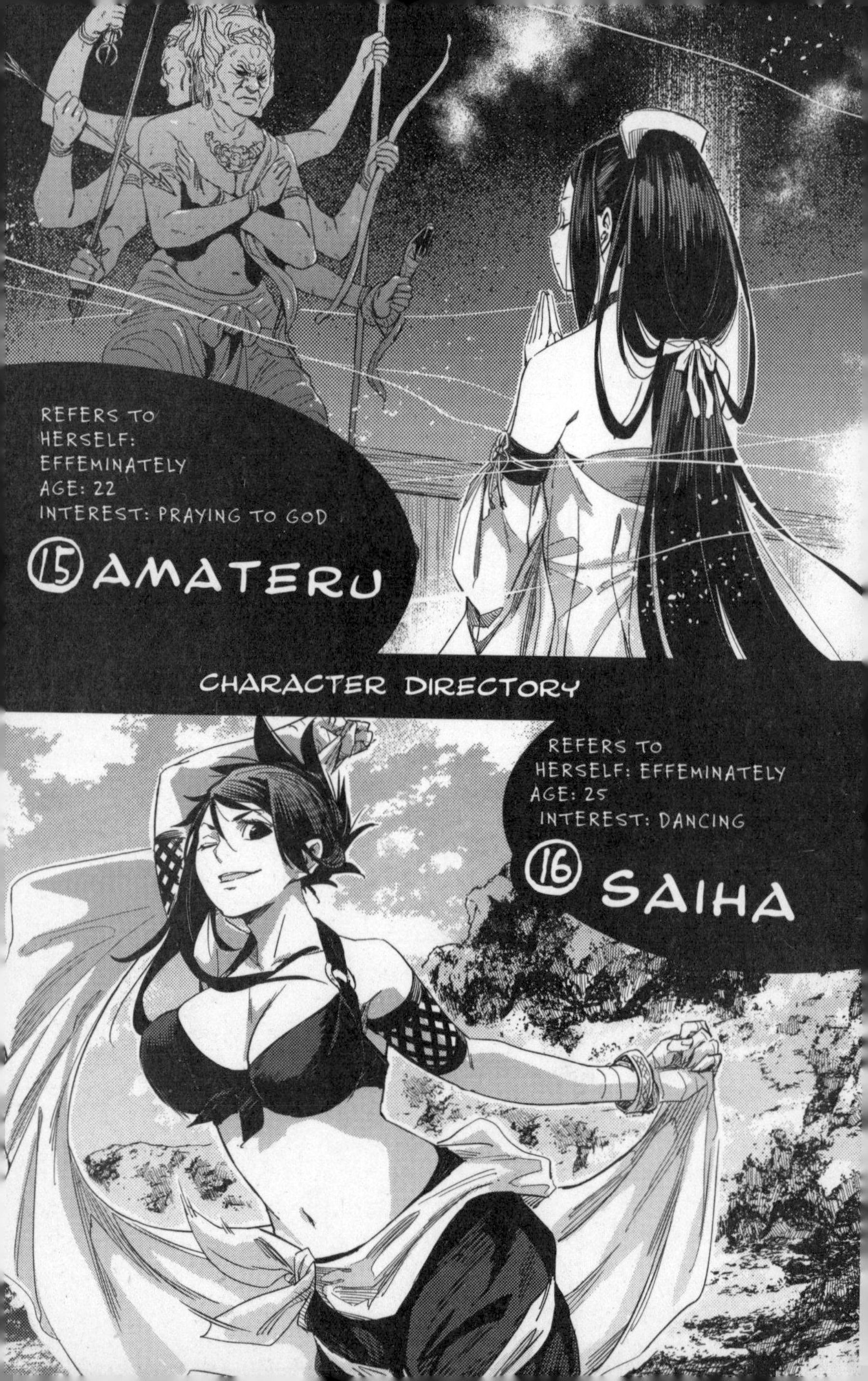
REFERS TO HERSELF: EFFEMINATELY
AGE: 22
INTEREST: PRAYING TO GOD
⑮ AMATERU
CHARACTER DIRECTORY
REFERS TO HERSELF: EFFEMINATELY
AGE: 25
INTEREST: DANCING
⑯ SAIHA